VINCENT DE PAUL

PRIEST AND PHILANTHROPIST

1576—1660

BY

E. K. SANDERS

AUTHOR OF
"ANGÉLIQUE OF PORT ROYAL," ETC., ETC.

WITH EIGHT REPRODUCTIONS FROM ENGRAVINGS
IN THE BIBLIOTHÈQUE NATIONALE

Copyright © 2018 Read Books Ltd.
This book is copyright and may not be
reproduced or copied in any way without
the express permission of the publisher in writing

British Library Cataloguing-in-Publication Data
A catalogue record for this book is available from
the British Library

CONTENTS

	PAGE
INTRODUCTION	v

PART I
VINCENT DE PAUL AND THE WORLD

CHAPTER
I. THE YEARS OF APPRENTICESHIP	3
II. IN THE SERVICE OF M. DE GONDI	22
III. M. VINCENT AND THE PRIESTHOOD	45
IV. THE ORDERING OF CHARITY	67
V. RENAUDOT, THE FRIEND OF THE POOR	91
VI. M. VINCENT'S FELLOW-LABOURERS	104
VII. THE QUEEN REGENT AND THE COUNCIL OF CONSCIENCE	120
VIII. THE FRONDE REBELLION	138
IX. M. VINCENT AND THE PEOPLE	160
X. CARDINAL DE RETZ	181

PART II
THE COMPANIONS OF VINCENT DE PAUL

I. MLLE. LE GRAS	207
II. THE RULE OF THE SISTERS OF CHARITY	230
III. M. VINCENT AND HIS DAUGHTERS	249
IV. THE LADIES OF CHARITY	261
V. THE COMPANY OF MISSION PRIESTS	281
VI. M. VINCENT AND HIS SONS	304
VII. THE VOCATION OF A MISSION PRIEST	328
VIII. THE FOREIGN MISSIONS	349
IX. S. LAZARE AND PORT ROYAL	367
X. THE LAST DAYS	389

APPENDICES

NOTES	409
LIST OF AUTHORITIES	413
CHRONOLOGICAL TABLE	415
INDEX	417

Vincent de Paul

INTRODUCTION

A RECENT work by a learned and brilliant writer contains the following passage: " It was the age of S. Vincent de Paul, patron Saint of practical philanthropists. The air was thick with orphanages and hospitals, with Sisterhoods of Charity, with schemes for evangelizing the inferior clergy. But practical philanthropists seldom escape a touch of superficiality. They may be content with little, with small profits and quick returns; but a brisk turnover they must have."*

This—if we can eliminate the note of scorn—is representative of the popular view of Vincent de Paul. He is accepted as the pioneer of social reform and organized charity—the charity of Annual Reports and Balance Sheets. The biographical study contained in the following pages is an attempt to pierce the veil with which the celebrity of his achievements has enshrouded him. His own choice, undoubtedly, would have been to remain unknown, but as fame has been forced upon him, it is well to connect it as nearly as we may with the reality of his labours and of his aspirations.

An endeavour to show that he was not chiefly a philanthropist does not involve any denial of the value and success of his philanthropic labours. He was born in the sixteenth century, and by a combination of inspiration and experience he arrived at conclusions which are regarded as discoveries in the twentieth. He dealt almost single-handed with problems of destitution involving many thousands of lives, and devised remedies for some

* " Pascal," by Viscount St. Cyres, p. 266.

of the diseases of social life which are still in use. Of the difficulties that harass and discourage the benevolent there were very few that did not come under his eye, for the whole field of social service lay open before him. He realized and met the need for the teaching and tending of the young, the nursing of the sick, the aiding of the prisoner, and passed on to the more difficult enterprises that concern the fallen and the wastrel. In his old age a grateful nation hailed him as " Father of his Country," and in the ungodly Paris of the present day his effigy may still be seen presiding at the corner of those streets where the poor will find assistance for their wants.

His undertakings were in almost every instance crowned with the most astonishing success; but if they had all been failures, his life would still be worthy of record. To himself external success came to be merely an unimportant incident. He loved his fellow-men, and planned and laboured for them untiringly; but he did not claim to know what was best for their welfare, and he showed no anxiety as to the results of what he did. The self-devoted philanthropist or the eager social reformer of the present day may claim him as a comrade, but it is not with them that he has community of thought; the later years of his life—though they were passed in the midst of sensational events and pressing responsibilities that made demands on almost every hour—were dominated by the habit of prayer to a degree that lifted them into supernatural regions. In fact, if we would trace the real life of M. Vincent, we must be prepared to revise both the standard of value that is ordinarily applied to human existence and the accepted division betwixt the real and the unreal; we shall not need to discount his reputation for charity, but we shall find that the full meaning of his charity is the " ascent of the ladder of love " of which Ruysbroeck writes, and that his labours were a fragmentary expression of something much greater than themselves.

It is essential, moreover, to remember the importance

of his priesthood. He held the Catholic faith simply and sincerely, and he was a priest. From this it follows that external events, however sensational, did not affect him so deeply as the processes of his own interior development, and his vast undertakings were never so engrossing as to distract him from his life-long endeavour after self-purification. "*Ruinez en moi Seigneur tout ce qui vous y déplaît.*" Those words—on his lips in his extreme old age—represent the aspiration of his later years. To overlook, even momentarily, the spiritual bias of all his actions is to fail in comprehension of their purport; to remember his charitable achievements and to forget the hours of prayer in which they germinated is to miss the real interest of his life. It is, after all, only a colourless semblance of M. Vincent that is familiar to pilgrims on the broad highway of social service. He may have power to inspire new endeavour and to deepen perseverance in those who have only partial knowledge of him, and it is certain that his name is revered by many who have no understanding of his true purposes; but if we would find the real Vincent de Paul we must seek him on the steeps of Carmel, it is there only that we shall hear even an echo of his message.

Vincent de Paul had no advantages of fortune. He was the son of a peasant proprietor in the South; and though an attempt* has been made to prove that he was of noble descent, and that his repeated references to his humble origin merely show his humility, the case for the advocates of aristocracy remains, to say the least, not proven. There are, indeed, many incidents in his long career that support his own assertions. He was born when the conflict between Henry of Navarre and the Guises was raging, and through the distracted period preceding the accession of that gallant monarch to the throne of France was calmly pursuing his studies at Dax, at Toulouse, and at

* See " Recherches sur la Famille de S. Vincent de Paul." Oscar Poli, 1879.

Saragossa. In all probability, the horrors enacted in Paris and Touraine reached him only as a distant rumour, and stirred him neither in experience nor in imagination; in after-years he makes no reference to them. During the twelve years of reconstruction, extending from 1598 to 1610, the course of his destiny had no connection with the history of his country. He was the bearer of some message from Rome to Henri IV. in 1608, but we have no knowledge of the nature of this business, nor had it any notable effect on the fortunes of the messenger. Then and for yet another decade the life of Vincent de Paul was hidden; other men had time to rise to eminence, to win a place in history, and pass out of the world, while he was still serving his apprenticeship. The confusion that prevailed during the minority and youth of Louis XIII. touched him as little as did the miseries of the Valois rule; he had lived nearly half a century before he had part in the national life, and yet before his death he had rendered more effectual service to his countrymen than any Frenchman of that epoch.

A remarkable feature of his transition from insignificance to an important place in social and political life is that his ascent was not self-chosen; it was an unavoidable consequence of an aim in another direction. The reason of his settling in Paris was the foundation of the Congregation of Priests of the Mission, of which he was the original Superior, and the object of that foundation was completely spiritual. A few priests gathered together to journey into isolated country villages and preach Christ to the working people; they were given a house in Paris for their headquarters, and endowed with a small income for their support. In their journeyings they gathered knowledge of the lives of the people outward and inward, and of the immensity of their need. They could not have embarked on their original enterprise if they had not possessed enormous faith; and to their faith in God it was necessary that they should add a certain confidence in their fellow-men. Their Mission work could hardly have been sustained without an assurance that no sinner has gone so far as to be hopeless.

M. Vincent's confidence in the virtue latent in human nature gave him a power of another kind. Seeing wealth on the one hand and destitution on the other, he assumed that the selfishness of the rich was merely the result of ignorance, and that they would welcome a summons to give of their superfluity. It is difficult at the present time to realize that such a theory could possibly be true, but when M. Vincent came to Paris the divisions of class were so profound that the distresses of the one were outside the limit of ordinary consideration for the other. Undoubtedly he was able to become a link between the two. He had the wisdom to demand personal service as well as money from those who were able to give, and the instinct of sympathy, once stirred, spread rapidly. We hear of "Madame la Princesse," mother of the great Condé, insisting on carrying a bowl of soup with her own hands to a needy invalid in a garret, and coming home with her clothes caked with the mud of the streets; and, despite an element of absurdity and exaggeration, there is plentiful evidence of an awakening to the conception of charity that brings all classes into community of love and labour. The awakening found its first expression in simple things and under normal conditions. In town and country Confraternities were started for the assistance of the sick and unfortunate; the idea of organizations for relief became familiar, and in the years of distress to which France presently doomed herself there was opportunity to discover the worth of M. Vincent's regulations.

It was by the widening of the great circle of charity he had devised that M. Vincent came into touch with Anne of Austria, first as Queen Consort, and afterwards in the days of her misused power as Queen Regent. There were no outward experiences in the whole life of M. Vincent so painful as those which he owed to his connection with the Court, but, though even a passing association betwixt him and Mazarin is unseemly, the taint of the Court did not affect him; he was as much the simple Mission Priest at the Palais Royal as at S. Lazare. It was the strain of the *dévote* in Anne of Austria which accounts for his summons thither, but that strain did not prevent her from being a type of the voluptuary. She desired comfort for her own soul, and she desired physical comforts for those that needed them; but these desires had no weight against the ruling passions of her existence after she became Regent. Only, in moments of spiritual uneasiness, it seems to have been a source of consolation to her to reflect that in affairs concerning the Church she had asked the advice of M. Vincent, and that occasionally she had taken it.

To M. Vincent the contact with the life of the Court involved by giving advice to the Queen was a source of endless misery. He was a witness of the whole deplorable struggle of the Fronde; it is likely that he understood the sins and weaknesses on all the contending sides which were responsible for it, and assuredly he had fuller knowledge than anyone else of the appalling suffering it brought to the thousands who had no desire or comprehension of revolt. The years of the Fronde rebellion were hard ones in which to maintain the vision of universal charity; M. Vincent was seventy before the Fronde began, yet it was in those years—when all the natural leaders of the people were fighting each for his own hand—that he was given power to proclaim the real meaning of charity; for he had the simplicity that strips obligation bare. It was through no fault of their own that the peasantry were dying of starvation during the civil wars, and to a proportion of them it was possible to supply food if money were forthcoming. But the numbers to be fed were enormous, and the sums needed of corresponding immensity. The disasters that meant actual death to the poor meant lessened incomes and consequent discomfort to the rich, and the civil dissensions in progress were of a ind to rouse all that was worst in human nature. It was an unpropitious moment for an appeal to the instinct of generosity, but to M. Vincent the necessity of giving was so obvious that response was a foregone conclusion. A follower of Christ must sacrifice vanity to save the lives of fellow-Christians. If a woman had jewels that were her own to give, she could not retain them when their price would give food to those dying for lack of it. It must be remembered that there was no complication in the position; it was extremely simple. The soldiery wrought havoc in the provinces; houses were burnt, farms destroyed, cattle driven away. There was literally nothing to eat, and no means of obtaining clothes. But the people could be gathered in the towns; food could be prepared in vast quantities and at the smallest possible cost, and supplied to all who were destitute. The distribution of relief was organized by M. Vincent; it was under the close supervision of persons appointed by him and under obedience to him; it was he who made known the intensity of the need for funds. Probably the power of his personality had much to do with opening hearts and purse-strings, so that the stream of beneficence was kept in flood until the time of agony had passed. For more than twenty years it had been possible to watch M. Vincent in all his doings; he had had enemies and slanderers, and had shrunk from no criticism, and he was known as a righteous man. Therein lay his power. He was not afraid to proclaim the real consequence of Catholic belief, for he accepted it himself, and he could not admit that there was any alternative. The man or woman who would not sacrifice personal desires was repudiating membership with Christ. To those who came under his influence—and they were many—it was this simplicity in his demand that made it irresistible, and as a result the lives of the poor were saved by the bounty of the rich.

It was just that the miracles of generosity of which

France was witness in her hour of trial should reflect glory on M. Vincent; he was acclaimed as the Father of all who suffered, and when peace came, and there was leisure to see what he had accomplished, all Paris rang with applause. But, in his view, the work which stirred his fellows to enthusiasm was the least of the tasks that God had given him. The same power that moved the rich to prodigies of liberality he had used in other fields, and its hidden work was incomparably greater in real importance than all the organizations of relief for the victims of civil war and famine which was attracting the world's acclamation. It seems that the true vocation of M. Vincent was as little recognized by his contemporaries as it is at the present day, but if he had evaded it, he would have failed to accomplish those philanthropic feats that are the obvious sources of his fame. As has been pointed out already, the root of his power was his complete sincerity. He was given vision for the misery and degradation of his countrymen, and his life was thenceforward consecrated to the endeavour to help them. But he was a priest; the treasures offered by the Church to him were priceless, and the bodily needs of the poor had far less importance in his eyes than their spiritual desolation. Through every quarter of France, almost without exception, the people were as sheep having no shepherd. There were no vacant benefices, it is true, and in time of peace an authorized person would administer the rite of baptism, of marriage, and of burial, according to the ordinances of the Church, and would also exact payment for such service. The Church had representatives everywhere, and almost everywhere an ignorance more dangerous than that of the heathen was left unremedied. "It is the priests living as most of them live to-day who are the greatest enemies of the Church of God"—that was M. Vincent's verdict after years of wide experience.

To raise the priesthood from its degradation came to be his chief desire. He began by an attempt to do some of the work that had been left undone, to proclaim the Church's message to Christians who had never heard it. " I have only one sermon," he said in the early days of his preaching, " and that is on the fear of God "; but he soon realized that he and his fellow-labourers could only touch the fringe of the work that needed doing. It was not sufficient to awaken sleeping souls; there must be provision for their future sustenance and encouragement, and that provision could be made only by those who lived amongst them, by the curé who was in truth responsible for the progress of his flock. When this knowledge dawned on M. Vincent he came at once face to face with an enterprise whose difficulty far exceeded that of the most baffling problem of relief. He had the highest ideal of the sanctity of priesthood, and believed himself to be altogether unworthy of its privileges, and he was forced to regard in detail the practices common to the priests of that period. In his eyes, the one hope for his countrymen lay in the revival of the true spirit of sacerdotalism, but only an actual and living faith that with God all things are possible could have given him courage for his attempt to cause such a revival. As his life unfolds itself we obtain increasing knowledge of the vast scope of his vocation as a spiritual reformer, but it was a point of infinite importance to the fruitfulness of his labours that the handful of fellow-workers who had settled with him at his first establishment in Paris were of the type to inspire imitation. Year by year their numbers increased, until the Congregation of the Mission was known, not only in every part of France, but far beyond her frontiers. And it was the part of the Congregation of the Mission to train and teach the teachers of the poor as well as the poor themselves, and to show by their own lives that the idea of sacerdotal holiness was not impossible of realization. As they laboured with that intent, other fields opened before them; but M. Vincent cautioned them that their original objects must never become secondary. Under a rule of poverty and humility, their lives were always to be devoted to the service of the poor and the sanctifying of the priesthood.

It is in the foundation of the Congregation of Mission Priests that we find the real centre of M. Vincent's lifework. It was in and through them that his influence was most deeply felt in his own day, but it is characteristic that that which was most intimate in connection with him should be most hidden; his Sons of S. Lazare were nearest to his heart, but in our knowledge of his relations with them we may penetrate only a little way. That which we know, however, in its revelation of strength, of courage, and of insight, is immeasurable in its value, and the reserve which guards the closest records of his life from publicity is in accord with the spirit of personal reticence that ruled him while he lived.

On the other hand, his intercourse with the other great Company which bears his name has been generously laid open, and M. Vincent, as he stands among the Sisters of Charity, teaching, consoling, and reproving, becomes so vivid and human a personality that it is hard to realize how great is the lapse of years which divides us from him. The Sisters of S. Vincent de Paul came into being to supply a need felt, on the one hand, by the generous upper class whose method of giving it was difficult to regulate, and on the other by the Mission Priests whose spiritual labours were hampered by the constant claim to minister to bodily necessities. We shall find that the Mission Priests, individually and collectively, reached heights of self-devotion and heroism where they may hardly be surpassed; but the Sons of M. Vincent, if they were true in their vocation, had the constant spur of the sense of their priesthood, and their sacrifice of self deepened and renewed the realization of their privilege. If we turn from them to regard M. Vincent's Sisters of Charity, the difference between the privilege of the one order and the deprivation of the other is notable.

INTRODUCTION

The Company of Sisters of Charity—which was even more humble and more indefinite in its beginning than that of the Priests of the Mission—was formed of persons belonging to the working class. A Sister of gentle birth was the exception in their early period. They performed the duties of parish nurse and Mission woman; when the hospitals in provincial towns had fallen into disorder, they were sent to reform them, and afterwards in many instances were established as the permanent staff for nursing and supervision. As charitable institutions of various kinds grew up in Paris, their services were continually demanded to secure good government. In time of war they were called upon to face the horrors of military hospitals; in time of famine or of plague the organization of relief and the struggle against death was carried on under their leadership. It was a lawless and unsettled period, and a Sister of Charity braved many dangers besides those of infection. The work required of her was incessant, and often was so much beyond physical capacity that many a Sister seems to have died from sheer exhaustion. She was vowed to an extreme practice of poverty. If any chance gave her an interval of leisure, she was exhorted to employ it in working for her own maintenance. The obedience required of her was of the most searching kind. Although her duty took her into the streets and gave her intercourse both with rich and poor, she had no freedom and no right of independent action even in her own most personal and spiritual concerns. And yet she was not a Religious, and was often reminded that she must not claim the privilege of the religious life. Her obedience was due, not only to her recognized Superiors, but to all and sundry of the benevolent ladies who supplied funds for the assistance of the poor (and many of them were difficult to please). If she was in attendance on the sick, it was her duty to carry out the orders of the doctors in every detail; if she was attached to a parish, she was to follow the directions of the curé. And a Sister of

Charity whose aptitude for her duties made her so friendly with the people that she identified herself with the little circle of the hospital or the parish was immediately removed elsewhere. If, having sacrificed herself, she looked for human solace, her sacrifice was regarded as of none effect. "I tell you," said M. Vincent to them, not once only, but many times, "that you will never be true Sisters of Charity until you have sifted all your motives, have rooted up every evil habit, and stamped out every personal desire." Nevertheless, by the free acknowledgment of M. Vincent himself, there were very many true Sisters of Charity.

It is well to consider this Company of women—a large proportion of them unable to read, almost all lacking in any sort of culture—banding themselves together for the service of God and of their neighbour, accepting every sort of physical hardship as part of a daily routine, and, when occasion offered, vying with each other in eagerness to accept posts that involved the acutest danger to life. There was no promise, nor even any possibility, of reward. They did not retire out of sight and sound of the world's allurements; they escaped no outward difficulty or toil, and, even to the most imaginative, it must have been hard to invest their rough and arduous conditions with any halo of the picturesque. But the Company of Sisters of Charity grew very rapidly, and the vitality which has preserved it to the present day was evident while its original members were still living. These facts, regarded dispassionately, present a problem, and its solution bears close relation to the comprehension of M. Vincent's life.

The teacher and first Superior of the Sisters of Charity was Louise de Marillac, known as Mlle. Le Gras. The nucleus of them gathered beneath her roof; she vowed herself to their service long before they were bound together by a common vow, and she watched over their interests, both spiritual and temporal, with scrupulous and unremitting care. But, though she was possessed of

INTRODUCTION

remarkable capacity for government and organization, she referred every decision to M. Vincent, and it was at her suggestion that in 1634 he gave the first of his "Conferences" to the Sisters assembled in the Church of S. Lazare. Thenceforward, until within a few weeks of his death, more than twenty-five years later, the "Conferences" were continued, and not only do they bring him as a person nearer to us than any other record, but they convey the homely persuasiveness of his method, so that its charm seems to be still alike. We may picture him standing in the midst of the rows of grey-gowned Sisters, clearing his mind as he regards them from all the crowded interests and anxieties of his own difficult life, and gathering all his knowledge of their aims, their sorrows, and their temptations. It was his habit to give notice of his subject and to elicit the ideas of the Sisters before he conveyed his own; by this means he got into touch with them, and formed an estimate of their limitations. The "Conferences" were friendly gatherings. The Sisters would sometimes volunteer observations; occasionally they seem to have interrupted. They were given an opportunity of revealing difficulty or distress, and very often they made use of it. There is nothing rigid or formal in the proceedings—M. Vincent is as a father among his children. Nevertheless, it is in this familiar intercourse that we learn the meaning of the spirit of austerity as M. Vincent understood it; it is here that we grasp what was involved in the vocation of Mission Priest or Sister of the Poor according to M. Vincent's vision, and simultaneously we may discover the secret of attraction in that undeviating routine of self-repression. M. Vincent does not vary in his standpoint in all the course of the "Conferences" (though a quarter of a century separates the first from the last); there is always a naked reality in his representation of the claim on the Christian which he will not drape or shelter. As for the great lady, it was a matter of obligation that she should not cling to her jewels while her neighbour died for lack of bread, so for the man or woman who had entered on the special service of Christ there could be no reservations. We find in him a severity which is only deepened by his sympathetic understanding of the weakness of his listeners. He has the courage to refuse to humour them; he shows them their temptations one by one, depicting each with graphic touches; he declares to them the motives that have caused their sin, and will palliate nothing. In his hands life is stripped bare of every small indulgence, not only in the domain of external enjoyment, but in the hidden world where self-love snatches delight even from the practices devised for its own undoing. There could be nothing simpler than the form of these discourses, yet they sum up all that is tragic in the life of penitence :

" *Quoi ! dira quel qu'une, toujours se mortifier ?*"
" *Oui, toujours !*"

M. Vincent knew that that question must occur to the minds of many of those who heard him, and his answer is always unflinching. That undoubtedly is the reason of his power; yet, though he was not afraid to accept and to insist on the full consequence of a real belief in Christ and in His teaching, he can—having so insisted—show the joy that underlies the hardness. " Remember that mortification is not so bitter as it seems, and holds more of comfort than of pain for those who practise it for the love of God. Yes, there is no greater delight than that of a soul that is really mortified. You ask how that can be. Ah ! my Daughters, this comes to pass when privation is not a thing of itself, but is united with the desire to please God. When it is the expression of love for Him, God so touches the soul as to fill it with happiness far greater than that which it renounced. Thus renunciation ceases to be difficult. In truth, what joy can be so great as the thought that we have done something that pleases God ? There is a sense of happiness in this which nothing equals."

The Sisters, as they listened, knew that they had the

opportunity of practising; instead of the grumbling and bickering that often soiled their service, they might raise their daily toil and hardship, and test the truth of M. Vincent's assurances. They must have known that he was speaking from experience, and, as he stood among them, the great force of his conviction infected them. They went back to their diverse tasks and responsibilities, to dangerous journeys, to new undertakings of infinite difficulty, but they took with them the sense that their renunciation—if it was complete—was their privilege. A tenderness that would have softened their conditions and have given them relaxation could not have kept them steadfast. "The spiritual life," says Père Grou, "is of the nature of a bargain." In that truth we find the explanation of the Sisters of Charity. It was the completeness of self-offering that brought recompense: "a sense of happiness that nothing equals."

M. Vincent did not hesitate to spur them on towards endeavour which may seem beyond the limit of human capacity. "Hold yourselves always in the presence of God," he said to them, "and remember that that which will always preserve and sustain you as a Sister of Charity is to keep God always as witness of your thoughts and actions, and to do everything for love of Him."

As we come to more detailed knowledge of all that they accomplished and endured, we realize that these " *pauvres filles des champs* " (as their Founder loved to call them) required the supernatural atmosphere in which he strove to place them. They rendered practical service to the poor, and that was the nominal reason of their being; but if their outlook had been limited to the practical, they could not have continued. To Vincent de Paul that fact was so obvious as to need no assertion, but, looking back towards him, it is worth remembering that the great foundation which still does honour to his name was due to his position as a man of prayer. His compassion for the poor—great as it was—was not a force sufficient to generate and support a movement so vast and so permanent in its importance as the institution of the first uncloistered nuns. " The thought of this was never mine; this is the work of God; man has no part in it." This was his own constant protestation regarding his own supposed successes.

M. Vincent lived to be eighty-five, and he passed nearly forty years in Paris. He came in contact with many celebrated personages, and the course of his later life is in touch with the developments of history, so that we cannot trace his career without linking it to the politics of his period. But though we must follow him into the Palais Royal and on his journeys to Saint Germain in obedience to the call of duty—although the cause of charity drew him to one and another of the great houses in the Luxembourg and Marais Quarters, in all of which he was welcomed and revered—yet it is not enough to recognize his public life or to catalogue his achievements. He cannot live for us again unless we can win entrance to the circle of those who were not content to revere, but attempted also to share with him. Among the Mission Priests and Sisters of Charity in their labour and suffering he does to some degree reveal himself; for them his fifty years' apprenticeship bears fruit, and he attempts to impart what he himself has learnt. He gave them no golden rules that would lessen the difficulty of prayer; he did not show them how they might dispense with any of the toil of the spiritual life; nor, in practical matters, has he any simple theory for the relief or prevention of destitution. From his knowledge and vast experience there is very little that could be gathered for a handbook on any subject, and he never wrote anything for publication. Much has been recorded of him, however. A great collection of his letters has recently been issued. His utterances, as set down by his listeners, have been carefully compared and guarded. The voluminous biography which was compiled by Louis Abelli, his personal friend, from the contributions of those who shared his daily life, was published only four years after his death, and seventy years before he was canonized. It will be seen, then, that there is no lack of material for an attempt to find him as he was to those who knew him.

And in the end, when all available authorities have been studied and the great mass of information falls into some sort of shape, there emerges one idea, overmastering all details, definite, infinitely impressive: here is a man who has learnt humility. His charge to his Sons and Daughters as they listen for his teaching, or kneel to receive his blessing, is constantly repeated, and varies but little in its form.

" As for us, we are of no account; we are ignorant and sinful, and we must remain hidden as being of no use in ourselves, and unworthy of a thought."

That was the effect of all the praise he heard on the lips of rich and poor, of all the acknowledged success of his enormous labour, and in him it was no simulated virtue; his self-abasement is consistent and unfailing. If proof were needed that all his wisdom was learnt in those hours that he spent upon his knees, we should find it in his humility. The man who had achieved as he did, and allowed himself the thought that his achievement was due to his own brains and energy, could not continue humble.

PART I
VINCENT DE PAUL AND THE WORLD

VINCENT DE PAUL

CHAPTER I

THE YEARS OF APPRENTICESHIP

THE parents of Vincent de Paul were natives of the South. His father, Jean de Paul, owned a very small property called Ranquines, in the parish of Pouy, near Dax, and married Bertrande de Moras in 1572. Vincent, their third child, was born April 24, 1576. It is clear that from his early childhood he was required to work, but his father was thrifty, and the family enjoyed a certain prosperity. Jean de Paul seems to have been in the position of a small farmer; besides his house and the land surrounding it, he owned cattle and sheep, and it was as shepherd to his father's flocks that Vincent was initiated in the meaning of work and duty.

Afterwards he would have liked to forget the humble surroundings of his childhood. We know by his own testimony that when he was a student in the College at Dax, and received a visit from his father, he was ashamed to acknowledge him before his schoolfellows. It was a period when good birth was an enormous advantage, and a peasant origin a heavy handicap to any advancement, therefore the temptation is an obvious one; but the memory of this weakness remained with M. Vincent, and he never wearied of reminding those who treated him with reverence in later years that he was a peasant, and the son of a peasant.

Tradition says that he was generous in giving before his right to give was well established. In touching on the childhood of a Saint, it is wisest to leave detail to tradition, and in the case of Vincent there are no authentic incidents to mark the first decade of his long record. At twelve years old his father took him to Dax, to the Convent of the Franciscans, that he might be educated. This fact suggests that he had shown intellectual and spiritual capacity beyond that of his brothers, and that his family destined him for the priesthood. But in this there was nothing remarkable; many a country priest was of peasant origin, and the lot of such persons was not an exalted one. The country folk, indeed, were given but poor provision for their spiritual needs in those latter years of the sixteenth century, and the parish priest who really attempted to represent his Master would have to take a line that differed sharply from that pursued by his fellows. But it was not required of Vincent deliberately to choose his way of life; his progress—begun under such peaceful auspices—was curiously chequered, and it needed no effort of his to make his course distinct from that of others who had sprung from similar conditions. Circumstances imposed upon him the test of violent experience; it was in his use of it that he gave proof of his qualities.

Moderate good fortune attended his student years. He worked hard under the guidance of the monks, was selected as tutor to the two sons of M. de Commet, a legal magnate in the town of Dax, and for four or five years retained this post, which enabled him to continue his studies without expense to his parents. In December, 1596, he received the tonsure in the church at Bidache, near Bayonne. His further education was pursued first at the College of Saragossa, and afterwards at Toulouse. To provide for these new expenses his father sold a yoke of oxen, but—though this may have meant considerable sacrifice—the provision was insufficient for a college course of four years, and Vincent was obliged to find more pupils. He seems to have had several boys under his care during a part of his sojourn at Toulouse, and the

THE YEARS OF APPRENTICESHIP

death of his father in 1599 must have forced him to support himself; but the records of this period are indistinct.

On September 23, 1600, he was ordained priest in the chapel of Saint Julien (now known as Château l'Évêque) by François de Bourdeille, Bishop of Périgueux. There is nothing to give any real indication of his character before this date. Apparently he was an eager student, and, although it was his habit to refer contemptuously to his own mental equipment, he did, in fact, acquire a deep fund of learning, but of his inner life we have no knowledge. At the moment of his ordination we get the first suggestion of the Vincent de Paul of the future; the awe of his own privilege so far possessed him then, that his first Mass was said in the solitude of the little mountain chapel of Our Lady of Grace at Büzet, where he had no witnesses but a priest and a server. He was only on the threshold of life, and subsequent events betray that he was very far from his own future standard of what a priest should be; but even then he was untouched by the lax custom of the times, and his Offering at the Altar was the chief event of every day. Almost fifty years later he wrote this message for two of his Company at their ordination:* " Tell them, if you please, that I have prayed, and shall still pray, that Our Lord may give them an ever *new desire* for the Sacrifice, and grace that they *may never offer It merely from habit.*"

For the next four years there are no data from which to construct an idea of M. Vincent except the fact that he remained as a student at Toulouse, and took a degree there in 1604. He was then twenty-eight, and unless he pictured for himself a career very different from that of the ordinary country priest, he would hardly have devoted so long a time to the acquisition of learning. It is likely that he had already given tokens of unusual capacity, and was fired with ambition; but in after-life he never gave a hint of the nature of his early dreams. We know only

* April 25, 1648. "Vincent de Paul et le Sacerdoce."

that at the close of his University life there lay before him a possible prospect, which, although shrouded in mystery, indicates that worldly advancement was not without attractions for the young priest of the Bearnais. For some reason Vincent was summoned to Bordeaux, and his visit there involved him in expenses that were far beyond his means. This fact is established, but the explanation is not forthcoming. One of his friends, M. de Saint-Martin, declared that there was question of a bishopric, and of an interview with the Duc d'Epernon as a preliminary thereto. If this be true, it would throw an interesting light on the change that time and circumstances wrought in Vincent's point of view, but there is no evidence to corroborate it; it can stand only among probabilities.

Something there was, however, that tempted him to overstep the boundary of prudence, and he returned to Toulouse no richer in preferment, and burdened with debts beyond his power to pay. An unexpected solution of his difficulties was presented at this moment by a legacy from an old woman who had profited by his ministrations. The position is best recorded in his own words:

"You shall now be informed," he wrote to M. de Commet,* " of my discovery, when I returned from Bordeaux, of a will made in my favour by a good old woman of Toulouse. My inheritance consisted of some furniture and of a little property that had been assigned for 300 or 400 crowns owed by a bad debtor. I went thither to effect the sale of it, by the advice of my friends and by reason of my pressing need of money to discharge the debts I have already incurred, also for the great expense in which I shall be involved if I want to bring about the affair which I don't dare name. Having arrived there, I found the rascal had left the neighbourhood by reason of a warrant the old lady had out against him on account of these same debts, and I was told that he was doing very

* "Lettres," vol. i., No. 1, July, 1607.

well at Marseilles, and had plenty of money. Whereupon my attorney advised, and the condition of affairs demanded, that I should journey to Marseilles, and by arresting him possess myself of 200 or 300 crowns. Not having the money to do this, I sold the horse I had hired at Toulouse, intending to pay on my return. My ill luck in being so delayed is as great as my dishonour at allowing my affairs to be so tangled. It would not have happened like this if God had given me the success in my venture which it seemed to promise. I went to Marseilles accordingly, caught my man, had him imprisoned, and afterwards released for 300 crowns, which he was then glad enough to pay."

This letter is of extraordinary interest if we consider it in connection with the Vincent de Paul of S. Lazare. Sixteen years of smooth development and mild success lay behind him when he wrote it; his mind was full of his own interests and of " the affair which I don't dare name " —perhaps the possible bishopric—and in pursuit of these things he ceases to be scrupulous either in kindness or in honesty. It may be that even at that moment he was better fitted for ecclesiastical preferment than most of those who obtained it, but France lost nothing because the force of a real destiny swept Vincent de Paul out of reach of the goal of his ambition.

On his way back from Marseilles he was persuaded to journey as far as Narbonne by sea. For the description of the sequel we still have his own words, addressed to M. de Commet:*

" The wind would have been sufficiently favourable to bring us to Narbonne, fifty leagues, the same day, if God had not permitted three Turkish sloops coasting the Gulf of Lyons to give chase to us, and make so sharp an attack upon us that two or three of us were killed and the rest all wounded, even I myself receiving an arrow wound which has left its reminder for all my life. We were thus

* "Lettres," vol. i., Nos. 1 and 2.

constrained to yield to these pickpockets, who were fiercer than tigers, and, as a first expression of their rage, hewed our pilot in a thousand pieces to avenge the loss of one of theirs. After seven or eight days they set sail for Barbary, the robbers' den of the Grand Turk, where, when we had arrived, we were put up for sale with a certificate of our capture on a Spanish vessel, because otherwise we should have been freed by the Consul who is kept there by the King to safeguard French trading.

"We were paraded through the streets of Tunis, where we were brought for sale, and, after having gone round the town five or six times with chains on our necks, we were brought back to the ship that we might eat, and so show the merchants that we had received no mortal injury.

"I was sold to a fisherman, and by him to an aged alchemist, a man of great gentleness and humility. This last told me he had devoted fifty years to a search for the Philosopher's Stone. My duty was to keep up the heat of ten or twelve furnaces, in which office, thank God, I found more pleasure than pain. My master had great love for me, and liked to discourse of alchemy and still more of his creed, towards which he did his best to draw me, with the promise of wealth and all the secrets of his learning. God maintained my faith in the deliverance which was to be an answer to my continual prayers to Him and the Virgin Mary (to whose intercession I am confident my deliverance is due).

"I was with this old man from September, 1605, to the following August, when he was summoned to work for the Sultan—in vain, for he died of regret on the way. He left me to his nephew, who sold me very soon after his uncle's death, on account of a rumour that M. de Brève, the King's Ambassador, was coming—armed with powers from the Grand Turk—to emancipate Christian slaves. I was bought by a renegade from Nice in Savoy, and taken by him to his dwelling-place among the mountains in a part of the country that is very hot and arid. One of his three wives, a Greek, who was a Christian, although a schismatic, was highly gifted, and displayed a great liking for me, as eventually, and to a greater degree, did another of them, who was herself Turkish, but who, by the mercy of God, became the instrument for reclaiming her husband from his apostasy, for bringing him back within the pale of the Church, and delivering me from slavery. Her curiosity as to our manner of life brought her daily to the fields where I worked, and in the end she required me to sing the praises of my God. The thought of the *Quomodo cantabimus in terra aliena* of the children of Israel, captive in Babylon, made me, with tears in my eyes, begin the psalm, *Super flumina Babilonis*, and afterwards the *Salve Regina* and other things, in which she took so much delight that it was amazing. In the evening she did not fail to say to her husband that he had made a mistake in deserting his religion, which she believed to be a very good one by reason of the account of our God which I had given her, and the praises of Him which I had sung in her hearing. In hearing these she said she had felt such pure delight that she could not believe that the paradise of her fathers, and that to which she one day aspired, would be so glorious, or afford her anything to equal this sensation. This new representation of Balaam's ass so won over her husband that the following day he said he was only waiting for an opportunity to fly to France, and that in a short time he would go such lengths as would be to the glory of God. This short time was ten months, during which he offered me only vain hopes, but at the end we took flight in a little skiff, and arrived on the 28th of June at Aigues-Mortes, and soon afterwards went to Avignon, where Monseigneur the Vice-Legate gave public readmission to the renegade, with a tear in his eye and a sob in his throat, in the Church of Saint Pierre, to the glory of God and the edification of all beholders.

" Monseigneur kept us both with him till he could take us to Rome, whither he went as soon as the successor to his three-year office arrived. He had promised to gain entrance for the penitent into the convent of the *Fate ben fratelli*,* where he made his vows, and he promised to find a good living for me. His reason for liking and making much of me was chiefly because of certain secrets of alchemy which I had taught him, and for which he had been vainly seeking all his life."

The rest of the letter is occupied with business directions in connection with the papers of his ordination, and the old distress touching his creditors (among whom one may hope the horse-dealer of Toulouse was numbered), for whose satisfaction he intended to devote a sum of about 100 crowns given him in proof of gratitude by his former master. The story of these two years thus briefly given claims an effort on the part of the reader for realization of the suffering, mental and physical, which it represents. In it there is no record of sensation, no self-conscious excitement in the memory of past endurance; there is little, indeed, that is not a statement of fact, but in the fact there lies a clue to the real character of the writer, which no deliberate attempt at self-expression would have afforded us. The venerable priest whose influence was a terror to Mazarin—who had power to work miracles in the social order of Paris—is one with the Christian slave labouring for his pagan owner without apparent hope of deliverance. In both the mainspring of thought was a reliance on the will of God, so simple and unswerving that no detail of life escaped its influence; and that early discipline — so terrible in possibility that the modern imagination fails in grasp of it—secured for Vincent the foundation of certainty in the Divine protection and guidance which made his great heights of after-achievement possible to him.

But his deliverance from captivity, wonderful though it was, did not bring with it deliverance from the difficulties in which his mysterious rashness, three years

---

* Name commonly given to the Fraternity of S. John the Divine.

earlier, had involved him. In spite of the generosity of his repentant master, his letters show that the burden of debt weighs on him to the exclusion of other considerations. His ruling desire is "*quelque honeste bénéfice en France*," and he gives an ingenuous description of the means by which he enlisted the interest of Pierre Montorio the Vice-Legate. Apparently, the dignitaries of the Church then resident in Rome had a taste for curious arts, and the lore that Vincent acquired from the Turkish sage, who had been for many months his owner, was eagerly sought after. Among the thousand other things which he had learnt, and which his patron was eager to acquire, there was a trick whereby a skull appeared to speak; and so great was the value set upon these secrets, that he was discouraged in holding communication with anyone else, Monseigneur being anxious to keep a monopoly of them and have the satisfaction of producing them for the edification of His Holiness and the Cardinals.

Possibly, while he imparted one form of knowledge, Vincent was imbibing another. He who originated the Congregation of Mission Priests may have found a part of his incentive in the memory of his experience in Rome. A desire for reform can spring only from knowledge of an evil, and the thought of the good living, the cure of souls, that was to be his as reward for tricks learnt from a heathen wiseacre must have given him some insight into the levity with which spiritual responsibilities were incurred. It is evident that his own ruling desire at that time was the honourable satisfaction of his creditors, and he could not have fulfilled his vocation of ministry with a clear conscience until his debts within his family, as well as outside it, were paid to the last farthing. The difficulties in obtaining certificates of his ordination combined with Montorio's pleasure in his society to delay preferment, and finally, when he left Rome (early in the year 1609), it was as envoy on secret business from the Pope, Paul IV., to Henri IV. Such a mission would, to many a young clerk of high ability, have been the first step in a swift upward progress, but Vincent's gifts needed the leaven of worldly wisdom, and he failed to secure any of Fortune's prizes for himself. In fact, his stay in Rome was fruitless in visible benefit; he brought away nothing except experience and such learning as he had acquired in a year of study with the Dominicans at their College of La Sapienza. The thread of natural advancement in the diocese where he had been ordained was snapped by his period of slavery, and his peasant origin left him unsupported by family interest. Therefore, at the time of his return to France, he being then thirty-three years old, his prospects were gloomy; no opportunity to employ his fine abilities presented itself, and every hope that arose ended in disappointment.

Vincent seems to have accepted discouragement with the same valiant spirit that had supported him in captivity. Already, it may be, the instinct that made him pre-eminently the servant of the poor was alive within his breast, and, eschewing the cultivation of interest where he might have been secure of finding it in the household of Cardinal or Bishop, he gave his services to the Hospital of Charity* in Paris, and so began his ministry to the sick and suffering. The task he set himself was one to be fulfilled in obscurity, and its interruption must have been completely unexpected. The manner of it brings us into contact with that juxtaposition of extremes which characterized the Paris of the seventeenth century.

It is an indisputable fact that if deliberately we seek acquaintance with the Saints of those dark days, we cannot fail to come in contact with the sinners. Thus at the opening of the real life of Vincent de Paul stands Marguerite de Valois.

Even a superficial survey of the years prior to the birth of Vincent, and those during which he was passing through his childhood and his studious youth, reveals the

* Built by Marie de Medici.

peril that threatened the existence of France as a separate kingdom; and the historian, gravely considering the swift yet vigorous growth of the power of Spain, and realizing the probable effect of Spanish despotism and Spanish bigotry on the history of European nations, is moved to exalt the King of France, who as a soldier and a statesman was the deliverer of his country, into a hero with an unquestionable claim upon the homage of mankind. The lover of romance with equal justice applauds the gallant figure of the Gascon Prince as he stands contrasted with the degenerate and miserable Valois brothers. Henri IV. is a popular hero, and it would be an invidious task (even if its fulfilment were a possibility) to depose him from his pedestal. He, the first of the Bourbon Kings, was born beneath a lucky star; to those great capacities as General and as diplomatist which he possessed was added the magic of personal charm that bewitches a man's contemporaries into a conspiracy to deceive posterity. In fact, Henri IV. did not rise a hair's breadth above the corruption of his age. The poisoned deformity of social life under the dominion of the Queen-Mother might be found reflected in the Huguenot Court at Nérac, and the son of the Puritan Jeanne d'Albret was not behind the sons of Catherine de Medici in supplying material for the most lurid pages of the Court chroniclers.

Marguerite de Valois becomes less isolated in ill-repute if we realize how far Henri was impregnated by the prevailing corruption, but in that year (1610) when M. Vincent crossed her path it is difficult to conceive of any link between them strong enough to make their connection more than momentary. It was only five years since Marguerite had been permitted to return to Paris, and, although old age was very near, her way of life even then did not tend to edification.* M. Vincent could not have failed to have some knowledge of it, and it is not without

* A description of the life of Queen Marguerite in Paris is given by Lestoile (" Journal de Henri IV.").

an impulse towards regret that we find him enrolled among the number of her dependents. No doubt Queen Margot desired to salve her conscience with charity, and preferred that the charity itself should be administered in the best possible way. But it was a proof of singular discrimination, either in herself or her advisers, when she singled out the humble peasant priest to be her almoner.

Almsgiving, perhaps, was but a doubtful virtue in one whose debts were always far beyond possibility of payment, but this was by no means the only time in his life when M. Vincent's tolerance was strained by the doings of exalted personages, and he was far more likely to serve his generation by the practice of an exaggerated charity than by any violence of criticism. To realize his position towards Queen Margot, and afterwards towards Anne of Austria, we must remember the extraordinary force of Royalty. These ladies were on a different plane from the human beings for whose moral condition he might be more or less responsible, and the fact that the divorced Queen had never deviated from her profession of the Faith gave her an additional claim upon him. He might justly have been moved by pity for her also. She was a lesson in the vanity of earthly glories. Her father, three of her brothers, and her husband had been Kings of France, yet the kingdom can hardly have contained a more unhappy woman than she was in those days. For her the sharpest bitterness of living lay in the fact that she had been so often within sight and hearing of the happiness which she perpetually missed. She was, in the common phrase, her own worst enemy, but she was what her birth, her surroundings, and her consciousness of her own brilliant wit and beauty made her. She had been bred to bigotry, to that abhorrence of the heretic which was in part superstitious and in part political. She was forced into a marriage that outraged principle and inclination, and found, when it was once accomplished, that she

THE YEARS OF APPRENTICESHIP

had been utilized as the bait to lure her brother's enemies into the trap prepared.

The wedding of the Valois Princess and the Huguenot King, and the crime of S. Bartholomew's Eve, were matters of very long ago history, when Queen Margot and Vincent de Paul came into contact. At this time she had recently left the Hôtel de Sens (the residence allotted to her by the King when she was allowed to return to Paris), and was established south of the river near the Hospital of Charity. It was in a hospital ward that one of her household noticed M. Vincent, and by reason of his good offices to the sick that he was appointed to be her almoner. Probably, he did not have very much personal intercourse with his patroness, but he was eminently fitted for the administration of charity, and must surely have earned her respect; and she—though she was a divorced Queen and of sensational reputation—was also by birth a Princess of France. It is not unlikely that the magic touch of her royalty did clear away some of the shadows that hid M. Vincent from the notice of those who could help him to use his great capacities. The employment she gave him was the first he had received since his captivity, and for all who can read the stained pages of Marguerite's romance with commiseration there is a certain charm in the thought that she, as she neared the last of her many years of thriftless self-pleasing, was allowed to be of service to Vincent de Paul at the time when he was friendless and unknown.

There is no record of the details of M. Vincent's life in Paris at that time; contemporary letters and memoirs make no reference to him, and his later celebrity failed to awake any reminiscence of him in former days. He was an unnoticed unit in a city where there were many things and people worthy to attract notice, and he did not aspire to be anything else. The one letter written at this period* that remains to us may be taken as a real

* "Lettres," vol. i., No. 3, February, 1610.

indication of his desires for the future. It is addressed to his mother:

"My delight in the assurance which M. de S. Martin gives me of your good health is as great as is my distress at finding myself unable to offer the service that I owe you. The necessity of retrieving my fortunes, which have been so disastrously injured, keeps me in this city, and I have great confidence that by the grace of God my efforts may be blessed, and I may soon be given the possibility of retirement, that I may spend the rest of my days near you. I long to know all the news of home, and if my brothers and sisters and the rest of my friends and relations are well. I wish that my brother would make a student of one of my nephews, but my misfortunes and inability to be of any service to the family may, very naturally, quench his desire to do so. He must remember, however, that present distress may lead to future prosperity. I pray constantly to God for your health and for the welfare of all at home."

It is quite clear that the Vincent de Paul of those days aspired only to do his duty in peaceful retirement, and assist his relatives as soon as he had opportunity in return for the sacrifices that had been made for him; the ideals which were so clear to him in after-years were not then outlined in his mind. We do not know by whose interest he obtained the Abbey of S. Leonard des Chaulnes, in the Diocese of Saintes, but he held it from 1610 to 1616, and probably derived his living from it during that period; for the dependents of Queen Margot were ill-advised if they relied on any salary from her. At first he had a lodging in the Rue des Saints Pères, that he might be near to the Hospital of Charity, the scene of his ministrations. He shared it for a time with a lawyer from Bordeaux who had come to Paris on business, and, in consequence of this temporary fellowship, found himself involved in a very painful experience. He had remained in bed on account of illness while his companion went out.

THE YEARS OF APPRENTICESHIP 17

The doctor came to see him, and brought a boy to carry his medicines. While the doctor was engaged with the patient the boy extracted from an unlocked drawer a considerable sum of money which had been left there by the lawyer. When the loss was discovered, M. Vincent was held responsible. There was no proof of his guilt, it is true, and after one denial he refused to make any protestations of his innocence; but the impoverished lawyer, moved by a natural desire to vent his indignation, told the story wherever he could find a listener, and sought out especially those who had any acquaintance with the supposed culprit. Vincent de Paul was insignificant of origin, and had achieved nothing that could bring him reputation. Dishonour of this kind might well have proved a serious drawback to his career, and his calmness in the face of it is remarkable. " God knew the truth," he said; but it was only after six years that the confession of the real culprit gave proof of his innocence.

When thirty years later the " Conferences " at S. Lazare gave opportunity for illustrating a principle by a real experience, he told the story in the third person. " If the offence of which we are accused has not been committed," he said, " let us remember that we have committed many others, on account of which we ought to welcome disgrace and accept it without justifying ourselves, and without having the smallest resentment against our accusers. Let us acknowledge, my brothers, that in ourselves we have capacity for all evil, and let us leave to God the charge of declaring the secrets of guilt and of innocence."*

The significance of the adventure lies in the opportunity it gave to M. Vincent to put in practice in the earliest years of maturity the principles which were the root of his teaching in later life. Complete resignation, complete humility—these may be necessary qualities in the fol-

* " Vie du Vénérable Serviteur de Dieu, Vincent de Paul," par. L. Abelli.

lowers of Christ, but it is rarely that the Christian can produce them to meet the exigency of an unexpected test. In the insignificant priest who neither trembled nor cried out under the whip of calumny we find in embryo the character that afterwards had force to brave the enmity of Mazarin and to withstand the Queen when royal wishes clashed with principle.

But in those days there was no foreshadowing of an important future. M. Vincent probably knew that his family had formed great hopes from the promise of his studious youth, and that they must regard him as a failure; and he was not buoyed up by any secret reliance on his own capacities.

We do not know what the circumstances were which brought him into contact with de Bérulle, the future Cardinal and founder of the Congregation of the Oratory in France. Their first meeting was an important event to M. Vincent, for de Bérulle became his guide in affairs both spiritual and temporal, but with characteristic reserve he makes no reference to it. In November, 1611, de Bérulle and four other priests took up their abode at the Hôtel de Petit Bourbon in the Faubourg S. Jacques, and two years later the Papal Bull sanctioning the establishment of the Oratorians in France was given by Paul V. For a time Vincent de Paul lived with de Bérulle and the new-born Congregation, and his adoption of a standard of rigorous austerity in personal life may be traced to this experience. Moreover, his connection with the Oratorians was important to his career in its external aspect; for one of them, Père Bourgoing, resigned the cure of Clichy when he joined de Bérulle, and the vacant post was given to M. Vincent. The two years which he spent at Clichy as a parish priest may seem to be merely an insignificant episode in his history; they have no direct bearing on any event that came after, but it is likely that the memory of them influenced him enormously in the days—then so very far ahead—when he was Superior at S. Lazare.

His knowledge of the needs of a poor parish might have been supplied by observation, but he could only gauge the possibility of satisfying them by actual experience. That the true status of the parish priests should be recognized appeared to him a point of infinite importance, it was on them that the spiritual welfare of their flock depended, and he was strenuous in imposing on them a very rigorous standard. Such an endeavour is apt to arouse the wrath of the easy-going, and if his own conduct during his time at Clichy had been open to criticism, his exhortations to others would not have passed unchallenged. But, in fact, the deliberate devotion and consecration of his life to the service of his Master had begun. He pictured a parish priest as one who was at once the leader and the servant of his flock, who held every capacity that God had given him—of energy, of physical strength, of mental endowment—as a trust for the use of those he served. His own love of his people took form in the spending of himself for them. He studied their material interests and laboured for their spiritual awakening. He won their friendship, he taught them, he prayed for them. The ideal that he set up seems to have been fulfilled. It should, however, be remembered that he held his charge for a period of many months, but not of many years, and therefore was not able to prove that an isolated individual can go on maintaining so strict a personal rule and so rigorous an attack upon the devil.

Outwardly, as well as in the hidden life of the little town, the sojourn of M. Vincent at Clichy was memorable. He found the church in ruins, and those who desired to worship there could not supply the funds to save its downfall. As it stands now, it is the memorial of his presence, and also of his amazing power in awakening the rich to a sense of their responsibility. Many years later that power was in perpetual use in a time of exceptional misery, and to it was due the preservation of unnumbered lives; but at that more peaceful moment it was the needs of the poor folk of Clichy for opportunity of prayer and worship that the rich citizens of Paris were required to supply. It is possible that at that time money was supplied to him more freely because he had been almoner to Queen Margot, but it was by reason of a personality that unconsciously claimed implicit trust that then and always his demands were acceded to when those of others were fruitless.

If it is possible to judge of a situation so long passed by modern standards, we should pronounce that M. Vincent had found at Clichy a niche for which he was admirably fitted, that from the little town his influence and his example might go out far and wide, until at length, by some direct development of events, a larger sphere for which his parochial life had been a preparation opened before him. But the life of M. Vincent cannot be adapted to any human design. Superficially there is no coherence between its stages; in fact, the design was so far beyond human conception that conventional systems of cause and effect were bound to prove at fault.

As he laboured at the work for which he was so pre-eminently suited, another door was thrown open, and he was invited to pass through it into a field of endeavour that had had no attractions for him hitherto, and of which he had not the smallest experience. Monseigneur Philippe de Gondi, Comte de Joigny and General of the Galleys, needed a tutor for his children. The need was represented to de Bérulle. He was director to Vincent, he had befriended him in Paris and sent him to Clichy, there was much outward reason for the strength of his influence; but its true root was the spirit of submission which M. Vincent had fostered in himself, till it grew into real humility. The proffered post had great external advantages. Many a priest stepped from the humble footing of chaplain or tutor in rich and noble houses to high ecclesiastical preferment, but Vincent was without this species of ambition. He loved the people and his work among them. To leave

Clichy for a more arduous task might have been matter for regret, but to leave it for conditions of ease and of soft living was the sharpest test of self-surrender imaginable. It was this that was required of him. To those who looked on, the experiment must have seemed a strange one. Even to the most far-seeing there was no clue to its eventual result.

CHAPTER II
IN THE SERVICE OF M. DE GONDI

WHEN Vincent de Paul joined the household of Philippe de Gondi, General of the Galleys, he was, ostensibly, quite as far from the discovery of any clear purpose in the use of life as when he depended on the patronage of Montorio in Rome. He was nearing his fortieth year, and there was not as yet the least indication that his development was of any importance to his fellow-countrymen. Except in the pulpit at Clichy—which was then in the country and out of touch with Paris—he does not seem to have delivered a sermon; he was certainly as unknown in learned circles as he was among the frivolous, and his link with Royalty in the person of Queen Margot was not conspicuous enough to lend him dignity in the eyes of ordinary persons. De Bérulle, who was only one year senior to Vincent de Paul, held a position among French ecclesiastics which was second only to that of François de Sales, and for twelve years he had been eminent. The contrast between the two contemporaries is remarkable, and assuredly at the moment that M. Vincent abandoned Clichy and returned to Paris (with his personal possessions on a hand-barrow, as Abelli tells us) he appeared a most unlikely subject for celebrity. Even then there lay before him eight years of uncertainty, but these contained the events that were to give him his directions for the future. The experiences that lay behind him when he accepted his post as tutor to the children of de Gondi, had been educational and fruitful of result for himself rather than for others. As we consider that long apprenticeship, we find

IN THE SERVICE OF M. DE GONDI 23

reflection of it in certain words of his spoken forty years after it ended in a "Conference" with the Sisters of Charity.*

"Let us see," he said to them, "why God allows those who serve Him to suffer. My daughters, we are each like a block of stone which is to be transformed into a statue. What must the sculptor do to carry out his design? First of all he must take the hammer, and chip off all that he does not need. For this purpose he strikes the stone so violently that if you were watching him you would say he intended to break it to pieces. Then, when he has got rid of the rougher parts, he takes a smaller hammer, and afterwards a chisel, to begin the face with all the features. When that has taken form, he uses other and finer tools to bring it to that perfection which he has intended for his statue. Do you see, my daughters, God treats us just in this way. Look at any poor Sister of Charity, any poor Mission priest, when God drew them out of the corruption of the world they were still as rough and shapeless as unhewn stone. Nevertheless, it was from them He intended to form something beautiful, and so He took His hammer in His hand and struck great blows upon them."

Disappointment, captivity, and failure had done their work on M. Vincent; he was ready to be treated by the lighter tools; the time had come for the features of the statue to disclose themselves beneath the hand of God; but it is clear that he was not aware that he had found at last the opportunity for his true development. At Clichy his work was congenial, and it was only under obedience that he left it; he was out of his element among magnificent and luxurious surroundings, and he does not seem to have possessed special aptitude for teaching and training children. The two boys placed under his care were described by their aunt, Mme. de Meilleraye, as "*vrais démons*," and there is not the faintest evidence that Vincent de Paul obtained any influence over either of them.

* No. 65, July, 1656.

The younger did not survive his boyhood, and the only record of him that remains is his expressed desire to be a Cardinal, that he might take precedence of his brother; the eldest was a brave soldier, but he was not distinguished for piety. There was also Jean François de Gondi, the most celebrated representative of his race, but he was not educated with his brothers. He was very much the youngest, and could not have shared with them; therefore it would be unjust to attribute the training of the future Cardinal de Retz to M. Vincent. The result of a strong influence in childhood, nevertheless, is often felt through life, and the notorious Cardinal was not a credit to the associations of his infancy.

It becomes evident, then, that Vincent de Paul did not find his vocation in his office as tutor; he must have seen at once that he was not suited to his new position, and, though we have no reminiscences of that period, he would hardly have been human if he had not felt the chill of deep discouragement. Yet perhaps the understanding of vocation which was afterwards so strong in him was then taking hold upon his mind. For him vocation—a term that is constantly made synonymous with conscious aptitude and strong desire—meant the fulfilment of God's will, and as life advanced he tried to be true to it in complete simplicity. At that moment of upheaval it may have become real to him for the first time, and his feet at length were set on the right path. For he was not merely submissive; his acceptance was so complete that with every successive step his will seems to grow a little nearer to the Divine Will. It should be recognized that it was not by the spur of a fine and pure intention for the future, deliberately conceived, that he kept himself steadfast to his vocation, but by the continual withholding of intention, by a most faithful yielding of himself.

His direct connection with de Gondi lasted for a period of ten years. It was in November, 1613, that M. Vincent left his labours at Clichy, and was established in his new

Philippe de Gondi.
(General of the Galleys.)

capacity at the Château de Montmirail. His patron was one of those aristocrats of France over whom history casts a glamour hard to define and impossible to dispel. The Courts of Henri IV. and of his successors were unspeakably licentious. We know that coarseness of speech matched depravity of morals, and that the reality would inspire abhorrence, if by bridging the centuries it were possible faithfully to reconstruct it. But an impression of brilliancy is quite independent of all sober and reasonable conviction. Neither Gui Patin nor Tallemant des Réaux, nor any of the other witty scribblers who have perpetuated the ugliness that surrounded them, can rid us of the half-envious admiration we accord to their glittering contemporaries. In spite of everything, the French aristocrat of that period remains superb, and that quality of superbness, of complete and unassailable self-assurance, has its own historic value. It was not only for posterity that they were impressive; in the eyes of the class below them—that bourgeois class which was so much better endowed intellectually—they were possessors of a magic with which no power that a man may acquire for himself can possibly compete.

And here it is well to prepare ourselves for the unquestionable fact that to accomplish those great and far-reaching schemes which were to revolutionize the social life of Paris Vincent de Paul contrived to use the magic of the noble. Possibly it was easier for him to use it by reason of the enormous width of the gulf that separated his natural position from that of his clients, and dispelled any misgiving on their part lest he should presume upon their bridging of it. The bourgeois priest, however spiritual, had more prejudices to overcome before he could attain to satisfactory terms with the aristocrat than had the peasant. But Vincent's relations with other men were too unusual to be affected deeply by considerations of convention or of class. Even in those early times he was learning to be humble, and the exterior manifestation of his humility gave him from the first a special security of foothold. He went to the Château de Montmirail in the position of a dependent, but he so ordered his ways that it would have been impossible to cast a slight upon him. He would never appear among the great folk of the Château unless specially sent for; when his young charges were not in need of his services, "*il demeurait dans cette grande Maison comme dans une Chartreuse,*" says a contemporary. He laid down as a maxim for his own guidance that among the many perils and temptations surrounding him, his sole protection was the choice of silence and retirement whenever choice was possible, and his room became to him as the cell of the Religious. This choice of retirement, however, was in no wise slothful; he was on the lookout for every duty that had relation to his office. His own position towards the many grades of servants in that huge establishment might suggest great possibilities of difficulty, but he was so self-forgetful that he ignored any such trammels, and he applied himself to the task of winning their confidence. When a great festival approached, he tried to assemble them and remind them of their privilege as Catholics and all that it entailed. Such an enterprise demanded courage. Under the most Catholic monarchs who ruled France while Vincent lived it did not, perhaps, present such insurmountable obstacles as would a similar effort with a Reformed Church in the twentieth century; but lackeys in all places and at all times have a tendency to scoff, and the peasant priest gave signal proof of entire self-abnegation when, in the new world on which he had just entered, he made this venture.

Here, again, it is quite clear that he was not consciously training himself for the future that did, in fact, lie before him. There was an after period of uncertainty and doubt which shows conclusively that he had no prevision of his career. And such experiences of his as seem to have been a preparation for his destined work were so utilized by reason of the extraordinary spiritual energy that was developing within him. To such a development no circumstances are a hindrance, but the Château de Montmirail did not offer any notable advantages.

Philippe Emmanuel de Gondi was not distinguished for special saintliness of life. He held the office of General of the Galleys, and from boyhood stood high in Court favour. It is true that his uncle, his brother, and afterwards his son, were Cardinals, and the episcopal throne in Paris was held in succession by four members of the de Gondi family; but, without detailed study of Church history in France, we may understand that preferment was possible without corresponding spiritual endowment, and, in fact, the de Gondi furnished examples of just such abuses in the Church as Vincent de Paul in later years made it his mission to attack. But if Philippe de Gondi was not the ideal patron for a man of Vincent's calibre, his wife* soon showed herself capable of appreciating the privilege de Bérulle had obtained for her and her children. She was still a young woman, but she had reached the fourteenth year of her wedded life, and, in spite of the temptations of her high position and great personal beauty, she seems to have kept herself unspotted by the world. She was by nature a dreamer, one of those beings whose purity of soul is admitted and admired, but who hold themselves so far aloof from ordinary experience that as a rule they accomplish nothing. The records of fact which concern her are quite sufficiently explicit to show the transformation which was wrought—not suddenly, but in process of years—by Vincent de Paul. Some months after his arrival at the Château de Montmirail, the birth of her youngest and most celebrated son, Jean François, took place, and it was during her time of physical weakness that she discovered the degree to which Vincent was worthy of her confidence. The natural outcome of her

* Françoise Marguerite de Silly, daughter of Antoine, Comte de la Rochepot.

growing trust was her choice of him as spiritual director, but she seems to have had sufficient discrimination to foresee that he would not welcome such a suggestion, and to obtain his compliance she resorted to the intervention of de Bérulle. Vincent was thus coerced by a double claim of obedience, and he accepted the charge; but it is evident that he was never entirely reconciled to the delicate position it entailed.

The fashion of professing sanctity did not come into vogue till some sixty years later, when Mme. de Maintenon reigned at Versailles, and the doings of the Ladies of S. Cyr furnished inexhaustible topics for the chatterers; but even in those early days of Marie de Medici's regency, as in the wild times of the Valois, the instinct of the *dévote* (which is never eradicated in the French nature) declared itself in unexpected quarters. And at all times the *dévote* is difficult to deal with. When—as in the Château de Montmirail—we find a high-born lady, possessing every advantage that this world can give, living in comparative seclusion, with one of her dependents as confessor, we recognize elements of danger. Vincent's own development had hardly reached the point that would teach him to be moderate with others. Already he ruled himself by a law of sacrifice before which ordinary human nature quails, and in his new penitent he had just the material out of which might have been made one of those astounding examples of conversion in high places with which Fénelon and Bossuet and the Directors of Port Royal edified their contemporaries. We may search in vain, however, for anything sensational in the record of his dealing with Mme. de Gondi. The charge which he accepted in fear and trembling he held in a spirit of complete personal humility.

It is much to be deplored that there is no record of this period of M. Vincent's life. His failure with the children was counterbalanced by success with their parents, but the gradual process by which that success was attained is

IN THE SERVICE OF M. DE GONDI

hidden; his references to the years at Montmirail are very rare, and all they convey is the impression that he avoided any sort of self-assertion, and regarded the authority of his employers as of Divine appointment. Abelli gives us one incident, nevertheless, which proves his courage. It was the age of duelling; Richelieu was not yet in power, and no attempt to check the savage practice had been made. De Gondi was a notable duellist, but the influence of his wife or his years of association with M. Vincent had drawn him into practices of piety. With the childlike inconsistency that distinguished the Catholics of that period, he went to Mass on a morning when he proposed to fight. M. Vincent celebrated. When the other worshippers had gone, M. de Gondi remained—praying, perhaps, for success in the forthcoming contest. It was then that the duty of the priest became so clear to M. Vincent that his own natural diffidence was put to flight.

"Monsieur," he said, approaching the kneeling figure, "will you let me say something—with all humility. I have heard on good authority that you intend to fight a duel, but I tell you as a message from my Saviour, Whom you have just beheld, Whom you have been adoring, that unless you will renounce your intention His judgment will fall on you and on your family."

He was the dependent admonishing the seigneur, the priest interfering in affairs of which he had no knowledge. In either aspect the attempt was dangerous, for the Church had grown loose in discipline, and the great nobles were imperious. Yet he succeeded. Probably the honour of M. de Gondi was unassailable, and he approached a duel in the spirit of the sportsman rather than in that of the bully, so that for him there was less difficulty in refusing a contest than for many others; but he would not have listened to the suggestion of a priest in such a matter unless a foundation of respect for the priest as an individual and for the Church he was representing had been laid. M. Vincent desired that his life during those years at Montmirail should be hidden, and his desire has been fulfilled, but we know by his effect on those who were with him that he must have lived in the practice of personal holiness.

It was natural that Mme. de Gondi should wish to share with others the privilege that she valued so highly, but she had reason to regret her generous instinct. M. Vincent was not fully occupied by his duties to his charges, for they had much to learn in the department of sport and swordsmanship, and therefore he had many hours of leisure. At first he remained in retirement, but the march of events forced him into prominence, and the deep respect with which he was regarded by Mme. de Gondi increased the difficulty of his position. One incident in particular that was to have great effect upon his afterlife had immediate influence at this juncture; it is, indeed, as important to the development of his character as of his actions, for it seems to have come as the most searching test of his humility. It was in humility that he found himself wanting, and in agreement with S. Augustine he believed that this was the essential virtue of the spiritual life. The form of his temptation and his violent method of dealing with it shows us that he had reached a stage when his regard for the progress of his own soul was paramount over every other consideration.

The momentous incident occurred in 1617. He had accompanied Mme. de Gondi to the Château de Folleville in Picardy, and, while there was summoned to the bedside of a peasant in a village on the estate. The sick man was respected by his neighbours and believed to be a faithful son of the Church, but when M. Vincent came to him and he knew that death was near, the bonds by which for years he had confined his conscience snapped, and the fear of hell possessed him. Vincent de Paul, in the ministrations that are part of the ordinary duties of a parish priest, was awakened to a new understanding of the possibilities of human nature. This Folleville peasant

IN THE SERVICE OF M. DE GONDI   31

had not neglected the Sacraments, but he had misused them; he had lied to God and to himself, and the deadly poison of this constant secret sacrilege had almost destroyed his soul. The depth of his repentance, however, spurred him to an act which had results of immense importance. His shrinking from confession had involved him in the most fatal form of deceit, but having recognized his sin, he was not content with the shame of the confessional. He desired that Mme. de Gondi, as representing his liege lord, might come to him, and to her he made open acknowledgment of his misdoing. Of the nature of his original crimes we know nothing, nor is there any record of his name. Having played his unconscious part in the development of future events, he died.

Mme. de Gondi and M. Vincent shared this experience, and it made a vivid impression on them both. It was not a matter of hearsay; they had each been personally concerned, and actual touch with such a spiritual tragedy as this suggested to the minds of both the possibility of a great spiritual need for which there was no provision. The imagination of the devout Catholic shrinks from contemplating the fate of those who, by making a practice of untrue confession, deprive themselves of every means of grace. The idea that thousands of souls might be in such a plight was brought home to the minds of these two, to whom the Church's Sacraments were so much more precious than life itself. It seems that M. Vincent received a sudden revelation of the spiritual conditions under which the peasantry of France were living, and that the course of his life was altered in consequence.

At the moment he took action. On January 25 he preached a sermon in the church at Folleville, on the reality and necessity of the Sacrament of penance. While he meditated on his theme, Mme. de Gondi prayed that he might be inspired by the Holy Spirit. This was, in fact, the first of the Mission sermons, and its effect on those who heard it was so great as to suggest that

M. Vincent had found the remedy for a wide-spread disease. Great schemes for the sanctifying of all the country folk on her vast and scattered estates filled the brain of Mme. de Gondi. Her enthusiasm knew no bounds, and it would seem that it reached beyond the schemes themselves, and was fixed on the personality on which, as she believed, success depended. M. Vincent found himself the object of an admiration which was no less intense because completely spiritual.

Simultaneously he was becoming conscious of the call of his real vocation. It had not taken definite shape; it may have appeared to him as the stirring of ambition, for we know absolutely nothing of the progress of his thoughts at that period, but it is clear that it made a claim on him which could not be satisfied without action. The action which he took was sensational. In the July following his first Mission Sermon, he left his post in the de Gondi household, and established himself at Châtillon, in the province of La Bresse. Mme. de Gondi took leave of him without any suspicion that he would be absent more than a few days. His excuse—which was a true one—that his personal affairs called him away deceived her completely, and he was settled in the parochial work of his new cure before the truth dawned on her. For two months she was expecting his return from day to day, and then in September a letter from her husband—who was then in Provence—opened her eyes. The best record of the position is to be found in this letter, and others succeeding it, which Abelli has preserved:

"I am in despair," wrote M. de Gondi,*" over a letter which M. Vincent has sent me, and which I enclose in the hope that you may find a means to avert such a misfortune as his loss would be to us. I am utterly astonished that he should have told you nothing of his resolve and that you had no warning. I beseech you to use any means to keep him with us, for if the reasons he gives be the real

* Abelli, vol. i., chap. ix.

ones, they do not seem to me worthy of consideration. There are none of them so important as is my salvation and that of my children. I know that he will some day be able to aid us in this, and will help me in those resolutions of which I have often spoken to you, and which I am now more than ever eager to make. I have not yet replied to him, and shall wait to do so till I hear from you. You must decide whether my sister, de Ragny—who is not far from where he is—would do good by interference. But I think the best hope is from M. de Bérulle. Tell him that even if M. Vincent has not the gift of teaching children, that he may have a man under him; and that in any case I desire most ardently to get him back under my roof, that he may live there as he may choose; for, if he is with me, I myself shall some day live as a righteous man."

By his eagerness and incoherence, M. de Gondi shows us what deep importance he attached to M. Vincent's presence in his home; but to him, in the midst of a busy and active life, the shock of their sudden loss was not so overwhelming as to his wife. Of her we are told that for days she did nothing but weep, and could neither sleep nor eat. She had accustomed herself to accept M. Vincent's decisions in the spirit of obedience, but it is plain that resentment very nearly mastered her. A confidential letter to an intimate friend discloses her mind to us:

"I should never have thought it possible," she wrote. "M. Vincent has shown too great charity towards me to desert me like this. God be praised, however, I do not blame him—far from it. I believe he has only acted under God's special guidance and touched by His grace. But it is very strange, truly, that he should have gone away. I confess I can see no reason for it. He knows how greatly I need his direction and all the business on which I ought to consult him; the sufferings of soul and body which have been the result of losing him; the good which

I am longing to do in our villages, but which can come to nothing without his help. In short, I am in a most pitiable state. You know how indignantly M. le Général has written, and that my children are losing ground daily; that all the good he was doing in my household and among the seven or eight thousand souls on the estate has come to an end. Yet are not these souls bought by the Blood of Our Lord as truly as are those in Bresse? Are they not equally dear to Him? I do not know how M. Vincent regards it, it is true; but to me these things seem so important that I shall spare no means to get him back again. He only desires the Glory of God, and I desire nothing that is against His Holy Will; but I do beseech Him to give him back to me. I pray the Holy Mother, and should pray even more vigorously, if my own personal need was not so intertwined with that of M. le Général, of my children, our household, and our tenants."

The pendulum swings rapidly betwixt the mood of submission, which was an acquired virtue, and the imperious wrath, which was the natural instinct of one of her class. Mme. de Gondi shows herself very human in this outpouring, and it is hard to understand how M. Vincent reconciled his conscience to a desertion that seems strangely unfeeling in its method. He had, without question, received abundant kindness from his employers; they had made a visible effort to conform their way of life to his standards, and the extent of his influence could not have been hidden even from his own eyes. We cannot arrive at any explanation with complete certainty, for we have only outward facts by which to judge his conduct; but it is possible that M. Vincent reached the crisis of his life in that year of the first Mission, and that the stirring of his soul towards his real life-work brought him to that deep spiritual experience which is termed Conversion. If this was indeed the case, he was impelled to his sudden flight by a force that he could not resist; he had no choice. The Call of God had come to him to leave the familiar things among which he had prospered so notably and to sojourn among strangers, that he might test the standards of his life. It was imperative that he should obey, for his sense of vocation was synonymous with such obedience, and the great enterprise of the Missions — which he seemed to be evading — may have been dependent on the complete submission of his will.

Whether this is the true explanation of his action or not, his use of the years before and after the experiment at Châtillon seem to prove that his sensational escape was not the result of a sudden whim or a desire for novelty. The episode remains mysterious, but, considered in its practical aspect alone, it has immense importance. It lasted less than six months, but it gave M. Vincent knowledge of the conditions of a provincial town which it would have been hard to acquire otherwise. It brought him into touch with a class of persons who were new to him, and—as we shall see in connection with the foundation of the Confraternities of Charity—it was while he was curé at Châtillon that he received a suggestion from which sprung vast undertakings in the future.

The hope cherished by M. and Mme. de Gondi that de Bérulle's authority would restore M. Vincent to them was a fallacious one. In fact, de Bérulle was the confidante of M. Vincent's intention, and procured for him the cure that made fulfilment of it possible; and Châtillon was an admirable field for his energy. There were many priests attached to his church there, and they seem to have been lively persons addicted to field sports and the wearing of lay attire. His conception of the obligations of priesthood must have come as a surprise to them; but, if tradition may be trusted, his influence and example brought them back to duty. At this time only did M. Vincent win celebrity by effecting some of those sensational conversions of private individuals, which suggest Port Royal rather than S. Lazare. He found the society of a little town frivolous, undisciplined, and silly. He came with all the force of novelty as well as the fire of conviction, and some of those he touched were not again what they had been before he came to them. The popular fashion—against which M. Olier at S. Sulpice afterwards made war—of attending Mass in the most extravagant attire, and chattering behind a fluttering fan during its progress, was prevalent at Châtillon, but it was one for which M. Vincent had no tolerance. He tried the experiment of insisting upon outward seemliness. The power of the priest appeared almost to have lapsed through the habit of laxity in the confessional, but the inheritance of the faith, even in the most frivolous of Catholics, is an incalculable force. Where reverence for Divine worship was in question, M. Vincent became severe, and the result of his severity was a sensational reform, not only in the outward appearance, but in the private life of the chief ladies of the town. Philanthropy took the place of amusement, and some of them seem to have accomplished useful work, which was continued when the direct personal influence of M. Vincent had been withdrawn. There was the case, also, of a certain M. Beyrier, a young man in whose house M. Vincent hired a lodging. He was so celebrated for his riotous hospitality that the priest was urged not to countenance him; but perhaps the fact that he had been brought up a Huguenot and had abjured those errors, even though he did not attain to the full practice of any other faith, gave him a special claim. M. Vincent remained under his roof in spite of the expostulations of the well-meaning, and in due course the young men of the town awoke to the unwelcome knowledge that the gayest of their playfellows was taking life seriously, and becoming a devout Catholic, as well as a good and sober citizen.

And, finally, to this short episode in M. Vincent's career belongs the romantic story of the Comte de Rougemont the great seigneur of the district, who had been cele-

IN THE SERVICE OF M. DE GONDI

brated far and near for his wild life, and was one of the most notable of duellists. From the lurid and rather fantastic tradition regarding this gentleman's youth, it would seem that he had not the least respect for any principle of mercy or of charity; as a type he presented as sharp a contrast to M. Vincent as is conceivable. That fact in itself may possibly have had an effect on him. The new parish priest, whose influence was stirring the town of Châtillon, was animated by aims and instincts that were altogether outside the experience of that magnificent personage, Balthazar de Rougemont, Baron de Chandes. Out of curiosity, he joined the congregation that gathered to hear one of M. Vincent's sermons; still, it may be, out of curiosity, he sought personal intercourse with the preacher, and the force of contrast between this man's life and his own, the promise of magnificent usefulness in the one and the certainty of evil effectiveness in the other, impressed and absorbed him. Little by little the man of peace conquered the duellist, the estates of Rougemont were sold—with a recklessness characteristic of their owner—and the proceeds were given for the support of works of charity; the festivities of the Château de Chandes where he made his abode ceased for ever, and the only guests were the needy. The most severe of the Hermits of Port Royal could not have outdone him in rigour of renunciation. It is told of him—and if the story is inaccurate in detail, it is true in spirit—that when his conversion had gone far and he had learnt to deprive himself of all those desires and possessions which had been his by right, he made the discovery that his sword, the companion of his adventurous career, was very precious to him; and thereupon he drew it from its sheath and struck it against a rock until it fell in fragments. So great was the sacrifice that afterwards he had no difficulty in obeying any demand his conscience might make upon him; for him the joy of life was represented by his sword, and without it the only way was that Way of the Cross to which it seemed that Christ had summoned him. M. de Rougemont did not live to old age, but while life lasted he maintained the practices of asceticism and penitence he had adopted.

Records of this kind are rare in biographies of Vincent de Paul because it was only at this stage that he had close connection with the class whose conversion appeals to the imagination. The poor and ordinary were the chosen objects of his spiritual energy, and these had no individual history. In his intercourse with the rich it was his part to guide those who were already the declared followers of Christ, rather than to retrieve those who forgot Him; and in his dealing with the priesthood it is likely that he was himself responsible for the careful concealment of well-known names.

During these months of labour in new fields he seems to have shown no sign of compassion for the distress of Mme. de Gondi; but his silence did not check her in her efforts to win him back. She went to Paris and succeeded in enlisting M. de Bérulle in her cause. She devoted all her thoughts and energies to it, and all her projects of benefiting her tenants slipped into abeyance. Her state of mind is represented by the following letter which she wrote to M. Vincent:

"I told you often of my fear of losing your help, and it was not a vain fear, because now I have indeed lost it; I could not bear the misery of it if it were not for a special grace of God of which I am unworthy. If it was only for a time I should not be so unhappy, but when I reflect on all my need of direction and advice, for dying and for living, my distress overwhelms me. Do you think either soul or body will be able to bear this trouble for very long? I am not able to seek or to accept any help elsewhere, for you know very well that it is only to very few that I can disclose the needs of my soul. M. de Bérulle has promised me to write to you, and I call on God and on the Blessed Virgin to restore you to us for the salvation not only of my family, but of so many others who need your charity. And once again I beseech you to extend this charity of yours towards us, for the sake of your love for Our Lord. I yield myself to His Will, even though I fear greatly that I shall not be able to continue to do so. If you still refuse me, I hold you responsible before God for all the evil that may come to me and for all the good I fail to do for lack of help. You expose me to the risk of being often deprived of the Sacraments because in my great distress there are so few who are able to help me. You know that M. le Général has just the same desire (with which God has mercifully inspired him). Do not forego the good that you might do in helping towards his conversion, for it might at some future time affect so many others. I know that my own life, being only an offence before God, there is no reason that it should not be endangered, but my soul needs preparation for death. Do you remember my terror in my last illness when I was in the country? I am on the verge of even greater misery, and the dread of it alone does me so much harm that I fear—unless something counterbalances it—it may kill me."*

There was no immediate result from this appeal, and it is extremely likely that it obtained no reply. M. Vincent held strongly to the view that no soul can depend on individual direction, that all help of this kind is fallacious unless it be recognized as derived from God and given or withheld according to His Will. It was on M. de Bérulle that Mme. de Gondi made an impression. We have no means of knowing the extent of his interference. In October M. Vincent began to show signs of wavering. He had worked hard, and would have been content to remain working hard in his retreat; but probably, when the pressure of distractions that had preyed upon him was removed, he was able to see his life in truer proportion. As the weeks drew out and the appeals from those he

* Abelli, vol. i., chap. ix.

had left behind grew more and more insistent, some misgivings may have been mingled with his relief. He consented to see M. de Fresne, secretary to M. de Gondi, and at his suggestion he went to Lyons to discuss his position with the Superior of the Oratory there. The hopes of Mme. de Gondi may well have risen at the first rumour that M. Vincent was reconsidering his decision. The arguments for his return to her and to all the work she offered him were far more weighty than the claim of Châtillon on its new curé. But the Superior at Lyons was prudent and discreet, and by his advice there was to be further time taken for reflection. As a result of their interview a letter was despatched informing M. de Gondi that before the year ended Vincent de Paul was coming to Paris to take counsel with certain devout persons there. The reply was prompt:

"I received that which you wrote me from Lyons two days ago, and I note your resolve to make a journey to Paris at the end of November. I am greatly rejoiced at this, hoping to see you then, and that you will grant—at my entreaty and at the advice of your best friends—the favour that I ask of you. I say no more, because you have seen the letter I wrote to my wife; I only ask you to remember how likely it seems that God wishes that the reform of the father as well as of the children should be effected by you."*

For another two months the people of Châtillon had the benefit of M. Vincent's presence, and then he bade them farewell and started for Paris, arriving there December 23. Ostensibly he sought the advice of M. de Bérulle, but the substance of that advice was not doubtful for M. de Bérulle had joined forces with Mme. de Gondi, and on Christmas Eve Vincent de Paul returned to the de Gondi household, under a pledge to remain the spiritual director of its mistress so long as her life lasted.

In fact, M. Vincent's retreat had made him a far more

* Abelli, vol. i., chap. ix.

notable personage than he would have been if he had accepted the ordinary progress of events. He had been the theme of endless discussion and correspondence, and his subsequent position with the employers he had deserted could not have been that of an ordinary dependent. The step taken to break up his growing reputation had just the opposite effect; on his return he found it more firmly established. But, whether his flight from Montmirail was, or was not, an error, it must be regarded as a landmark in the career of M. Vincent. After it there is no longer any uncertainty in his progress; he had definite ends before him, and he went forward steadily in pursuit of them.

Mme. de Gondi had awaited his aid to put into shape the shadowy ideas awakened by the incident at Folleville. She had seen the plan of a Mission spring—almost of itself—from the actual and intimate experience of an individual need, and its success had made a deep impression upon her. She was weighed down by a sense of responsibility towards the large numbers of tenants on her husband's estates, and she thought she recognized a Divine summons to provide for their spiritual necessities by the assistance of M. Vincent. The Folleville sermon that had so stirred the hearts of the people was to be the first of a long series; the personal influence which had done so much to deepen its after effect was to touch as many as possible of the thousands who were needing it. There was no shadow of self-glorification in her scheme. From the haven of her home M. Vincent was to go forth on his mission of succour to famished souls. All the material support he needed she and her husband were to supply, but in the work itself he, and he only, would be God's agent. Her purpose only grew stronger during that long autumn of suspense, and when M. Vincent was at last restored to her, she lost no time in attempting to fulfil it. She offered to endow—with the sum of 16,000 livres—a band of preachers who would engage to make a complete circuit of her estates in the course of every five years. Vincent approved the idea; he was ready to assist, but he considered himself unworthy to lead, and he recommended that these preachers should be chosen from some existing community. He approached Père Charlet, a Jesuit, in the hope that he would undertake the work, but sanction could not be obtained from Rome; and when he turned to his old friends the Oratorians, among whom it seemed certain that exactly the right persons might be found, he was met by direct and uncompromising refusal. These and other tentative negotiations with existing bodies of Religious spread over years without producing any result, and Mme. de Gondi chafed at the delay. It was obvious to her that Vincent himself was the fittest person for the post he was inviting others to fill, and that the discouraging reception that was accorded him was an acknowledgment of this fact. In her eyes, indeed, he was the only person able to bring the idea to the fruition that she pictured, and as she had at her command just the ecclesiastical influence most likely to be serviceable, she brought it into play.

The See of Paris had become almost an hereditary possession of the de Gondi. Jean François, who held it at that time, was the first Archbishop, and to a son of the Church, as loyal and as humble as was M. Vincent, his authority would have infinite weight. With him M. and Mme. de Gondi held conclave, and there and then their plan took form. A new Congregation was to be founded, having for headquarters the Collège des Bons Enfants, which stood near the Porte S. Victor. Its members were to be persons who renounced ecclesiastical preferment, and devoted their lives to preaching in the villages. They were to avoid towns of any importance, and were to be wayfarers defraying the necessary expenses of travel from a fund held in common. Their selection was to be made by their Superior.

Mme. de Gondi and the Archbishop then made a joint

appeal to Vincent to be the first Superior, and his consent was a foregone conclusion. The scheme was in accordance with his most cherished desires. Clearly it was only humility that withheld him from volunteering to inaugurate it. In March, 1624, the Archbishop made over the Collège des Bons Enfants to be prepared for its new uses. Just a year later M. and Mme. de Gondi executed the Contract of Foundation. The clauses of this contract embodied the original scheme, and were simple and uncomplicated. The Founders were sincerely desirous of providing for the spiritual needs of the poor, and, departing from the usage of their kind, made no demand that Masses should be said for their own welfare. But all the holy zeal with which Madame was animated did not lessen her need of Vincent's support and actual presence, and the deed that sets forth the duty, responsibility, and authority vested in the " Sieur de Paul " provides that he shall, notwithstanding, make his abode continually and actually in the house of the Founders, to the end that he may continue to render to them and to their family the same spiritual guidance as for many long years they have received.

Since the summer day when he had fled from temptation, M. Vincent had grown in spiritual capacity. If he was sincerely anxious that the new Company should fulfil the purpose of its Foundress, he must have deplored a provision that condemned him to certain inefficiency; but he was able, from its earliest beginning, to confide it and its development to God. And events proved that it was the Will of God that it should grow, and that it should grow under his guidance. A new Order will not prosper under a Superior who is perpetually an absentee, and Vincent was pledged to remain with Madame for the rest of her life. She was greatly his junior, so that the prospect was not promising. But two months after signing the Contract of Foundation the Foundress was taken ill, and died in a few days. She had Vincent with her, and her end was peaceful, though her husband was far away in Provence. When she was laid to rest in the Carmelite Convent in the Rue Chapon, the Superior of the new Congregation hastened south to break the news to M. le Général, and through the sadness of that mission there glowed the welcome certainty that the chain which bound him to the uncongenial life of these noble persons was finally broken.

In vain had Mme. de Gondi attempted to command the future by her Will, and with the force of a voice from the dead implored Vincent to remain with her husband and her sons, while with equal fervour she laid a last command on those nearest to her to " keep him with them, and to remember and to follow all his directions." There is extraordinary pathos in this woman's confidence in the power of the pure soul it had been her lot to encounter, to shield those whom she loved against all evils that might beset them; and she is essentially womanly in her disregard for all consideration of proportion when she claims to monopolize this power in the interest of her own family. But the attempt was ineffectual. By the free consent of M. de Gondi, Vincent moved to the Collège des Bons Enfants a few weeks after the death of Madame, and so entered upon the fulfilment of his real vocation. Two years later the magnificent General of the Galleys abandoned all his state and dignity, and was admitted to the Congregation of the Oratory.

CHAPTER III

M. VINCENT AND THE PRIESTHOOD

VINCENT DE PAUL was now forty-eight years old. He stood high in the estimation of those who knew him, but he had earned no great renown; his name was known to a small circle only. For ten years he had been a dependent in a rich man's household, and although he had made for himself an exceptional position, he could not escape some of the drawbacks attendant on that state. He was a peasant by birth, he had never held a post of any importance, and had he died at the end of fifty years of a devout and rather toilsome existence there would have been nothing notable to record about him. But, in fact, that fifty years was his apprenticeship. In action and in judgment he was deliberate; he had not been less so in development.

At their end he accepted a divine commission to revive the faith. He had seen the fields lying ripe for harvest, and he entered almost alone upon the labour of gathering. No great and penetrating appeal, such as might arouse the sluggard heart and conscience, was made from the pulpit of Notre Dame. No Court influence spread the knowledge of the need. There was nothing stirring or eventful to mark an epoch of reform. Vincent went to the Collège des Bons Enfants, and his faithful friend, M. Portail, joined him. It is well that we should have the description of their inauguration in his own words.

"We had with us a good priest to whom we gave 30 crowns a year," he told the Company thirty years later,* " and we went about all three together from village to village preaching and holding missions. When we started we gave the key to a neighbour, and asked him to go and sleep in the house. Such was our custom when certain other priests bore witness that the blessing of God was on our labours by wishing to join us."

The new recruits were du Coudray and de la Salle, and on September 4, 1626, a formal Act of Association was drawn up between Vincent de Paul and his three first companions by which they all pledged themselves to the service of the poor in the country according to the Foundation, and to live together as a community; and the three companions promised obedience to Vincent de Paul as Superior, and to his successors in that office.†

A few months later their numbers were doubled, but there was no excitement about them, no moment when a crown of volunteers was knocking for admittance at the great doors of the house in the Rue S. Victor. Their growth was gradual but it was steady, and in January, 1632, the Company was so far established as to receive formal recognition from the Pope (Urban VIII.). Thenceforward it was to be known as the Congregation of the Mission.

It was at this early stage in the history of the Congregation that the Superior was also the leader in the actual work of country missions. Later, as was inevitable, it became very difficult for him to leave Paris, and his responsibilities were too great and too numerous to allow of a wandering existence. Probably, those early days were a cherished memory, his references to them in afteryears are frequent. The cause of the poor from the point of view of spiritual neglect and ignorance was very dear to him, and he said that when he decided to return to Paris, after a course of village missions, it seemed to him as if the gateway of the city ought to fall on him for

* Conference, May 17, 1658. † See Appendix, note 1.

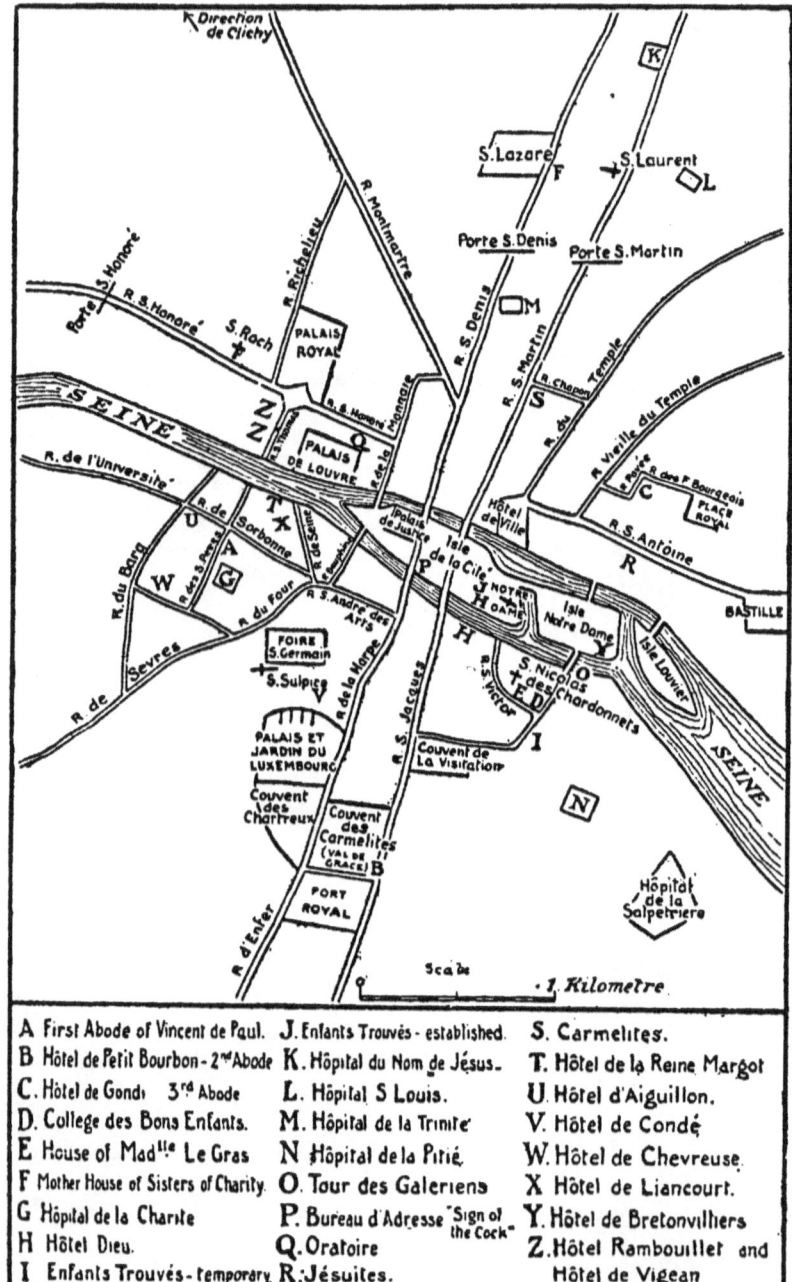

A First Abode of Vincent de Paul.
B Hôtel de Petit Bourbon – 2nd Abode
C Hôtel de Gondi   3rd Abode
D College des Bons Enfants.
E House of Mad^{lle} Le Gras
F Mother House of Sisters of Charity.
G Hôpital de la Charité
H Hôtel Dieu.
I Enfants Trouvés – temporary.
J Enfants Trouvés – established.
K Hôpital du Nom de Jésus.
L Hôpital S Louis.
M Hôpital de la Trinité
N Hôpital de la Pitié.
O Tour des Galeriens
P Bureau d'Adresse "Sign of the Cock"
Q Oratoire
R Jésuites.
S Carmelites.
T Hôtel de la Reine Margot
U Hôtel d'Aiguillon.
V Hôtel de Condé
W Hôtel de Chevreuse.
X Hôtel de Liancourt.
Y Hôtel de Bretonvilliers
Z Hôtel Rambouillet and Hôtel de Vigean

THE PARIS OF VINCENT DE PAUL.

M. VINCENT AND THE PRIESTHOOD

turning away from the innumerable souls whom he left in need.*

He would have been content to pursue his work on a humble scale, but his Foundation was destined for a certain outward greatness. In 1630, two years before the Papal sanction had been given, there came one day to the Collège des Bons Enfants an ecclesiastic of position and repute—M. Adrien le Bon, Prior of the Augustinian Order of *Chanoines Réguliers*, established at S. Lazare. This gentleman desired a private interview with M. Vincent, and M. Vincent, being at all times humbly accessible to those who had need of him, the private interview took place forthwith. It was memorable in the history of the Company, although the visitor who had sought it went away downcast. Long afterwards the details of it were made known. M. le Bon—like many another Prior in that period of lax discipline—had had difficulties with the Community. Possibly some cross current of new idea set afloat by de Bérulle or by Vincent de Paul had been wafted to him, and his eyes had opened suddenly to irregularities practised habitually under shelter of his jurisdiction. Possibly he was precipitate in acting on the impulse of the new revelation. It is clear that he found his authority inadequate to accomplish a reform which he conceived to be necessary. In his dilemma he went to M. Vincent with a suggestion (to which the Community must have agreed) that S. Lazare should in future be the headquarters of the Mission priests, and that the new-born Company should join forces with his Augustinian monks. He thought—with some reason—that the inducements he could offer for his scheme were, to say the least, worthy of consideration by the head of a small and struggling Order, but Vincent's refusal was direct and absolute. The time had come at last when he saw his aim in life clear-cut and definite, and he would not deviate from the pursuit

* Abelli, vol. ii., chap. i., sect. 3.

of it. There might be need of reform among the Augustinian monks of S. Lazare, there was great likelihood that the influence of his own small band might accomplish much that was needed, but he did not recognize the claim: his little company had more work than it could do already, and even at that early stage he grasped the necessity of concentration. Many a time in after-years he heard the call of work that needed doing, of work that probably he could have done, but which lay outside the limit of that which he had undertaken; and always he stood firm, realizing—as smaller minds cannot—that only by the rigorous preservation of the limit that he recognized could he fulfil the gigantic task assigned to him.

In 1630, therefore, M. le Bon failed to obtain any help in his difficulties from the Superior of the Collège des Bons Enfants. But he seems to have been notably pertinacious, and he enlisted others in his cause. There was a learned Doctor of the Sorbonne, M. de Lestocq, who set to work to break down M. Vincent's resolution touching the proffered establishment at S. Lazare. Against the offer in its original form Vincent's decision was unalterable, but the offer was changed, and the advocates of acceptance were persuasive. "We cried after him," says M. de Lestocq in describing the affair, "as did the woman of Canaan after the Apostles." The strange suggestion of amalgamating the two Orders was dropped, and instead Vincent and his Company were invited to take up their quarters at S. Lazare. There was no valid reason for refusal, and at length he consented to refer the question to another Doctor of the Sorbonne, M. André du Val, and to abide by his decision.

No impartial judge could have hesitated. The Company of Mission priests was growing steadily, it showed every sign of life. The Collège des Bons Enfants which had sufficed for the pioneers was quite inadequate as the headquarters of an important movement. S. Lazare, on the other hand, was so finely situated, and carried with it so much of the dignity that was adherent in the seigneurial buildings of Paris, that its occupation by an Order that had become demoralized and effete was in itself a subject for regret.* To the onlooker it seemed that M. le Bon had been directly moved by the inspiration of God in furtherance of the designs of Vincent de Paul. But then and always, as we shall see, Vincent himself held back, lest an appearance of success should tempt him into presumption. It was more than a year after the original proposition before he showed any signs of wavering, and when, after the advice of M. du Val, he could no longer shirk acceptance, he showed no desire to inspect the splendid property which was so miraculously given into his hands. At the last moment, indeed, it seemed likely that he would break off negotiations on a clause in the agreement that to others seemed of infinitesimal importance. M. le Bon desired that his monks should have the benefit of association with the Mission Priests, and sleep in the same dormitories; but on this point Vincent was obdurate. To him his Company appeared as a sacred trust from God for a sacred purpose. His indifference to their temporal fortunes was sincere; he knew that his responsibility towards them was the development of his ideal for their inner life, and their outward establishment was nought in comparison. Years of varied experience lay behind him. He had acquired knowledge of human nature, he knew the temptations to which his Missioners would be exposed by the roving and unsettled life which was part of their vocation, and here at the very beginning of his appointed work he stood firm. The rule which had protected him amid the distractions of a ducal household he now laid down for them. "The true Missioner," he said, "must be as an Apostle in the world, but as a Chartreux at home,"

* Tradition says that in 1630 the only occupants of these vast buildings were eight Augustinians and five imbeciles.

and no advantage to be gained from the possession of S. Lazare would compensate them for the injury of association with demoralized Religious. But S. Lazare was the destined home of the Congregation of the Mission, and M. le Bon gave in on every point. In January, 1632, Vincent de Paul entered into possession, and although before the year was out his right was disputed by another community, no power proved strong enough to oust him.

This great change in outward circumstances opened a new field of labour. For eight years the Mission Priests had travelled from village to village striving to awake the country people to spiritual life. M. Vincent declared that no one knew so much about the peasantry of France as did his Missioners, and there was good reason that that statement should be accurate. But this knowledge went beyond the people themselves, and touched those on whom lay the real responsibility of their ignorance. It was the experience gained in country missions that showed Vincent de Paul the need for the reforming of the clergy, and it is necessary to cast a glance at the conditions prevalent, before we consider M. Vincent's measures for dealing with them.

In 1628 a Bishop, writing to him of his own diocese, declared "*Qu'il y a presque 7,000 Prêtres ivrognes ou impudiques qui montent tous les jours à l'Autel et qui n'ont aucune vocation.*" The extent of evil conveyed in that short sentence is baffling to the imagination, but many contemporary records bear out the same impression. The monasteries were centres of licence and disorder, their Superiors were appointed solely for mercenary reasons, and the idea of obedience became an absurdity. Henri de Bourbon, son of Henri IV., was Abbé of S. Germain des Prés, and held ecclesiastical authority over that quarter of Paris; he held other preferment of the same nature, and became Bishop of Metz. He was never a priest, however, and in his old age he married.* The priests of gentle birth were more likely to prosper if they were well known in society and welcome for their wit; the humbler sort were not hampered by complete ignorance of their duties. M. Vincent, addressing his Company,† put on record the experience of Mme. de Gondi in this matter. "My late lady," he said, "having made confession to her curé, noticed that he did not give her absolution. He murmured something between his teeth, and did the same again at other times when she confessed to him, which troubled her somewhat. At length she asked a Religious who came to see her to set down in writing the formula of absolution, which he did. And the lady, when she next went to confession, asked the curé to give her the words of absolution on the paper, which he did. And she continued to do this every time she confessed to him, always giving him the paper, because he was so ignorant he did not know the words that should be used in absolution. And having heard this, I began to pay more special attention when I myself confessed, and I found that it was really the case, and that there were some who did not know the words of absolution." But it was not only for the administration of the Sacrament of Penance that elementary knowledge was lacking, M. Vincent drew the attention of the Company also to the variety of methods of celebrating; he describes the diversity of ritual, the rearrangement of the Canon. "I was once," he said, "at S. Germain en Laye, and I saw seven or eight priests all saying Mass in a different way."

He was speaking, in 1659, of a period forty years earlier, to the end that his sons might know how imperative the need had been when the Company first entered on its labours; and, over and over again, he made the evils of the time the theme of his discourse. "The Church has

* See Rohrbacher, "Hist. de l'Église Catholique," vol. xxv., p. 244.
† Conference, May 13, 1659.

no enemies so dangerous as the priests," he told them. "It is due to the priests that the heretics have flourished, that vice has gained its mastery, and that ignorance is so prevalent among the people. Is it not worth any sacrifice that you can make, Messieurs, to help to their reform, so that they may live in conformity with the greatness and dignity of their calling, and by this means the Church may be delivered from the contempt and desolation that has come upon her?"*

Such utterances as these show us how deeply M. Vincent was affected by the revelations of depravity that came to him. He maintained always that "those who celebrated the Sacred Mysteries were unworthy if they fell short of perfection, for the holy profession they had made demanded nothing less." He could not be content with mediocrity either in himself or in others; he demanded the perpetual struggle and no less perpetual failure of those who aim at perfection, and yet everywhere he was confronted by the spectacle of vice and hypocrisy—for the diocese that had 7,000 priests possessed by the devils of intemperance and immorality was not an isolated instance.

In fact, it was M. Vincent's fate to see human nature in its extreme of savage ugliness. Not only was he witness of the exceptional horrors that were evolved by the Fronde Rebellion, but many of the enterprises that were part of his vocation brought him into touch with the degradation of life in the byways and hidden places of great cities, with all the infamy that infected the convicts and galley slaves in a period of authorized brutality. And in what he saw there was no inherent material for hope. It must be remembered that he could not look to a phalanx of philanthropists with possible energy to gather up what he might leave undone. In those early days there were no benevolent societies, there was no organization, there were very few priests who

* Conference, May 6, 1658.

recognized that they had any duty towards the poor; yet poverty and ignorance, with all the evil that breeds from their alliance, prevailed alike in the cities and in the country districts, and M. Vincent heard the call to meet the needs he saw, temporal and spiritual, and for him that call meant leadership as well as personal labour. The odds against success were so great that reason must have suggested despair; but it was the hopelessness of the case that taught M. Vincent the remedy. " For you by yourself the task is certainly too great," he wrote to one of his Mission Priests who was overburdened by responsibility; " but for you, with the help of God, nothing is too difficult." That was his discovery and the source of his continual courage.

It was with the sense that nothing was too difficult for God to make plain that M. Vincent approached the problem of the degraded priesthood. While he was still at the Collège des Bons Enfants he had made an attempt to re-establish the Ordination Retreats which had fallen into disuse, and during his last year there the Archbishop of Paris issued an order that every candidate for priesthood should make a Retreat with the Company of the Mission before his ordination; but it was only after the removal to S. Lazare that this work could assume its fit proportions. In days before the duties of Superior to the Company had become absorbing, Vincent de Paul went many times to Beauvais at the invitation of its Bishop, Augustin Potier, a man who regarded the misdeeds of the ecclesiastics under his jurisdiction as bringing disgrace upon himself. The two held long discourse over the terrible disease that was so apparent to them both, but it was the Bishop who suggested the remedy. It was a suggestion that bore witness to his wisdom. In face of a crying evil it is a natural instinct to resort to some drastic measure, and only a really wise man will direct his energies to prevent it in the future, instead of wasting them on a vain endeavour to correct in the present. In those days it seems that the conversion and reform of a depraved priest was regarded as a miracle; the contagion of drunkenness alone had spread so widely that no one cherished a hope of cure, and it was only from a new generation of priests that the people would again receive guidance and example. To secure a change in the new generation Bishop Potier and Vincent de Paul reorganized Ordination Retreats.

The scheme was first put in practice at Beauvais in 1628, and it was then that the Directions for Ordination Candidates* were drawn up. These directions point to strictness of life of the most searching kind; the young priest who really followed them would have no possibility of slipping unconsciously into laxity. The complete consecration of life at ordination was to be followed by the scrupulous ruling of every hour, and by submission not only in outward things to the Bishop, but also to a Director, who was to be given knowledge of every spiritual difficulty. M. Vincent was well aware that the time of test would always come after the vivid impression of the Retreat was over and all excitement had subsided, and it was his ambition to sow a seed that should be long in springing and deeply rooted. At Beauvais, in the Rue S. Victor, and afterwards for many years at S. Lazare, M. Vincent conducted the Ordination Retreats himself; he set the standard of simplicity which was to be the characteristic of the Lazarist, and upheld the greatness of responsibility involved by this task of theirs. Again and again he made these Retreats the theme of his "Conferences" with his sons, urging on them the humility that was essential if "this paltry Company" was to be worthy of its charge. "It is not by knowledge that you will do good," he told them, "or by the fine things that you can say to them; they are more learned than we are. Very little they can get from us would be new to them; they have read or heard it all before. They say them-

* See Appendix, note 2.

selves that it is not in that way they are touched, but by the strictness of life that they see in practice here.".

These Ordination Retreats may well have served as a spur to the Mission Priests themselves for the perfecting of their individual lives, and from the first it seemed as if the new Company had been endowed with a special vocation for its task. It was on their quiet intercourse with the Retreatants that their Superior depended. "If you are filled with that which is Divine," he told them, "and if each one of you is struggling continually after perfection, then, though you may seem to have no capacity for helping these gentlemen, God will be able to use you to light them on their way."

"You must know," wrote Vincent de Paul to du Coudray,* "that the goodness of God has bestowed a blessing—so great as to be almost beyond belief—on our Ordination Exercises; so great is it that all those who have been through them—or almost all—are leading lives such as a good priest should lead. There are some who are notable either for their birth or for other qualities that God has given them, who live as strictly by rule as we do here, and are more spiritual than many of us—more so, for instance, than I am myself. They have a time-table, and are regular in mental prayer, in saying Mass, in self-examination, even as we are. They devote themselves to visiting hospitals and prisons, where they preach and catechize and hear confessions; they do this also in the colleges, and are very specially blessed in doing it."

This letter was written only a year after the Company was established at S. Lazare, and it shows us what immense encouragement Vincent de Paul received in his early undertakings as Superior. It shows also how closely he grasped those things which he undertook. S. Lazare was not merely a hostel where these future priests might gather on the eve of ordination, and go through a certain spiritual routine; it was a centre of

* "Lettres," vol. i., No. 18, July, 1633.

real inspiration, and to stay there meant personal touch with M. Vincent, and the after-knowledge—for each one who sought such a privilege—that his thoughts and prayers would go with them in the new life, on the threshold of which they stood. In that time of low standards it would be hard to exaggerate the possible effect of such an experience. M. Vincent, in spite of his homeliness and humility, had an ideal of priesthood that was never lowered to meet the difficulties of any individual; he was impossible to satisfy, but his unreasonable demands stimulated instead of discouraging, and it was sustained intention rather than complete fulfilment that he expected of them.

" It is our will that in each of the four Seasons of the Year M. Vincent de Paul and his Company (without hindrance to their Missions) should receive and provide for the Candidates for Ordination in the diocese of Paris sent by us, for a fortnight, that they may go through the Spiritual Exercises." So runs a clause of the deed by which the Archbishop of Paris established the Mission Priests at S. Lazare; and large donations from other quarters for the expense thereby involved testify to the widespread recognition of the value of the enterprise. And, indeed, it is not hard to understand that M. Vincent's influence, brought to bear at the right moment on characters not yet distorted by the habit of evil-doing, might have been lifelong in its effects. The careless youth coming for ordination indolently, the weak who allowed himself an optimistic view of a future that would somehow be better than the past, the calculating for whom the priesthood opened a gateway of ambition—to all these the voice of M. Vincent had power to sound a note of warning.

It was always possible that those days might prove the most important in a man's life. Many there were, no doubt, who accepted and went through the Exercises as through a course of lectures; who made notes of the instruction in the earlier hours of the day that was devoted to the outward duties of priesthood; who asked intelligent questions at the conferences that succeeded such instructions, and were able to employ the time for relaxation in real repose. Such as these took away with them a memory that might fade completely, or might in the far-off future stir the desire for understanding of that which had once been in their reach. The Archbishop of Paris gave the order that all whom he ordained should go into Retreat, but no reasonable person, lay or clerical, imagined that the fifteen days of retirement would transform dross into gold by magic. They were " to conform to the ancient practice of the Church," so ran the Archbishop's command, and by fifteen days of study and seclusion they fulfilled what the Church required. It was to the few and not to the many that M. Vincent was sent. He had many listeners to the discourses that he gave every evening of a Retreat on the deep things of the inner life; and to one here and there his words rent away the veil that hid reality, and the meaning of their vocation stood revealed. It was an ordinary thing to the world that a young man should become a priest. A great many priests were needed, and as there were not enough candidates for ordination among the more educated classes, a well-to-do peasant would select the most studious of his sons (as M. Vincent himself had been selected) that he might enter the priesthood, get preferment for himself, and push the interests of his family. Indolence or ambition were frequent substitutes for vocation, and it was not likely that a higher ideal could survive the pressure of accepted custom unless support was offered to it.

When we come to consider M. Vincent in his intercourse with individuals, as shown by his letters, we shall see the measure of his sympathetic understanding. For his task of direction in these Ordination Retreats, this was the power that was most essential. His own view of the sacerdotal vocation had no relation to prevailing opinion;

in his old age he declared himself to be unworthy of it;
"*Si je n'étais pas prêtre je ne le serais jamais.*" But it was
not so much his part to present impossibilities to those
whose career was already chosen and approved, as to show
them how they might meet the claim the future inevitably
would make upon them. They would need stupendous
strength and courage, and only from the Master Whom
they professed to follow could they draw it. The deepest
of the demands of their Retreat was that of honesty with
their own conscience, and it was to the few who made of
their ordination the turning-point of their lifetime that
the full meaning of such honesty revealed itself. To
these the idea of taking up their office was awe-inspiring,
and it was a natural instinct among them to turn to
M. Vincent for a continuance of help. It was to meet
this need that there was instituted *Les Conférences du
Mardi*.* On June 25, 1633, a number of young priests
met together at S. Lazare and formed themselves into a
species of guild. They were pledged to complete detachment from self-interest, to a pure and direct intention of
making the offering of self to God, and to maintain a fixed
resolve to serve Him in the person of the poor, the sick,
and the captives. There were to be weekly gatherings,
and membership was not very easy to obtain. M. Vincent
required that the individual life of each member should
be known to the officials of the " Conferences " (of whom
he was himself the chief), and that his participation
should have practical effect upon their actions. Very
soon after their first assembly he called upon some of
them by way of test to preach a Mission to the workmen
employed on some new buildings near the Porte Sainte
Antoine,† and at all times he seems to have regarded
them as an auxiliary force for Mission work. At the
weekly gatherings discussion was encouraged. The subject of debate was always announced beforehand, so that

* In 1642 the day of meeting was altered to Thursday.
† See " Vincent de Paul et le Sacerdoce," by a Mission Priest.

M. VINCENT AND THE PRIESTHOOD 59

there might be time for reflection, and the real part of the Director was left to the end, when he summed up the points of the previous argument, and gave a few words of counsel.

It was this personal touch with Vincent de Paul that gave the " Conferences " their attraction and their influence. In his lifetime 300 members were enrolled, and among them were numbered Jean Jacques Olier, Bossuet, and M. Tronson, each of whom became himself a centre of inspiration. If this work were the only one accomplished by M. Vincent, it would establish him as the benefactor of his generation. The power of the priest for good or evil was so far-reaching as to be illimitable, and it was being used chiefly for evil. To belong to the " Conferences " demanded reality in practice as well as in profession; the conduct of the members was so scrutinized that a defaulter would inevitably be found out; yet their number increased steadily. There is a tradition (the truth of which is borne out by after-events) that Richelieu sent for M. Vincent and asked him for a list of the members of his " Conferences," with a mark against the names of those whom he thought suitable for a bishopric, and that the list was given, but only after the Cardinal had pledged himself to secrecy, lest the taint of self-interest might ruin a pure endeavour.

The work of S. Lazare—which at this time was almost sensationally successful—may seem to suggest that M. Vincent and his associates were the first to realize the great abuse under which society was groaning. This was by no means the case, however. Every conscientious priest of that generation was forced to admit the degradation of his order, and various theories were promulgated from time to time by those who sought a method of reform. There was a certain M. Charles Godefroy, who in 1625 presented to a conference of Bishops in Paris a scheme for facilitating the practice of Retreat among the Clergy, for bringing them within reach of spiritual discipline, and also for training aspirants for priesthood. His scheme foreshadowed much that was afterwards accomplished by the Company of the Mission. It was approved by the assembly of Bishops, but the author died almost immediately, and it bore no fruit.* The Ordination Retreats and the "Conferences" admittedly did not accomplish more than a fraction of the reform that was needed. At their first institution both depended largely on M. Vincent, for it is impossible to doubt that much of their success was due to his personal magnetism; but though this power is useful in inspiring the immediate change of conduct that means defeat of inclination and of custom, it is a dangerous substitute for principle and conviction. It was plain to any reasoning mind that a fortnight's spiritual exercises, even under the care of Vincent de Paul, was not sufficient preparation for the responsibility of priesthood, and the view that a long training was desirable was in accordance with the decree of the Council of Trent, which had provided that every Bishop should have a seminary for the future priests of his diocese.

There is in theory very much to commend the ancient idea of the seminary which admitted boys from twelve years old, and kept them apart, marked by tonsure and cassock, as separate from their fellows; but in practice the seminaries did not produce good priests, and the Bishops abandoned any attempt at obedience. François de Sales, who was not likely to evade a responsibility without reason, declared that he had spent seventeen years trying to train three good priests, and had ended by producing only one and a half!† At Bordeaux and at Rouen, where special efforts were made, the failures were lamentable, the young clerks under training all returning to the world when their education was complete, and pleading their youth at the time of admission as excuse.

* "L'Origine des Grandes Séminaires et M. Charles Godefroi," par l'Abbé Adam.
† Rohrbacher, "Hist. de l'Église Catholique," vol. xxv., p. 249.

Nevertheless, the need of special training remained, and many minds were exercised over the difficulty of providing for it. At the accession of Louis XIII. no seminaries were in existence in France, but de Bérulle began, soon after the foundation of the Oratory, to admit a few young men who were already in deacon's orders, and so gave the suggestion of a new idea. His charges for the most part became Oratorians, however, and the real idea of the seminary was not yet revealed. M. Vincent, moved by the instinct of obedience to the Church that so often prompted his actions, began, at the Collège des Bons Enfants, a seminary of the type suggested by the Council of Trent, and failed as completely as those who preceded him in the same attempt. It was not until 1642 that he decided to eliminate all who were not in holy orders—to keep his seminary, in fact, for those who were already committed and likely to prove steadfast. Through the four stages of ordination these priests of the future were to have every assistance from teaching, association, and influence, and the lads whose vocation was still uncertain were removed to another house in a suburb of Paris, that they might not distract their elders in the solemn years of preparation. This was the beginning of the Lazarist seminaries, and by a simultaneous inspiration, M. Olier began at Vaugirard the seminary that was to obtain—in its after-establishment at S. Sulpice—such vast celebrity. It is impossible now to estimate the importance of this movement, the honour of which is shared betwixt S. Lazare and S. Sulpice. The darkest hour for the Church was over when the new seminaries were opened and accepted, and they were the safeguard of reality in its reform. The age of Bossuet and Bourdaloue was coming, and priests and people were awakening. We need only regard the later years of that century, and contrast the general attitude towards religion with that in vogue when Henri IV. was King, to understand the change that had come to pass. When Mme. de Maintenon reigned at Versailles, society was not guiltless of hypocrisy. It was the fashion to be pious, and fashionable piety is tawdry. But if that smoke were offensive, there was still a fire behind it with capacity for burning clearly —a fire kindled from ashes that barely smouldered ninety years earlier. There had been many manifestations of that fierce desire for goodness which flashes forth even when mankind is at its lowest, and many influences had been at work; but the spiritual influence of M. Vincent must be recognized in this connection. It was, in fact, far more important than his labour for those definite institutions which are responsible for his fame and reputation. What he most desired was that a new standard of living should prevail, and the success of his sons in training others went far to accomplish his desire. The self-repression that he inculcated increased their power in this direction (though this is among the hidden things that may not be weighed or valued), for it should be remembered that they might easily have used the new institution of the seminary for the aggrandizement of the Company of Mission Priests, if their Superior had not forbidden any such use being made of it. The temptation avoided has no necessary place in the record of a life, yet there is no higher proof of this man's greatness than his abstention in this matter. It was in 1642 that Cardinal Richelieu endowed the Collège des Bons Enfants as a place of training for ecclesiastics, and in the years that followed priests from all parts of the country, and of every type, came there. There were some who belonged to the nobility, and some endowed with the qualities that insure power to their possessor; there were among them a few with that capacity for self-devotion in obedience which is the root of strength in a Community, and they were all at a period of transition. It was for that reason that they found themselves at the Collège des Bons Enfants. They had definite things that must be learnt, and, for some at least, things equally definite to be unlearnt; and around them, in touch with them at every moment, were the Priests of the Mission, men whose experiences were of the same order as their own, and who had found peace under a special rule. A suggestion of a possible vocation for the Company dropped at such a moment was likely to bear fruit.

But Vincent's outlook was far too wide for him to permit this simple process of benefit to his foundation. His sense that the Company was of Divine origin did not for a moment blind him to its position as only one among many endeavours for the service of God and of mankind, and its success in the eyes of the world never gave him an exaggerated view of its importance. It had its work to do—by Divine commission—but other work was needed equally, and must not be encroached on in its interests.

Therefore he exhorted his children never to let a word escape them that might attract a listener to the Company. " It is for God to give that summons. And I go farther, even if there should be any who come to you unfolding a desire to join us, beware lest you give them any encouragement. Charge them to make it a subject for communing with God, for it needs much reflection. Impress on them the difficulties they will have with themselves, and that they must be prepared for long delay if they accept our conditions of suffering and of work for God. Let us leave all to God; for ourselves it is only necessary that we should have humility and patience as we await the orderings of His providence. He has mercifully allowed that this should be the method of the Company thus far, and we may feel that we have only what God has given us, and that we have sought neither men nor goods, nor importance. In His Name let us keep to it, and leave all to God. Let us wait for His commands, and not try to forestall them."*

The secret of this man's effective work is in this principle of waiting, so constantly sustained. Not only in his

* Abelli, vol. i., chap. xxxiv.

foundation of the Company of Mission Priests, but in the long catalogue of his achievement, his rule remains invariable: " Let us leave all to God." So far did he carry this reliance that he wrote to one of his Missioners* that he had not dared in twenty years to pray for the growth of the Company, because, if it was the work of God, it must be left in His hands completely. Nevertheless, the more adventurous spirit of a younger generation so far affected him that he recognized their wish to pray for more labourers as being legitimate. That naïve confession, though it may not be defended in relation to the Church's theory of prayer, is nevertheless consistent with Vincent's point of view. Strong as was his faith, it wavered when confronted with the success that in the eyes of men had crowned so many of his enterprises. The blessings showered upon him aroused in him a certain instinct of misgiving and apprehension. We shall see his tendency in his old age to exaggerated self-abasement. He was acutely aware that the applause of human voices implies separation from the Master Who was despised and rejected of men, rather than union with Him.

" Our Lord died as He had lived: His life was hard and painful, His death was violent and agonizing, unrelieved by any human consolation. Many of the Saints, therefore, have been glad to die in loneliness and desolation, knowing that they would have God to comfort them." So he wrote,† with the knowledge that the world was eager to do him honour clear in his mind. In that knowledge, which was never dimmed, lay his safeguard against the snares that surrounded him. The vividness of contrast between his lot and that which was accepted by Christ on earth continued always as a matter for regret and self-reproach, so that he seems strangely to have been disciplined by his moments of outward triumph. But, though he could not escape notability, he was able to

* "Lettres," vol. ii., No. 306, November, 1655.
† *Ibid.*, vol. i., No. 38, 1639.

preserve an order of daily life as laborious and austere as that of the humblest workman. Every day he rose at four, and spent three hours in church, adhering to this habit, although the pressure of business might tempt him to divergence. All day long he was the prey of visitors, who came to consult him, and to all he tried to give a patient hearing. As the years passed, he became so deeply connected with affairs in distant parts of France and of other countries that his correspondence must have been overwhelming. In Paris itself there were many claims upon him which kept him out sometimes for many hours. In the evening he said Office on his knees, and without haste, and afterwards was at the disposal of any of the Company who might desire to consult him. Often, we are told, his business kept him up till a late hour of the night. In that daily routine at S. Lazare, with the pressure of overwork continually upon him, the need for patience is particularly evident. Those who knew him testify that he acquired such a measure of this quality as was almost inexhaustible. In the perpetual interviews required of him he learnt to be brief in giving counsel, but would listen without interrupting. For one whose time was precious, no better opening for self-conquest is conceivable; so large was his charity, and so many the real proofs of it preserved, that it is likely he reached the supreme attainment of the few and suffered fools gladly. In his correspondence there is indication that he did so at least without complaint.

The history of his accomplished work contains developments which Vincent himself referred to as miraculous, but, in fact, nothing more worthy of that term appears than the detail of his own personal doings. When he entered into possession of S. Lazare he took over the responsibility of three or four miserable idiots who had been entrusted to the care of M. le Bon, and made it his practice to serve them himself, although they were distressingly afflicted, and were sometimes dangerous; and if disease broke out under his roof, he was prompt in personal attendance, braving infection himself before consigning the care of the sick to others. We are told that when he had been ten years at S. Lazare, at Christmas-time, 1642, he invited two old beggars to dine with him, and sat between them attending to their wants; and it was characteristic of him that, having once had an opportunity of giving this literal interpretation to his idea of charity, he should hasten to repeat it. Ere long it became the custom to entertain two guests of this type daily at S. Lazare, albeit, "*infirmes et quelquefois assez dégoûtans*," as a contemporary expresses it, and Vincent frequently was seen welcoming them when they appeared, and helping them up the steps of the refectory. Such things as these, if practised by the Father Superior of a monastery whose duties were limited to the control of his Order, might command admiration; but Vincent was not only the founder of his Company, the regulation of which was sufficient to occupy all the energies of any man, but he was the centre and originator of the chief charitable enterprises of his day. He was consulted by the great folk of the Court and by Ministers of State. He was the confidant of innumerable private persons, and he was the head of the new Order of Sisters of Charity which still bears his name. In him these individual kindnesses, to render which it was necessary to step off the beaten track of unremitting labour, are among the miracles of the grace of God.

CHAPTER IV

THE ORDERING OF CHARITY

WE have glanced at the life within the walls of S. Lazare, and at the spread of its influence over the hidden things that touch the souls of men, but all the time that that inward life was developing the great world of Paris seethed and shouted within sight and hearing of the old building and the tragedies that spring from disease and vice and negligence were being enacted hourly in the crowded streets of the city where the poor congregated. In his vocation as a priest M. Vincent held himself to be dedicated to the service of the Church, but, to his understanding, the service of the Church was synonymous with the service of the poor. " The poor our masters," was a phrase constantly on his lips, and he regarded his practical labour for that which would now be called social reform as not less spiritual than the endeavours that related directly to the Church.

In his dealing with the two great Companies he founded we shall, it is true, come closer to him in his personal character than in any other relation; but for proofs of his more visible and startling effectiveness it is necessary to turn away from the austere surroundings of his daily life, and regard that social world of Paris and the provinces which has so much both of likeness and of contrast to the social world of to-day.

The year which gave him the inspiration of his country Missions was also the year of his first great discovery in practical philanthropy. This last was made during his brief ministry at Châtillon, and the occasion of it reveals the simple methods of the charitable 300 years ago, and is therefore worthy of record. The monastic system of giving food at stated times to all who asked for it not only encouraged mendicity, but checked any attempt at rational application of relief. It prevented real destitution, however, and so long as the religious Orders remained wealthy and generous the problem of poverty was kept in abeyance. But the civil wars of the sixteenth century reduced all revenues, and the wide flow of charity dwindled to a trickle that seldom reached those who most needed it. In this notable instance at Châtillon a whole family in a farmhouse were so laid low by illness that they reached the border of starvation. As M. Vincent was about to preach on a Saint's day, a description of the miserable plight of these persons was given him, and in the course of his sermon he made an appeal on their behalf to his congregation. Then, after Vespers that same evening, he set out to visit the unfortunate family himself. The farm was about three miles distant, and at intervals along the road he met groups of his flock at Châtillon returning homewards, while others, overcome by heat or fatigue, rested under trees by the wayside. It appeared that most of those who had heard his appeal had responded to it in the most practical manner, and started there and then to relieve the wants of the sufferers.

No better object-lesson to expound the necessity of organization in the giving of charity could have been devised. The family at the farm could not consume more than a small fraction of the food that had been lavished upon them; the surplus was inevitably wasted, and in a few days their want would have been as great as before if M. Vincent had not taken their case in hand. From this experience came his idea of the Confraternities. In the Archives of Châtillon may be found the rules of M. Vincent's first Confraternity of Charity. Any woman —so long as she was a Catholic—might belong to it if she had the consent of the male relation who claimed

THE ORDERING OF CHARITY 69

authority over her movements. Officials were to be elected from among them, and they were all to be under the authority of the curé. Their first duty was the care of the sick, their second the relief of poverty. "The Servant of the Poor will do her nursing lovingly, as though she tended her own son," so ran M. Vincent's recommendation. The idea of the early Christian Community was to be revived, so that poverty might lose all shadow of shame, and the rich be only fortunate because of their greater opportunity for giving.

As we have seen, M. Vincent's coming had meant a great awakening at Châtillon. Capacities that had seemed paralyzed were stirred, ideas undreamed of were suggested, to many of his flock the reason of their being seemed to have altered. It was well for them that, with their new awakening, there opened for them a new field of interest. Imbued with M. Vincent's idea of the claim that life made upon a Christian, they turned with zeal to the practical service of their neighbour; and afterwards the inward work of a Mission, wherever held, was never felt to be complete if it had not resulted in the outward activities of an established Confraternity.

But in a small country town, far from any of the populous centres, it was not difficult for M. Vincent to instil the practical observance of the Christian rules of brotherhood and fellowship, and the idea of the Confraternities, properly carried out, was a satisfactory solution of the problem of almsgiving. It was in the cities that the question assumed an entirely different aspect.

At Macon, a little later, M. Vincent beheld pauperism in its most degraded forms. He was passing through on his way elsewhere when his attention was arrested by the enormous number of beggars who infested streets and churches. They were of the most depraved and abandoned type, without any desire for improvement, and his religious instinct was specially offended by their presence in the churches, where they were heedless of all reverence for holy things. There seems to have flashed upon him, as with the force of a sudden revelation, the sense that he could find a remedy. Instead of continuing his journey, he asked for further hospitality from the Fathers of the Oratory, and remained with them three weeks. It was Père Desmoulins, their Superior, who put on record what was accomplished in that time.* M. Vincent began by the practical measure of drawing up a register of all indigent persons in the town. (And here it should be noted that the Patron Saint of Charity was opposed to promiscuous almsgiving. He considered that the able-bodied were in need of work as well as of food, and created useless labour for them rather than leave them unemployed. It is told of him† that he utilized a tract of marshy ground near Paris that had been given to the Company to occupy the men who begged of him in the streets. They were set to dig a deep ditch at fifteen sols for the day's work. In course of time the job was completed, and the overseers came to M. Vincent for instructions. He had never wanted the ditch, and he still wanted to provide employment, therefore he directed that a second ditch should be made alongside, and the first filled up. Economically, such a system is unsound, but M. Vincent's action proves that he did not sanction the old monastic custom of free giving.) When he had ascertained the numbers with which he had to deal, he arranged that assistance should be given on fixed days to those in need; but if they were found begging in street or church, they were to be punished and the alms withheld. For those who passed through the town lodging for one night only and two sols were to be provided. For the aged and the sick he recommended ample and generous provision.

Organization at Macon demanded virile qualities, and

* Abelli., vol. i., chap. xvi.
† See *Revue des Deux Mondes*, Mai, 1894: " L'Assistance par le Travail," Comte d'Haussonville.

M. Vincent founded a Confraternity of men. It was their business to distribute relief, to watch over the shelter given to vagrants, and to arrange that destitute children should be taught a trade. A Confraternity of women on the usual lines was founded also, but the duties of each were distinct. We shall find that the associations of men for the protection of the faith and the assistance of the poor which were being formed in all parts of France at this time were not the direct result of the work of M. Vincent, but at Macon he was responsible for a complete reconstitution of the social conditions of the town. " So well did he manage both small and great," says Père Desmoulins, " that everyone was eager to contribute in money or in kind, so that nearly 300 poor obtained sufficient provision."

Ignorance as well as poverty seems to have reached an extreme in the city of Macon. The beggars, old and young, with whom M. Vincent held conversation had not the most elementary knowledge of religion, but he left a special charge that they should be taught and given an incentive to lead a better life.

Macon itself did not have a second visit from M. Vincent, but he took away from it a provision of experience that was afterwards of infinite use to him.

There awaited him in Paris so many problems to be solved, so many abuses to be faced and conquered, that if in his provincial experience he could have looked forward, it would seem that even his high courage must have been daunted. But with the vast array of difficulties there awaited him also such a measure of support as could not be foretold. The description of his capacity for managing others given by Père Desmoulins shows us the key to a part at least of his power. In response to his touch, purses were opened and personal service offered, not only conscientiously, but eagerly. To regard him as the wise dispenser of charity is to catch but a narrow glimpse of him. He was essentially the inspirer of others, and none of the sick and starving people for whom he laboured owed more to him than did the great ladies of his day in Paris. It was his part to wake them, as he had wakened the frivolous women of Châtillon, and then to see that the work they undertook was really for the service of God and of His poor. Among all the changes and chances of those turbulent times, his task was not a light one; but method and means grew as he needed them, and his miraculous achievements in the midst of war and famine were brought to pass without evidence of sensation or excitement.

The amateur enterprise destined to have such immense results was first set in motion by the needs of the patients at the Hôtel Dieu. The great hospital that still stands at the very centre of ancient Paris was—as its name denotes—a definitely religious institution. By regulations that were drawn up in 1227, careful provision was made for the lives of those who served the sick within its walls.* These were to be limited to thirty lay brothers, four priests, four clerks, and twenty-five sisters. They took vows of chastity and renounced their goods, and were under obedience to the Chapter of the Cathedral of Notre Dame. Three centuries later the thirty lay brothers were replaced by Religious of the Order of S. Victor, and the Sisters seem also to have been under a definite religious Rule. Probably the original institution required modification to suit the times, but though the provisions for the staff were altered, those which concerned the patients remained.

Now, the pious souls who were responsible for the original foundation of the Hôtel Dieu attached more importance to spiritual than to temporal needs, but they approached the difficult question of combining the two with a simplicity that may move the religious philanthropist of later times to envy. A sick person desiring the tendance the Hôtel Dieu offered must make confession

* Félibien, "Hist. de la Ville de Paris," liv. viii.

and receive the Blessed Sacrament. After that, he would be regarded as master of the house; before, he would not be able to claim any assistance. The theory that lay behind the rule was pure, but its purity was impossible to preserve in practice. About 25,000 patients passed through the great hospital in the course of a year, adherence to the rule became a mere formality, and the formality was sacrilegious. When an abuse of this kind is of long continuance, interference demands great courage, and the criticism of the established work of other religious bodies was a task which M. Vincent at all times declined. The mission to the Hôtel Dieu associated with his name was actually the work of one of those intrepid women who become oblivious of all other considerations in a passion of desire for one particular reform.

In 1634, Mme. Goussaulte, wife of a well-known magistrate, discovered the light usage of the Sacraments at the Hôtel Dieu, and was appalled. She went in haste to M. Vincent. The evils she saw were so flagrant, and, in her estimation, productive of such poison to the souls of all concerned, that she was assured that the Superior of S. Lazare would intervene. But he, characteristically, deprecated any idea of responsibility for what might occur at the Hôtel Dieu.

"I have neither position nor authority to check abuses which may exist there as they exist everywhere else," is the answer attributed to him. "One must hope that those who undertake the management of this great institution will make the alterations that are needed."

The reply had sufficient finality (coming from a priest of M. Vincent's standing) to check even the reforming energies of an enthusiastic woman. But Mme. Goussaulte's enthusiasm was very deeply rooted, and she would not be daunted. She turned (as Mme. de Gondi had done) from the hopeless task of persuading M. Vincent to the comparatively easy one of cajoling his ecclesiastical Superior. In due course the Archbishop of Paris wrote to Vincent de Paul, urging that he should make an effort to ameliorate the lot of the patients at the Hôtel Dieu.

M. Vincent was as ready in obedience as he was backward in interference. He set himself at once to study the need that was to be met, and organize a scheme for meeting it, and in this connection he made his first real appeal for help to the great ladies of Paris. He summoned them together at the house of Mme. Goussaulte that he might tell them what he wanted. The assembly seems to have resembled the drawing-room meeting of the twentieth century, but it was aided by the magic of the unusual as much as by the convincing reality of need. Those who listened responded with a precipitation which was not in keeping with the maxims of M. Vincent; but though the first form of their response was afterwards modified, there is no evidence that many of them repented of their haste. If there were a few who enlisted under the charm of novelty, and then fell away, their unworthiness may be left in oblivion.

There was no vagueness about the purpose of these ladies. The sufferers in the great hospital and the sick poor in Paris were in sore need of comfort, corporal and spiritual. For their assistance a guild was formed, and three officers duly elected—Superior, Treasurer, and a Keeper of the Wardrobe—who was to have charge of stores other than money. The guild bore some resemblance to the Confraternities that had long been in existence, but it had essential differences in its constitution, and must not be regarded as only an aristocratic form of the same movement.

Vincent de Paul regarded this new development with the deepest satisfaction. He described it in glowing terms to M. du Coudray, his representative at Rome, and betrayed at the same time a simplicity which suggests that as the years passed his experience of the realities of human nature would deepen. There were, he says, about 120 ladies of quality in this new Association, who

THE ORDERING OF CHARITY

went in parties of four to cheer the sick, taking them soup and jellies and other luxuries, in addition to their ordinary rations. Some 800 invalids were given comfort of this sort, and this, he adds, is done to incline them to make a general confession of their past life, that those who are dying may be well prepared to leave this world, and those who recover may begin life again with good resolutions.

It is plain that the persuasive methods of these ladies were not free from the element of bribery. We shall see that this difficulty arose and was faced during M. Olier's parochial labours at S. Sulpice. But at the Hôtel Dieu the original abuse had been so immense that the Ladies of Charity, with their soup and jellies and soft words, were a lesser evil. Their charitable purpose, moreover, was supported by a personal sympathy that was absolutely sincere, and hearts hardened by long adversity and the injustice of the ordinary world may have been touched into reality by contact with love of a kind never before experienced. There were no rival possibilities of profession, moreover, no struggle between sects where those who had most to offer might gain most adherents. The Huguenots, if they gained admission, gained it by a fraud that must have been very easy to discover. The patients were Catholics, and therefore in all of them the faith was there, dormant. The influence of good suggestion might be transient, but that which responded to it was a part of themselves; they were not summoned to accept a novelty, but were recalled to recognition of their inheritance.

The work of the Ladies of Charity at the Hôtel Dieu was, as a whole, a magnificent object-lesson in the possibilities of real charitable effort. M. Vincent's influence guided them clear of the pitfalls lying ready for ignorance and excessive zeal, and smoothed the difficulties between the newcomers, in their first glow of enthusiasm, and the Grey Sisters who had tended the patients of the Hôtel Dieu for so many years that their work of charity had become a matter of routine. But though the beginning was admirable, the drawbacks that attend amateur philanthropy soon became apparent, and the Members of the Association of Ladies of Charity ceased to be regular in the fulfilment of the duties they had undertaken. It was natural that a great lady who had been stirred by the new and beautiful idea of serving Christ in the persons of His poor should discover—with the subsidence of first fervour—that delicate fingers were less capable of service than stronger and rougher ones, and that her novel occupation could only be regarded as an interlude in the employments and amusements of ordinary life. Goodwill towards the objects of their charity remained unaltered, but reasons of health, interference of husbands, claims of Court duties, intervened; there were a thousand reasons against fulfilling their tasks themselves, and many of them turned to the obvious resource of the wealthy and paid a substitute. It was easy to send a servant when it was very difficult to go in person; but that which had been a glorious work of piety to the mistress was, unfortunately, only a disagreeable duty to the maid. Very little profit accrued to anyone from visits or from gifts, and the fire of Mme. Goussaulte's great scheme bade fair to flicker down into dull and uninspired ashes.

It is at this point—in 1638—that the world of Paris had its first real knowledge of the Sisters of Charity, or Servants of the Poor. In a quiet house in the parish of S. Nicholas Chardonnet, Mlle. Le Gras (the widow of a Secretary of Marie de Médici) had gathered round her a small number of young women from the country to aid her in her own efforts for the service of the poor. She herself had long been working under the direction of M. Vincent, and the story of their friendship belongs to the record of his deeper and more intimate life. The needs of the poor around her had been her inducement to seek helpers, and because the tasks required of them were laborious and homely, her helpers were of the lower class;

THE ORDERING OF CHARITY

but in gathering them she had no great scheme in hand, only the fulfilment of a pressing and immediate claim. M. Vincent, confronted by the instability of great ladies, turned to these unpretentious Servants of the Poor, and called on them to carry on the work their more favoured sisters had discovered, but not sustained. Mlle. Le Gras reorganized the scheme of Mme. Goussaulte, eager interest and liberal funds were forthcoming, and the Company of the Sisters of the Poor justified its existence.

It was many years before their Founder sought for them the sanction of the Church, but their actual growth was extraordinarily rapid. The numerous and inevitable failures of the Confraternities and the weaknesses of the Ladies of Charity demanded the settled force of a trained band of workers pledged to regular service, if the fruit of many fine and high aspirations was to benefit the people. The experience of Mlle. Le Gras had convinced her that the work that needed doing could only be done by women of dedicated life, that the spiritual responsibility entailed was too heavy to be borne by persons of divided interests. " It is of little good for us to hurry about the streets with bowls of soup," she said, " and do such service as regards the body, if we do not look on the Son of God as the object of our effort. If we lose hold—ever so little— on the idea that the poor are members of Him, inevitably our love for them grows less."

The root of their strength and influence lay in that suggestion. Their method of approach to the poor they tended, whether at home or in the hospitals, was a novelty, and they were recognized as doing good in the Name of Christ. They were homely persons, not endowed either with eloquence or education; if they made converts, they did it not by their words, but by their lives. Nor were their first beginnings attended by any excitement or applause. The degrees by which Mlle. Le Gras formed them into a Sisterhood are indeed hardly perceptible. We may take the year 1629 as that of the first arrival of helpers at her house, and eleven years later they were given a peranment Rule; but at the outset their future as a Community was not considered, each of the little band was to be content with a sense of individual consecration. Before the giving of their Rule they had made their headquarters at La Chapelle, outside the gates of Paris, the private house of Mlle. Le Gras being too small for them, and, while there, the Company was joined by some of those Sisters whose devotion and endurance—proved amid the terrors of civil war and invasion—laid the first stones of its reputation.

The Sisters of that first generation were, almost without exception, of the lower middle class; among them were peasants of special capability, but novices of noble blood were not accepted. This rule was afterwards modified, and the standard of service was not lowered because there were women of high lineage among the Servants of the Poor, but its existence at the beginning defended the Company from the invasion of persons to whom novelty was an attraction. Complete obedience and unity of purpose were necessary, for in times of great distress it was often their difficult task to organize and administer relief, and in the seventeenth century the problem of destitution was no less pressing than in the twentieth, while the laws and machinery of charity had not come into being.

The problem that made sharpest appeal to the hearts and minds of the Ladies of Charity was that most difficult one of the habitual vagrant. That which had been a remediable disorder in a provincial town, such as Macon, assumed a more sinister aspect in the capital. Any semblance of protection for the public that had existed during the reigns of Henri IV. and Louis XIII. was extinguished during the War of the Fronde, and as soon as the daylight hours were over the streets could not be traversed by a peaceful citizen without the gravest danger to life. The testimonies to this condition of

THE ORDERING OF CHARITY 79

things are countless. If we go no farther than the writings of Boileau or Gui Patin, we may find it graphically depicted. No doubt many of the robberies were committed by the soldiery or the lawless servants attached to the households of the nobility, but the difficulty of dealing with the question was greatly increased by the hosts of homeless persons who crowded the streets, living on alms which were often extorted by force. An individual male ctor of whatever degree was impossible to trace amid a crowd which was a species of nursery for the galleys, and it was generally accepted that an able-bodied beggar only required opportunity to change from supplicant to robber. The citizens were so habituated to the danger from these marauders that they seem to hav ecognized them as possessors of certain rights.* The were places of refuge scattered a out Paris where the ggårs might congregate unmolested, and which cam o be forcing-houses for every species of crime. There were companies of beggars having different headquarters and a species of organization to aid them in preying on society, and the evil—a lamentable one even on the smallest scale—grew with alarming rapidity. When justice continually miscarried, and the general distress was so great that honest men and their families perished of want, the incentive to vagabondage is obvious, and the first deliberate effort to check the spread of this infection does not seem to have been made until in 1667 Colbert appointed Nicolas de la Reynie Lieutenant of Police, and under his supervision the beggars' sanctuaries were raided, and that simple expedient for the safety of the public, the lighting of the streets, was troduced. Summary justice by drastic means the city of a disease that undermined its prosperity, which, being once cured, was cured for ever.

But there are symptoms of debility hardly less dange that cannot be disposed of by violent remedy, and are

* See Caillet, "De l'Administration en France sous Richelieu."

not expelled from the system by the natural process of civilization. Laws wisely made and carefully administered may be successful in checking crime and in diminishing the number of the criminals, but though moral deficiency may be thus dealt with, no law has yet been made that will lessen the number of victims to another evil that is hardly separable. In every community there exists a race of persons who may be classed as Na re's failures. Deficient in some faculty, and yet not so entirely deprived as to be the objects of charitable effort; seeing but dimly, hearing indistinctly, yet not blind or deaf; limping and misshapen, with speech that is only half articulate, yet not either a cripple or a mute—these unlucky beings start in their race heavily handica ed, and in most cases lose even the humble place they have won for lack of courage to compete against th Add to their numbers the melancholy company whose mental faculties are shortened, whose is not systematically controlled by any reasoning process, yet who are not within measurable distance of insanity— the aggregate presents the hardest problem that can confront the student of social questions. Because the line of division is so hard to draw betwixt deficiency and indolence, and mental weakness verges so closely upon criminal intention, therefore indulgence towards inefficiency tends to widen the ranks of wastrels, while ordinary justice applied where the sense of responsibility is only half defined becomes inhuman.

London in the twentieth century groans under the ravages of the disease, and finds no remedy. Paris 300 years ago was less resigned and more In a city whose total population was much 500,000 there were, in 1650,* 40,000 beggars. The law, by making vagrancy a crime, had already done what it could to cope with the difficulty. In January, 1545,†

* Félibien, " Hist. de la Ville de Paris," liv. xxix.
† *Ibid.*, liv. xx.

THE ORDERING OF CHARITY

an edict was passed forbidding anyone to beg on penalty of a whipping, the second offence to be punished with perpetual imprisonment; and at the time some attempt must have been made to enforce it, as we hear of a difficulty touching the care of children whose parents —as second offenders—were thus summarily disposed of. The same edict required the regular distribution of alms to the sick poor. Both provisions became a dead letter, the latter probably from lack of funds, the former from the obvious impossibilities attaching to it at a time when the prisons were constantly overcrowded, and the State could not afford to feed those whom it debarred from seeking for support.

The enterprises of Vincent de Paul in many directions had prospered so amazingly that it was a natural instinct in those whose eyes were opened to the degraded and dangerous position of the street beggars to turn to him for direction in their hard effort. The Ladies of Charity seem to have attributed to him an almost miraculous power, and had no misgivings as to success in their stupendous task, provided they might rely upon his guidance. M. Vincent knew more than they did, and was more anxious that any scheme of this kind should be allowed time to mellow than that it should receive speedy acceptance and popular support. But the Ladies of Charity were not under obedience, and they were full of fervour. His efforts to control them were only partially successful, and eventually M. Vincent decided to go with the tide rather than exhaust his influence in a futile attempt to stem it.

It is easy to imagine how the infection of pity—originally suggested, probably, by some particularly miserable group shivering at a street corner—had spread among a society of wealthy women who had been for years encouraged in the principles of charity by Vincent de Paul, and how they formed a plan for the extermination of cold and hunger, with very little notion of the vast issues that were involved. But M. Vincent had the experience thay lacked, and knew that if the plan was to be effective it would eventually have to be carried out on a large scale. If he was forced to go with the current, he kept his hold upon the helm, and the result was due to his guidance rather than to the generous haste of the Ladies of Charity. He laid the matter before the Queen Regent, and obtained a grant of the buildings and grounds known as La Salpêtrière, on the banks of the river opposite the Arsenal. At first the delight of the Ladies was great, and they had to be restrained from going out into the streets and driving every beggar whom they met into the home that was henceforward to await the homeless. M. Vincent exhorted them to begin on a small scale, and to go forward slowly, not only for reasons of prudence, but from the highest motive, that it was more reverent to wait for God's fulfilment of their desire. Probably his arguments would have prevailed with them, as they had done before, even if the power of the law had not intervened and made patience a necessity. It was impossible to begin a charity of this description without reference to the magistrates, and to some of these the advantage of the plan was not self-evident. Something of the kind had been attempted under Henri IV., and had been very unsuccessful. It was two years before their objections were overcome, and when at length the expediency of the new idea was generally admitted, instead of giving permission to its originators to carry it out, the magistrates undertook the matter themselves. The Ladies of Charity were loyal in support, but the actual result must have been very different from their dream. They had intended to be the hostesses of that wretched class who knew none of the happiness of a kindly welcome and gentle treatment, and the possibility that by such charity they might increase the numbers of those whose existence was as a wound to their soft hearts did not occur to them.

THE ORDERING OF CHARITY 83

In fact, the Salpêtrière became the enforced retreat for beggars. All who asked for alms in the streets of Paris must go thither or leave the city; there was no other alternative, and it is probable that those who loved their freedom, and to whom custom had softened the hardship of a vagrant life, were not disposed to gratitude towards those benevolent ladies whose suggestions had so effectually deprived them of their liberty. But Paris had cause to bless M. Vincent, as Macon had blessed him many years earlier, for the fame of the new regulations reduced the number of homeless poor within its walls to 5,000, and these were no longer to be found inciting pity in the streets, but in the Hôpital Générale of La Salpêtrière, provided with such work as they were able to do. On May 7, 1657, it was given out in every pulpit in Paris that in a week the new order would begin, and the doors of the Salpêtrière were thrown open to all who cared to come. On the 13th, instead of the persuasions of the Ladies of Charity, the insistence of the City Archers collected all who did not prefer to try their fortune in the country. The numbers for whom it was necessary to provide increased as time went on, and four establishments were required. In the main building young children, women, and 250 aged married couples (who were each provided with a room), were housed. Bicêtre was reserved for men of all ages. At Notre Dame de la Pitié were boys under twelve, and the establishment of S. Marthe de Scipion was used for the offices of the commissariat, necessarily on a vast scale for this enormous colony. It was provided by the regulations that the children should be educated and taught to work, while all able-bodied men and women should be obliged to do their share of labour.*

The Ladies of Charity had complained at the dilatory methods of the magistrates; they had been obliged to exercise patience for two years, and endure the thought

* Félibien, "Hist. de la Ville de Paris," liv. xxix.

that hundreds of men, women, and children were exposed to rain, wind, or frost night after night throughout two winters within the immediate neighbourhood of their own well-appointed homes; they thought the delay unnecessarily prolonged, but posterity is astonished at the precipitation with which so immense a scheme was launched. M. Vincent's position towards it is a curious one. He, whose choice of action was ruled always by the spirit of caution, was possessed of fuller knowledge of the difficulties of this enterprise than any of the officials of the law. Before La Salpêtrière was actually opened he wrote to a friend that "Begging is to be abolished in Paris, and the poor all gathered together in a place specially prepared for them, and taught and set to work. This is a great undertaking, and very difficult, but by the grace of God it seems to promise well, and everyone applauds it." Yet his hopefulness was tempered with misgiving. It was true that this huge affair had sprung from the plan concerted between himself and the Ladies of Charity, and that the poor folk were to have special facilities for receiving instruction as well as for useful employment. Ostensibly, the lines he had laid down were followed, and in the letter already referred to he says that he finds himself and his Mission Priests appointed as the spiritual guardians of the new institution, while the Sisters of Charity were to be the recognized servants of the poor thus congregated. Colbert, as representative of the King, was ready to defer to M. Vincent, and to undertake that this work should be done for the advancement of the kingdom of God. Such a foundation for such a purpose would seem to be ideal, yet he who was its originator hung back. Neither he nor any of his Company were to be found in the vast halls of the Hôpital Générale attempting to bring those messages of hope which they loved to carry to the most miserable. Yet they never shrank from labour, and their hearers would have been pre-eminently of the class which it was their mission to serve. The explanation may perhaps lie in the element of compulsion, which was an essential part of the system. For one week only had there been a chance of accepting an offer, made in the name of charity, by free-will; afterwards force had stepped in.

M. Vincent was the apostle of charity. Many years of experience had taught him an understanding of the poor man's point of view—an equipment seldom possessed or desired by those who have to regulate the poor man's lot—and the indiscriminate treatment of vast numbers is not compatible with that respect for the individual which, according to M. Vincent's theory, is the right of every Christian. Before many years had passed there were instances of men guilty of the worst offences being sent to the Hôpital Générale to share the lot of those whose only crime was poverty, and, although M. Vincent could not foresee all this in detail, a long life had given him the opportunity of studying the tendencies of popular movements, and he had reason for grave misgiving.

He had already, with a sum of money given to him, founded the hospital known as *Le Nom de Jésus* for forty aged and penniless persons, and tradition says that the benefits there bestowed nourished the souls no less than the bodies of the inmates. So far as in this later case his own ideas took form, they suggest that he meant to persuade the poor and miserable to accept shelter, with the sincere intention of working for their spiritual benefit, and that their removal from the streets by force because their presence was undesirable was not a measure consistent with any of his theories. M. Vincent did not regard the most hopeless wastrel as beyond reach of the grace of God; he believed each one might be turned into a loving servant of the Master whom he served himself. But it is not astonishing if his plans appeared fantastic and impracticable. To have tested them by lending them the support of all the law's machinery would have meant on the part of the magistrates a faith in God's guidance of affairs equal to his own—an unimaginable consummation. Yet without the law's support no adequate measures could have been taken against this particular species of distress. La Salpêtrière was therefore, humanly speaking, the best provision possible for a class in itself degraded and notably dangerous to others; and its effect was found to be so greatly for the benefit of the State that similar institutions were founded throughout the provinces. M. Vincent, loving his country as he did, rejoiced, one may be sure, at all the good that had been by this means allowed to come to it, and, as was his method, could resign into the hands of God that scheme of loving-kindness which was not to be fulfilled.

The attention attracted by the opening of the Hôpital Générale may have gone farther than its original object, so that a little of the melancholy knowledge with which M. Vincent and those about him had long been familiar became public property. To ascertain the immense number of the homeless poor in Paris was to open the door to speculations that went far beyond the evil indicated by the fact itself. We have seen that, a century earlier, compliance with the edict of 1545 respecting mendicants had thrown the care of the children of imprisoned beggars upon the State, and it may easily be understood that the greater the difficulty in obtaining the means of living, the less welcome did a child become to parents of the necessitous class. In the dark and crowded streets there was no difficulty in depositing a child where it was not altogether hidden and in escaping before the desertion was observed. This practice became so common that, in 1552,* a law was passed providing that all infants found in the streets should be brought to the Hospital of the Trinity and placed in the charge of a woman especially appointed for the care of them. A little later, further and more elaborate arrangements were made for their benefit, and two houses in the Rue

* Félibien, " Hist. de la Ville de Paris," liv. xx.

THE ORDERING OF CHARITY   87

S. Landry* were rented for their reception. A sort of committee was appointed, and the actual supervision entrusted to three married women of the respectable middle class. The treatment of the question seems to have been well considered and humane, but, once disposed of, was allowed to pass out of the range of public interest. The number of the unfortunate babies found in the street increased as the years passed, but the supplies for their support did not increase in proportion. In the year 1638,† the house in the Rue S. Landry was occupied by " a certain widow," who, with two servants under her, received and disposed of some 400 babies annually. It appears to be generally admitted by contemporary chroniclers that of these the only survivors were those who were bought and nefariously substituted for others who had died. The rest were exterminated by various methods, most often by administering a soothing draught which effectually quieted their cries; but as they were sold to any buyer for a very small sum—about a franc—there were some whose fate was far less merciful.

The most familiar and the most picturesque presentation of Vincent de Paul commemorates his action with regard to the deserted children of Paris. The suggestion that he rescued individual children and carried them through the streets to a haven of care and kindness is not borne out by evidence; but, if inaccurate in detail, it is founded on reality. In a very true sense he carried the foundlings from certain death to safe protection. The varied avocations of the Superior of S. Lazare took him to every part of Paris, and brought him into contact with all sorts and conditions of persons. In course of time his attention was directed to the horrible system in use at the Couche S. Landry. So abominable were the practices of the widow and her servants that it is hard to understand M. Vincent's delay in dealing with her. There

* On "l'Ile de la Cité" near Notre Dame.
† Félibien, " Hist. de la Ville de Paris," liv. xx.

was no sudden raid and summary expulsion of the offenders. M. Vincent adhered to his law of prudence, and by degrees withdrew the unhappy infants from hands unworthy to have care of them without any public sensation or excitement. Eventually he abolished the horror and organized a noble substitute, but he meditated on the best method of advance, and waited for God's guidance long after he discovered the abuse, and when he began to act it was very slowly.

The Ladies of Charity were sentimental as well as generous, and here sentiment had full scope. He could rely on their support of his new enterprise. Each child rescued from the *couche* in the Rue S. Landry was saved from death, and—as they were all believed to be unbaptized—their salvation appeared to a true daughter of the Church to be not only for time, but also for eternity. A house was hired and made ready outside the Porte S. Victor, in the near neighbourhood of the Collège des Bons Enfants, and as a beginning twelve babies were established under the care of the Sisters of Charity. It seems to have been generally understood that this foundation was specially dear to the heart of M. Vincent. It is told of him that he would appear among the babies at all sorts of unexpected times, that he knew each individually, and mourned the death of any of them with a definite regret. That his adopted family should increase and the house in the Rue S. Landry become tenantless was his constant desire, and even the liberality of the Ladies of Charity could not keep pace with his enthusiasm.

If we remember that when the foundlings were under normal conditions the mortality among them was no longer great, and that almost every day brought a fresh claim, it is easy to understand that the most generous of women might draw back from so immense a burden. But M. Vincent's persuasions at length proved irresistible; those who already gave so much taxed themselves further, and the Ladies and the Sisters of Charity under-

THE ORDERING OF CHARITY

took the entire charge of the foundlings in Paris. The Queen's interest was aroused, and a subscription came from the royal purse. Mme. de Miramion, one of the most notable of that large-hearted band without whose help M. Vincent's reforms must often have been baulked, gave lavishly, and the scheme was definitely set on foot.

For thirty years this immense burden was supported by those who made of it a labour of love. There could be no stronger tribute to the power that M. Vincent wielded than the fact of their perseverance in it. To him the life of each one of these children was precious.

There was, it must be acknowledged, a moment of crisis when the work had lost all novelty and the hearts of those who supported it were stirred by the miseries of the starving people in Lorraine. Money was needed to save those who suffered from the horrors of an invaded territory, and money that was spent in one direction could not be given in another. The expense of the foundlings was steadily on the increase; they were costing 40,000 livres, and the Ladies of Charity were looking towards other fields.

M. Vincent summoned one of those assemblies which, under his management, seldom failed to fulfil their purpose. He gathered his Ladies of Charity and represented to them the necessity of a definite decision.

"You are free, ladies," he said; "but before you make up your minds I ask you to consider what it is you have done, and what it is you are going to do. Your loving care has preserved the lives of a great number of children, who, without your help, would have been lost in time, and, it may be, also in eternity. These innocent beings have learnt as their first lesson to know and to serve God. Some of them are beginning to work and to be independent of anyone's assistance. So good a beginning surely foretells results that will be even better." But on this occasion the Ladies of Charity were unusually hard to convince, and M. Vincent was moved to make an appeal which has become celebrated. "Remember, ladies," he said, " that out of compassion and charity you adopted these little ones as your children. You have been their mothers by grace ever since their natural mothers deserted them. Make up your minds now if you will desert them also. You must cease to be their mothers and become their judges. It is for you to say whether they are to live or die. I will ask you to give your votes; it is time to pronounce sentence on them and to make sure that you have no mercy to spare for them. They live if you continue to take care of them; they must (on the other hand) perish inevitably if you give them up. It is impossible to deny what you know by experience to be true."

M. Vincent won his cause; the resources of the Ladies of Charity were taxed a little farther, and the Foundling Hospital continued.

Not until 1670 did the State resume its responsibility. The foundlings were provided for on the same foundation as the children of the Hospital of the Trinity, and the two establishments in the Faubourg S. Antoine and in the vicinity of the Hôtel Dieu ceased to depend on voluntary support. The relief to the resources of the Ladies of Charity was great, but so closely had their charge become interwoven with their life that, when it was withdrawn, they were resentful, and only resumed their visits to the children after a considerable interval. By that time M. Vincent himself had been dead for nearly ten years, and that extraordinary fervour of personal love and personal service which animated all who were within the range of his influence had become no more than a memory in the minds of a few. The principle of charity remained and bore good fruit, but the idea that Christ Himself was to be found in every suffering atom of humanity was no longer a burning truth that made all counter-argument or calculation frivolous. And the future of the foundlings was therefore safest with State officials who would now be impelled to do their duty by an awakened and watchful public.

Théophoaste Renaudot.

CHAPTER V

RENAUDOT, THE FRIEND OF THE POOR

TRADITION has been formed by a very simple method in relation to the philanthropy and social reform of the seventeenth century. Vincent de Paul, having been once recognized as philanthropist and social reformer, becomes responsible for all the good works undertaken; anything that was accomplished outside the range of his influence has either been attributed to him or else ignored as unworthy of serious attention. His contemporaries were probably quite sincere in their presentation of him, and his achievement was so astounding as to give sufficient excuse for ignoring the attempts of others; nevertheless, his life bears such close relation to his time that it can only suffer by the suppression of fact. During the years of his greatest activity we must recognize that the instinct of reform in social conditions was alive even where it received no stimulus from the Church's law of charity. It was prompting vigorous activities in those who were not outwardly pledged to the service of Christ, and undoubtedly labour in the service of others was separable from religious practice in the days of Vincent de Paul, even as it is to-day.

It is well, then, to find the real place held by M. Vincent among the philanthropic movements of his time, and incidentally to pay tribute to the independent effort of a layman in the cause of far-reaching social reform. In any picture of those days it should be impossible to overlook the personality of Théophraste Renaudot,* that

* See Eugene Hatin, "Théophraste Renaudot." Gaston Bonnefont, "Un Oublié—T. Renaudot, 1586-1653." Gilles de la Tourette, " Renaudot d'après des Documents Inédits."

learned doctor and gentleman of Louvain whose originality and enterprise gave birth to schemes of such practical value that one can hardly set a limit to their development. The sympathies of M. Vincent were drawn in just the same direction, but he and Renaudot never seem to have come in touch. This fact has its own significance, for it points to the very clear division between the work of the social reformer and that of the priest. Whatever M. Vincent did had as its ultimate purpose the conversion or confirming of souls; all his pity for the bodily sufferings of the people was overshadowed by a supreme desire to share with them the spiritual joy which was his own. He could not ignore their bodily necessities, and he was so true a servant of Christ that he suffered in the sufferings he witnessed, and was constant in his attempts to solve the problem of poverty which in its most ghastly form was presented to the thinkers of the seventeenth century. But the desire for that solution was never all-important; always there was present with him the conviction that the knowledge of Christ is a benefit far greater than deliverance from pain or satisfaction of earthly desire. It would be better to depose him from his place as the leader and patron of practical philanthropists than to forget for a moment that he was in the truest sense a mystic, holding things unseen incomparably more precious than any good that might be accomplished by the most devoted of charitable workers under the most perfect of committees.

This was not the point of view of Théophraste Renaudot. But though it was applied to securing tangible benefits, and those only for his fellows, the self-devotion of the doctor was hardly less than that of the priest. The priest, coming to Paris while Marie de Médici held the reins of government, was appalled by the indifference of the people to such things as concern eternity; the doctor was seized with consternation at their ignorance of practical matters affecting their immediate welfare. Both held that the evils they deplored were remediable,

RENAUDOT, THE FRIEND OF THE POOR 93

and faced the vast array of difficulties bravely, the priest relying on direction and support from God, the doctor appealing to his generation in the name of humanity and common sense. Their paths, therefore, remain parallel, till that of Renaudot was blocked, and his enemies succeeded in deposing him from the pedestal of public benefactor on which he had fairly earned his place. To realize the true value of his attempt, it is necessary to picture an industrial population without employment agencies, without advertisements, without auction-rooms where a private owner could dispose of his goods, and without pawnshops. None of these things had any real existence when Renaudot came from Louvain to Paris. One attempt had been made, it is true, to establish an office where workmen from the country could hear of work, but as those for whom it was intended did not know of its existence, it was not of notable utility.

When the harvest was bad, or when the army had passed by, destroying crops and commandeering cattle, the country-folk had to face starvation or seek refuge in the towns. In the provinces their lot was less desperate, but Paris had no hospitality to spare for new-comers; and though their course of action was an inevitable effect of public and universally recognized disasters, no effort seems to have been made to provide for the victims or prevent them from becoming ensnared by the gangs of malefactors of both sexes infesting the poorer parts of the capital. It was not the fashion to give much thought to such people, and in those days of the first Regency there were many absorbing topics for the thoughts of those who held power or ever hoped to hold it. Sweeping regulations to expel or shut up all thieves and wastrels might be passed, and from time to time enforced, but, as we have seen, there was no idea of treating a vagabond as an individual, or of offering him the chance to win back his place in the social order, lost very frequently by reason of national calamities.

Théophraste Renaudot belonged to a profession which did not aspire to power in the State. The nobles and the prominent lawyers—the *noblesse de la robe*—might struggle for control over the affairs of the nation, but the doctors went their own way on a path that was often both lucrative and pleasant. In Louvain and the surrounding country Renaudot won for himself great respect and popularity. He had a capacity for independent thought and for encouraging others to use their brains, and his fame became familiar to Père Joseph, and was brought to the notice of Richelieu. His practice had given him knowledge of the needs of the people, and he wrote a "Traité des Pauvres." Richelieu's mission was first of all to exalt and protect the throne, and afterwards to raise the condition of life for the rank and file of the King's subjects. He found in Renaudot a man whose ambitions caused no misgiving, and whose station gave him opportunities of knowledge denied to the most astute of First Ministers. In 1625 Renaudot obeyed the summons of the Cardinal and came to Paris. He was to be Commissaire Général des Pauvres and an honorary physician to the King. Thus he could begin his experiments with the support of royal patronage. The first of these was the establishment of the Bureau d'Adresse. This was the practical exposition of his most vigorous theory on the social question—namely, that it is a grievous infringement of the rights of the individual to force him to an employment without possibility of choice, as was done by the regulations for the treatment of vagrants.

He chose as headquarters a house at the corner of the Rue Calandre, which looked on the Marché Neuf. Here, at the Sign of the Cock, in the very centre of labouring Paris, he entered on his tremendous task.*

At the Sign of the Cock, from eight to twelve in the morning, from two to six in the afternoon, advice was

---

* A statue of Renaudot commemorates the site of his house on the Ile de la Cité.

given to all who desired work. Employers were welcomed and the details of their needs entered in a book. Masters of workshops were invited to send notice of their vacancies; those who were changing their abode might register their new addresses; those who were desiring a tenant might come in contact with those that sought a habitation. Advice on every subject of practical utility might be obtained, and infinite pains were taken to make the advice the best available. For those who could afford to pay, a charge of three sous was made; but to the very poor, for whose benefit the Bureau was originally conceived, its help was given gratis. There is no room for doubt that Renaudot was inspired throughout his career by an earnest wish to lessen the suffering that is the fruit of ignorance, and to encourage self-respect and self-reliance in the class where those qualities are most uncommon. His methods show that he had grasped the disabilities of his poorer neighbours, had weighed them, and formed his judgment with a justice and precision that would have qualified him to take his place as a leader among social reformers in a later age. A glance at the prospectus that heralded the opening of his Bureau d'Adresse reveals his point of view:*

1. " To prevent poverty and mendicity in the future," he wrote, " the best precaution is the prompt supply, to those in danger of these evils, of employment for their industry and skill, so that none may be forced into the miserable last resource of begging for lack of other means to help themselves."

2. " According to S. Bernard, really good advice is the greatest benefit we can confer on anyone. This does not apply only to the poor, but the poor, being the most in need, may receive most assistance from it."

3. " It is for this reason that we begin with a petition to each and all to suggest everything for the help and assistance of the poor that may be of service either to

* See Eugène Hatin, " Théophraste Renaudot."

their general condition or to particular individuals—anything that may aid them to obtain shelter, food, clothing, attendance in sickness, or the means to earn their living, which last is the most necessary of all charities."

With the actual dispensation of charity the Bureau would have nothing to do, but the charitably disposed might leave an address to be given to a necessitous person of whatever type they chose. The kindling of the spirit of charity and the extension of the knowledge of the poor was, indeed, one of Renaudot's objects, but his office towards the poor was to be kept carefully from connection with almsgiving. He meant that, in a modern phrase, "they should be helped to help themselves."

The Bureau won immediate celebrity. It is curious to turn from the tentative methods of Vincent de Paul, to whom success came always as a surprise, to Renaudot, with his flourish of trumpets, his sensational ventures, and swift plunges into notoriety. The Bureau d'Adresse was amply sufficient to satisfy the instinct of enterprise even in a man of energy. Its utility grew. All newcomers were sent, by the King's authority, to register their names there if they were not provided with work. The difficulty of arranging bargains when owners and purchasers lived at a great distance from each other suggested a sort of auction-room; the desire to borrow small sums on security of goods that might be kept in pledge inaugurated a sort of pawnshop. These institutions were afterwards separately adopted and perfected. Renaudot, who had been in Italy, had seen the beginning of the *monte di pietà* there, and he applied the principle to the needs of the people with whom he was in constant intercourse. It was natural that the offices in the Rue Calandre should become just such a centre of usefulness as Renaudot had pictured, and that a stream of men of greatly differing types and fortunes continually passed through them. Watching them as they came and went, talking to them as he transacted business, listening to snatches of their talk one with another, Renaudot became inspired by a new idea.

At all times scandal flies as swiftly as ill news, and in those days the knowledge of a pungent and satisfactory scandal was assisted in its course by the circulation of evil little leaflets known as "*Nouvelles à la Main.*" These, albeit their authorship was always hidden and their contents were flagrantly libellous, were bought and eagerly discussed, but beyond these there was no method of purveying information that concerned the public. To Renaudot the interests of his fellow-citizens was synonymous with the interests of his Bureau. He saw the need for an accredited journal of events, and at the same time the host of applicants at his sale-rooms suggested that a price list of their contents would be of service to intending buyers. He had easy access to the secret counsels of Père Joseph and the Cardinal, and he laid his new idea before them. Richelieu listened, comprehended, and approved, and undertook to incline the King to do the same. Another royal patent was issued to Théophraste Renaudot, and on May 30, 1631, the first *Gazette*, containing current news and a catalogue of goods for sale, was issued from the Sign of the Cock in the Rue Calandre. This was the birthday of journalism in France, as well as of the system of advertisement. In England and in Italy the need for news was at the same moment producing the first attempts at a newspaper, but Théophraste Renaudot was the first to combine advertisement with the supply of news. Probably there was not one of the citizens of Paris who could understand what an important movement was being heralded from the Sign of the Cock. Renaudot himself was as anxious about the notices furthering bargains between his clients as about the news that preceded them, and Richelieu, absorbed in his endeavour to disentangle the royal prerogative from the criticism and contempt that had been earned for it by Marie de' Medici, never showed a full realization of the power

of the new weapon put into his hands. Possibly the true
spirit of journalism is in its essence combative, and cannot develop without opposition. Renaudot had been
granted a monopoly. No news was to be circulated in
printed form except by the *Gazette*, and the news in the
Gazette came fresh from the Louvre and the Palais Cardinal. Loyal subjects thus had the privilege of buying
for the modest sum of one sou the literary efforts not only
of the First Minister, but of the King himself, and might
rest assured that all the information imparted to them
was made public with the full approval of their rulers.
So long as the *Gazette* had no rival, it answered its purpose
of pleasing the people and strengthening the influence of
Richelieu, but to maintain the monopoly of so brilliant
an enterprise required the support of the law. Other
news sheets were issued and found a ready market, and
Renaudot could not hope for justice in the courts, because,
as the partisan of the Cardinal, he was the enemy of the
noblesse de la robe.

The whole position is difficult to realize after a lapse of
nearly three centuries. The flagrant corruptness of the
magistrates is hardly less astonishing than the short-sightedness of the autocrat who thought that all editorship could be vested in one individual. Renaudot himself seems to have had some gifts as a leader-writer, but
when keen wits were pitted against him, and the tremendous claim of his other avocations made it hard to compete in a war of words, he did not attempt to employ
mercenaries for his defence. Not until his sons reigned
in his stead did journalism become a bread-winning trade
for starving genius, and by that time the city had settled
down to the calmer times of the Great Monarch's maturity.
Renaudot's fortunes were bound up with the *Gazette*.
He retained it when he lost all else, and so far as he is
remembered at all, it is in connection with it that his
memory survives. But though it was effective in lessening the gulf between differing classes by increasing the

interests that could be held in common, it had not that direct bearing on the daily life of the poor which characterized every other enterprise of his. Of his real achievements the last, still to come, was at once the most useful to the poor he loved and the most fatal to himself.

As agent, as man of business, and as journalist, Renaudot acquitted himself well, but he never ceased to be a doctor or to regard the sufferings of humanity from the point of view of one who seeks to cure. He was not a religious man, and close scrutiny into the detail of his life reveals that some crusades against abuses undertaken on the purest motives were maintained in the spirit of fiercest rivalry and partisanship. He was born and bred a Huguenot, and the fact that State patronage was necessary to carry out his projects is likely to have accelerated his conversion to Catholic belief. Nevertheless, when confronted with distress that had no necessary connection with his own interests, and no natural claim upon his sympathy, he was moved to efforts for its relief so strenuous and so self-denying that no follower of Vincent de Paul could have outdone him. With his ardour, too, went practical knowledge such as was rarely possessed by the religious enthusiast. If a Catholic Confraternity could have so enlarged its limits as to benefit by his experience and power of initiative, the rugged outline that is left to us of Renaudot the Combatant might have been softened by the gentler traditions of fellow-workers, while his work itself, supported by the tremendous influence of the Church, might have weathered the fiercest violence of opposition.

For his last undertaking, far more than for his Bureau and Pawnshop, or even his *Gazette*, survival under the best auspices was desirable. To Renaudot the doctor, the needless suffering caused by neglected illness made a special appeal. But in his day the Hôtel Dieu was so overcrowded that patients admitted were not likely to profit by their sojourn there, and numbers were turned away for lack of space. The medical profession occupied itself with those who could offer a fee rather than with the rejected applicants at the hospital, and there was actually no means by which a poor man could obtain medical assistance. The parish doctor, the dispensary, and the hospital out-patients' department, were unknown, and the amateur suggestions of the herbalist of a religious house was the only resource for those who could not afford a doctor's fee.

Renaudot required another of those royal patents which it was so easy for him to obtain; he required also the practical support of learned doctors who sympathized with his experiment. It was a result of his work during the foregoing years that he could command all he needed, and in 1640 there was opened the first "Consultation Charitable" in the largest room of his premises at the Sign of the Cock. Here every Tuesday morning (at a later time it was every day) certain doctors assembled, sometimes to the number of fifteen, and the afflicted persons desiring to consult them were admitted. If the case were serious, the doctor to whom the patient had applied could claim to consult with others, but the proceedings were very carefully ordered. Every applicant had a numbered ticket given to him, and by that number was summoned to take his turn, and medicines were supplied from a dispensary in the house. In due course arrangements were made for seeking out the sick in their own homes, but this was chiefly out of regard for the needs of the women (no women were admitted to the consulting-room at the Sign of the Cock), and the real utility of the "Consultation Charitable" was as an established centre of medical advice. When we consider prevailing conditions, it is not without reason that we term it the crowning achievement of Renaudot's career. It was also an instrument of his downfall. Already his success in other directions had won him a host of enemies, and this tremendous innovation on the practices of the medical profession left him open to the attack of a powerful clique. While the "Consultation Charitable" was still a novelty, Cardinal Richelieu died, and Renaudot found himself without protection. The Cardinal contrived to maintain a hold on the small affairs that concerned the citizens of Paris, while he directed the destinies of nations, and it was in the petty interests and intrigues of professional men and scribblers that the removal of his iron hand was felt the soonest. All those who had resented the ascendancy of Renaudot found themselves free to turn on him, and those of his own profession were eager in their onslaught. He was overwhelmed in a storm of opposition, and the great work for the lightening of the poor man's burden, which he had carried on at the Sign of the Cock, came to an end.

Public opinion would not permit the suppression of the *Gazette*, but only this was left to him. The "Consultation Charitable" took form under another name and in other hands, and some of his best endeavours seemed to be lost in utter failure. Yet there can be no doubt that Paris was the better for the years he spent in the Rue Calandre, and the clamour that raged round Renaudot and his inventions may have carried to some deaf ears a new suggestion of the duty a man owes to his neighbour. Perhaps, also, when his enemies trumpeted round the city the news that he was dead, and that he—the celebrated favourite of the Cardinal—had died "*gueux comme un peintre*," the scornful phrase may have borne with it the thought that this was the most honourable ending to the life of the poor man's friend. Thus, neglected and almost beggared, robbed of all credit from work that was destined to benefit ceaselessly those whose need was greatest, Théophraste Renaudot came to the end of his task. He is worthy of remembrance, not only for the new ideas which by his courage and cleverness were made into pivots of national life, but because he himself was the originator of a new type. He stands in complete independence of all established works of charity. Indiscriminate almsgiving, which was always the practice of religious houses, had no place in his schemes to help the poor. He desired that the rich should learn respect for the individual, and that the poor, carefully guided to the means of self-support, should merit such respect. The monks distributing food and money broadcast at their convent gates, or the pious ladies forcing all and sundry to accept their largesse in just the form they chose for its bestowal, had not as yet the faintest inkling of the high ideal of social amity towards which Renaudot was striving. But in those days an innovator could not hope to stand by his own strength. The waves of party feeling ebbed and flowed too strongly for a solitary figure to keep foothold. The benefactors of the poor were introduced to the people by the Church, and Renaudot, though he was protected by Richelieu, deferred to him as First Minister rather than as Cardinal. His philanthropy, we must repeat, was not connected with religion.

The full force of that fact is obscured by the vast numbers of his prototypes in the more recent centuries, but it had tremendous significance at the time. Practical piety was the fashion, even in high places, and the "Consultation Charitable," as well as other efforts dear to their founder's heart, might have had support strong enough to baffle all attack from jealous doctors or pettifogging lawyers. But Renaudot would not be pious. It is probable that his close knowledge of the poor revealed to him the prevalence of hypocrisy where charities were administered in the customary way, and he kept sternly aloof from the Church or the Church's methods. Later generations have discovered that the religious and the utilitarian spirit are not necessarily inimical, but it is idle to speculate on the possible result of combination between Renaudot and M. Vincent. Without *éclat* or eventual profit to himself, the layman struggled through his task, and because of the limitations that he set for himself, was freed from many complications. The priest, aiming higher, was oftener deceived, and had, perhaps, more reason for deep discouragement; yet, allowing for the power he derived from the Church, and the special patronage lavished on him because he was a priest, it must still be admitted that the sum of his accomplishment was infinitely the greater of the two.

CHAPTER VI

M. VINCENT'S FELLOW-LABOURERS

THERE is certainly no opportunity for confusion of result between Vincent de Paul and Théophraste Renaudot; their ambition and their field of labour are so distinct that the biographers of each make no allusion to the other. But this is not the case with all the contemporaries of M. Vincent; there were some who worked on the same lines as he did, and yet worked independently, and there is every reason to believe that of the reforms attributed to him a certain number were brought about by other agencies.

The difficulty of determining on the borderland between his achievements and those of others is due to the fact that there existed, at the time of his greatest activity in Paris, a body of persons, like-minded with himself in general aim, who had agreed to envélop all they were doing for the welfare of their neighbour in the profoundest mystery. While they worked secretly, Vincent de Paul was striving for the same objects under the eye of the public, and it was inevitable that he should obtain credit for success which was really theirs. It would be an impossible task to select from the list of his philanthropic triumphs those which from the first depended wholly on himself; but no faithful chronicle of him should ignore the great society of fellow-labourers bound to him by common sympathies, yet separated from him and from S. Lazare by many essential differences of opinion and intention.

It was in March, 1630, that four friends arranged

Jean Jacques Olier.
(Curé of S. Sulpice.)

together to meet weekly at the Capuchin Convent in the Faubourg S. Honoré. One of them, Philippe d'Angoumois, was himself a Capuchin; another was a priest (destined in the future to be a Bishop); the other two were laymen, Henri de Pichery, gentleman of the King's household, and M. de Ventadour, who was celebrated for his austere piety. Their intention was to found a Society of priests and laymen pledged to protect the faith and labour for the poor. They invited others to join them, and a year after their first meeting a name was decided upon: they were to be the *Compagnie du Très Saint Sacrement de l'Autel*, which title took a shorter form as the *Compagnie du Saint-Sacrement*.* At the same time they fixed their Constitution. Every three months a Superior, a Director, a Secretary, and six Councillors were to be elected from among their number. The Director was a priest, but the Superior was generally a layman; he acted as chairman of their weekly meetings, and was responsible for carrying out the resolutions arrived at. The meetings opened and closed with prayer; the business was laid before the assembly by the Secretary and discussed; in cases where relief was needed the amount to be given was put to the vote. The practical was followed by the spiritual; when the end of the agenda was reached, a passage, previously decided on, from the Bible or the " Imitation of Christ " was read, and two of the associates gave their reflections upon it. It will be seen that these meetings bore very close resemblance to the " Conferences " at S. Lazare, the chief external difference being the exclusion of laymen from the latter; and it appears curious that the scheme that centred at S. Lazare should have had such extraordinary influence when we reflect that it came into being after the Company of the Holy Sacrament was firmly established.

* The full history of this institution will be found in a volume edited by R. P. Beauchet Filleau, " Annales de la Compagnie de Saint Sacrement par le Cte. René de Voyer d'Argenson," and in "La Cabale des Dévots " (Raoul Allier).

The object of the Company is set forth in an official circular as follows:

"To undertake the promotion of all that is good, and the suppression of evil in every way possible, at all times, in all places, and in relation to every sort of person. The Company has no limits or restrictions save those of ordinary prudence and caution. Its work is not only the relief of the needy, the sick, the prisoner, and the unhappy, it is concerned with assisting missions and seminaries, with the conversion of heretics, and the propagation of the faith all over the world; it must also endeavour to abolish every sort of abuse, impiety, and blasphemy; it must, in short, aim at preventing or remedying every evil; at furthering all that is for the good of the public or of individuals; at charging itself with all good work that is difficult and has been neglected or given up."

There was sufficient " abuse, impiety, and blasphemy " practised to give ample scope for the energies of the Company; there were, besides, conditions of misery to which there is no real parallel in modern times—cruelty and injustice in the prisons, horrors of neglect in the hospitals, a huge submerged class for whom there was no chance of self-support or self-respect, and therewith an ignorance of all useful knowledge, both temporal and spiritual, which left a human being on a level with a beast. It is plain that the fortunate class was awakening to a sense of its responsibilities, and that it had strong men as leaders; yet where so many influences were tending in the right direction, it is impossible to determine on the particular inspiration of any individual movement. But all reforms contain an element of offence, and the true conservative will never have difficulty in finding flaws in an untried and novel system. The Company of the Blessed Sacrament existed to defend the weak, but it was also part of its programme to attack the strong, and there is no period of social history wherein the strong have shown themselves resigned to concerted and serious attack. Under Richelieu, and during the Regency that followed, passions were stirred easily, and were apt to find violent expression; beneath the surface of elaborate manners were the instincts that brought about the orgies of the Fronde. It is easy to see, then, that an open crusade against the extortion of landowners and the oppressive judgments of the magistrates would have resulted in such warfare between parties of differing opinion as must infallibly have counteracted any benefit that the aggressors were seeking. It was, however, the distinction of the Company of the Blessed Sacrament that it did not engage in open warfare or make appeal to public opinion: it was to labour secretly, and each one of its members pledged himself to conceal the fact of its existence. Outside its limits no one knew who its members were, and when a blow was struck in a good cause, or some flagrant injustice exposed and counteracted, no one could say for certain whether a member of the secret society was responsible or not. This rigorous and almost miraculous preservation of secrecy explains the silence of all memoir writers concerning it, and the lack of any reference from M. Vincent. It is supposed that he was himself a member of the Company, but when we remember his own weekly "Conferences" at S. Lazare, and regard also the vast responsibility that rested on him as the head of two growing Communities, we can only consider his membership as nominal and honorary. Among the active companions, however, may be numbered two of the intimate friends of M. Vincent—de Condren, Superior-General of the Oratory, and Jean Jacques Olier, afterwards the celebrated Curé of S. Sulpice—and the fact of their membership is sufficient of itself to prove that the aims and practices of the Company, at least in its early years, were above reproach.

As its name implies, the Company was more spiritual in its rule and object than a Confraternity of Charity; it was its essential charge " to promote the adoration—at all times and in all places—of Christ present in the Blessed Sacrament," and it was part of the spirit instilled into its members that even as the Presence of Christ was hidden in the Blessed Sacrament, so was His Presence with them to be hidden by their semblance of ordinary life, and yet to go out as a conquering force against the sins and miseries of the world.

It is not very easy—in a more prosaic period—to picture the situation; most probably every pious layman in society was a member of the Company when it was at its highest level. There was an infection of piety in the air; the austere adherents of Port Royal, as well as the devout parishioners of S. Sulpice, belonged to a race that could not have maintained existence in the Court of Henri IV., but was able to breathe freely in the atmosphere of mingled licence and devotion that surrounded Anne of Austria. And the man who, by original instinct or violent conversion, was devout, obtained through the Company a new zest for life. Instead of facing a long future that was, by a process of self-repression, to be made barren of excitement, he found himself armed with a constant incentive both to watchfulness and activity. The lively imagination of a cultivated Frenchman was touched by the mystery of the pledge he had taken, and his powers of observation were sharpened by the thought that any moment and any incident of his ordinary avocations might reveal a claim by which to prove his mettle and show himself worthy of his membership. When M. Vincent's schemes depended on the influence of the magistrates and the tolerance of the nobles, it is very likely that he owed to the Company the astonishing compliance and support that he met with; the Ladies of Charity could hardly have persisted in their novel and unconventional pursuits if the Company had not prepared the way by accepting for themselves a law of personal service; and many a great enterprise, in the provinces as well as in the capital, must have been stifled

M. VINCENT'S FELLOW-LABOURERS

at birth for lack of funds if there had not been a spring of generosity, out of the sight of the public eye, that supplied each need as it arose. Some circumstances in the career of M. Vincent, that strain credulity if regarded by themselves, are explained by the existence of the Company of the Blessed Sacrament. Reformers and philanthropists in every other generation are met with such baffling forms of opposition that the constant support accorded to Vincent de Paul may seem to throw a shade of unreality over the chronicle of his labours. But, in fact, in outside achievement he must often only have gathered what others had sown. If there were need, we might find here another reason for insisting on the superiority of his hidden and spiritual service over that which had earned him his renown; for, great as he was in originating and organizing, there are years when it is impossible to decide how much of the success of his philanthropy was due to himself and how much to his mysterious assistants.

The Company of the Blessed Sacrament was not destined for long life. It was the expression of thoughts latent in many minds that might without it have borne no fruit, but it was the movement of a generation, and when the best years of its founders were passed, it had not, as an organism, the strength to control the ill-directed zeal of some of its members. The spirit of the Samaritan was exchanged for that of the inquisitor, and the energies of the Companions were directed to the pursuit and conviction of the heretic rather than to the relief and consolation of the oppressed. It was Cardinal Mazarin who suppressed the Company on the plea that secret associations were illegal, but when he did so the moment was already reached when Society could no longer tolerate the Companions and their methods. The suppression of evil was as much a part of their original programme as the promotion of good; but the man who will denounce an associate, as soon as their intimacy gives him sufficient evidence to do so, is apt to be regarded as a spy, and the excellence of his motive will not protect him from subsequent unpopularity.

The real glory of the Company had departed long before its actual end, and it was commonly referred to as *La Cabale des Dévots*, which scornful nickname is adopted by the most recent of its historians. Death or disagreement had removed from its roll of membership the strong men who could have preserved its original purity, and the fine enthusiasm which it had fostered for a while vitalized other fields of labour in which it had no part; this, rather than the despotic interference of Mazarin, must be regarded as the reason of its downfall.

The degree to which the Company affected the age must always remain a matter of conjecture; probably it was very important, and the lay element in its membership lent it a strength that could not have been attained through a movement that was solely ecclesiastical. It stood for the recognition of Christian obligation, and so long as such recognition was confined to the clergy, there was small hope of social progress. Vincent de Paul—except during his brief experience at Châtillon—avoided what is known as Society, his touch with the leisured class depended on their initiative; the natural course of his life never brought him into contact with the heedless majority. It is therefore plain that there was immense scope for labour altogether outside his domain, while at the same time his enterprises were so far-reaching that any movement that made for righteousness could not fail sooner or later to affect and further his purposes. This, vague though it be, seems the only satisfactory summing-up of his relations with the Company of the Blessed Sacrament. That during his lifetime there was no rivalry or suggestion of rivalry is absolutely clear. Again and again we find the Companions—lay or clerical—working in intimate union with the Mission Priests, and the Convict Hospital at Marseilles, which was founded by the Company of the Blessed Sacrament, was placed from the first under the direction of the Lazarists.

There would appear to be something inherent in historical research that fosters a spirit of controversy, but Vincent de Paul is an ill-chosen object for attack, and the learned writers who in recent times have set themselves to prove that he was not responsible for the charitable movement of his age, or for the attempt to educate the priesthood, forget that he would himself have deprecated any credit that might accrue to him from the success of any enterprise. To defend his reputation, it is sufficient to let the well-established facts connected with him speak for themselves, even if in considering them, it is well to remind ourselves that his efforts were not isolated, and that the prominence that has been given to him by popular sentiment as well as formal sanctification is somewhat deceptive. We admit freely that among his contemporaries there were men who would have stirred their fellows to an effort for reform—social and spiritual—if he had never escaped from slavery. Of the laymen enough has been said already, but there remains a priest whose mark on life in Paris has never been obliterated; he was the friend of Vincent de Paul, the partner in some of his strongest desires, yet a labourer in a somewhat different field—Jean Jacques Olier, the Founder of the Seminary of S. Sulpice.*

South of the river there lay a populous and much-frequented quarter comprised in the ancient parish of S. Sulpice. Here stood the Hôtel de Condé, and the Palace of the Luxembourg, owned by Gaston d'Orléans, the King's uncle; here also dwelt M. de Liancourt, the celebrated adherent of Port Royal, and Mme. d'Aiguillon, to whose generosity M. Vincent's charities owed so much, besides many other magnificent personages. But it was also the home of a very different race of beings—the worst houses that Paris contained in a period of extreme

* See " Vie de Jean Jacques Olier " (l'Abbé Faillon). 2 vols.

depravity were to be found there, and year after year, when the Fair of S. Germain was held so near the church that the din could be heard within its walls, a fresh stream of evil poured in for the poisoning of the people. Inside the church, moreover, there were abuses that were not less deplorable because they had grown customary. Timorous ladies who desired the minimum of risk in their pursuit of adventure used it for assignations; the clatter of tongues never ceased during the celebration of Mass, and the congregation emerging from the sacred building was greeted in the porches by vendors of disreputable books and pictures, and by the touts of drinking booths and gambling hells. Paris was full of evil, but the parish of S. Sulpice was notorious as the centre of corruption.

According to public opinion then prevalent, the curé of a parish had no real responsibility for its condition; the Curé of S. Sulpice for many years was M. de Fiesque, a gentleman who made no pretence of residence, but spent the considerable emoluments of his office in other parts of the city. He may have had some misgivings as to the habits of his flock, however, for in 1639 we find that the priests of S. Lazare were persuaded to make an exception to the Rule that confined their work to the country and to preach a Mission there. The fullest knowledge of the iniquities prevailing in the quarter would by this means have reached M. Vincent, but we do not know what part he played in subsequent events. M. Olier had at one period been under his direction, and withdrew from it because M. Vincent urged him insistently to accept a bishopric which was offered him. His own instincts were so strongly against obedience in this matter that their relations could not continue on the same footing, but their friendship never wavered, and their divergence of opinion indicates that M. Vincent would have chosen him for a post of difficulty. By some means M. de Fiesque was induced to surrender his office to M. Olier, the Seminary which already he had opened at Vaugirard was removed to the neighbourhood of S. Sulpice, and in 1642 M. Olier, with his two faithful friends, du Ferrier and de Bassancourt, took up his residence as curé.

The substitution of an energetic priest for one of indolent and luxurious habits in a populous parish is not ostensibly a sensational event. But in this instance there were elements that made it of immense importance. In the first place, the idea of a rich benefice like that of S. Sulpice being held by one who intended himself to do the work attached to it was something of a novelty. At S. Nicholas du Chardonnet M. Bourdoise, the intimate friend of Vincent de Paul, had set an example, but the church itself and the possibilities of its work were of far smaller extent than in the case of S. Sulpice. And even more astonishing than the initial fact of a curé in residence was the personality of the curé himself.

Jean Jacques Olier was the son of Olier de Verneuil, who held some Court appointment under Henri IV. He was thirty-four when he entered on his labours at S. Sulpice—an age when instincts of ambition are apt to be in the ascendant. He was brilliantly gifted, and had been very popular in society; his relations were clamorous in remonstrance at the step he was taking, and he must have been aware that it was an anxious experiment. He had had some success with mission work in the provinces, and the need at S. Sulpice was for a perpetual Mission; but in the interests of his own career it would obviously have been wiser not to step off the beaten track. It was regarded by general consent as degrading to a gentleman to hold the position he accepted, and for a man of his talents there was no difficulty in obtaining whatever preferment he might choose. As we know, however, he had refused a bishopric, and when he embarked on his enterprise at S. Sulpice he must have done so with some understanding of the immense difficulties that lay ahead.

Perhaps that curious question of the social position of

the curé was the first obstacle to be overcome; the great folk—and there were very many of these at S. Sulpice—were accustomed to look on the officiating priest as a dependent, and resented any suggestion of authority in virtue of his office. In 1643 a letter was written to Vincent de Paul petitioning him to draw the attention of the Queen to the outrageous conduct of a certain Seigneur de Berzian, who had knocked down a priest on the threshold of his church, and kicked and beaten him, and in the journal of a devout woman of this same period we find the following entry:

"It would appear that to the great personages in a parish the curé is merely as one of their lackeys. In truth, a good curé in his inward humility will consider himself as the lackey of Jesus Christ, but in relation to men he is their pastor, and, as such, honour and respect are due to him."*

It was necessary for M. Olier to assert himself against this position of the lackey before he could begin his work on either class, for without the respect and support of the rich the task of civilizing and purifying the neighbourhood was an impossible one. It is to the credit of his noble parishioners that they recognized his worth and forgave his lack of obsequiousness. The change wrought in a few years by M. Olier at S. Sulpice was very remarkable. It proves that men grow sick of licence, and turn with desire to reform. In many directions M. Vincent and the Mission Priests had the same experience, but it was not their part to reap the full harvest of their labours; their vocation was for movement, and they had no opportunity of developing a theory and watching the effects. The fame of M. Olier is chiefly due to his foundation of the Seminary of S. Sulpice. He has had so many imitators in his parochial experiment that he receives less than his share of honour on that account. But, in fact, it was his part to prove the possibility of a con-

* "Journal of Marie Rousseau," December 4, 1643.

dition that had never been recognized, or had fallen into disuse, and his work was carried on by others after his death, and strengthened by many successors who were worthy to maintain it. The influence of S. Sulpice has been felt through many generations; it is still aflame. He cherished an ideal—very difficult to apply under the conditions that he found—of teaching the miserable beings whom he drew into the great Church of S. Sulpice to regard themselves as a family of which he was, in a sense, the head; and he was able to show the possibilities of the relationship between a pastor and his people in an age when any pure ideal was strange, and to do it in such wise that it was understood as being a closer imitation of the method of Christ than the practice of the Religious. He lived in days when piety was constantly travestied, and excitement and exaggeration were often the main features of conversion, and he had always to keep such dangers in view. Most of his flock, moreover, were in the most abject ignorance, and in so far as the Church attracted them the attraction was due to the brilliancy of its ceremonies. The task of infusing the idea of discipline was one of superhuman difficulty; nevertheless, he regarded discipline as the indispensable foundation of any real success. Neither the Church nor the precincts of S. Sulpice were to be used for assignations, and the ladies who came to worship were not to come in the fashion of the day that exposed neck and shoulders to the gaze of their neighbours. The church was the sanctuary of the Blessed Sacrament; the first lesson for those who came there was that they came into the royal presence chamber—an idea that had vivid force even in the childhood of Louis XIV. But the image of respect for the Majesty of the King could not be carried out in detail. At one point it broke down. In this more sacred Presence there were no inequalities of rank; the claim of the humblest workman was as good as that of the owner of a palace. A commonplace such as this, however, was not accepted readily. The rich man stalked and the poor man cringed, and the fact that they were within the walls of a church made no difference in their mutual relations; even to suggest the possibility of equality was an offence to the ruling class. One measure that he adopted made him unpopular with the poor. The Sacrament of Penance had, until then, had direct connection with the giving of alms, but he ordered every priest who heard confessions at S. Sulpice to warn the needy that no money would be given to them. On the other hand, he checked the unlawful extortion of fees which had become customary, and so applied his discipline to himself and his colleagues as searchingly as to the laity. The fact that he roused indignant opposition does not prove that he was unduly violent in his methods, for the condition that he found required drastic treatment. He attacked the gambling hells and houses of ill-fame in the immediate neighbourhood with unflinching perseverance, and was openly desirous that the Fair of S. Germain should be suppressed by royal command, though it was an old-established institution, and had been patronized by princes and nobles, as well as by their pages and footmen, for generations.

Even so brief a summary as this will show that M. Olier's reign at S. Sulpice was not a peaceful one. There were constant intrigues against him and one violent outbreak, but his personal courage was self-evident. It was admitted that he stood for righteousness against those who upheld vice, and he earned the respect of rich and poor by the industry with which he regulated charity and all relief of suffering. He might make inconvenient demand for reality in others, but it was recognized that he applied the sharpest tests to himself, and at moments when his authority hung in the balance the testimony of his personal life turned the scale in his favour. No doubt the fact that he did not come of the same class as the parish priests to whom they were accustomed helped him with the people. He was a scholar and a gentleman. His contemporaries record that he was extraordinarily eloquent, and he had the gift of intuition, which taught him how to appeal to the many widely separated grades of humanity that came under his care.

Here, perhaps, it is worth noting a special point of distinction between Jean Jacques Olier and Vincent de Paul. The Curé of S. Sulpice, though he had been destined from childhood for the priesthood, and had been recognized by François de Sales as possessing special vocation for it, had not always held aloof from the life of the world. In common with many another young abbé of aristocratic lineage, he had not regarded his eloquence in the pulpit as a bar to the full enjoyment of the amusements that could be obtained by the laity. There is a legend that his conversion was partly the result of the exclamation of Marie Rousseau—a strange and devout prophetess of the *bourgeoisie*—who saw him standing at the door of a wine-shop when the Fair of S. Germain was in full swing, with three or four other young abbés in mauve satin doublets, all alike forgetful of the claim of their vocation. We do not know what impression was made on his companions, but the brief "*Ah, messieurs, que vous me donnez de peine!*" of the old *dévote* had extraordinary effect upon Olier. In the sequel he was ordained priest, and passed into the hands of M. Vincent. But he had knowledge of the renunciation that he claimed of others—a knowledge which M. Vincent could not possess in the same way. And as life went on and the mystic in him developed, the past that nothing can obliterate taught him a depth of penitence which, to those who knew him intimately, was a cause of wonder. It is likely that on those who had no intimate knowledge of him it had an effect so strong as to silence any need of explanation.

M. Olier remained ten years at S. Sulpice. He established there something which has survived, and he

trained a successor who could uphold the standard he had
set up. It is difficult now to realize that his severance
from S. Sulpice meant downfall and disgrace, but this
was actually his fate, and so heavy was the blow that he
did not long survive it. The nominal reason was due to
his own imprudence and ill-fortune. For years society
was divided by the Jansenist question, and religious
controversy was the theme for drawing-room chatter.
It was the Jansenist party—inextricably confused with
the adherents of Port Royal—who suffered ultimately,
and whose cause was the weakest. There was, however,
a brief period when they were in the ascendant. The
most popular preachers were the Jansenists preachers.
The Congregation of the Oratory—then very powerful—
supported them, and the whole de Gondi influence,
paramount in ecclesiastical affairs, was on their side.
This was the moment chosen by M. Olier to launch from
the pulpit of S. Sulpice a violent diatribe against the
teaching and the practice of the Jansenists. It was the
last sermon that he was permitted to preach there. The
Oratorians were already roused against him because,
believing that they favoured heresy, he had refused
them permission to establish a branch house within the
limits of his parish, and it required very little pressure
to induce the Archbishop of Paris to exercise his authority
over the offender. There was, moreover, a secret reason
—more potent than any that were declared—for the withholding of protection from the Court. The tumult of
the Fronde was hardly over, and while it was in progress M. Olier, moved to desperation by the miseries of
the people, had written to the Queen urging her—sternly
rather than persuasively—to part from Mazarin, and put
the welfare of the nation before personal taste. We shall
see that Vincent de Paul was made to suffer for a similar
venture, but the Superior of S. Lazare was too firmly
established to be displaced even by the machinations of
Cardinal Mazarin; the Curé of S. Sulpice was an easier

victim. Opposing parties combined that they might strike at him, and he fell.

Perhaps the astounding record of that ten years could not have been sustained for a longer period, and the interference of party strife in an enterprise so essentially spiritual is a sign of the times. The political conflagrations of the Regency were of such a nature that no French subject, however peaceful in intention, could be secure of keeping outside their limit.

CHAPTER VII

THE QUEEN REGENT AND THE COUNCIL OF CONSCIENCE

THERE is a very strong element of the unexpected in the life of Vincent de Paul. Events have none of the coherence which may be observed in the career of one who sets an aim before him and uses men and circumstances to serve it, and those occurrences which affected him most deeply and were the most sensational burst upon him without warning, and never seem to have been in accord with his personal desires. In so far as he formed any intention with regard to politics it was one of entire abstinence. A part of the Rule of the Mission Priests forbade discussion of public affairs, and their Superior, apart from any other motive, had quite enough to do in connection with his own undertakings without embarking on dangerous waters where his vocation did not call him. But M. Olier was probably in agreement with M. Vincent on this point when he went to S. Sulpice, and in his case circumstances proved stronger than his resolution, and in consequence S. Sulpice lost its curé. M. Vincent at one point was moved to an act that resembled that of M. Olier, and before and after that special crisis—during a period that lasted fifteen years—was deeply involved in public affairs.

The claim came upon him very suddenly. Until he had passed middle age he had succeeded in holding aloof. He must have been in Paris at the date of the murder of Henri IV., and in the years that followed, when the Regency of Marie de Médici was furnishing perpetual

THE QUEEN REGENT 121

scandal and excitement, it was impossible even for a humble priest to be completely ignorant of the affairs of the Court. M. Vincent left the capital only to find a place in one of those great houses where every national event must have been a subject of interested discussion. In those days the favourites of the Queen-mother and of the young King, Louis XIII., succeeded each other on a pinnacle of giddy eminence, and one after another lost balance and fell headlong, and royal personages struggled perpetually among themselves, distracting trade and agriculture by petty civil warfare. It was, indeed, a period when human nature, as seen in the great ones of the earth, was brought on the stage under the pitiless glare of the footlights, and humble persons might stare and wonder. M. Vincent's detachment can hardly have gone the length of ignoring the extraordinary drama that was being played by the hereditary rulers of his country, but he never refers, even distantly, to the history of that time. When he was established in Paris as Superior of the Mission Priests an age of comparative quiet was beginning. It was in 1624 that Richelieu became chief of the King's Council. To every citizen of Paris—whether he realized it or not—that event had immense significance, and to one who, like Vincent de Paul, threw himself whole-heartedly into the life of the people, the dawn of Richelieu's despotism could not have been indifferent. But we have not from his own lips or his own pen any testimony that he was oppressed by that overshadowing presence, or that, on the other hand, he was grateful for the rule and order that resulted from its dominance. The influence of Richelieu was the most important external factor in the career of Renaudot, but, though it touched him faintly at certain points, it affected M. Vincent very little. All through the years of the great Cardinal's administration Vincent de Paul contrived to carry on work that was so far-reaching in its scope that the limits of the kingdom did not limit it, and yet to avoid all visible connection with the Courts either of King or Minister. Probably he anticipated that he would always be granted the skill and the good fortune to remain hidden, and it was chance rather than the deliberate intention of any individual that drew him into the sort of publicity he shunned.

Cardinal Richelieu died in the autumn of 1642. In the following April the news that the King also was very near his end began to spread through Paris. The account of his last days has been written by Saint-Simon, who seems to have had an honest admiration for him; but there seems no reason to believe that his subjects generally felt any violent grief at the prospect of his death, nor that he had given them reason to do so. He was not noble either in his private life or in his rulership, but beneath his weakness and his folly, and in spite of the cruelty of which he had from time to time been guilty, he had a deep understanding of religion. It was this quality in him which links his name to that of Vincent de Paul. The Mission Priests had been in existence for eighteen years, and had never been chosen for special royal favours, and their Superior had not any of the methods or the manners of a courtier; nevertheless, when the King lay dying, it was to S. Lazare that he sent for help. The clouds were gathering before his eyes, and a great desire seized him to have M. Vincent at his side to give him courage.

The Court was at S. Germain, and it was necessary for M. Vincent to leave behind him all familiar surroundings, and to plunge into a world that was completely uncongenial. Probably there was no moment in his life when he so greatly needed to concentrate his mind on the high essentials of his religion. The idea of Royalty in those days, to loyal subjects, was connected with exaggerated reverence, and Vincent the peasant would regard the surroundings of a King with bated breath. But Vincent the priest was able to forget his

THE QUEEN REGENT

awestruck regard for kingship in his sympathy for the human being who, remembering the past, was afraid to face the future.

Their intercourse was not limited to one visit. M. Vincent remained more than a week at S. Germain, and then, because the patient seemed to be recovering, returned to Paris. The improvement was very brief. Once more the King saw death approaching, and another messenger was sent to S. Lazare. During his last three days he kept M. Vincent near him, and tradition says that he died in his arms. It is, of course, impossible to have any authentic knowledge of what passed between them, yet the fact of that brief intimacy shows us Louis XIII. in a new aspect. We forget the vindictive son and husband, we cease to condemn the weak ruler who could yield up all authority to other hands; we see only the King accepting his share of the suffering of humanity, yet crying out for help in his desolation. It is proof that there was in him a quality of which history can tell us nothing that he sent for M. Vincent. He had courtier priests at hand, devout and learned men, who were ready to give him spiritual consolation. When he sent his messenger to S. Lazare he was breaking through convention and grasping at reality.

"I have never seen in anyone who had reached this condition greater reliance upon God, greater resignation, or more evident distress over the smallest actions that might be sins,"* wrote M. Vincent to a Mission Priest when the King was dead, and from him we hear no more of that strange episode.

If he could have followed his own wishes, he would have left the Court for ever when the service that had called him thither was complete; but, though Anne of Austria, as Queen Consort, had never disturbed him in his labours, and only displayed interest in them at rare intervals, as Queen Regent she claimed a large share of

* " Lettres," vol. i., No. 72.

his time and powers. When she entered upon her Regency, Vincent de Paul was actually in the Palace, therefore, when her heart was stirred by the great change that had come into her life, the thought of him was fresh in her mind, and it was natural that she should turn to him to help her to carry out the good intentions which for a time possessed her.

In Saint-Simon's account of the last days of Louis XIII. the dying King is reported to have said to M. Vincent that he would wish for the future to have no Bishops appointed in France who had not spent three years at S. Lazare. There is an echo of this wish in the Queen's endeavour to appoint a "Council of Conscience" to regulate the disposition of all ecclesiastical preferment. In France this rested almost completely with the Crown, and even with the support of a high tradition the responsibility would have been a very grave one. Enough has been said already to show that the tradition had become deplorably degraded. The provision of the Council of Trent, that the holder of any benefice should be a man of sufficient learning and assured virtue, received no attention, and the spiritual degradation of the land was the result. The Council of Conscience was to consist of five persons, on whose advice the Queen intended to act, and as one of the five she chose Vincent de Paul. His experience and his character made him admirably suited to this office, and infinite good might have resulted but for the fact that Cardinal Mazarin was associated with him in the Council, and that the aims of these two were impossible to reconcile. The Italian diplomatist was as intent on his chosen life-work as was the Mission Priest, but its accomplishment required the encouragement of the conditions and the standards which M. Vincent constantly endeavoured to break down. It was by understanding and utilizing the vices of humanity—the cupidity, the passion, the meanest order of ambition—that Mazarin built up his fortunes. Observation must have given M. Vincent a measure of understanding of these vices, but its only use to him was as an incentive for himself and others to renewed struggle against the forces that made for evil. And of human forces in those dark times the strongest and most fruitful was Mazarin himself. M. Vincent was no match for him. Even after three centuries the fact that their names were ever coupled is matter for regret. The unambitious peasant, versed in the methods of dealing with God's poor, apt in guidance of the rich and gifted who desired to qualify as Christians, had no understanding of real statecraft; and when at a moment of crisis conscience bade him testify, at all costs, against the selfishness that was ruining his country, he only forfeited the confidence of the poor he loved without altering by a hair's breadth the action of those great ones whom he sought to influence.

But that climax was not reached until he had endured other, and perhaps severer, tests of his singleness of purpose. It is likely that Anne of Austria was partly actuated in her selection of M. Vincent for her Council of Conscience by a desire to reward a priest who worked so hard in the service of others. She was a good-natured woman. "*La reine est si bonne*" was the phrase on the lips of many in the weeks that succeeded the death of Louis XIII. She gave freely (sometimes with so little understanding of the value of her gift that it was necessary afterwards to take it back), and M. Vincent, who had comforted the last hours of the dying King, received a post that most men would have coveted. It meant the command of patronage and, in consequence, of almost illimitable power. The man who had a hand in bestowing preferment would be courted everywhere; if he was clever, he could make his own terms with his suitors. It was only a question of bargaining, and it was an accepted custom. M. Vincent, as he was so devoted to the poor, would no doubt use his power to obtain benefits for them, and all good people would be pleased. This, according to the standards of the day, was the natural point of view of the Queen Regent, and she was not prepared for the refusal of her councillor either to use or recognize the power with which she had endowed him.

Once persuaded that it was his duty to accept responsibility, Vincent de Paul was unflinching in upholding his principles with reference to the Church. But it was one thing to deplore upon his knees before the altar at S. Lazare the abuses from which she suffered, and quite another to withstand their continuance against the wishes of the Queen Regent and her first Minister. His first plea for reform appears culpably moderate, but its moderation indicates the point of corruption that had been reached.

He stipulated that in future children should not be Bishops, and that a bishopric should be given to persons who had been priests for at least a year; that the rich endowment of an abbey should not be conferred on a person who had not reached the age of eighteen; that a cathedral Canon must be sixteen years old, a Canon in a college fourteen; that it should be impossible to divert the revenues of a bishopric to a *seigneur ;* and that the system of granting *un dévolu*, whereby a priest was guaranteed the reversion of a benefit, should be abolished, because it was found to cause the aspirant constantly to watch for an opportunity of denouncing the man in possession, to the damage of Christian amity.

These demands do not appeal to the modern mind as being specially heroic. It is obvious that they leave abundant scope for irregularity; but before we condemn M. Vincent as pusillanimous, it is well to remember that Mazarin, before whom they were made, was not a priest, nor even a deacon, but that he was Bishop of Metz and the holder of thirty abbeys.* The Church of France could not be reformed in a moment by a solitary champion, but

* "Coups d'Etat des Cardinaux," A. Richard.

it was no small thing that the Superior of the Priests of the Poor had courage to throw down his gauntlet in full view of the first Minister of the Crown. It is hard to say how much he actually accomplished; it is possible that Mazarin purposely increased the difficulties of his position, and it is most unlikely that the Cardinal was ever prevented from carrying out any serious intention by the interference of the priest. But the interference had its value; the gossip of the Court spread the tidings of M. Vincent's protests, and men began to ponder on the reasons for them and to understand the rottenness of the existing system.

M. Vincent himself was called to new understanding of the devious developments of human nature. Probably at the time of his first visit to the Court he was ignorant of many events in the lives of the royal personages whom he saw there, which were matter of common knowledge. The mind of Vincent de Paul was too much occupied to give space to gossip, and he had no premonition that the character of Anne of Austria would ever be of signal importance to himself. He owed to it, however, some of the bitterest of his personal experiences as well as the vicarious suffering due to the distress of others. It was the character of the Queen Regent which was mainly responsible for the disasters of the Regency; but before judging the Queen Regent, it is fitting that we should glance at the Queen Consort.

Anne of Austria, as the wife of Louis XIII., had a just claim to pity. She had come as a young girl to a strange Court, and instead of being guarded and cared for by the King, she was persistently neglected. Her ill-fortune gave her as companion the wife of the Constable de Luynes, and she could hardly have encountered a more pernicious influence. As Mme. de Chevreuse, Mme. de Luynes, in a later reign, won celebrity as a leader of revolt; but in the earlier stages of her career her rebellion was against the laws of morality and seemliness rather than against those of the State. She looked on life as on a great feast spread out before her, and would recognize no hindrance to helping herself from any dish that caught her fancy. The young Queen was thrown into intimacy with this woman at the most impressionable stage of her development, when the novelty of her surroundings and her own isolation gave her a special craving for sympathy, and their subsequent separation did not undo its effects. Dumas has perpetuated the romance of the Queen Consort and thrown a certain halo over her relations with George Villiers, Duke of Buckingham. Probably a trap was laid for her; possibly her own conduct was innocent throughout; but with such a confidante as Mme. de Luynes she was not likely to be conspicuous for prudence. Whatever truth there may have been in the original scandal, it is certain that the Queen suffered very severely for her part in it. It placed a weapon in the hands of Richelieu, who was always her enemy, and he used it against her mercilessly. As the years passed, her position grew more and more miserable. There came a time, indeed, when, by the King's orders, no man might be admitted to her apartments save in his presence. When she became the mother of the Dauphin the worst indignities to which she had been subjected were removed; but while Richelieu was dominant it was hopeless for her to assert any of her rights as Queen. Then, within six months, death removed the Cardinal and the King; her son was a child of four, and she, as Regent, was supreme. There is no room for wonder that her years of Regency were not well used, and that she fell a prey to the most brilliant adventurer in history, Jules Mazarin, the Italian pupil of Cardinal Richelieu.

It was not his skill in diplomacy, nor the courage and finesse with which he could play a desperate game, that won for Mazarin his supreme dominion over France; it was his understanding of a woman's character, his capacity

THE QUEEN REGENT

for holding the balance steadily, and knowing when to flatter and when to rule, when to be the counsellor and when the lover. The long years, barren of all delight, on which the pleasure-loving Queen looked back had been the most perfect preparation for the success of Mazarin's schemes. He began by encouraging her in her amusements, and from time to time gave her an entertainment, as a wise tutor will give a child a treat. It was his object to divert her more and more from thinking of affairs, and to teach her to think of him as inseparable from all those things that gave her happiness. He had both the patience and the pertinacity that his task needed, and he succeeded in it. The time came at length when he was indispensable, and the Queen Regent would have forfeited the kingdom rather than consent to a permanent separation from him. The actual terms of their alliance remain a mystery, but at its best it was degrading to the Queen and a demoralizing spectacle for her subjects. It was a strange freak of destiny that brought Vincent de Paul into touch with this sinister romance, and one which he had every reason to regret. Yet he had no free will in the matter. The Council of Conscience was the direct result of the Regent's good intentions, and when he accepted his place on it Cardinal Mazarin had not attained to his supremacy.

In eighteen years of rule over others as Superior of the Mission priests the character of M. Vincent had had opportunity to develop, but those whom he had ruled—though we shall find how widely they differed in individuality—all came under his authority because they desired to serve God and their neighbour in a special way. The duty which the Queen laid upon him put him in quite a different position from any which he had ever occupied, and he had to win fresh knowledge of human frailty. In the Council Chamber at the Louvre the burden of his new appointment was a very heavy one. He had to withstand Mazarin, and, as time passed, this endeavour became more and more hopeless; he had to avoid association with the great folk who tried to flatter him, and even his shabby cassock was no protection from their importunities. But he knew when these hours of difficulty would come, and could arm himself against them; he had to face the sharpest test to nerve and brain when he was outside the limits of the Court, and the detail of some of these has its own curious interest.

By the original constitution of the Council of Conscience nominations for ecclesiastical preferment were to be submitted to M. Vincent, that he might report on the qualifications of the nominee. His knowledge of the individual lives of the younger generation of priests was enormous, and for the fulfilment of the true purpose of the Council no plan could have been more perfect. Mazarin disapproved of this purpose because he required bishoprics and abbeys as bribes to wavering adherents, therefore the Council eventually was a failure; but in its first years the real responsibility of selection rested upon M. Vincent. It is a theme for wonder that the Superior of S. Lazare was able to carry out this task with the thoroughness and devotion which is ascribed to his performance of it. His place as the centre and director of immense organizations, to each of which he gave the most minute attention, seemed to preclude the possibility of bearing this additional burden without a stumble. Yet he did so. His unusual capacity for detachment, and that mental self-conquest of his, the most precious of attainments, explain in some measure his comprehensive power. He could banish completely the harassing questions that made judgment of the fortunes and characters of other men so difficult, and turn to a letter of encouragement to a Sister of Charity in a far-away provincial town or to the selection of preachers for a country Mission, or to the consideration of the latest scheme of some impulsively disposed Confraternity; and because he had this capacity it was possible for him at the same time to continue his own enormous labours and direct the patronage of the Crown. His success does not indicate immense intellectual vigour so much as the real power that results from consistent submission to the will of God. M. Vincent, confronted with the persons and circumstances most calculated to oppose his purpose, wasted no time or energy in quarrelling with them, but merely sought for greater confidence that his purpose was the right one, and so went on, indifferent to the likelihood of recognized success. For him personally, indeed, success and failure seem to have had no existence. The thing that God could use might flourish by the will of God, and he, to whom it had been given to sow the seed, looked on and humbly offered up his thanks for what he saw. In learning to withdraw himself, he learnt how to establish and confirm the work he had been inspired to begin, and it was this same capacity for withdrawal of personal interest that made him able to sustain without disturbance the attacks of the envious when they were directed towards him.

It was, according to the custom of those times, natural to regard the possession of interest as a source of wealth. M. Vincent's position on the Council of Conscience had great pecuniary value, and by its judicious exercise he might have gathered large sums for the use of the Company and the benefit of the poor. He might have done this without countenancing any appointment of which he disapproved, because the most worthy of candidates for preferment might give a bribe, under some other name, without infringing any law of conscience. But M. Vincent's idea of morality was not in unison with that of his generation. The financial resources of S. Lazare suffered by his singularity, and he was the less popular. He missed also many an opportunity by which he might have strengthened the position of the Company in Paris and the provinces by conciliatory methods towards those in power that would not have outraged any principle. But he would not. He was for the whole of his ten years of office uncompromising in repudiating the smallest claim on personal interest. "The Company will not perish by reason of its poverty," said he; "it is far more from lack of poverty that one fears its downfall."

When preferment was wrongly given by the will of the Queen (or, rather, by the will of Cardinal Mazarin), Vincent bowed to the inevitable, but if any loophole was left by which the abuse might be prevented, he did not hesitate to take it. Thus, on one occasion, Mazarin having written to him from S. Germain that it was the Queen's pleasure to present a certain most important bishopric to a young priest whose father merited special reward and distinction, M. Vincent, knowing the matter had gone too far to be stopped by authority, resorted to persuasion, and went himself to the father, representing the unfitness of the son for this sacred responsibility. It is certainly to the honour of the gentleman in question that the Mission Priest was well received, and his interference carefully considered. It is not to be wondered at that his plea was unsuccessful, but it was not roughly pushed aside, and perhaps the new Bishop might have been roused by remembrance of it to justify its refusal by his zeal and energy. He died within a few weeks of his consecration, however, and those who agreed with M. Vincent regarded his death as a judgment on himself and on his father.

The difficulty of vigorous intervention was enormous; the Church was regarded as the natural haven of the impoverished or inefficient noble. Claimants of all conditions, armed with a recommendation from the Queen or on their own initiative, constantly attacked him. The first were, of course, the most difficult to deal with, but it is not hard to picture the uneasiness of the peasant priest, conscious, as he always was, of his own humble origin, when he found the great ladies of the Court currying favour with him, and had not skill to check them before they had laid themselves open to discomfiture. In fact, the prospects of their sons and nephews were only injured by their attempt to make interest in this quarter, but such attempts were so far the rule that a rebuff—especially from an obscure person in a very shabby cassock—was altogether intolerable.

In connection with the Bishopric of Poitiers, M. Vincent had an opportunity of learning the entire indifference to the claims of justice and of righteousness that distinguished the leaders of the great world. A well-known Duchess, *dame du palais* to the Queen, desired it for her son, and, as a clever woman who had had ample opportunity of watching how affairs of this kind came to success or failure, she approached the matter very carefully. She went first to the Queen, representing that the See was of very little value, but that the family estates in Poitou made it desirable that they should hold the bishopric. The Queen, whose conscientious scruples on questions of this kind were intermittent, professed herself quite ready to sign the appointment if M. Vincent would bring it to her in fitting form at Court the following day. The Duchess repaired to S. Lazare, and, declaring that she was very much pressed for time, gave the Superior the Queen's order that the nomination paper should be made out in her son's favour. M. Vincent, aghast at the bare suggestion, implored her to stay and talk it over with him; but she declared that there was nothing to be added to the fact of the Queen's command, and hurried away. The simplicity of the arrangement made the position of M. Vincent extremely difficult. To him personally there would come no discredit because an unworthy Bishop held the See of Poitiers; he was not in the least degree responsible for the choice, and if he opposed it he was braving the sort of enmity that was most dangerous and most far-reaching. It was a situation calculated to tax the resolution of a saint; to an average person the simple path of submission was the obvious one.

M. Vincent duly appeared with his roll of paper at the Court, in obedience to the royal command; but when the Queen took it for signature she found that it was blank, and her councillor was obliged to explain that he felt it impossible to take any part in such a transaction. It appears that Anne of Austria was never roused to anger by M. Vincent, and in this case she was distressed. She believed herself bound by her word, and yet was uneasy as to the possible consequences of her impulsive promise. M. Vincent did not hesitate to overcome her scruples by assuring her that the fulfilment of such a promise was nothing short of a crime. The young abbé who aspired to episcopal dignity was an habitué of the lowest haunts of the city, and so confirmed a drunkard that he was constantly picked up unconscious in the streets. His family, justly ashamed of him, desired an excuse for getting him out of the capital, but their method of so doing was not one in which a lover of the Church could give assistance.

The Queen was convinced, but her courage was not equal to the task of explaining matters to her lady-in-waiting. M. Vincent might appoint whom he would to Poitiers, but it must be his part to interview Mme. la Duchesse. If we would realize what such a commission entailed, we must consider the respect with which the lower orders were trained to treat the nobility. In an unassuming nature that tradition would be impossible to eradicate, and M. Vincent needed all the strength of his great conviction to support him. He spoke plainly, and did not leave Mme. la Duchesse, who had met him with a welcome, long in doubt as to the nature of his errand. It appears that she forgot her dignity in her anger, and ended a torrent of abuse by throwing a footstool at his head. He left her house with the blood streaming from his face, and had much difficulty in calming the Brother who had accompanied him by explaining that this ungovernable rage was part of a mother's affection for her son. How far, indeed, it proceeded from that sentiment, and how far from the fury of the aristocrat whose path is obstructed by the plebeian it is impossible to say, but certainly reverence for the dignity of the Church or the sanctity of religion had no place therein, and those who had no such reverence to give, were not likely to look with favour on M. Vincent. For them the fact of his position, and even of his existence, as a matter for notice was offensive and unintelligible.

To catalogue the struggles of this kind which he carried through, more or less successfully, would be an interminable task. Besides the appointments of the clergy there were the Religious to be considered. There had grown up a sort of heredity in the command of some of the monasteries. Daughters of the same house held them in succession, and sometimes each succeeding abbess insured the use of the monastic building and pleasure gardens to her relations when they needed recreation and change. These abuses were far-reaching, and had brought the religious life into dishonour; it was extremely difficult to reform them. The work of the Abbess Angélique of Port Royal had set an example, and M. Vincent was anxious to find and to obtain the appointment for such women as would have strength and courage for the task, rather than for one whose father could claim for her the dignity and comfort of provision by the Church revenues. He guarded himself always from any close connection with religious houses. It was only at the express desire of François de Sales that he undertook the direction of the mother-house of the Order of the Visitation, and he was never the referee—as de Bérulle had been—for the Religious or the Superior whose spiritual distresses were baffling the convent confessor. Therefore it was easy for Churchmen to urge against him that his experience of the religious life was not sufficient to justify the vigorous line he took towards the system of preferment in it. He maintained (and his judgment agrees with that of the lay mind) that the true spirit of such a life was so delicate that it must not be exposed to the risk of injury from contact with a worldly motive, and that authority over souls could not rightly be a privilege of certain families, but must be vested in persons who had proved themselves worthy to wield it. The plea of his opponents was that the fact of the appointment of a certain person to a position of responsibility proved that an overruling Providence had intended her for her post, that family interest would not have been bestowed upon her without reason, and that to question the system which custom had established was to question Divine wisdom.

Aristocratic privilege, especially on such lines as these, had many powerful supporters; nevertheless, while M. Vincent held his place in the Queen's Council, it was impossible to obtain the royal consent to the appointment of girl abbesses or of those whose pursuit of pleasure had demonstrated their ignorance of the only possible motive for their profession.

No great knowledge of human nature is required to estimate the danger braved by M. Vincent in thus outraging the susceptibilities of the ruling class. They claimed the right to establish the daughters whom they could not afford to marry in the command of religious houses. M. Vincent not only criticized their motive in exercising their right, but actually deprived them of the right itself. Even he, however, could not defy tradition with impunity. His reputation was too firmly established, it is true, for open assault, but the stab in the dark may always be delivered, and false charges of a kind incidental to his office were urged against him. It was said that the Superior of S. Lazare, though he inveighed so fiercely against simony, had, in fact, been known to accept a percentage of revenue and a gift of books from one who desired, and had received, a benefice from the Crown. The story, with full detail, was whispered about Paris until it came to the ears of M. Vincent. His first instinct was to challenge his accuser and to make open declaration of his innocence. But a strife of tongues or of pamphlets was not to be reconciled with his chosen standpoint towards life. We are told that he flung down his pen in bitter self-abasement, and would make no effort for his own defence.

In fact, he had lived his years of service to such good purpose that those who knew him were moved only to anger by the whispers of calumny, and the number of his friends was great enough to silence his enemies. Through that trial—a dangerous one for a man who had any joints in his armour—he passed scathless, but the malice that prompted such an attack remained unappeased, and the time was coming when, by his own imprudence, M. Vincent gave his foes their desired opportunity.

CHAPTER VIII
THE FRONDE REBELLION

IT is difficult to connect the Court of Anne of Austria with the real spirit of Vincent de Paul, and there is equal difficulty in realizing that the devout persons who carried out the social reforms suggested at S. Lazare, or were members of the secret company of the Blessed Sacrament, were of the same rank and race as those on whose shoulders rests the guilt of the Fronde Rebellion. Many of the heroes and the heroines of those wild years sought refuge at Port Royal, and they found fit environment among the hermits and nuns, for the violence of Port Royal in its self-abnegation and its penitence is clearly the right antidote to the unbridled licence of the Frondists.

But M. Vincent's teaching was very different from that of S. Cyran and Mère Angélique. Natures nourished for a lifetime on excitement could find nothing to satisfy them at S. Lazare, for it was by a rule of charity that the Lazarists were guided, and the necessary preparation for that rule is the gradual development of years of Christian living. On the first awakening of penitence it may not be understood. The practical service of others in matters temporal as well as spiritual was the object of M. Vincent and his followers, and, of a truth, nothing could be more opposed to the aims of those who ruled in Paris during the Regency. In periods of civil warfare, however false in origin, the spirit of heroism and of sacrifice is seldom lacking; but in those miserable years of strife it is hard to find a suggestion of devotion or of loyalty among the combatants. The picture is among the strangest that history presents. All who might claim to high estate and to the power that went with it—from the Queen downwards—had been schooled and disciplined by Richelieu into an impotence so universal as to be unrealized. The death of the autocrat had no immediate effect; his methods had been too well adjusted; the machinery could continue for a while without him. It is possible, indeed, that Louis XIII. might have had skill to keep this machinery in working order—he had been the nearest witness of its construction—and with skilful treatment the habit of submission inculcated by the great Cardinal might have endured for a generation. But death made the skilled hands impotent, and Anne of Austria was like the boy owner of a great estate who finds himself released from the tutelage of guardians. The King's death signalized the end of her minority, but to have prolonged it another twenty years would not have made her more fit for independence, and the severity of her past experiences gave greater impetus to the swing of the pendulum.

If, at the time of the King's death, there were onlookers who gave any thought to the future, it must have been clear to them that the Government of France would not long be directed by the Queen; but for a time it was not possible to be certain whose hands would hold the reins. Perhaps that period of uncertainty was partly responsible for the tempest that made this Regency so memorable. Unreasonable as well as natural ambition was stirred by a sense of possibility. The influence of Richelieu so far survived that the Queen was afraid to adopt an obvious course, and give her confidence to Condé, who was by far the strongest and most capable of her subjects. According to Richelieu's doctrine, he was too near the throne and too much admired by the people for any extra elevation; but the fact that he possessed the qualifications for the place of Queen's Councillor when the place was vacant, and that he did not attain to it, poisoned his nature, and helped to make a traitor of him. In sharp contrast to the great General stands de Beaufort, one of those left-handed kinsmen of the King who complicated Court society in bygone times. At the beginning of the Regency he made use of his personal attractions to win the Queen's favour, and dreamed of power. He was, however, singularly incompetent as a statesman, and was hardly less indolent than the Queen herself. Gaston d'Orleans, the young King's uncle, was also precluded by feebleness both of will and intellect from ruling; and de Gondi, the only one of the contemporaries of Mazarin who might aspire to rival him, was not, at the death of Louis XIII., in a position that gave him the opportunity of competing on equal terms with the Italian Cardinal.

It is characteristic of Mazarin and of Anne of Austria that for many months their consultations were held every evening in her private oratory, and that in consequence his rise was imperceptible. By the time the general public had discovered whose will was expressed by the Queen's actions, and disapproval of the foreign interloper had grown into definite form, his authority over the Queen was established on a basis even stronger than her wish to be relieved of trouble, and all the power of France, though there were moments when it seemed concentrated against him, proved insufficient to oust him from his place. The revolt which darkened the youth of Louis XIV. was primarily an expression of indignation against the dominion of the royal favourite. There was much more involved. There were many leaders and many causes; there were the plots brewed in whispers round the couches of intriguing women, of which jealousy or pure love of excitement were the inspiration; there were those set on foot by the few who had some definite personal ambition in view—by Condé, by Jean François de Gondi, or by de Beaufort; and there was the continual counter-plotting, the ingenious weaving of complicated webs to entrap his enemies, by Mazarin himself. But at the root of everything lay fury with the Queen for imposing the Italian on her subjects, and therewith lay the dangers that are latent in the challenge of authority; for in the middle of the seventeenth century, as at the end of the eighteenth, the people of France were an oppressed and suffering people. And then, just as a hundred and fifty years later, they were strong enough to overwhelm their oppressors had they had a leader able to reveal and to direct their strength.

The attempts of the few, such as M. Vincent and Théophraste Renaudot, to remedy the ills beneath which the poor were groaning, did probably direct the thoughts of those who had energy left to think to the injustice of prevailing conditions. Such suggestions were an ominous preparation for the Regency. Richelieu spent the public money freely, and was callous to the distress of the French people so long as France herself reaped glory. Anne of Austria also spent the public money freely, and was heedless of the sufferings of the people, but no magnificent motive excuses her. She was frankly eager to enjoy herself, and to indulge her favourite in the very expensive species of display which he affected. The wars on the frontier went on giving occupation to dangerous persons, but they also drained the State coffers, and left many a humble household bereft of the breadwinner. The peasantry, starved out of their natural homes, tramped to the towns, and met starvation in the streets or a miserable death in the prisons. Actual famine devastated many parts of the provinces, but the refugees who managed to escape and to find their way to Paris had the privilege at their journey's end of beholding a display of magnificence which should have indicated wealth and prosperity.

Mme. de Motteville, the most naïvely honest of memoir-writers that ever wielded pen, pictures for us the life of the Palais Royal in these early years of the Regency.

It appears to have been characterized by an astonishing levity rather than by actual vice. The austerity of Louis XIII. had been due partly to his feeble health, and partly to his natural disposition, but it had resulted in the suspension of Court society, and the younger generation had never learnt to connect amusement with the royal presence. The Court of the Regent might, perhaps, have been livelier if she had possessed more energy; but while it was a novelty, it satisfied the pleasure-seekers. Anne of Austria was not imbued with the restless spirit of the age. She liked a great deal of repose, and made it a habit to sleep till ten or eleven in the morning. A certain amount of business was transacted before she got up, and courtiers of both sexes paid her their respects. As a rule, she spent twelve hours in the twenty-four in bed, and it was her practice to remain there for a day or two at a time if any special pressure of business had been forced upon her. It is likely that she began her reign with good resolutions—her Council of Conscience is, indeed, a proof of this—for she had always a certain desire to do her duty, and was sincerely attached to her children; but, as Mme. de Motteville expresses it, " her resolutions were undermined by her desire for ease and her aversion to the multiplicity of business affairs, which cannot be separated from the Government of a great kingdom." As time went on, she grew more indolent. She desired always that the royal will should be supreme, but would not realize that even royalty requires a measure of knowledge for the direction of its will. It is possible that, though he could hardly have secured the same stability of rule merely by his skill as a politician, Mazarin might have enslaved the Queen without the power of sex; for a master of statecraft such as he was able to save her from the constant friction of small anxieties, which she abhorred, and in great things to leave her with the impression that her decisions were all-important.

Yet Mazarin, despite his cleverness, was not in touch with the French people. He was quite incapable of gauging the force of public opinion, and was, in fact, the worst of advisers for the Queen Regent. In 1647, on the eve of the outbreak of revolt, Mme. de Motteville tells us that " the most considerable affair at Court and the things which were chiefly thought about were diversion and pleasure." The Queen's enjoyment of comedy was so great that in the early days of her mourning she sought a place at each performance where her ladies could shield her from observation, while she herself could see the stage. Being free at last of such conventional hindrance, she indulged her taste to the full, and every alternate day there was a performance either in French or Italian. The cost to her of these performances was very great, for they were held at the Palais Royal, and she entertained the Court. They were an offence also to many serious persons. A priest, whose name we do not know, remonstrated most earnestly with her on this subject, and did not desist even in the face of her displeasure. There was a difference of opinion with regard to it among the Doctors of the Sorbonne, to whom the matter was referred, and the Queen chose very wisely to place her confidence in the judgment of such Bishops and theologians as were able to sanction the indulgence of her tastes. The Court blamed Vincent de Paul, who certainly had not interfered personally, but may safely be assumed to have shared the opinion of the nameless priest, and the comedy continued.

The Saturday before Lent in that same year Cardinal Mazarin began a series of entertainments. He had brought singers from Rome and experts in machinery from all parts. His Comedy was so elaborate that the Court could talk of nothing else, and it was essentially Italian. It was in honour of the King and Queen, and designed to meet the taste of the latter; but it was of a character to outrage the section of the *dévots*, and these, even at that period, were not altogether negligible. It was well known that visits to the Carmelite Convent at Val de Grace were part of the regular routine of the Queen's life. Before the great festivals she would retire thither for a species of Retreat; at all times she was scrupulous in keeping the fasts prescribed by the Church. (although she was frankly fond of good living); and references to her prayers are frequent in the reminiscences of her intimates. Her attitude on this point was, therefore, an anomaly, but so, indeed, was her whole position towards Cardinal Mazarin, and it is possible that to his tortuous Italian mind this method of setting public opinion at defiance made special appeal. Even as early as 1647, when the full peril of his position had not yet declared itself, he had realized that there was danger for him in the Queen's pious proclivities,* and that it was well to assure himself that in a moment of crisis he could rule her conscience as well as her heart and her intellect. Therefore, he applied his test, and afterwards had no further misgivings on that score. If, however, the reception of this celebrated Comedy was intended to prove to him the unassailable nature of his supremacy over the French people, as well as over the Regent, it was less satisfactory. It was a dangerous experiment. The country was desperately impoverished, and, as he was known to have come to France as an adventurer, all the money that he spent so lavishly was drawn from a starving people, and only if they looked on without murmuring could he in future have confidence that he stood above criticism. Such confidence, if he ever cherished it, was short-lived. Serious people were moved to indignation by a display of wealth at such a moment, and even the pleasure-lovers at Court were on the verge of revolt at the self-assertion of the Queen's Councillor. All favours were at his disposal, and Mme. de Motteville

* See his entry "Carnet," No. iii.: "Tous ces prétendus serviteurs de Dieu sont en réalité des Ennemis de l'Etat."

THE FRONDE REBELLION

describes how the great nobles were forced to stand in his antechamber if they desired an audience of him, how they murmured at the arrogance that kept them waiting, and then, like grumbling servants, became mute and obsequious when he passed among them to his carriage and drove away.

Such conditions were too unnatural for long continuance, but the result was as distorted and unhealthy as its cause. In her years of light-hearted indulgence Anne of Austria prepared a time of misery not only for herself, but for her subjects, the effect of which was wholly evil for the kingdom. In the struggle which taught her son to be a despot, the opening stages were far the most dangerous to her prerogative. The *Parlement* and the Crown disagreed first on a question of taxes, then on one of privilege. The disagreement revealed behind the *Parlement* a possibility of force, behind the Crown a suggestion of weakness. The *Parlement* and the people it represented were not alone in possession of grievances; scarcely a noble about the Court but had a grudge against the Queen or the Queen's favourite. The routine of the Palais Royal had grown monotonous. The Regent grew more and more indolent, the Cardinal more and more autocratic, and imaginations that had long languished for excitement were fired with the bold idea of taking the side of the people in a struggle against the Crown.

It is unlikely that among the great crowd of noble personages who in 1649 joined forces with the *Parlement* there was one who had deliberately considered what effect their action might have upon their country's history. They saw only the glorious novelty of the immediate present, and the future did not concern them. And so, amid much patriotic sentimentalism, the Duc de Longueville confided his wife and children to the keeping of the people of Paris, and Anne Geneviève de Bourbon, sister of Condé, Princess of the blood royal, bore him a son in the Hôtel de Ville itself. By such means the real struggle, which might have served a great purpose had it been waged on its true issue, was turned into a travesty. Great lords and ladies practised knight-errantry, turning from melodrama to farce and back again until they were weary of sensation, and the people paid in blood and tears.

That establishment of an aristocratic nursery within earshot of the deliberations of the judges was a type of the fantastic nonsense that was fashionable. The excitement of a game of hazard bore no comparison with that thrill of the blood which is stirred by the acclamations of a mob. High-born women, who, until then, would hardly have admitted the bond of a common humanity betwixt themselves and the toiling multitude, ogled the astonished citizens and posed to the crowd, making their bid for a popularity which they might barter for some other privilege. This most amazing form of sport would be merely a subject of pleasant study for the historian, but for the dread facts that lay behind. If the Fronde had been a tournament of rival lords and Princes, in which the King himself was forced to imperil his dignity, and that only, it would claim no more than passing notice, and it is under this guise that it is very often represented. But it had a different aspect for those who care to look behind the tinsel of noble name, and the glitter of amorous adventure to the sombre lives of the common people. The conditions of these lives are worthy of consideration. It was recognized that the passing of an army (which always depended for its sustenance on the supplies levied from the inhabitants of the district through which it passed) impoverished the country almost to the point of famine, and in twenty years many armies, hostile and friendly, had marched through France and left their tragic traces. Nevertheless, the taxes never lessened. In 1647 (the year of the Cardinal's celebrated Comedy), when, in addition to the expenses of the war, the Queen wanted money for herself and her First Minister, she demanded that they should be increased. The previous year the prisons of France contained 23,000 inmates, whose crime was failure to pay their taxes. In the country districts the people existed as those do who have no hope, and they had almost passed beyond the capacity for dread. No threats and no persecution could wring from them money which they did not possess.

Omer Talon and Mathieu Molé, men learned in the law, the latter holding the office of *Premier President* in the *Parlement*, presented their humble remonstrance to the Queen in these terms:

" Madame, give a thought to the distress that prevails everywhere. To-night, in the solitude of your oratory, consider the misfortune that has overtaken the country districts. It will be revealed to you there that neither the glory of our victories and of our newly-conquered territory nor the hope of future peace is sufficient sustenance for those who have no bread."

" The working men will soon be obliged to give up their work, to leave their families and their homes, to beg their bread from door to door. Every sort of violence is resorted to to extort payment of the taxes. If some remedy be not found speedily, the country will soon be a desert."*

It was thus that these two—as near to the type of the City Fathers as France could produce—wrote to the Regent. But she had sunk too deep in the habit of sloth to be stirred. She left such affairs to Mazarin, and Mazarin was not likely seriously to disturb himself for the sufferings of a French peasant or the remonstrance of Parisian magistrates. The Fronde Rebellion, therefore, sprang from the indolence of the Queen and the recklessness of the Cardinal. It was, despite its name, in its true origin an expression of the despair of the

* See Omer Talon, "Mémoires," Petitot Coll., vol. lx. (January 15, 1648); and de Barante, " Le Parlement et la Fronde " ("Vie de M. Molé").

people, not of the rivalry of the nobles. In addition, it is a tragedy not only by reason of the appalling suffering of which it was the cause, but because its true import has been shrouded by the vain futilities of irresponsible persons. Because there was not a man in France who could join to the capacity for leadership the clear brain and the true heart, without which a popular hero is merely a danger to the State, a great opportunity was missed, and misery and injustice continued to hold their sway until, in 1789, the day of retribution dawned.

If the *Parlement* could have stood firm—if, following the lead of Mathieu Molé, they had as a body represented the people and striven to guide the Queen to justice and moderation—the Regency would have stood for ever as a golden epoch in the social history of France; but they had not the required strength either as individuals or as a body. Misled by traditional respect for the ruling class, they welcomed the intervention of the nobles, only to find that the cause for which they were prepared to sacrifice fortune and life was of no account in the minds of the leaders they had chosen. The people had yet to learn their need of representation; there were no labour leaders even in embryo. Théophraste Renaudot, who, of his contemporaries, had been most fitted for that position, had had so many enemies among the *bourgeoisie* that his only possibility of existence depended on the protection of the Court. De Gondi, though he had the genius of the democrat, had none of the self-devotion which would have been necessary in a real champion of the people's rights; and the others who, at differing epochs, played for and caught the fancy of the populace, desired it and used it solely to serve some evanescent, personal ambition. The strongest cause was that of the *Parlement* against the Crown—this was indeed the cause of a suffering people—but the self-interest of individuals destroyed any hope of a contest on a straight issue, and it would have been difficult for an honest man to choose a party and be loyal to it, for the objects of each of the many parties that opposed the Queen seem to have been interchangeable.

Enough has been said already to show that M. Vincent's sympathies were bound up with the interests of the people. His touch with the Court left him with the same opinions as he had always maintained—that is to say, with an abhorrence of luxury and self-indulgence, and a deep respect for rank. When the Fronde began, he was unavoidably on the side of the people; it was, indeed, impossible for a priest who lived among them as he did to hold aloof from their concerns. M. Olier, during his ministry at S. Sulpice, became a keen politician, and— until the agitation of rebellion had reached fever pitch— he had considerable influence with his aristocratic neighbours in the region of the Luxembourg. But M. Vincent was in a more difficult position. He had made it one of his rules of life that he and his company should have nothing to do with politics, and in the light of the opposing point of view of the Frondists it is well to recall his maxims, as he had written them a few years earlier to Le Breton, Superior of the Mission at Rome :

" 1. It is not fitting for poor priests like us to interfere, except in the things that concern our vocation.

" 2. The business affairs of Princes are mysteries which we should respect and not spy upon.

" 3. Most people offend God by sitting in judgment on the affairs of others.

" 4. All choice of action is questionable unless it be such as Holy Writ decides; outside that, no opinion is infallible.

" 5. The Son of God preserved silence on questions of politics."

But we must remember that he was living in Paris, and Paris was in an uproar.* In the autumn of 1648 the

* For description see Mme. de Motteville, "Mémoires pour servir a l'histoire d'Anne d'Autriche," vol. ii.

Queen had been rash enough to imprison Broussel, a magistrate who was a favourite with the people, because he opposed the royal will, and she was afterwards—by the threats of the infuriated mob—forced to release him. The Palais Royal offered no security for the Royal Family; a courtier recognized in the streets was in peril of his life, and the air rang with scurrilous ballads against the Queen and the Cardinal. For the moment authority had lost all meaning, and the right was undoubtedly on the side of disorder. So great, indeed, did the danger of a revolution appear that the *Parlement* might have extorted any terms so long as they held the person of the King in their power. They failed to maintain their advantage, however. The Queen was clever enough to escape by night to S. Germain, taking her son with her, and once they were both outside the gates of the rebellious city the aspect of affairs was completely altered.

Perhaps the news of what was happening in England was useful to the Regent. Condé hated Mazarin, and it is conceivable that he might have held aloof from a dispute that centred upon the general abhorrence of the Italian; but the people had more provocation in France than in England, and if they had found a leader they might have been equally successful. And Condé would not at that time have thought his hatred of Mazarin was sufficient justification for leaving the monarchy in jeopardy, and he had not the slightest feeling for the people. He joined forces with the Regent and the Cardinal, therefore, and on January 6, 1649, laid siege to Paris, that the audacious *Parlement* might be terrorized into complete submission.

It was at this point that the reality of M. Vincent's self-abnegation was put to the test. He had always been clear that a hidden and retired life was essential to the spirit of the Mission Priests. The Company had been tested once already. In August, 1636, when the Spaniards entered Picardy and were within ten leagues of

THE FRONDE REBELLION

the capital, M. Vincent wrote to M. Portail with undisturbed composure: "There is a rush of the countryfolk inside the walls, while the terrified citizens fly from the city. Our army is far away, and everyone is volunteering. The drums begin beating at 7 a.m. The Company has gone into Retreat, that each one may be prepared to go wherever he is sent."*

That last sentence summarizes the fitting attitude of the Company. To remain untouched by public excitement, but to be prepared to respond to any call, was the ideal held up before every Mission Priest, and it was as clear to them in 1649 as it was thirteen years earlier. But for their Superior the difficulty was to determine whether the call to action was a certain one. It seemed that the moment had come when piety was no longer separable from politics, but in the interests of S. Lazare the wisest course was to abide by those maxims of his, and to allow " the business affairs of Princes " to remain mysterious. If he maintained a neutral attitude, he could depend on the protection of the Queen, if the Court party triumphed; and his services to the people were so well known that the wildest mob would restrain itself before his gates. He was essentially a man of peace, and he had seen enough of the Court to know the complication of motive that lay behind the movements of the royal will, and the impossibility of inducing the Queen to form and follow an unbiassed judgment.

It is well to review the evident objections to the course chosen by M. Vincent at this juncture, for it is certain that he must have realized them himself. It is clear that if safety was possible to anyone in France, it was assured to him and to his companions at S. Lazare; and that he was under no obvious obligation to depart from his ordinary routine—by adhering to it he could have brought much assistance within reach of the distressed people inside the city walls, and retained the favour of

* "Lettres," vol. i., No. 27.

the Queen at the same time. But a vision of the horrors of civil warfare banished every other consideration. His knowledge of his fellow-countrymen told him that it was imminent, and he—not being touched himself by the fever of revolt—could measure the ghastly consequences once it should be declared. At that stage the struggle was not complicated by the innumerable cross-currents of ambitions and opinions that afterwards were interwoven with it; to M. Vincent it appeared that the only insuperable obstacle to peace was the presence of Cardinal Mazarin, and that no reasonable person—if the position were clearly represented to them—could fail to see the necessity of Cardinal Mazarin's withdrawal. But from the fact that the Queen was at S. Germain surrounded by courtiers and prejudiced advisers, he deduced that the position was not likely to be clearly represented, and that the supreme disaster he was dreading might come to pass merely by reason of her ignorance.

We have had opportunity of noticing his slowness of decision and habitual prudence, but here was a crisis when, if he was to act at all, he must act quickly; while the fear of implicating others in dangerous responsibility withheld him from taking counsel. On his knees in the church of S. Lazare he could seek guidance, and there he came to the decision that meant complete self-sacrifice. The bitter cold had added to the miseries of the famished people, and his love of them had suggested his great venture. In the night of January 12, 1649, he mounted his horse in the courtyard of S. Lazare and rode forth to seek the Queen at S. Germain, and lay before her the true dangers of the situation and the extent of her responsibility towards her people. There is a child-like simplicity in his conception of this enterprise. It was a marvel that he ever reached his destination. His only companion was his secretary, and the prevalent disorder was so great that travellers by night were regarded as suspicious persons, and were liable to arrest by any of the self-constituted guardians of the peace who might be about. As he rode into Clichy before dawn he was waylaid by some of the townspeople, and only their discovery of his identity saved him from rough usage. At Neuilly the Seine had risen so that it covered the bridge, and it was necessary to ride through the water (a feat which caused Ducourneau, the secretary, by his own confession, " to shake with terror "), and they were soaked to the skin when they gained the farther bank. S. Germain was reached without further mishap, and we are told that the Queen, imagining that M. Vincent had come as an emissary from the rebels to make terms with her, gave him an immediate audience.

That dangerous night ride does not appear the best preparation for an interview which was intended to have infinite importance, but one may be sure that Vincent de Paul was praying for guidance throughout the weary journey, and came into the Queen's presence as composedly as if he had had many quiet hours for reflection. In fact, he regarded his case as a very clear one. To him the claim of the people was immeasurably stronger than that of any individual, and the indignation of the Queen towards her subjects seemed a small thing compared to their calamities. He explained himself with that simplicity of speech which he could always command, and—as it appears—without full understanding of the odds against him. He had ridden from Paris to S. Germain to ask Anne of Austria to deprive herself of the company of Cardinal Mazarin for the sake of the people who had defied and insulted her, and he cherished high hopes of success. Probably the result of his mission modified his regard for his royal mistress, and gave him knowledge of a type of human nature—that of the spurious *dévote*—with which he had had no previous dealing.

The Queen listened while he made his plea, and she did not then—or at any other time—show the least resentment at his plain expression of opinion; but though her manner was gracious, the point of view which he strove to represent to her did not move her in the slightest. She heard him to the end, and then referred him to the Cardinal, and at that even the sanguine spirit of M. Vincent must have acknowledged defeat. The Cardinal was suave and smiling, and, though it is said that he never forgave M. Vincent, he was in no real danger from so honest a foe, and could well afford to be generous. The real demand of the Mission Priest was that the Regent and her First Minister should, at a moment of crisis in political affairs, set an example of self-sacrifice and humility; that, in plain words, the maxims of Christ should be applied to their methods of government. Such an idea cannot have failed to move the Cardinal to covert mirth, however great his indignation at the outspoken suggestion that he should withdraw from France; but in fact, in propounding it, M. Vincent was only following that principle of faith in the character of his fellow-men which guided him to success in so many difficult enterprises. In this instance, however, the sole result was damage to himself; and of this the first token came from those on whose account he had risked his personal peace and well-being.

When he left Paris he despatched a letter to Mathieu Molé, explaining his design and his reasons for keeping it a secret, and the news soon leaked out that M. Vincent had joined the Queen at S. Germain. At that crisis of tense excitement the bare fact was enough. The record of all his years of service to them was insufficient to hold for him the confidence of the people with whose true interests he was identified more closely then than at any other moment. Because he had gone to S. Germain they believed that he had betrayed them, and S. Lazare —hitherto exempt from all depredations—was pillaged by the mob. Twenty-four hours seemed to have destroyed the fabric of reputation which it had taken thirty years to build, and to have altered the position held by M. Vincent entirely. He had brought his misfortunes upon himself; by his own deliberate act he had forfeited his favour at Court and flung away his popularity in the city, and he gained nothing either for himself or for anybody else. Nevertheless, as he left S. Germain he told Ducourneau that he had said to the Queen and her Minister " that which, if I was at my hour of death, I should have wished to have said to them."

It is impossible to doubt that he felt himself impelled to his hopeless venture by a force stronger than human judgment, and that he would have known no peace if he had preserved his security and left the Queen to pursue her way without remonstrance. Long afterwards, when he looked back, he wrote: " I meant to serve God in going to S. Germain, but I was not worthy "; and if that was a reminiscence of his mood at the moment, he must have added personal discouragement to the sense of outward failure. It is, indeed, the temptation of the devout man to believe that if his cause is good, the fervour of his prayer must bring its accomplishment. And therefore failure means more than the disappointment of a hope; it may involve the pressure of self-questioning and the despairing avowal of unworthiness, or it may mean the far more intimate and poignant misery of doubt as to the foundation of his faith. It is hardly possible that M. Vincent's courage could have borne him through his tasks if any cloud of uncertainty had ever descended on him; their difficulty and multiplicity needed the support of an absolutely simple faith; but when he was pressed by failure, he attributed it to the corrupt condition of his own mind, and strove to maintain a closer watch upon himself than hitherto.

No episode in his life gives us a more impressive instance of his command over himself than this. He had reached his seventy-third year, and his only personal desire was for seclusion and repose. He had made a great and valiant attempt to further the welfare of others, and in return had been met with contumely on all sides. Almost inevitably he must have felt the temptation to lay down his arms and cease to serve, because his service had been flouted and he himself was infinitely weary. Instead, he made the moment an opportunity. Throughout every enterprise he had imputed all success to God Himself; now, under this semblance of disgrace, he showed, as he had never shown before, the degree to which he was the servant of God, and not of man, and that human disapproval had no power to daunt him. Ousted from Paris, he turned unhesitatingly to labour in the provinces.

It was no light matter in those days for a young and active man to ride from end to end of France with one attendant; in one who had fulfilled his threescore years and ten it meant fortitude and determination of the highest order. Vincent de Paul was provided with a passport which the young King himself had signed, but even such authentic royal sanction was not security, and his real protection came from his courage and his poverty. It was his object to utilize his hour of misfortune by visiting some of the many branches of the two Companies, and seeing for himself what a Mission Priest or a Sister of Charity could accomplish when in exile from the mother-house.

From S. Germain he went to Villepreux; from thence to Valpuiseaux, in the neighbourhood of Etampes. Here, early in his pilgrimage, came great encouragement. The country was already feeling the grip of famine, and the Sisters had responded to the call to suffering, and were denying themselves to the point which nears starvation that they might have the more to give away. "They are more and more united," wrote M. Vincent, "loving their vocation and fulfilling it."

He had time to judge. It was early in February and bitterly cold, and his journey was delayed. He utilized the time to preach a Mission in the village—" by way of preparation," as he explained, "to help these good people to give themselves to God during the miseries that lie before them."

This, being written to Mlle. Le Gras, was certainly an expression of his real feeling, and it is significant. We may have reason to wonder how a man of his vivid capacity for sympathy could survive the horrors which he was obliged to witness in the years that followed, but his idea of a preparation for that which he foresaw furnishes us with a clue. They "must be helped to give themselves to God." If he could accomplish this for them—if he could make them see, as he himself saw, beyond the terror and the ghastliness of life, the Will of God as an absolutely perfect explanation—then he could leave them to their earthly fate without misgiving.

For the consistent believer in Divine guidance this is, of course, the only logical position; but absolutely consistent belief is probably a rarity, and in face of the worst forms of suffering faith in the perfection of a Divine ordinance is difficult to maintain. In fact, the experience through which the French people were passing made brutes rather than saints. Here was no simple issue—no obvious motive of attack and defence by which the spirit of patriotism and of endurance might be aroused; probably those who suffered most had least opportunity of understanding the burning questions that brought their suffering upon them, and were given no chance to choose a side or to remain neutral. The poor were merely the prey of both opposing forces. At the approach of the soldiery every farm and cottage was deserted. The people took refuge in the woods, and were fortunate if they were able to remain hidden, and to escape death or mutilation. All that they possessed was stolen or destroyed, and when the storm had swept by and they crept back to the ruins of their home, it was to face the terrors of famine. Accounts of this sort are common to every history of civil war or of invasion—so common that they convey little to the imagination. Present-day problems of overcrowding and of unemployment are apt to present themselves to the philanthropist as of greater difficulty than any question that disturbed former generations. But in the middle of the seventeenth century, when there was not in France anything representing a Poor Law, when the financial resources of the country depended chiefly on the contributions of the working class, and when for immense districts there was no possibility of deriving benefit from the farms because of the completeness of the devastation, it must be allowed that a position of difficulty was reached to which the twentieth century affords no parallel.

M. Vincent was the better able to meet it when the time came because he could speak with the authority of his experience of these country places. We find him at Marseilles, at Nantes, at Angers, at S. Méens, at Richelieu. Never was travelling more difficult. He was old and broken in health, and it is not surprising that at S. Méens and at Richelieu he was delayed by definite illness. In the autumn he returned to Paris, because the Queen desired his presence there. Mme. d'Aiguillon sent a carriage and pair to fetch him from Richelieu, and so feeble was he that his usual resistance to such luxuries was overcome.

During his exile the people had had time to discover what he meant to them. The siege of Paris had lasted till March, and then the starving citizens made terms. In the August following the young King, with Mazarin on one hand and Condé on the other, rode into his capital as a conqueror. The whole sequence of events had been a contradiction of M. Vincent's ideal of the relations of governors and governed, and even from a distance he had been an agonized spectator of the ruthless cruelties of Condé and the indifference of the Regent. While the siege lasted he had written to implore the Queen to send supplies of grain to the starving poor within the walls; but though in good-humoured compliance she gave an order, her energy was not sufficient to see that it was carried out, and M. Vincent was too far off for effective insistence.

Doubtless he returned to S. Lazare with relief. When the people were suffering they needed him, and he was not deceived by the nominal peace. It was not difficult to read the signs of the times, or to foresee that the future held promise of disasters as great as any that had yet been experienced. The fitting place for Vincent de Paul at such a moment was Paris.

CHAPTER IX

M. VINCENT AND THE PEOPLE

THE subjugation of the rebellious citizens of Paris in 1649 was due to Condé, and the Queen soon awoke to the fact that her state and dignity was likely to suffer more from the arrogance of her kinsman than from the insolence of the magistrates. The prestige of his military genius was dangerous in a prince of the blood-royal; by a reminder of it Condé always had the power to stir the common people to enthusiasm, and they realized that the protection given to Mazarin was only temporary, and that their conqueror shared their detestation of the Italian Cardinal. Possibly the fact that he had been too strong for them and had had power to bring the King back to Paris in triumph, added to his impressiveness, and for a year the outward manifestations of his power increased steadily. During that year Anne of Austria was forced to look on while he and his family indulged in pomp and circumstance that dimmed her own, and the Palais Royal was deserted that the courtiers might throng the galleries of the Hôtel de Condé. But at length the moment came when her own pride and the Cardinal's forebodings prompted decisive action. An order was given for the arrest of Condé, and with his brother de Conti and the Duc de Longueville he was imprisoned at Vincennes.

The tradition of imprisonment as a remedy for those who were offensive to the Crown had been well sustained in France since medieval times, yet no force of tradition could make it anything but a dangerous remedy. The patients were apt to develop an after-disease of a more serious nature. " I went into my prison innocent, I came out of it guilty," is the traditional saying of Condé himself. For all his arrogance he had been a patriot, and he was the most skilled commander of his time. His country owed him a debt of gratitude, and with the recollection of that debt vivid in his mind, the humiliation of imprisonment made a traitor of him.

After his arrest there was no escape from civil war. Turenne led the Spaniards into France, and the friends of the imprisoned Princes joined forces with them. Mazarin and the Queen were dexterous in choosing those who had power with the people as their supporters, but they broke faith repeatedly, and so alienated the allies who had been admitted to their councils. The thirteen months of Condé's imprisonment were full of danger for all parties and all interests; the scale wavered perpetually. When his release was determined, Mazarin himself fled.

It made but little real difference to the people which party was in the ascendant; there was, it is true, a deep-seated and general desire to expel Mazarin from France, and between January, 1651, and the following December, this purpose was achieved; but Condé proved himself as inhuman as a leader as he had been as a foe, and they never suffered more than when he held Paris against the King. The horrors of anarchy turned the city into a hell, and a longing for peace became universal. The citizens at length, in the autumn of 1652, invited their King to come back to them, and though they would give no invitation to the Cardinal, the cry of "*point de Mazarin*" grew fainter. Nothing that could be inflicted on them by an Italian favourite could be worse than the treatment they received from their own Princes. So they decided, and in February, 1653, Mazarin was triumphantly reinstated in the capital, and a great banquet at the Hôtel de Ville itself celebrated the victory of autocracy and the final humiliation of the people.

From beginning to end of the five years of misery Vincent de Paul had desired peace; probably it would be true to say that he desired it at any price. No man in France understood the people as he did, no one had so true an estimate of their grievances; but without an honest leader they had no hope of winning fair terms by honourable means, and he foresaw their ultimate discomfiture if the Queen was bent on enforcing her will and keeping Mazarin with her in face of all opposition. It is said that he tried to exert personal influence with the young King and to intervene among the aristocratic leaders of the mob; but his message was always, in one form or another, a call to sacrifice, and the ears of the Frondists were not open to it. When in August, 1652, the misery of the people, both in Paris and in the country, had reached its climax, he turned—like the good and simple-minded churchman that he was—to the Holy Father for assistance, and the following letter was despatched to Rome.*

"Most Holy Father,†—

"Kneeling humbly at the feet of Your Holiness, I—the most wretched of all men—once more offer, devote, and consecrate to your service, myself and the little Congregation of Priests of the Mission, of which I have been made the Superior-General by the Holy See, although I am most unworthy. Further, I am venturing—confiding in the fatherly goodness with which you receive and listen to even the least of your sons—to lay before you the miserable and pitiful state of France.

"The Royal Family is torn by dissension, the people are divided in rival factions, the towns and the provinces alike are made miserable by civil war; villages and cities are devastated, ruined, burnt; the labourers do not reap what they have sown, and no longer sow for future years; everything is at the mercy of the soldiers; from them the people have to fear not robbery only, but actual murder and every sort of torture; most of those who

* "Lettres," vol. i., No. 235. † Innocent X.

dwell in the country perish of hunger if they escape the sword. Even the priests are not spared, but are cruelly treated, tortured, and put to death. Every maiden is dishonoured, and the nuns themselves are exposed to the wild excesses of the soldiers; churches are profaned and robbed and ruined, and almost all those which are still standing are deserted by their pastors, so that the people are left destitute either of Masses, or of the Sacraments, or of any spiritual consolation. Also that happens of which it is horrible to think and even more to speak, the most Blessed Sacrament of the Body of Our Lord is treated with utter contempt even by Catholics, for they throw the Holy Eucharist to the ground and trample It underfoot that they may steal the sacred vessels that contain It. And how far do the heretics go who have no sense of this Mystery? I dare not and will not enter on description. Yet it is not much to hear of these things or to read of them, it is necessary to be an eye-witness. I know that Your Holiness has good reason to charge me with audacity. I am a mere nameless individual, and I am daring to set forth these things to the Father and Chief of all Christians, with all his wide knowledge of the doings of every nation—especially the Christian nations. In fact, most Holy Father, there is no remedy for our misfortunes unless it may come from the affection, the fatherly kindness, and the authority which Your Holiness possesses. I am aware that you have been greatly troubled by our sufferings, and that very often you have endeavoured to check civil wars at their very birth, that Pontifical Letters have been issued for this purpose, that the most reverend Nuncio has been bidden to interfere in your name, and that he has laboured abundantly so far as lay in his power for the service of God and of Your Holiness, although hitherto without result. But, Most Holy Father, there are twelve hours in a day, and that which has failed once may succeed on a second effort. Moreover, the arm of the Lord is not shortened, and I have a firm belief that God may have reserved to crown the labour of the Pastor of His Church the glory of winning rest for us after all our toil, blessing after so many miseries, and peace after strife; of reuniting the Royal Family, of comforting the people who are crushed by the long war, of giving subsistence to the poor who are nearly dead of hunger, of coming to the help of the devastated country, of rebuilding the ruined churches, and of bringing back to them the priests and the shepherds of souls; finally, of giving life once more to us all. Will Your Holiness condescend to do this?"

The mixture of courage and simplicity is characteristic of Vincent de Paul. He is ready to incur blame for audacity towards the Pope for the sake of the suffering people, and his faith that the Holy Father had power to still the strife and to save France is perfectly sincere. But if Rome had any power either with Queen or Cardinal, it was not exercised, the slow course of affairs dragged on, security and peace depended on the return of the young King to his capital, but the presence of Mazarin continued—as has been said already—to be the obstacle.

During his years of danger the Cardinal (freed by circumstances from the drag that had been imposed upon him by the assemblies of the Council of Conscience) distributed ecclesiastical preferment freely, paying for the support of powerful families by bestowing an abbey or a bishopric where it was asked. M. Vincent's hopes for the future of the Church in France were thereby ruined, and it was for him the bitterest form of failure. The fact that Mazarin had been completely triumphant in this matter proved how complete his ascendancy over the Queen had become, and the consequent peril of incurring his dislike. But Vincent de Paul—having written to the Pope in vain—refused in this matter to accept failure; he mustered his courage, and wrote the following letter to the Cardinal:

*September 11, 1652.

"Monseigneur,—

"I take the liberty of writing to Your Eminence. I beseech you to permit the liberty, and to allow me to inform you that the city of Paris is returning to its natural state, and is crying out for the King and Queen. Wherever I go I find no one who is not of this mind. The Ladies of Charity, who are of the highest in the kingdom, tell me that a veritable regiment of ladies would go out to receive their Majesties in triumph.

"This being so, Monseigneur, I suggest that it would be worthy of Your Eminence to advise the King and Queen to return and take possession of their city of Paris and of all the hearts awaiting them within it. But because there are many drawbacks to this course, I set down those that appear to me the chief and the arguments that balance them, for which I humbly ask the consideration of Your Eminence.

The first is that, though there are many good folk in Paris whose inclinations are such as I have described, it is said that there are also many of the opposite opinion and some who are undecided. To which, Monseigneur, I answer that I think there are only a very few that are ill-disposed, for within my knowledge there is not even one, and the indifferent—if such there be—would be infected by the enthusiasm of a crowd representing the greater part of Paris.

"Then there are some who will possibly assure Your Eminence that Paris needs punishment, to the end she may learn wisdom; but to my thinking it were well for Your Eminence to look back on the methods of those Kings against whom Paris has revolted in former times. You will find they have been gentle and tolerant. Only Charles VI., by the punishment of many rebels and the confiscation of the chains that can be stretched across the streets, poured oil on the flames, and so increased

* "Lettres," vol. i., No. 239.

them that they continued for sixteen years, and the enemies of the State won many allies.

"And there are some who will urge upon Your Eminence that for the sake of your individual interest the King should not enter Paris, or allow his people to have access to his presence, unless Your Eminence can be beside him. They will say this to prove that it is not the intervention of Your Eminence that is the cause of strife, but the malignity of rebellious persons, and that, in fact, it is worth while for you to entangle affairs yet further and to encourage warfare. To which I answer that once the King is himself established in Paris, he will be able to recall Your Eminence whenever it pleases him, and of this I am absolutely convinced. Moreover, if it should be known that Your Eminence—whose chief concern is the good of the King and Queen, and of the State—helped to reunite the Royal Family and to bring Paris back to its allegiance to the King, you, Monseigneur, will win all hearts and will speedily be recalled.

"It is this, Monseigneur, that I am bold enough to lay before you in the assurance that you will take it in good part. I have told no one what I am writing to you, but I live and die in the obedience I owe Your Eminence, and I remain always, Monseigneur,

"Your very humble, very faithful, and very obedient servant,

"VINCENT DE PAUL."

It was an injudicious letter. Vincent de Paul would not have been true to himself if he had not made these desperate ventures, but their sole effect was to prove the incapacity of an honest man to influence affairs. When he went to S. Germain he weakened his hold on the Queen, when he wrote to the Pope he must have disheartened himself, and when he wrote to Mazarin his unvarnished statement of unpalatable truth was calculated to weight the balance against his wishes. The

King did enter Paris without the Cardinal, it is true, but it was nearly six weeks after M. Vincent's petition had been delivered at Compiègne, and during those weeks the suffering of the poor—who were the prey of the lawless ruffians that Condé had brought into the city—increased in horror daily. The rashness of M. Vincent is not a matter of regret. It is in such crises of baffling contradiction and bewilderment that the real mettle of a man is proved, and there was then so much opportunity for time-serving and shuffling that it was very easy for a priest to adduce sufficient laudable motives for moving with the times. But, as we know, it was not only the Congregation of the Mission that showed itself to be intrepid in the face of danger; across the river in his Clergy-house of S. Sulpice, M. Olier suffered with his suffering people, and lived in hourly peril in this the worst quarter of the city. And he also, moved to extreme measures by the agonies he was witnessing, despatched a letter to Compiègne. He showed even greater boldness than M. Vincent, and wrote in plain terms to the Queen herself. The conclusion of the letter indicates the purport of the whole:

" Madame, you could settle every difficulty and turn this far-reaching insurrection into peace by dismissing the object of your people's resentment. By sacrificing to God the service you accept from this person you would pay Him the homage that He prizes, and would win for yourself the love and respect of your subjects, which you ought to desire more than anything else."*

It was no wonder that M. Olier was ejected from S. Sulpice at the first opportunity, and that M. Vincent was no more consulted in the distribution of ecclesiastical appointments; the frankness of these comments and suggestions of theirs were not likely to find favour. Anne of Austria had lost her desire for the love and respect of her subjects, and M. Olier's idea of her obligation in that

* l'Abbé Faillon, "Vie de M. Olier," part ii., liv. 8.

direction did not restore it to her; her feeling towards them was one of animosity. She feared the mob, and was ready to show clemency towards all past offences because she feared it; but she judged truly enough that at the extremity to which she had arrived, the only person deserving of confidence was he whose fortune depended entirely upon herself.

And finally, as we already know, events unfolded themselves much as M. Vincent had foretold. The King and Queen were welcomed by their people, and within a few weeks the Cardinal himself returned amid the plaudits of the populace. Of all the great personages concerned in those five years of uproar, Mazarin, and Mazarin only, emerged at the end in a somewhat stronger position than he had held at the beginning. When we remember that among many grievances, the grievance against him was admittedly the chief, that the sole point of unity amid contesting factions was hatred and distrust of him, that for this reason fertile provinces had been laid waste and thousands of lives sacrificed, the record of his return and of the subsequent Feast of Welcome in the Hôtel de Ville takes rank among those flashes of irony with which history sometimes provides us.

Vincent de Paul has left no statement of his own opinion either of the political or moral aspect of the Fronde in its progress or in its conclusion; he has only set down the horror of its effects as he witnessed them, and even out of those effects he made an opportunity. In his instituting of his Confraternities we see the intention of bringing the true condition of the poor to the notice of the rich; the sensational sufferings of vast numbers of the French people in the years between 1647 and 1653 brought the attainment of his object nearer, for it served to level differences of rank and to convince the aristocrat that the peasant was of the same human nature as himself. Although this new impression was not received universally, there is evidence that it was widespread, and after the Fronde M. Vincent was able to reckon on the capacity for generosity in the rich with greater certainty than before it. The amount of relief given in the years of the nation's most poignant distress was stupendous, but no claim can be made that it was all collected and administered from S. Lazare. The Company of the Blessed Sacrament laboured diligently and gave freely, the nuns and hermits of Port Royal sheltered refugees and distributed food and clothing, there was also in all probability a great deal of private benevolence in the provincial towns; but the onus of organization on a large scale fell on M. Vincent, for it was he who had applied his mind to problems of poverty long before the nation was overwhelmed by the special disasters of the civil war. It seems, indeed, that he became imbued—after years of association with the poor of Paris and study of their conditions—with social theories that were far in advance of the opinion of his times. He applied them unobtrusively but very vigorously, and to this day the traces of his industry and of his discoveries remain. But while he dealt to good purpose with the city, the condition of the country-people was not greatly altered. It had become the custom to regard the succour of the peasant as the monopoly of pious persons. The pious gave relief, and added an exhortation to accept distress as a visitation from the Almighty—the fitting chastisement for sin—but there were probably many occasions when neither relief nor exhortation supplied the real needs of the recipient—bodily or spiritual—there were probably many needs also which were never supplied at all. Almsgiving generally took place at convent doors, and those who desired it learnt to loiter through hours of waiting in the certainty of eventual reward. No more fatal lesson can be taught, and it is one which pious persons after the lapse of centuries are still teaching. Thus, on the one hand, the race of beggars was nurtured and encouraged, while, on the other, the system of taxation destroyed the spirit of enterprise. When the civil war came upon them, the people were unfit both morally and physically to act for themselves. There may have been moments when it was possible to combine for their own protection, or at least to find some hopeful method of escape; but in every account they appear to have shown no more initiative than would be expected from flocks of sheep.

Circumstances rather than natural incapacity were responsible for their degradation. They had never been trained to think for themselves. It is significant that agricultural interests were not represented either in Paris or in the provincial *parlements*. The lawmaker was invariably a citizen, and all his energies were concentrated on the protection of commerce from the aggression of the aristocracy. The noble lords of those days were landowners on the most enormous scale, but very rarely did one of them find time to give a moment's consideration to the conditions of life on his estates. The wars were constant, and it was the duty of a gentleman to fight. Year after year, with the coming of summer, all those whose time was at their own disposal turned their backs on the frivolities of ladies' society and rode off to the frontier. They were thus preserved from effeminacy and from interfering unduly in home politics. But warfare as it was then practised did not nurture the milk of human kindness; they might acquire endurance and resourcefulness, but they became so inured to the spectacle of suffering that it ceased entirely to move them. And in those days there were no connecting links between the differing classes. There were the aristocracy, the *bourgeois*, and the poor. There was also—and in the seventeenth century this was becoming a very important development—the *noblesse de la robe*, the product of many generations of cultivated intellects and of moderate wealth. Life demanded of them that they should strive to retain and augment inherited benefits, and this tradition of striving resulted in a keenness of wit and vigour of character not to be acquired by a race whose part was merely graceful acceptance. Of the *noblesse de la robe* came the Arnaulds, the Pascals, Descartes, Corneille, Racine, Boileau, and Colbert himself—to name only a few of the many who were the true strength of the nation in that period. Superficially, we find a correspondence to the English upper middle class of the twentieth century; but in fact there is an essential divergence, and in that divergence is the spirit that made for so much misery in the France of long ago. For this class, which possessed the largest share of wisdom and wit and intuition, was a citizen class; the movements to which it led were in the interests of the cities. The home-keeping country squire and his family, whose interference in the affairs of their neighbours and enthusiasm for county business may be so unfailing a source whether of irritation or improvement, had no existence. In his place there was the great *seigneur*, spending his time between Court and camp; and in a specially favoured district might be found his pious lady, who would stay some months at the ancestral château and dole out charity, sometimes with a generous hand, but who would never dream of helping those toiling, hopeless wretches to rise above the squalor and the drudgery to which they had been born. The idea of encouraging self-respect was against the spirit of the times, it held a suggestion of heresy. The divine right which gave a noble his possessions fixed the dimensions of the gulf between him and the *canaille*, and any attempt to lessen it was tampering with the decree of Providence. That was the sort of doctrine with which far-seeing ecclesiastics checked any tendency to dangerous innovation, and so it came to pass that the peasant, half-starved in body and wholly starved in mind, continued for many generations to accept in silence the fate allotted to him.

But to M. Vincent, though he was obedient to the Church and loyal to the Throne, and paid all the respect that was due to rank, every man, whether serf or *seigneur*, was equally an individual, equally the possessor of a soul. And therefore the conditions that he found in the country even before the days of the Company and his own experience as a wandering preacher, were very disquieting. The miseries of the people in Lorraine in the earlier years of the Regency stirred his compassion, and taught him to rouse the sympathies of others, and when similar or even worse horrors were inflicted on French subjects in all parts of the kingdom by foreign mercenaries, he lost no time in applying the same organization by which Lorraine had long been benefited.

There are detailed records of the tortures in which the Fronde involved the poor, but they are so ghastly as to be unfit for reading. Yet the facts must have been widely known at the time, and neither the Queen on the one hand, nor the rebellious *noblesse* on the other, were moved thereby to relent and modify the course of action they intended, to check the sufferings for which they were responsible. It was well for M. Vincent in those days that he had acquired a philosophy of life that enabled him to act, to love, and to pity with all his generous heart, to maintain the attitude of the Christian towards his fellows, and not to criticize the attitude of others. Had he allowed himself to reflect upon the cruelty and indifference of those who dwelt in high places at the time when he was most closely in contact with human agony, his courage must surely have failed him; but, instead, he set himself to discover his own office in the general confusion, and to concentrate every power he possessed upon it. His months of enforced exile from Paris at the very beginning of the Fronde established his position as the friend and helper of the poor. Wherever he went in his travels he left the kind of memory which starts into vividness in the moment of distress. When every hope was failing, when the population of each little country town and its surrounding district were perishing

M. VINCENT AND THE PEOPLE 173

of want, the wise heads of the community came to the one conclusion that was fruitful, and sent tidings of their plight to M. Vincent.* The Priests of the Mission and the Sisters of Charity became the heralds of returning life. It is literally true that thousands of lives were saved by their ministrations, and although the general misery baffles the imagination, that which was accomplished was miraculous. From S. Quentin in Picardy—to take one instance only—there came a letter describing how the food distributed by the Mission kept more than 1,000 persons from starvation. "The want is so great that in the villages no one has even any straw left to lie on. There are some who used to be possessed of 200,000 crowns who are now without bread, and have starved for the last two days."†

Ruin so complete only overtook the wealthy in the districts devastated by the soldiery, but every class suffered in those dark years, and if the Ladies of Charity had elected to tighten their purse-strings, the plea of "bad times" would have had obvious justification. It was very difficult to fulfil their obligations in Paris; the support of the foundlings and the many claims of their immediate neighbours in that period of famine imposed a very severe strain on their resources. But Vincent was ruthless in his demands—his was the spirit of the early Christian who must perforce share all that he has if his neighbour be in need. It is a spirit difficult to impart, especially to those who have family claims continually present, and M. Vincent failed to impart it in its entirety, but he was able to achieve what to others seemed impossible. He summoned his Ladies of Charity together and read to them the appeals he had received, and in making record of their response he acknowledges all that it meant. "The difficulty these ladies have in sustain-

---

* For official recognition of his position, see Appendix, Note III.
† From M. de La Fons. See Feillet, "La Misere au Temps de la Fronde," chap. x.

ing the weight of their immense expenditure is hardly to be believed."

We hear of jewels and precious personal possessions sacrificed. It is easy, when much already has been given, to resent a further claim, and to find a conscientious scruple to support refusal. It is hard, too, for a woman, even though she be devout and ready to renounce all vanities, to part with her diamonds, and it is in contemplating such results that the effect of M. Vincent's personality becomes apparent. The small establishment of Mission Priests and Sisters of Charity planted here and there about the kingdom stood forth as the most important of philanthropic agencies, and the influence over a certain section of the wealthy class which M. Vincent had gradually acquired became suddenly the chief hope of vast multitudes of starving refugees.

And to these great ladies the invitation to charity was (we must reiterate) given without any of the inducements that are generally appended. The rivalry, the self-aggrandizement, the innumerable cross-issues that confuse every philanthropic effort of modern times, were swept away, but with them went every misgiving lest the gift might be misdirected and do harm to its recipient. Once again came the question of the beloved disciple, " Whoso hath this world's goods, and seeth his brother have need, and shutteth up his bowels of compassion from him, how dwelleth the love of God in him ?" It came with absolute and direct simplicity; there was no evading it, and the sincerity of the *dévote* was never put to sharper test. But M. Vincent was in personal touch with those in whose hearts he had stirred the embers of charity years before—his demand on them had been continuous—and any who were not able to bear it had long since drifted away. In this supreme moment his confidence in his followers was that of the General who can lead to victory against overwhelming odds.

The hard fact of actual statistics is necessary to understand the full effectiveness of these efforts.

From 1635 onwards depopulation had been going on steadily in the country districts. Those who held real authority acted for the moment only, and the ultimate effect of a system of government which ignored industrial questions and concerned itself only with the bribing or the bridling of the nobles was never made a topic for serious consideration. The cloth manufactories at Lille and Elbeuf were the first to close; the glass-makers in Burgundy and in Lorraine, and the woollen industry in Picardy followed. In Champagne and Burgundy the wine trade was at a standstill. The taxes were so enormous that it was hard to pay wages, and the wage-earners could only continue to keep the barest subsistence for themselves by concealing the amount they were receiving. If common sense was the property of any French subject, it was not utilized in the processes of government. The elementary wisdom which teaches us not to slay the goose who lays the golden eggs was completely ignored. An immediate desire for goose outweighed the future need for her product. Political exigencies required the continuance of warfare and the maintenance of an army, and the troops were quartered on the people. The indulgence of expensive tastes had emptied the royal coffers, and the people were required to replenish them. In those days the rich had no financial resources outside the kingdom, except as the result of military exploits, and therefore depopulation and ruin of trade must eventually be felt by the great landowner, however persistent he might be in his indifference to responsibility. In some quarters a tenth of the small towns and villages that had been centres of industry disappeared entirely. This was the case in Burgundy and in Lorraine, ordinarily prosperous and populous districts, and often one farm, or a mill where two or three miserable refugees had found shelter, was all that remained of the homes of a hundred households.

The description of these deserted places is less poignant in horror than the facts concerning those where the people congregated. The pressure of actual hunger was of long standing. In 1633 the Ladies of Charity had begun to send relief from Paris to distant places. In nine years Frère Matthieu Renard, of the Congregation of S. Lazare, journeyed fifty times from Paris to Lorraine, driving his donkey before him, and passing on many occasions through the ranks of the soldiery. There was careful organization of the relief, and the emissaries of M. Vincent were spared pillage, even in those lawless times. In 1639 the general need became greater, and some difficulty was experienced in meeting it. This, it should be remembered, was eight years before the Fronde. To such places as Nancy, Verdun, Metz, Toul, Bar-le-Duc, an allowance of 500 livres a month for food was made; at S. Miluel, at one period, 1,100 hungry persons were fed daily; at S. Quentin there were 1,500 sick requiring support. With the civil wars of the Frónde complete destitution took possession of these country districts, but the Ladies of Charity had for years been supporting many thousand souls whom they never saw, and who had no nearer claim than that of a common nationality. To increase a demand that was already so exorbitant might have abashed a less humble man than M. Vincent, and he had to go beyond the circle of his Ladies of Charity in his exploitation.

It was computed at the end of the war that he had distributed 12,000,000 livres. He made application to the Queen herself, although her sympathies at that period were not at the disposal of her people, and obtained from her on two several occasions jewels amounting in value to 25,000 livres (these gifts, if we regard them as a salve to qualms of conscience, are characteristic of her). So miraculous was the response that even this most notable of beggars was astounded. In Paris the shopmen brought goods to the door of S. Lazare. Not only did the great ladies, who were themselves feeling the pinch of poverty, bring jewels and plate, but their humbler neighbours offered clothing they could ill afford to spare. The infection of generosity spread from one to another, destroying the acquisitiveness natural to human nature—an infection hardly less irresistible than that which had destroyed all scruple and all self-control among the women of the Fronde, and, if the truth be told, hardly less sensational in its effects. Even at the Court the Maids of Honour had a confraternity for the assistance of the people who rebelled against their mistress. Wisdom and folly were intermingled, but the chaos of the times prevented orderly procedure. At the quay by the Hôtel-Dieu, barges arrived continually laden with the sick and wounded from provincial districts where the soldiery had worked havoc. The Hôtel-Dieu was so overcrowded that the lives of its inmates were endangered, and the homeless sufferers were landed, only to be left on straw by the river's brink. To them came the Ladies of Charity, causing them to be carried to their own homes, and there tending them as best they could, in literal obedience to Gospel maxims—a proceeding attended by many risks, social and sanitary—and Mme. de Bretonvilliers gave up her house on the Ile Notre Dame for the storage and distribution of the goods intended for the refugees. It is not difficult to picture the glow of enthusiasm with which these devout ladies (who were so near akin to the women of the Fronde) threw aside established custom and all the tradition and etiquette of well-appointed lives, and sacrificed rest and food, as well as luxury, that they might succour the brother who had need. The divine spark of charity animated them, and there was also in them, as in their lawless sisters, that tendency to weariness, to the condition which later generations have termed " boredom," which was their inheritance from a generation nourished on excitement. The quiet progress of the pious from the cradle to the grave could not satisfy the great lady whose grandmother had been of the Flying Squadron, whose father had fought and feasted with Henri IV. Latent in them all was the thirst for excitement, but in the colleagues of Mme. de Chevreuse it was slaked by excess of self-gratification, in the adherents of M. Vincent by an exaggeration of self-suppression. In both camps reigned the imperative need of the abnormal, no less in the assumption of responsibilities than in the frenzied negation of them.

Therefore, while we pay full tribute to the magnificent generosities and the real self-devotion of the Ladies of Charity, we must accept that it was not permitted to them to touch the highest level. They gave personal service as well as largesse, but it was reserved for the more immediate companions of M. Vincent to show what glory of self-devotion can be inspired by extremity of suffering. It was not enough that food and funds should be provided; in those troublous times there was great difficulty in their distribution. The little settlements of Sisters of Charity were utilized in this arduous task. They prepared the soup that kept so many thousand starving folk alive (one of M. Vincent's letters gives the receipt, with bread, dried peas, lentils, herbs, salt, and butter for ingredients); but, in addition to this new duty, the demand on them in their ordinary vocation as parish nurses became overwhelming. Wherever there was a town the survivors of rapine sought refuge there, and, as violence and hunger had done deadly work upon them, they all needed tending. The Sisters were unremitting in their toil, and some died at their posts. In its detail the toil itself was probably abhorrent, for all that was most loathsome in disease was bred by the prevailing wretchedness of the people, and the impossibility of fulfilling everything that was needed of them added the element of despair to the weight of labour. Great as was their heroism, however, it is the Mission Priests

M. VINCENT AND THE PEOPLE

who bear off the palm of victory in that amazing competition of self-sacrifice.

They were the envoys of the Good Samaritans of Paris, and ran the risk attendant on bearing money and valuable commodities across a country infested by lawless soldiery. But in this they only fulfilled a duty demanding natural courage; their service to their country in its darkest moment was one needing qualities of a higher order. The barbarities of the troops upon the country-folk had left ghastly traces in the human remains lying by the wayside as a prey to wolves or vultures, or across the threshold of deserted homesteads. They meant a chance of pollution for the living as well as the desecration of the dead, and such things cried for a remedy; but the case was worse when civil warfare became widespread, and the bodies of men and horses rotted by hundreds where they had fallen.*

In the prevalent disorder no public effort was made to meet this horror. It was left for M. Vincent to devise a means, and but for the spirit that animated the Company, even he might have been baffled. The task was hideous, and one after another those who volunteered for it forfeited their lives. It was, indeed, a service that would have rejoiced the heart of Francis of Assisi. The acme of sensual mortification, and each one of the Company who devoted himself to it, paid a glorious tribute to the Superior to whom he owed his inspiration. " These are most truly martyrs!" cried M. Vincent proudly.

Throughout all those dark years, wherever the horror was greatest, wherever human cruelty and human suffering had been brought to their farthest point, there would be found the sons of M. Vincent labouring steadfastly to comfort and to remedy. And in Paris itself the work of S. Lazare went on unceasingly. The national misfortunes broke routine, but gave new opportunity.

* It is recorded that near Rethel 2,000 corpses lay for two months unburied.

The parish priests from all quarters of France, flying for safety to Paris, appealed to M. Vincent. Many of them were of that lax type whose reformation was among the objects of the Company. "We give them subsistence," wrote the Superior,* "together with training in those things that they should both know and practise." The mass of refugees also were just those persons to whom the Company ministered habitually, and at the moment when it became impossible to reach them in the country they were brought into contact with their appointed helpers in the city. "Not being able to hold missions in the provinces, we are resolved to hold them for those who have taken refuge in Paris," says M. Vincent, "and we have begun to-day in our own church with 800 poor folk lodging in this neighbourhood. Later we shall go elsewhere. Some of us also are beginning at S. Nicholas du Chardonnet."

The practical side of M. Vincent's action during the Fronde is so prominent that it is well once more to be reminded that these spiritual opportunities were those which he prized and valued; for these he sought even when the burden of organization was weighing most heavily upon him, and through them he derived the only comfort that was attainable. For, in truth, all the knowledge accumulated in his long life, all the courage won in the thousands of hours spent in prayer, were needed to help him to fulfil what this stage of his journey demanded of him.

* "Lettres," vol. i., No. 226.

Jean François de Gondi.
(Cardinal de Retz)

CHAPTER X

CARDINAL DE RETZ

WITH M. Olier and his Congregation of S. Sulpice labouring early and late for the starving citizens of Paris, and Vincent de Paul organizing relief throughout the whole of France, it would seem that the Church won honour from the sensational disasters of the Fronde. And, without question, the personality of M. Vincent assumed by reason of it a dominance over the minds and hearts of the people that might not have been his without it, and the spiritual power of the Lazarists was thereby strengthened. But the Fronde was the most selfish, as well as the most confused, of revolutions; it was prolonged and sustained by vain desires rather than by any principle of revolt against abuse, and the two figures ranged against each other as leaders on either hand are Cardinal Mazarin and Jean François de Gondi, Cardinal de Retz.* The Church, therefore, does not reap glory from that complicated episode.

The cause of those who were leagued against Mazarin was so strong, and their desire for his expulsion from the kingdom so unanimous, that their ultimate discomfiture is not easily accounted for. It may be that de Retz was more responsible for the failure of the Fronde than for its origin (in spite of the testimony of some of his contemporaries), and is therefore an historical personage of the first importance; but it is not primarily on this account that he claims notice here. One of the objects

---

* See "Mémoires du Cardinal de Retz contenant ce qui s'est passé de remarquable en France pendant les premières années du règne de Louis XIV."

of M. Vincent's life-work, and one that was very near his heart, was to set up a standard for the priesthood, and to awake the understanding of the priests themselves to the infamy of their loose lives in contrast to their strict and pure profession. A vigorous crusade against an abuse has little meaning without knowledge of the abuse itself. The maxims and practice of the Lazarists, the unremitting efforts of M. Vincent to impress the necessity of spiritual life upon the priesthood, and the sanctity of the priest's vocation on every man and woman in France, can have no better explanation than the career of the Cardinal de Retz.

Probably Jean François de Gondi was not in intention an enemy of the State, but his intentions were indefinite, and he was, in fact, the possessor of the most dangerous of all powers—the oratory that can excite, but cannot control, a mob. As we know, there was reason enough for discontent, and, had there been unity among the discontented, there would have been little hope of triumph for the boy King. But there were as many parties as there were notabilities. The Duc d'Orleans, first of them all in rank and last in ability, struggled through years of anxiety, and landed himself in disgrace and banishment, without ever having adopted a definite cause or policy. Condé, soldier and man of honour, of whom de Retz himself bore witness that he had " *l'âme du monde la moins méchante*," played with treason, first in the assertion of overweening vanity, and afterwards in revenge for insult and imprisonment. There was de Beaufort also, a reckless fellow, who loved notoriety, and had inherited a capacity for winning hearts. He led revolt because Mazarin engrossed the favours of the Queen, and life at Court was not fruitful of excitement. And the women passed from one to the other, goading, inciting, entangling—Mme. de Longueville, Mme. de Chevreuse, Mme. de Montbazon, Mme. de Guéménée, the Princess Palatine, and many more—a long list of them. They had played at poetry and the fine arts at the Hôtel Rambouillet, and yawned behind their fans; they had endured as best they might the incredible boredom of the Coürt of Louis XIII., with his neglected Queen guarded and discredited. And then the glorious moment came when every bond might be snapped and no law of society or of the realm need be recognized.

It was a period when woman's influence was extraordinarily powerful. The idea of it had been artificially nurtured by Mme. de Rambouillet. She had intended to foster the purest instincts of human nature, to revive the spirit of chivalry, to inaugurate an age when strong men, led by high-souled women, should strive for noble ends, heedless of personal interest. She was a visionary and a sentimentalist. But being also a woman of peculiar power, she was no less effective because her effectiveness fell so wide of its intended mark. The women of the Fronde owed much to the tuition of Mme. de Rambouillet, but their way of life was entirely at variance with her intentions. In fact, she had formed her theory and acted on it without allowing for the element of the unknown, inevitable where new suggestion touches human character. Flames arose where she had not suspected anything inflammable, and the flickering light revealed new qualities in natures she had thought familiar, and speedily the fire spread till, to her dazzled eyes, the calm shining of her social theory and her reign of art and literary excellence ceased to be visible.

The Hôtel Rambouillet, taken by itself, can claim only a subordinate place in the history of any development, social or intellectual; but the Fronde is impossible to overlook in the barest outline of the history of France, and the Fronde owed its duration and its bitterness to the women who took part in it. Condé was at times the central figure, it is true, and Condé was less the tool of women than most of his contemporaries; but its leader and instigator just at those points where the peace-loving hoped that strife might cease was de Retz, first Coadjutor, and afterwards Cardinal Archbishop, the man who of all others of that day was most involved in the intricacies of feminine intrigues.

It would be absurd, therefore, to describe Vincent de Paul and his long struggle to uphold the sanctity of the priest's vocation and to ignore the great example of the evil against which he fought given by Cardinal de Retz. To understand the strength of the Congregation of S. Lazare, we must realize Cardinal Mazarin and his secretaries, Cardinal de Retz and his envoys to the Papal Court—priests all of them, except Mazarin himself. There were years when de Retz was better known and better loved in Paris than Vincent de Paul himself. And those who loved him best were not to be found among the courtiers or in the light-hearted throng who were his equals in age and rank, but among those who lived in the mean streets or crowded thoroughfares. It was the people, for whose welfare Vincent de Paul struggled and thought and prayed continually, who offered their allegiance to de Retz, and so made him for a time the most formidable of all possible enemies to the Crown.

The coupling of these names is not suggested merely by their contrast. Vincent de Paul began his experience of this world's pomps and vanities just at the time when Jean François de Gondi was born. In his subsequent intimacy with the whole family he must have shared in the notice and interest excited by the brilliant talents of this youngest hope of a great house. The future Cardinal was not the pupil of M. Vincent for very long, but memories must, nevertheless, have been connected with his brother's tutor, and the death of Pierre de Gondi (the first and chief disaster of his own life) affected M. Vincent closely.

Jean François de Gondi might have shone as a soldier. He was a fine type of a class not uncommon in his day— one of those intrepid cavaliers who revelled in display, in excitement, and in love-making of a flamboyant sort;

who treated the world as a stage, and rarely forgot that they were playing to an audience. Intellectually, he was superior to the clattering troop who were swept hither and thither in the various developments of the Fronde, and, had Fortune allowed him to be one of them, it would assuredly have been as a leader, and not in the rank and file. He was possessed of the literary faculty which is of service in any condition, and also of that more dangerous endowment, the instinct for the picturesque. As an independent gentleman, with his hand on his sword-hilt and a reputation for daring to keep him safe from insult, Jean François de Gondi would have found a satisfying range of experience within his reach. It is not difficult to imagine the man he might have been had he been given a helmet in place of a biretta. But Pierre, his elder brother, originally destined to succeed his uncle in the ecclesiastical dignities claimed by the family, died suddenly and tragically; and, in consequence, it fell to the lot of Jean François, soldier and gallant to his finger-tips, to become the most flagrant example of the evil that was poisoning the Church.

During the five years that the French monarchy tottered on the brink of ruin, the thread that is easiest to follow in the difficult and entangled history of events is that of the struggle between de Retz and Mazarin for supreme rulership of the State. Both were Italian by descent. The de Gondi were of the Florentine nobility, and established their fortune in France under Catherine de Medici. Mazarin was a new-comer, and belonged to the lower orders, but both were endowed with that capacity for cunning which Machiavelli sought to nurture and instruct, and both had the skill to use the elementary passions and desires of their neighbours for their own objects.

Their battle, when it was over and de Retz vanquished, was chronicled by him with matchless cynicism, and his vanity did not prevent him from setting down the most damning evidence against himself. His admissions on the one side gave a stamp of veracity to his accusations on the other, and the brilliant whole destroyed any shreds of reputation that remained to Cardinal Mazarin, while de Retz himself emerges as a clearly outlined figure, with all his folly, all his trickery, all his puerile complacency. He had no standard of morality or truth; he accepted the most solemn spiritual offices purely for self-aggrandizement; he was devoid of any sense of responsibility, and stands self-revealed as unworthy of the trust of others. Yet it is well to remember that Vincent de Paul was a spectator of most of his career, with every opportunity of real knowledge of events. M. Vincent was a lover of honesty, and the glamour of notoriety did not dazzle him. Still, to the end of his days, he was faithful in allegiance to de Retz. On a lower level there were many of the Cardinal's followers, not otherwise virtuous, who remained unshaken in their devotion, in complete disregard of their own interests. It would seem, therefore, that he was possessed of some unusual capacity to charm which destroyed the balance of judgment in those who came under his spell. Faintly the pages of his memoirs convey the impression which facts support. Here is one who, by his own confession, has defied the laws of God and man, who has tricked, and schemed, and lied, and sacrificed the lives and fortunes of innumerable innocent persons to the chance of satisfying his ambition; yet when his memoirs end we are fascinated rather than repelled, and we may believe that this same power secured for him allegiance and support when defeat and confiscation might have brought him to ruin.

His youth was spent in schemes to escape from the chain of the profession that was being forced upon him. When he discovered that open opposition was useless, he resorted to elaborate devices. He hoped to be so distinguished for his martial ardour that the absurdity of condemning him to a cassock would be self-evident, and he lost no opportunity of picking a private quarrel or of brawling publicly. He arranged a runaway match which, had it come to pass, must of course have been decisive, in some measure, of his future; but this failed, as did all deliberate attempts to convince his parents of his unfitness for the priesthood; and in due course he, self-confessed as "*l'âme la moins ecclesiastique qui fût dans l'univers,*" became Coadjutor to his uncle, the second Archbishop of Paris.

Richelieu had marked him while he was only a lad, had taken him into some sort of favour, and then withdrew his patronage, and would not advance him. Jean François himself believed that Richelieu's suspicions of him were aroused by reading a wonderfully able pamphlet which he wrote when only seventeen on the Conspiracy of Gian Luigi Fiesco. Herein one may observe a hint of the vanity of the young author, for it is far more likely that the keen-sighted Cardinal descried in de Retz himself the qualities which he considered to be dangerous, than that their existence was traced through the medium of his writing. Very strong support would have been needed to secure his nomination as Coadjutor if Richelieu had survived, and there was much cause for the citizens of Paris to deplore an appointment that proved as impolitic as it was scandalous.

But if there were any who knew Jean François de Gondi as he really was, they made no outcry at his appointment to high ecclesiastical office, and the majority were very ready to welcome him, for he had had periods when he thought well to play the priest, and he was as skilful in this part as in any of the others which he chose to adopt.

Among those whose eyes were blinded must be numbered Vincent de Paul. His discrimination of character had been proved again and again, but here the memory of much kindness to himself, all the force of old loyalty, all the gratitude for the first beginnings of his Congregation, was ranged on the side of generous tolerance. He did not regret that Jean François de Gondi was to receive the highest preferment that at the time was possible, and therefore we assume that Jean François had aped the appearance and practices of piety to some purpose. Before the Archbishop's nephew was quite secure of his appointment, he tells us that he cultivated the society of the most reputable ecclesiastics who frequented the archiepiscopal palace. "I did not pretend to great devotion myself," he says, "because I knew I should not be able to keep it up, but I showed great esteem for the pious, and this in their eyes is one of the greatest points of piety."

Court favour and ecclesiastical support united at the right moment, the Queen smiled on him, and, at thirty, Jean François was Coadjutor to the Archbishop, with the certainty of the succession. It was necessary, then, that he should be a priest, and Vincent de Paul had introduced the custom of Ordination Retreats. Perhaps it was not unnatural that de Gondi, who based his fortune on public opinion, should be guided by it at this crisis. Nevertheless, his admission at S. Lazare for the prescribed days of devotional retirement is an anomaly so great as to cast a stigma on M. Vincent himself; his own account of it is sufficiently suggestive.

"As I was forced to take orders," he says, "I went into retreat at S. Lazare, where I conformed outwardly in all things. Inwardly I was absorbed by the most profound reflection as to the best course to pursue. It was a very difficult question. I found the Archbishopric of Paris degraded in the eyes of the world by my uncle's meanness, and distorted in its position towards God by his negligence and incapacity. I foresaw innumerable obstacles in the way of its restoration, and I was not so blind as to overlook that the greatest and the most insurmountable lay in myself. I was not ignorant of the importance of moral conduct in a Bishop; I knew that the scandalous licence my uncle had permitted himself made the claim on me even more narrow and more insistent than on others; and I knew at the same time that I was not able to sustain it, and that no barrier set up at the bidding either of conscience or ambition would be much check to the attack of temptation. After six days of reflection, I chose to do wrong deliberately, which is incomparably most sinful in the sight of God, but also, without doubt, is wisest from a worldly point of view, because one may take precautions to cover it in part, and so avoid the unseasonable mingling of evil doing with pious practice which in our profession is such a dangerous absurdity."

Never has there been cynicism more complete. In the quiet chapel at S. Lazare, which for so many was full of hallowed memories, Jean François de Gondi reviewed the possibilities of evil and of good, and " chose to do wrong deliberately." He went out from his Retreat to the new life and the new honours that awaited him, and preached a series of Advent sermons in the Cathedral of Notre Dame to crowded congregations. It was the beginning of as curious a drama of human nature as history presents. The Archbishop was going into the country for a time, and full authority was in the hands of the Coadjutor. Fresh from his intercourse with M. Vincent, he set on foot a scheme for the purification of the diocese. The clergy were, by careful investigation and inquiry, divided into three classes—the virtuous, those whose practices were questionable but who might be reformed, and those whose depravity had become confirmed. The last were to hold no office, and the more hopeful were to be suspended until they showed plain intention of living more worthily. Such a project must have rejoiced the heart of Vincent de Paul, and de Gondi's powers as an administrator were sufficient to carry it through and to effect immense improvement in the deplorable conditions that prevailed. Unfortunately, however, his authority was not supreme, and the Archbishop on his return cancelled every regulation made by the Coadjutor. It was said that he did so with the approval of Mazarin, who seems to have been unswervingly consistent in opposition to all attacks on the libertinage of the priests, and de Gondi, who meant his reforming ardour to serve as one of the steps by which he climbed high in public opinion, began his collection of grievances against the Cardinal.

In spite of the failure in practical result, de Gondi's reforming enterprise scored heavily in his favour, for he had managed to impress the Queen. She required that he should conduct a six weeks' Retreat in a convent, and he acquitted himself admirably. In those early days he was not only celebrated as a preacher, but it is plain he took a pride in his preaching. One of his sermons on S. Carlo Borromeo was famous. Doubtless there were many who believed they derived spiritual benefit from his exhortations. He sets down the record of his doings in fulfilment of his exalted office with a measure of pride in his success. And all the time that other life, which was to be hidden for fear of " dangerous absurdity," was going on, and the record of this also he set down.

His forefathers had been the comrades and confidants of the Valois and Medici; the chain that was meant to bind him had not been of his choosing; Southern blood ran in his veins—these are the excuses for him as an individual. Around him lay a wealth of temptation. It was a moment of reaction. The Queen set a dubious example. No member of the Royal Family could have presented a clean record, and in every mind there lurked the recollection of life at Court under Louis XIII., of his high standard of morality—and its exceeding dulness. Virtue itself was not more lacking than the desire for virtue, and it is unlikely that a man of thirty could have maintained familiar intercourse with the notable personages of the day unless he shared their vices. If his contemporaries do not malign him, Jean François de Gondi was without external attraction. He was under-sized and ugly, and though he loved to make nocturnal expeditions in all a courtier's finery, with satin cloak, plumed hat, and jewelled sword, he was undoubtedly a priest, and condemned in daylight hours to be disfigured by cassock and biretta. Nevertheless, it is plain that he was a dangerous rival in love and friendship. Mme. de Longueville herself is numbered among his conquests, and there was a moment when he dreamed of ousting Mazarin from dominion over the Queen. There was something about him that won affection, and, where women were concerned, it is likely that the anomaly of his position, his youth, his episcopal dignity, and his phenomenal daring, were effective. It was an age that loved novelties, and the stranger they were the more welcome.

Thus, in that city of contrasts, of vast palaces guarded by their gardens and their quiet courtyards from streets whose misery and offence baffle description, Jean François de Gondi, the pupil of M. Vincent, employed himself openly in an endeavour to reform the clergy, exhorted his flock from the pulpit of Notre Dame to tread the narrow path of saintly life; and all the time was gathering together every shred of knowledge that would serve him, listening eagerly for scraps of information which might fall from the lips of the great ladies whom he courted, noting the jealousies that threatened to sever ties of blood or friendship, and marking the growth of ambitions or caprices that might be woven into a pattern of his own design. The levity, the sensationalism, the licence of the time, were at one with his natural temperament. A midnight séance of conspirators at the bedside of a Court beauty suited his fancy; and plots, begun in mockery, ended, under his guidance, in deadly earnest.

Even in England, in the Victorian Age, he would have created opportunities to dissemble and intrigue, because to him the zest of life lay in mystery, and no contrivance was too elaborate by which he could create a false impression. To make one individual regard another—who was, in fact, his close adherent—as his bitterest enemy was an artistic triumph; and so far did the Coadjutor carry his enterprises that his memoirs leave the reader in grave doubt as to the real intentions of any one of the many extraordinary personages who were the leaders of the Fronde.

But though the love of excitement and of intrigue was innate in him, and was fostered by the opportunities of his position, a very definite purpose lay behind his melodramatic practices. The power of the Crown was a real thing in France, despite the murmurs of the people and the protests of the princes, and, as has been shown already, it was wielded by Mazarin, not because—like Richelieu—he was supremely fit to govern, but because he was master of the craft that can win and hold a woman's favour. In that direction de Gondi knew himself to be highly gifted; he also held an office in the Church which would, nominally, protect the Queen from scandal, and he could use a disguise and the backstairs as deftly as could the Cardinal. He had, also, far clearer comprehension of the humours and jealousies that spell danger in a Court, because he could associate on equal terms with the *noblesse*, while Mazarin, the low-born Florentine, could only guess his way among them. In short, the Coadjutor felt himself eminently suited to the post of guide, philosopher, and friend to the Queen Regent, and was persuaded that France would not attain to real prosperity until the Queen embraced the same opinion.

The obstacle was a simple one. The place he coveted could not be shared, and it was already occupied. Cardinal Mazarin stood where Jean François de Gondi wished to stand. Cardinal Mazarin stood beside the

Queen, and against the Queen were ranged many conflicting elements of danger. The exact nature of these elements was known to none better than to de Gondi. He might have preferred to strike at Mazarin alone; but if Mazarin sheltered behind the Queen, then, rather than leave him unmolested, he must aim at the Throne itself. It was easy to foresee that there would be stages of astonishment, of consternation, in the end, probably of panic. Mazarin was to be routed, and then, in the guise of paladin and deliverer, de Gondi would restore peace, would uphold the monarchy and guide the trembling hands that held the reins of government.

Such a part appealed not only to his immense ambition, but also to his histrionic sense. If there be behind the Fronde a scheme that can be given definite form, it is here, and in such a scheme there lay great possibilities of triumph. Direct and unswerving adherence to so plain an issue would, in fact, have gone far to command success. But de Gondi was not able to give direct and unswerving adherence anywhere. He desired to be stage manager of the remarkable drama that was being played out, but also he desired to try many different parts, and the curtain went down on the last act before he had decided which rôle best became him. He was diverted partly by a cross-current of ambition. He desired to be First Minister and to oust Mazarin, but he desired also to be a Cardinal; and the two desires, though there was nothing contradictory about them, required a different order of manœuvring. To be a Cardinal he must obtain a nomination from the Queen, a most notable proof of favour, not to be obtained by one who waged open war against Mazarin. Thus the Coadjutor found himself on the horns of a dilemma. His claim to consideration was his hold upon the people, he played for popularity and played successfully; but that which bound them to him alienated the Queen, and to keep both was necessary to his ambition. Yet where many men might reasonably have found defeat, de Gondi discovered opportunity. He obtained a private interview with the Queen, and by a show of openness and candour seems to have won from her a measure of confidence which certainly he did not deserve. With the half-truths which are the strongest weapons of an accomplished liar, he represented himself as the unrecognized champion of the royal prerogative, who posed as demagogue, so that he might safeguard the Regent and the King from the unreasoning anger of the mob. It was a clever stratagem, ably carried out. Mazarin still had complete mastery over the Queen, but de Gondi had extraordinary influence when he came into personal contact with her. He could be assured of producing an impression, and for his purpose it was as useful to impress as to convince her. She knew that the air was full of the murmur of treasonable plots, and his frank avowal of his own connection with them and of their danger revealed him as a possessor of the power in which she was most lacking. He understood the people and their motives, to her they remained always a mystery. Therefore he stood out prominent as an individual among the many—most of whom she had cause to fear—and at length his nomination was forwarded to Rome.

In this, then, he was successful, but success at this point and at a later stage proved a curse rather than a blessing, because of its effect upon his character. He had been so adroit in his manœuvres, that thenceforward he put no check upon them, and over-reached himself. The Queen must be reassured as to his intentions, must be constantly renewed in her belief that the Coadjutor was a loyal gentleman greatly calumniated, and therefore he became more guarded in his intercourse with the men of his party, and more deeply involved with regard to women. Had his sway over them been merely intellectual, his course would have been wisely chosen. A clever priest, standing apart from the ordinary intercourse of noble lords and ladies, might acquire knowledge and wield an influence immeasurably superior in those unsettled times to that of the man of the sword. But we do not grasp de Gondi, or the class he represents, if we picture him as only using weapons of argument and wit. During the Regency morality sank gradually to a level almost as low as in the days of the Valois Kings; there was a clique of women notable, most of them, for high lineage, conspicuous talents, and good looks, who were completely and avowedly lawless. The Coadjutor set himself to win the hearts of those whose valuable support he needed.

His memoirs indicate the methods that he followed and the risks he took. If they are to be trusted, we may picture him with plumed hat, and the voluminous cloak of the period muffling his face, clanking down the dim streets till, near to the hidden door he wished to enter, his step grew stealthy, and by a mysterious signal he gained entrance to the dwelling of some mistress of intrigue. He was a curious offspring of the times. In the daylight hours when he was greeted as a dignitary of the Church, and would raise his hands to bless kneeling and expectant crowds, he was not backward in asserting the high dignity of his office; and lurking in his mind there was a clear conception, which now and again he has betrayed, of the type of man the holder of that office ought to be. It is this comprehension of his true obligations which makes de Retz unlike the ordinary charlatan, but he takes a certain delight in recording his own hypocrisy.

"On Christmas Day," he writes, "I preached at S. Germain l'Auxerrois. I discoursed of Christian charity without the most distant reference to the affairs of the moment. The women wept over the injustice of persecuting an Archbishop who had only tenderness for his enemies, and when I left the pulpit I knew, from the blessings showered upon me, that I was not mistaken in my idea that this sermon would serve a very good purpose. In fact, it was incredibly effective, and surpassed my most sanguine hopes."

Again, on Maundy Thursday he tells us how he prolonged the ceremony of blessing the sacred oils at the altar in the Cathedral, because he knew there was a tumult pending, and he wished to be in the centre of the business. When he left the altar he hastened to the Palais de Justice, that he might pacify the representatives of the people, and display his power as a leader. Always behind his confession of ambitions there lurks a sense of special glory in his command over the people. "What is a virtue in the chief of a faction is a vice in an Archbishop," he declares. It is as chief of a faction that he acts.. It was that he might maintain himself as chief that he studied the interests of the masses and learnt to catch their fickle favour. For this, perhaps, it was that he simulated devotion, and for this certainly he sought to become known as the most generous of almsgivers. The mob accepted him as they saw him, and for a time they adored him. His equals were more enlightened; the sword which he felt it necessary to hide beneath his cassock was called *le bréviaire de M. le Coadjuteur*. On that celebrated Holy Thursday he was told that the sacred oils blessed by him would be mingled with saltpetre. The society of the day knew all about him. Nevertheless, he influenced it. He was known to be a villain, but among his intimates he had a fascinating way of confessing to villainy.

From the standpoint of the twentieth century it may appear incredible that the nomination of Jean François de Gondi as a French Cardinal should have gone to Rome unchallenged. Yet if the Coadjutor had had the vision and, as its consequence, the command over himself which would have withheld him from his perilous attempt to lead the mob, he might, as Archbishop of Paris and as Cardinal, have reformed the priesthood by precepts which he did not practise. From such conduct he would have gained at Court and in the city a power of immeasurable strength. The position might have been clearly defined. Mazarin was the declared enemy of reform in the bestowing of preferment. The Cardinal-Archbishop, struggling against the Italian favourite for the purity of the national Church, would have won the support of the vast majority of Frenchmen, and, having won it, might have used it against the same antagonist in other conflicts. But if he saw the opportunity, its promise was less alluring than the exciting possibilities that lay nearer to his grasp. It was in the rush and fever of events that he desired to lead, not among the slow developments of well-considered schemes. Therefore, hampered rather than helped by his ecclesiastical dignities, and missing, by reason of infirmity of purpose, the dominion which he might have claimed over the wills of others, Jean François de Gondi, Coadjutor, Cardinal, and ultimately Archbishop, was ineffective save as a disturber, and owes his great importance in the history of the time only to his responsibility for its miseries.

But if we would judge him fairly, we must remember that it was customary to employ tortuous methods in obtaining a Cardinal's hat. Even when he had obtained his nomination from the Queen, he dared not fight straight lest she should withdraw it; while she, although most reluctant to let him obtain a dignity that would place him on an equality with Mazarin, feared his power with the people so profoundly that she dared not force him into declared antagonism.

Innocent X. held Mazarin in abhorrence, and from this fact the Coadjutor derived his strongest hope of success. Eventually there is little doubt that it was to this that he owed his coveted dignity. While the intrigues of Rome were in progress, Mazarin was in exile, and was representing in letters to de Gondi that his chief desire for his own satisfaction and for the good of the State was to see him a Cardinal. De Gondi, in response, expressed his earnest wish that Mazarin should soon return to France. Meanwhile, there were envoys sent by Mazarin to Rome, whose sole mission was to undermine the interests of the Coadjutor; and the Coadjutor refused to leave Paris, even temporarily, lest in his absence the ferment of the mob against the Cardinal might lessen.

The long contest ended with a curious suddenness. The principals in it were no less surprised than the rest of the world when, in the spring of 1652, Jean François de Gondi was made a Cardinal by Innocent X., to be known to the world thenceforward as the Cardinal de Retz. It was a signal triumph. Mazarin was in exile, but he still ruled the Queen, and was believed to hold many secret strings that guided the progress of events. Victory could hardly have been expected even by the victor, and it seemed to throw open the way to the fulfilment of immense ambitions.

In his youth we have seen that the Abbé de Gondi had made special study of Fiesco, a character whose name has very little place in history. When Andrea Doria had acquired despotic rule in Genoa, he had beside him a nephew and favourite who interfered greatly in the government of the city; and pursued any who sought to rival him with deadly malice. One of the ancient nobility of Genoa, Gian Luigi Fiesco, determined to overthrow the favourite. He won the hearts of the populace, and impressed himself as a leading personality among his compeers, preserving meanwhile, until his plans were ripe, the appearance of friendly relations with the Doria. Not till he was certain of his following did he strike, and never did a conspiracy come to more complete fruition. It was at the moment of success that a plank on which he set his foot gave way, and he was plunged into the waters of the harbour. For this reason only, if it is possible to form a true judgment of the complicated surroundings of that dramatic moment, his scheme broke down, and Andrea Doria continued to dictate to Genoa.

The story of this forgotten incident was told by de Gondi with extraordinary power. His imagination grasped the figure of Count Fiesco, and that which was so vivid to himself he made vivid for others. He realized that the leader of this rebellion was conquered by the hand of Death striking mysteriously and suddenly, not by any human intervention, and it cannot be doubted that the career of Cardinal de Retz was notably affected by the concentration of the young Jean François de Gondi on this dramatic episode. His position in Paris and his point of view towards the Queen and Mazarin, reflected in some degree that of Fiesco with regard to the Doria kinsmen in Genoa. He depicted Fiesco as a patriot, and he had moments when he endeavoured to feel that he himself was striving for the good of the people. He aspired to win Paris, and to rule it by a personal hold upon his fellows, as Fiesco might have won Genoa. The idea was not entirely fantastic; and with the fever of such aspiration in his blood, there was small hope that prudence would be allowed to join forces with ambition, and make of him the stately, all-powerful ecclesiastic who would prove the most dangerous rival to Mazarin.

No doubt the delight of his success unbalanced him at the outset, and as he no longer feared the Queen, it pleased him to keep her under menace of the evils that he might direct against her in Paris if he chose. Afterwards, when he wrote the story of his life, he made naïve acknowledgment of his own folly. As Coadjutor he had considered self-assertion and display as a necessity, because the dignity of the See had been so lowered by his uncle the Archbishop; but as Cardinal he was free from any vicarious obligation. Yet he seems to have pretended to a pomp and magnificence in excess of that maintained by Princes of the blood royal. On one expedition to visit the Queen at Compiègne he had a train of 200 gentlemen, and spent 800 crowns daily, an immense sum in the coinage of those days. He desired to impress the world with an idea (which he held himself in all sincerity) that his position was now impregnable. In point of fact, he had never been more defenceless than in this hour of his triumph. He considered himself to be above the necessity of any precaution because he was Cardinal de Retz and had wrested his honours from a supreme power in the teeth of Mazarin's opposition.

In April, 1652, de Retz became a Cardinal; in October of that year the King re-entered Paris, and Mazarin retired to the frontier. The fact of this withdrawal may have been deceptive, the completeness with which the royal prerogative retained its power was probably not so clear to the onlooker as it seems in retrospect. The magic of royalty has never been so entirely destroyed as in the France of 1790, but it was never more strangely exemplified than in the France of 1652. Neither defeat nor disgrace nor the lack of the external trappings that give the Crown its mystery and grandeur disturbed its potency. In proof thereof we find as the monument of the Fronde—instead of the record of safeguards and benefits for an overburdened people—the great palace at Versailles, erected that the Great Monarch, in his superb magnificence, might dwell aloof, out of sight and hearing of the *canaille* whose murmurs had disturbed his boyhood. His return to Paris at the invitation of his baffled subjects was the prologue to an age of despotism, but it required far-seeing wisdom to foretell that henceforward the royal will would prevail in all things. And de Retz was not numbered among the wise. He would have acknowledged readily that it was the royal will that Mazarin should return, but he was convinced that that return was impossible while he himself remained in Paris. From that conviction, in itself true and well-founded, he deduced that the game was in his hands. So he toyed with his enormous influence over Monsieur the King's uncle, he encouraged suggestions that he might join hands with Condé—the consummation that was most dreaded by the Queen—and Paris rang with stories of his haughtiness and self-assertion.

Meanwhile Mazarin, waiting on the frontier with couriers passing constantly to and from the capital, watched the progress of events and cultivated the patience of the diplomat. To him there must have been an element of uncertainty in the position. He knew the Queen to be weak of purpose, and, as he was debarred from witnessing the foolhardiness with which his enemy courted disaster; his rôle for the moment was unenviable.

A few days before Christmas Cardinal de Retz, having presented himself at the Louvre to pay his respects to the King and Queen, was arrested as he left their presence. He made no resistance, for, in spite of the reiterated warnings he had received, he was quite unprepared. He was driven through the streets of Paris to his prison in the fortress of Vincennes, and he who had once been the idol of the people was allowed to pass without a voice raised or a blow struck in his defence.

The imprisonment of personages whose conduct threatened to be dangerous proved itself once more to be an expedient prolific of inconvenience. In the case of Cardinal de Retz, as in that of Condé, there was no pretence at a trial; *le roi le veut* was the sole warrant. And with de Retz, as formerly with Condé, the sense of injustice added immensely to the suffering inflicted. In both it produced not only bitter resentment, but a distrust as to the setting of any limit to the measures taken by his antagonists. After nearly two years of misery and humiliation, de Retz escaped, and, in defiance of innumerable perils, conveyed himself to Rome. He did not meet with the support he had expected; he was crippled both in health and fortune, and ostensibly he was not a dangerous enemy. In his case it would seem that the policy of despotism had succeeded. His enemies were able to triumph over him, and Mazarin, once more the reigning power at the Louvre, might meditate in leisure moments on the complete discomfiture and degradation of his rival. Despite his own misfortunes, however, Cardinal de Retz retained his capacity to torment Cardinal Mazarin. It is possible that the victor, having suffered so much, yielded to an exaggerated dread of the vanquished, but there was a more practical reason for Mazarin's disturbance. While de Retz was imprisoned, his uncle, the Archbishop, died, and he, as Coadjutor, succeeded. A formal resignation was extorted from him, which, on the plea that he had not been a free agent, was annulled after his escape. The King had no power to depose him, and the Pope would not. He was an exile, his property was confiscated; if he returned to his native land his liberty, and probably his life, were forfeit; nevertheless he was, and he remained, Archbishop of Paris.

As such he was welcomed at the house of the Lazarists in Rome, and for this crime M. Vincent was compelled by Mazarin to recall his sons and check the work of the Company in the Eternal City.* But if it was a crime to recognize him, it was not safe to deal vigorously with those who did so, for in the eyes of loyal churchmen the Archbishop's case was a very strong one. The obvious course was to make terms and to barter for this prize—indisputably his—with advantages that would be enduring. And it is here that we find the effect first of his long experience of chicanery, and then of his abrupt arrest.

"*Le fond de la probité n'y est pas,*" wrote Mazarin of de Retz in the autumn of 1652. The same phrase applied conversely explains the refusal of the Archbishop to deal with the King's First Minister. For many years they had tricked and deceived each other, until any desire

* "Lettres," vol. ii., No. 283.

that either might have to enter on negotiations was frustrated by mutual distrust. Mazarin might pledge himself to an amnesty, might assure de Retz that his return to Paris and the restoration of his goods was secure if he would vacate his See; but under despotic government de Retz had no belief that the pledge had any meaning, while he knew that his part of the bargain—his resignation—once given, could never be withdrawn.

Therefore the pricking of the ecclesiastical difficulty never ceased during Mazarin's lifetime, and only when Louis XIV. was really monarch did Cardinal de Retz submit to the sovereign pleasure. He then returned to Paris, and lived his last years in the society for which he was always suited. He was meant to be a soldier and a wit, he might have made a statesman and a courtier, but as a priest he was the product of the worst evil of his times, and it is as a priest that posterity perforce must judge him. In the end, says tradition, he took life seriously, and gave himself up to devotion. All that is certain is that he lived in seclusion, although the world of the Court was once more open to him, and although he still possessed the capacity for apt and skilful speech which had been his before his time of misfortune.

"Your hair is grey, M. le Cardinal," was the young King's greeting to him when he returned from his years of exile.

"Those who are out of favour with your Majesty grow grey speedily," was his reply.*

* See Léonee Curnier, "Le Cardinal de Retz et son Temps," vol. ii., part iii.

PART II
THE COMPANIONS OF VINCENT DE PAUL

Mademoiselle Le Gras.

CHAPTER I

MLLE. LE GRAS

THE violent outward events that make up the history of his time affected M. Vincent; his life, as a whole, cannot be understood without consideration of them; but its deepest realities were independent of recorded events, and if we desire to see him amidst them, we must leave the society of the Court, and cease to make any reference to Cardinals. To know M. Vincent we must attempt to watch him in the spiritual relationship that forced revelation, and to mark the effect of personal failure and of bereavement upon his character. We must join ourselves to the Sisters of the Poor as they drew from his fund of common sense and from his more inspiring knowledge; we must share with the Ladies of Charity as he checked their waywardness and stimulated them to new feats of generosity; and, finally, among his Mission Priests we shall find him bearing the burdens that he imposed on others, setting a standard that did not stop short of perfection, but setting it as his Master had done in Galilee, with clear understanding of all the human weakness that made for failure. It is, then, in his life at S. Lazare, in the daily monotonous routine which is the test of faith, that we must seek him, if his message to the world has any meaning for us. .

He had to bear—increasingly after he settled at S. Lazare—the strain of the dependence of other souls upon himself. So close and constant did this claim become, that his capacity for response must have rested in the unsullied purity of his own character. It was the influence of his personality rather than individual direction in separate cases that worked such wonders, and any deviation from his practice of rigorous self-discipline must have been reflected in those whose advance seemed to depend upon his guidance. During the last twenty years of his life there was a very numerous company of men and women scattered at immense distances from each other who all equally gave obedience to M. Vincent, and would have regarded his decision in any matter as final. They had all made the choice which M. Vincent required of his children—they had all renounced the satisfactions that the world might offer them for a life of toil and discomfort. He set the example, and they followed. There is a curious simplicity in the picture. Neither to the Mission Priests nor to the Sisters of the Poor did he offer anything that would appeal to emotional instincts. The essence of their sacrifice was that it must be hidden; they were to have nothing that could excite envy or stir enthusiasm. And most of them lived through long years of quiet labour, and died in harness, content with the knowledge that they had been faithful servants. These were the real representatives of M. Vincent's spirit, and it is because in the Sisters of the Poor we find this spirit in its simplest form that they are specially his representatives before the world.

The Rule he gave them seems to summarize his theory of life, and the gradual development of their Company coincided with the development in himself of the power to mingle practical and spiritual capacity. For this reason its foundation has immense importance, and in connection with it we come upon an episode in the life of M. Vincent that is important to comprehension of him —the one instance of his friendship with a woman.

We have already referred to Mlle. Le Gras and the gathering of the first unrecognized Sisters of Charity beneath her roof. She was the ideal Superior for a Company that was not only new, but was an innovation on all established ideas for Communities of women. M. Vincent was nearly fifty years old when he and she first came in contact, and he possessed deep experience of that form of service which she desired to make the object of her life. For a long period they had no relation to each other except as priest and penitent; but in fact the work of each would have been incomplete without the other, and both seem to have been guided into that sane uniting of their forces which established the Sisters of Charity for the service of the poor.

Louise de Marillac, known to her contemporaries as Mlle. Le Gras, was a woman of deeply religious mind. In her youth she desired to enter the cloister, but she had not the contemplative vocation, and so many of the established orders had grown lax in discipline, that her guardians were energetic in dissuading her from this form of self-surrender. When she was twenty-two she accepted the alternative they desired, and married M. Le Gras, a man considerably older than herself, who was Secretary to Marie de Medici. There was no place for her in the society of the day. Eighty years later she might have been one of the intimate circle round Mme. de Maintenon, but a sincere *dévote* was at variance with the spirit of the Court where Concini held first place, and if Louise Le Gras had desired to shine in the eyes of others, it would have been necessary for her to alter her whole system of life. The possibility of such a choice does not seem to have occurred to her. As a married woman she held herself as still dedicated to the service of God, and her husband did not oppose her devotion to works of charity. Possibly, at a time when Court life was complicated by perpetual intrigues, his mind was so fully occupied with his official duties that he had no knowledge of the spiritual experiences which were so engrossing to her; but he was indulgent to her proclivities for visiting the homes of the poor as he might have been to a craze for any special form of amusement.

Outwardly, therefore, her years of married life was peaceful. A son was born to her, and she fulfilled her duty towards him and towards her household assiduously; there was no indication in the well-ordered routine of her daily life of the inward storms through which she passed.

For Louise Le Gras, reality, the possibilities of joy, of suffering and of defeat, lay outside her experiences as wife and mother and mistress of a household. She neglected none of her responsibilities, but her being centred on a secret combat in which she was assailed by the insidious temptations to exaggeration, to scruples, to spiritual insincerity, that can work such havoc among aspirants towards the life of prayer.

"Do not be so disturbed over things that do not matter," says a letter from her director, which has its own significance. "Withdraw your eyes a little from yourself, and fix them upon Jesus Christ."*

The writer was Le Camus, Bishop of Bellay, a man whose wisdom and tolerance fitted him for the difficult charge that had fallen into his hands. Circumstances arose, however, which prevented his return to Paris. He was aware of the dangers to which the fervour of his penitent exposed her, and he appealed to Vincent de Paul to undertake the office he was relinquishing. M. Vincent's consent was not given readily. He was then at that difficult transition period of his own life when he was still bound to the household of the de Gondi, and was also responsible for the first foundation of the Congregation of Mission Priests; and it is clear that he acceded to the desire of Le Camus with the utmost reluctance. He did not regard a task of individual direction as part of the service to which God summoned him, it presented itself as a hindrance to the great labours developing before him, and he had no prescience of the importance of this unwelcome charge to the very work it seemed to interrupt.

* Gobillon, "Vie de Mlle. Le Gras," edition 1676, containing Correspondence with M. Vincent and "Les Pensées de Mademoiselle."

MLLE. LE GRAS

To Louise Le Gras, also, the time of her first link with M. Vincent was a time of crisis. Her husband lingered through years of painful illness, during which his claim on her taxed her fortitude and bodily health, and then died. During her married life her mind had been full of aspirations after more complete self-dedication than was then possible. At his death she reached one of those difficult moments when vague aspirations must be moulded into definite intentions, or be recognized as dreams. She was overstrained, and had a tendency to religious exaltation. It would have been easy for her to lose balance and imperil her spiritual and mental powers in those exaggerated outward practices of piety of which (in that period of extremes) there are many instances. But M. Vincent was a good guide for one who might be tempted to overstep the boundaries of common sense. He noted the design of the new life that was to be consecrated to the service of the poor, and required that the spiritual preparation for it should be of the simplest.

"Don't overdo yourself with rules and practices," he wrote to her, "but rather be very sure that those you have already are well observed, that the actions and duties of every day are well done. And beware of those eccentricities of thought that have tormented you before; they are the trick of the Evil One to set you off on a false line." She agreed with herself to make in the day thirty-three acts of adoration in honour of the thirty-three years of Our Lord's life, but M. Vincent could not take this sort of pledge very seriously. "As to these thirty-three acts and other things of the same kind, don't be distressed when you have missed them. God is Love, and desires that we should go to Him in love. Do not feel yourself bound by any of these good intentions." Excessive fasting he forbade also. The form of self-immolation which he required was more searching than any self-inflicted bodily suffering; and he began his test of her as soon as she was established in the home she had chosen in the midst of the dwellings of the poor. Mlle. Le Gras desired to give her labour to aid the Priests of the Mission; this was her ideal of service. Every attempt to organize the Confraternities emphasized the need of women's work, and she offered hers in the spirit of sacrifice, without taint of excitement or emulation. Nevertheless, M. Vincent was not prompt in acceptance. The work these two were to do together was of Divine appointment, and it was required that it should be solemnly approached. This, probably, is the true explanation of the long delay between her secret self-dedication and her actual employment in the work of the Missions. Before Louise Le Gras, in the first years of her widowhood, there lay a great vocation, unrevealed as yet, but there was never to be for her a moment of decisive and sensational choice. She yielded gradually and consistently to each demand that God might make; she learnt to wait and to bear suspense, as well as to spend herself in the service of others; and so, by steps that were hardly noted as she took them, she mounted to the place that God intended for her.

Perhaps the hardest test was the period of waiting. M. Le Gras died in 1626, and she removed to the small house in the Rue S. Victor, which was to be the birthplace of the Sisters of Charity. For three years she lived alone, and did humble service to the poor in the miserable houses of that quarter. The objects of the Mission Priests possessed her imagination; she desired to be employed in their interests, and the need for work such as she could give was self-evident; but M. Vincent withheld the boon he might have given. There were not in those days any great organizations to which she could unite herself; she was obliged to work alone, and to bear the innumerable discouragements that are the lot of the solitary worker. And as she had not the protection of high rank or wealth, malignant gossip busied itself with her. In spite of her seclusion, it was rumoured that she had accepted an offer of marriage. To her sense of secret dedication this was an outrage, and her resentment was boundless. M. Vincent's expression of sympathy is worth recording: "How deeply am I grieved at your distress! But in fact what does it all amount to? Here is a man who says you have promised to marry him, and it is false, and people are making untrue reflections on you, and you fear you are continually talked about! That may be; but understand that on this earth you could not have a better means of being united to the Son of God, that by this you may touch self-conquest such as you have never before imagined. What a blow it will strike at self-complacency! What opportunity for self-abasement it offers! Be assured that it is altogether for your good—in this world and the next. Let that assurance be your weapon against your natural impulses, and the day will come when you will thank Our Lord for testing you just in this way."

The immediate result of this trial was increased eagerness to be recognized as set apart for the service of God. Delay and discouragement only intensified the sense of vocation in Mlle. Le Gras; and if M. Vincent had not been within reach, she must certainly have taken the obvious step for one in her spiritual condition and entered one of the religious orders already in existence. But he waited for Divine guidance concerning her, and she trusted him completely. The simplicity of their attitude towards life and towards each other is very remarkable. M. Vincent would not permit any indulgence of the imagination, any of that secret bargaining that claims the joy of self-contentment in exchange for self-oblation. We shall find him exacting the most rigid spiritual austerity from the Sisters of the Poor, but assuredly the discipline imposed on them was never more severe than that endured by their leader and first Superior.

For three years Mlle. Le Gras divided her days between

self-imposed labours for the benefit of the poor and her hours of prayer and worship, and then, in 1629, she received her first commission, and went to visit Montmirail, in the diocese of Soissons, to investigate the progress of the Confraternity established there by the Priests of the Mission. The Company of Sisters of the Poor was the high development of the schemes of the Confraternities. The idea of social service, inseparable from the teaching of the Mission Priests, was ineffective without sustained and careful organization, and the idea was so new that to maintain an immense number of isolated organizations on a good footing was a task beyond human capacity. M. Vincent was making this discovery when he sent Mlle. Le Gras to report on the state of things at Montmirail, and he knew that she would require tact and prudence. He gave her careful directions in writing that she might have the full benefit of his experience for her actual conduct, and, in addition, he sent her the following brief suggestion on the eve of her departure:

"Go, Mademoiselle, go in the name of Our Lord. Beseech Him that His blessing may go with you, that it may be your comfort on your way, your strength in your labour, and finally may bring you back in good health. You will make your Communion the day you start to do honour to the *Charity* of Our Lord, in memory of the journeys He took for the sake of charity, and the suffering, the rebuffs, the weariness, and the labours, which He endured; with the intention that He may give you this same spirit and help you to bear your suffering in the same manner as He bore His own."

This was the perfect encouragement of her great venture. The dangers might be great, and were certainly unknown, and this first embassy was the preliminary of others more difficult. To look upwards with complete simplicity was the one safeguard against the tremors and misgivings that might assail her.

MLLE. LE GRAS 215

No detailed record was kept of her sojourn at Montmirail, but its success is attested by her employment in a succession of similar visits of inspection. Travelling at its best involved hardship, and Mlle. Le Gras permitted herself no unnecessary luxury. She used any vehicle that could survive the jolting of the roads, and accepted the roughest entertainment on the way. She took with her one or two companions, who were ready to share her discomforts and help her in her labours, and she bore the heavy expense of the journey herself. When she reached her destination, it was her custom to summon together all those who had enrolled themselves in the Confraternity of Charity, and rouse them to a sense of the obligations they had taken upon themselves. Possibly a public display of eloquence from a woman was in those days so unusual that it failed to rouse admiration, but it is clear that the extraordinary effectiveness of her visits to the scenes of former Missions was due in large measure to her power of speaking; and M. Vincent, writing to her when she was at the height of her energies, expresses a hope that she will not strain her lungs. She was not content with exhortation, however. One of her first cares was to fulfil those labours which were the charge of members of the Confraternity, and visit and tend the sick in their own homes. By this practice she not only set an example, but—which was equally important—she was able to discover the degree of previous neglect, and the extent of the distress in each individual case. It is easy to imagine the opportunities for discord which such an enterprise afforded; but if Mlle. Le Gras had in her progress left a trail of grievances and indignation, M. Vincent would not have continued his commission to her. It seems certain that she had the secret of that correction which is without offence, and was made welcome by the very persons whom she came to condemn by precept and example.

It should be remembered that the Missions and their

after-fruit had no official support from Church or State. Vincent de Paul was recognized as a power for good, but his earlier efforts were not backed by any of the impressive paraphernalia of established authority. Therefore Mlle. Le Gras depended on good-will for her reception and for her opportunity of usefulness, and therefore there was added to her labours—in themselves sufficiently arduous—the strain of cultivating the good opinion of those who were to aid her in her efforts. The tasks entrusted to her, which she seems to have grasped in all their many aspects, absorbed all her energies, and she overworked until her health broke down. She had undermined her strength when she was young, and had no reserve to meet an excessive claim. M. Vincent awoke to the risk that her zeal might defeat its object, and wrote her a charge that has in it a touch of the tender wisdom of François de Sales. It occurs in a letter of congratulation on her safe return from a visit of supervision to Beauvais in the depths of winter.

"Thanks be to God that you have arrived in good health," he says. "Now, for the love of God and of His poor, do your best to take care of it. The Devil has a trick of urging good servants to do more than they can that they may be unfitted to do anything. The Spirit of God leads us to do as much as we can do reasonably, that we may continue and persevere in it. When this is your method of working, mademoiselle, you will be working according to the Spirit of God."

Immense interests seem at that moment to have depended on her health. Her efforts to reanimate the spirit of charity that had been inspired by the Mission Priests serve to reveal the failure of the Confraternities as they originally stood. The bond of mutual service— the brotherhood recognized by the first Christians, which taught them to hold all things in common—was to have been their abiding inspiration. The idea of them was received with enthusiasm at the moment of a Mission, but, as a rule, before many months had passed, all tasks of neighbourly service slipped into the hands of the very few whose fervour survived the test of monotonous demand. Of these few each one was, in fact, a free-lance. The elected officers found it hard to enforce authority over voluntary workers when the faithlessness of the majority gave exaggerated value to any service. The chaotic result discovered in many districts may easily be imagined, and the reports brought to him must sometimes have taxed even the strong hopefulness of M. Vincent.

Mlle. Le Gras is responsible for the first practical suggestion of a remedy. In the Missions which M. Vincent's Company were preaching constantly it was not an unusual thing for a woman, who had been till then content to take life as it came and do her duty, to wake up to higher aspirations that were hard to translate into practice. The Missions were not intended for the rich, and this sort of response came from women who had been brought up to work for their living. Their response was not to a call to the religious life in the common acceptance of the term, but the Mission Priests recognized the call as that of a special vocation. And women such as these were welcomed by Mlle. Le Gras at her house in Paris, and employed among the poor whose daily needs had engrossed her own energies until M. Vincent summoned her elsewhere. It is not possible to discover at what point her mind began to foreshadow the future importance of that curious household she had gathered round her. Some of those who came were sent for their own sakes rather than for hers. Dawning capacities in them might depend on the encouragement and guidance they received at the outset, and to the true Mission Priest the development of the rough-mannered peasant-maid had the same importance as that of the keen-witted demoiselle of the Marais. At first the rule of daily life was that of a well-ordered and pious household, and those who came to Mlle. Le Gras came without any vast resolve of self-abnegation. It was a simple matter—the gathering of a few young women from different parts of the country who had in common that awakening to possibilities of service which the Mission Priests had inspired. Belonging to the working class, a life of labour came to them by nature; it was the special dedication of the labour that was to be the work of grace.

Some of the Confraternities had been in existence for a long time when Mlle. Le Gras first opened her doors to the future Servants of the Poor, and their organization and discipline in ideal was known. The employment of these humble colleagues of hers was therefore a matter of simple transition from an undefined position to a recognized one. The urgent need of the Hôtel-Dieu and the partial failure of the Ladies of Charity made just the claim on them for which they were prepared. Their aim was identical with that which had drawn the Ladies of Charity to their first endeavour; theirs was not the grudging service that is done for payment, but they were better equipped for attendance on the sick than their magnificent predecessors. Thus the Company of Servants of the Poor found their place as the natural agents of the Ladies of Charity in accordance with M. Vincent's theory that their existence and development was wrought directly by the Hand of God. In their joy at the greatness of their task, it was natural that the Sisters should aspire to an outward token of their vocation. They wished—and Mlle. Le Gras led them in the expression of the wish—to have the bond of a common vow, to be recognized as dedicated to God's service. Such a step as this was not to be taken hurriedly under M. Vincent's guidance. Never has there been a more consistent advocate of delay than he, and the foundation of the new Order was a fixed object of desire to Mlle. Le Gras before he would admit that it was a reasonable possibility. Her plan was to bind herself to the service of the Sisters, and then to let some time elapse before any of them were permitted to enter on any engagement of the nature of a vow. She was to be the pioneer and to bear the brunt of failure, should failure be ordained. She had a real wish to pledge herself, believing, one may conjecture, that a venture of faith was needed to give vitality to her scheme. The Servants of the Poor were already depending on her capacity to train and to direct them, and she believed that that capacity would be deepened if she herself was dedicated irrevocably to this form of service. M. Vincent, however, was not clear that her idea was of Divine prompting, and was unmoved by her insistence.

" As to this undertaking," he wrote to her, " once and for all I bid you not to think of it until Our Lord has made it very clear that He wishes it; for the present my leading is all against it. One may desire many things, good in themselves, they may seem desires that are according to the Will of God; nevertheless, they are not so always. God permits that this should be, that our spirit may be trained to accord with His desire. Saul sought a she-ass, he found a kingdom; S. Louis sought to conquer the Holy Land, he found how to conquer himself and to win the Crown of Heaven. You wish to be the servant of these poor maidens, and God would have you be His servant, and the servant, perhaps, of many more persons than you could be in this particular way. And when you are His only, is it not enough that your heart should be conformed to the peace of Our Saviour's Heart and wait in readiness to serve Him? The Kingdom of God is the peace of the Holy Spirit; it will abide in you if your heart is at peace."

We shall find that Mlle. Le Gras had been inspired by M. Vincent to the mystic's aspiration after the constant sense of the Presence of God. But once more he put her to a severe test when he checked her wishes in this matter. She believed that her zeal was of God's prompting, that He showed her what He required of her; it must have been extremely difficult to let the precious months go by while she awaited a summons more definite than that which she felt she had already. It was the second time that she had been required to submit to the extremities of M. Vincent's prudence. Possibly, by the discipline involved, she was fitted to be herself the director of others, and her scheme was ripened by just those denials that seemed to hinder it. His dealings with her are a striking instance of M. Vincent's detachment in direction. He had great respect for her judgment and reverence for her character. Eventually he came to agreement with her original opinion, yet he had no misgivings in ignoring it until he was convinced of God's guidance of himself. The demand he made on others was at all times and quite clearly made as God's agent. No personal knowledge of those with whom he was in contact made any difference to his message, and the confidence with which he delivered it was therefore not self-confidence. It is noticeable that he never expresses any regret for delaying the undertakings which eventually he approved. In 1634, on Lady Day, Mlle. Le Gras was permitted to take a vow, and was thenceforward dedicated to the Company of the Servants of the Poor; but the individual members were not allowed the same privilege till eight years later, and then it was extended only to a few. The contrast to the precipitate spirit of modern times is very remarkable.' In the twentieth century many leagues and societies for differing forms of service come into being, shoot into celebrity, and are completely forgotten in the period required by M. Vincent to assure himself that a new idea was approved by God.

The solid foundation of the Company owes as much, however, to the faith and determination of Mlle. Le Gras as to the prudence of M. Vincent. She realized the need for the Sisters, and she would not be discouraged in her scheme. They were very rough, some of them

MLLE. LE GRAS

of the most rugged peasant type. In early days one had to be sent away for beating another, and almost all of them required rigorous training in self-control; but difficulty spurred the zeal of their Superior, and if she could not get all that she desired of encouragement regarding the future from M. Vincent, she was secure of his practical help in the present. The first of the Servants of the Poor were very ignorant, and if they were to use their opportunities for instilling spiritual knowledge, it was necessary that they should possess the faith in so pure and simple a form that they could find words for it. His training of them took the form of " Conferences." He questioned them to begin with, and afterwards addressed them. This system, begun in early times, was continued during their experimental establishment at La Chapelle, and became a great feature of the life at the motherhouse when the new Company fixed itself in the Faubourg S. Lazare.* In the records of these " Conferences " we get some of the most intimate details of the relations of M. Vincent with the Sisters, and of his point of view towards many a difficult question of the spiritual life.

It will be easily understood that the Sisters needed all the help that could be given them. Their very existence was an innovation of a startling kind. To their generation devotion to God's service implied retirement behind high walls, and the attempt to give it a more practical form laid them open to misinterpretation. At the beginning Mlle. Le Gras records that they could not appear in the streets without risk of insult, and the tone of society generally gave support to those who held that women should be shielded from contact with life as it was.

For the Servants of the Poor there was no shelter from the contagion of sin save that which they erected and maintained for themselves. They were—according to

* In 1641. The mother-house was swept away in 1793. The Boulevard Magenta covers its site.

M. Vincent's well-known definition—"a Community who have no monastery but the houses of the sick, who have for cells only a lodging or the poorest room, whose chapel is the Parish Church, who have the streets for cloisters. They are enclosed only by obedience, they make the fear of God their *grille*, and they have no veil but their own modesty." He had very clear and practical knowledge of life in those streets which were to be their cloister, and experience in the guidance of others helped him to form a true conception of the difficulties a Sister of Charity would find in her vocation. From the earliest days of the Company, the life its members adopted was a very hard one. A Sister must rise at four in summer and winter alike, she must eat only sparingly, and of the plainest food, and was to drink no wine. Her duties as a sick nurse were of the most arduous and trying description. At a period when medical science had not yet adopted the methods of alleviating pain that are now ordinary, she was forced to witness every horror of suffering. Moreover, she breathed an infected atmosphere continually, and was exposed to constant danger of contagion. And as time went on the demands for the service of the Sisters became more and more insistent, and they seem constantly to have been overworked. In that last detail lies a part of their claim to be regarded as pilgrims on the Way of the Cross, and the physical weariness induced by long hours of labour dimmed to themselves the delight of their vocation. The Religious who mortified herself in the still seclusion of a cloister had her reward in a certain spiritual joy, but the Sister of Charity who combated the griefs of the outside world risked the dread experience of spiritual inertia, and therewith that reaction from self-suppression to intense desire which may make contact with the world so perilous.

"There is this difference between the Sister of Charity and a Religious," wrote M. Vincent after thirty years' knowledge of them, " that while for the Religious the one aim is the attainment of perfection for herself, the object of the Sister of Charity is the comfort and salvation of her neighbour."*

It is generally accepted that the life of the cloister has its own dangers known only to those who have adopted it. Not less is this the case with the woman dedicated to a life of service. The Rule as it was finally given to the Sisters of Charity demanded all the more—as M. Vincent himself attested—because it seemed to demand so little. It leaves no scope for any of the self-indulgences of piety, it requires that the little duties of a servant should be fulfilled day by day, and those obedient to it must recognize that they are set apart for rebuff rather than applause. The true Servant of the Poor must fix her gaze on a Light very far off; the joys of those to whom the contemplative vocation is accorded are not for her—indeed, her strenuous days need the inspiration of a faith too deeply rooted to be starved for lack of spiritual encouragement. Even the distinction of the dedicated life is not accorded to her. Her vow must be renewed every year; she may not rest in it with the security of consecration permitted to every Religious. Nothing, in fact, is left her for the fostering of self-esteem, and without real humility it is not possible that she should persevere.

The individual members of that first group had no high ideals for the future. They were simple people ready to do menial and arduous work without payment. Probably there were many in the earlier days who came and went away again, finding the test too hard. It was in July, 1634, that M. Vincent accorded to them the definite recognition of their life as a Community by recommending a preliminary Rule. Its chief provision is for the discipline of obedience. Wherever they worked in common, one must have authority, but the office of

* " Lettres," vol. ii., No. 550.

Superior was to be held by each in turn. In the early days the severity of the Rule depended on the amount of work to be accomplished; their work for others was the object of their lives, and hours of prayer and study were appointed with relation to its demands. At the beginning the figure of Marguerite Naseau stands out among these companions in labour as possessing in its purest form the spirit of devotion. In her girlhood she was seized with a desire to read herself and to instruct others. She seems to have taught herself by a method of patient questioning of all with whom she came in contact, and then to have journeyed from village to village trying to stir others to a desire for learning. She was heedless of physical hardship, and lived in constant fidelity to the service of her neighbour. M. Vincent found in her a finished model of the future Servants of the Poor, and she became—for the short time that her life lasted—the mainstay of her companions in service. She died, however, of the plague, caught from a patient she was nursing, before the new Community was recognized as having being.

But Marguerite Naseau was not a type. The task of Louise Le Gras would have presented little difficulty had there been many like her. The other recruits needed patient and continuous drilling, and their leader realized that all her hopes depended upon their response to training. M. Vincent realized it also. In his first " Conference "* he told them that they were bound, because they were the first chosen members of their Company, " to be irreproachable in conduct, and so set the example to all who might come after. When Solomon built the Temple of the Lord, did he not put precious stones into the foundation ? Sanctify yourselves, my daughters, that through you God may bless these beginnings."

The high ideal he set before them was inspiring, and

* July 31, 1634.

while they listened to him their spirits soared in sympathy with his; but in the wear and tear of daily life they sank to earth again, and Mlle. Le Gras was never free from the pressure of anxiety after she had once accepted the rôle of guide and teacher. The deep humility which was essential to the true Servant of the Poor has made the person of Louise Le Gras somewhat mysterious. As the Confraternities and her work in connection with them became more important, her advice was sought for so eagerly by those whose social position called them to hold authority, that it became necessary that she should hold in Paris meetings of ladies to whom she could give instruction, spiritual and practical. Her supervision in the provinces had, as we have noticed, tested and practised her in public speaking; but the woman-speaker—in days when her gift was not recognized as the common possession of both sexes—risked the development of a self-sufficiency inimical to the mental attitude required of a Sister of Vincent de Paul. Louise Le Gras could hold the minds of her listeners, and she must have reached a high spiritual level before she made her first essay in oratory if she escaped excitement as her power declared itself. There is no record of misgiving on her part, or caution on that of M. Vincent, and her immunity in this is doubtless due to the qualities that made her the ideal Superior for the Working Sisters. She had a capacity for prayer that brought her to the borderland of the true mysticism, and her passionate love of Christ made her snatch every moment that could be spared from duty, that in contemplation she might grow to nearer knowledge of Him. By her own experience she learnt that more was needed than the fervour of philanthropy to give the Sisters courage for their tasks.

In certain reflections that she wrote for them she may seem merely to be expressing the aphorisms of the devout life in simple language, yet to have read and accepted all that her words imply would equip the most faltering against the buffets of their difficult experience. "If you aspire to perfection, you must learn to die to self. Those words, my Sisters, contain tremendous meaning. Why may I not write them with my blood, or leave them to you in letters of gold? You must die to self, which means that you must destroy those impulses that come from your own capacities of soul or body, for they may conflict with the design of the Holy Spirit upon you.

"Try to preserve a quiet mind and a heart at peace amid all the painful chances that may occur. Make it your custom to accept all your little discomforts as from the Hand of God. He is your Father, and knows so well what is best for you. Sometimes you feel His Touch— to check or punish you; and sometimes to show you His great love by permitting your sufferings to give you a share in the merit of His Son.

"The lack of outward human help will serve to bring you nearer to the perfection of Divine Love, and will gain for you the special guidance of God. Do you know what He does to a soul that is deprived of all human comfort and support, if she has courage to profit by it? It is His pleasure to lead such a soul, and, though she may not be conscious of it, she may none the less be sure that, if she clings to Him with entire confidence, He will support her with His own Hand, and will never let her sink beneath the burden of her misery."*

These are not vague spiritual rhapsodies, they are definite instructions believed by their writer to be necessary for the training of the Sisters. There was to be no reserve. M. Vincent in one of his earlier "Conferences" asked them if they were ready "to go wherever obedience required them to go, without regard to their country or their friends, or to any thought of distance,"†

* "Pensées," chap. vi., liv. v. See Gobillon, "Vie de Mlle. Le Gras."
† "Conferences," No. 10, January, 1643.

and they had replied with one accord that they were ready for any order whatever it might be. Indifference as to the scene of their labour was symbolic of the deeper indifference Louise Le Gras required of herself and them. The immolation of self was to be real; the Sister of Charity might find herself in spiritual as well as actual loneliness, and she must not repine because she seemed to be exiled from all that fed or encouraged the growth of her inward life. When we reflect that the original inspiration of her self-sacrifice came from devotion to the Church, and that her perseverance was ordinarily due to suggestion and example, we can measure the severity of the discipline that left her in an unknown country town with perhaps one uncongenial companion, and no adequate spiritual guidance within reach. But a trial of this sort (part of the ordinary lot of a Sister of Charity) must be accepted as bestowed by the Hand of God. "He is your Father, and knows so well what is best for you," and she who has died to self must be able to resign herself completely to His Will.

The demands made on the Sisters by their Superior and by M. Vincent are always logical; but, if they seem sometimes a little inhuman, it is well to remember the knowledge and the tolerance that lay behind these counsels of perfection. The Sister of Charity might be denied all fulfilment of desire, but she was first trained to accept denial; and however great the space of time and distance that divided her from the Mother-House she knew that, so long as she remained faithful, she had the prayers and the silent sympathy of her Sisters there, and was doing her part in the service they had all accepted. It was this sense of corporate life that was the great support of the isolated unit, and, as the Company increased, their need of a bond stronger than that of a common aspiration became apparent. Louise Le Gras was pledged by a solemn vow to dedicate herself to the Company (every month she set apart a time of thanksgiving to God for this special privilege), and it was inevitable that the Sisters who aspired to a reflection of her spirit should be insistent in their demand to share it with her. The time came at length when M. Vincent encouraged a chosen few to give this outward proof of self-surrender. He was apprehensive of an attempt to make the Company into a new Religious Order, and never wearied of reminding them that they were not Religious; nevertheless, their need for the support of the threefold vow could not be denied, and on March 25, 1642, they were allowed to take it, on the understanding that they were bound by it for one year only.

"I, the undersigned, in the Presence of God, renew the promises of my baptism, and make the vow of poverty, of chastity, and of obedience to the Venerable Superior-General of the Priests of the Mission in the Company of the Sisters of Charity, that I may bind myself all this year to the service, bodily and spiritual, of the poor and sick—our masters. And this by the aid of God, which I ask through His Son Jesus Crucified, and through the prayers of the Holy Virgin."

Such was the purport of the bond accepted by the first four members of the Company, and before many years had passed it was the rule that every Daughter of M. Vincent must subscribe to it, for equality was as the alphabet of their education. Their real establishment dates, therefore, from Lady Day, 1642; their progress afterwards was the natural growth and development of the root that had been planted, and M. Vincent no longer felt himself bound to check it, for he saw that the need for them and their capacity to fulfil the need had been proved beyond dispute. In 1645, at the earnest wish of Mlle. Le Gras, he drew up a letter to the Archbishop of Paris asking that the Company might be formally recognized as an Order, " because labour in God's service ends with those who give it, unless there is some spiritual bond between all those who are thus engaged." And with their recognition he asked for sanction of the Rule that they were keeping and of their annual vow.

There was no opposition to the establishment of the Company with the full Archiepiscopal approval; they had no rivals and no enemies. Nevertheless, affairs moved slowly, and ten years passed before the Royal Letters Patent was accorded. During that ten years M. Vincent altered his mind regarding a very important point on which he and Mlle. Le Gras were not agreed. He had asked that the Sisters should be under episcopal authority; to her view their hope of stability depended on their direction by the Mission Priests. M. Vincent's humility was in all likelihood responsible for his original decision, but the fear that it would take effect was a continual tax on the faith of Mlle. Le Gras. In the ten years of suspense she did all that lay in her power to show the unity that existed between the two Companies, and the loss to the Sisters if they were formally divided. The wars of the Fronde raged over their heads, the Church in Paris was distracted by the disputes over the episcopal authority, Princes and Princesses were driven into exile, and the Italian Cardinal lost and resumed his dominion over France; but the Sisters worked on steadily, and their Superior, though she was torn with misgivings and anxieties as to her own fitness for her task, never slackened her prayers that the disaster with which their Founder seemed to threaten the Company—a disaster more terrible to her than any national calamity—might be averted.

At the eleventh hour M. Vincent yielded. Jean François de Gondi was in exile at Rome, but he was Archbishop of Paris, and he was ready to accord any boon to Vincent de Paul. In 1654 a new application was made, and in January, 1655, Letters Patent were issued to the Sisters of the Poor, sanctioned by Church and Crown, and placing them in perpetuity under the authority of the Mission Priests. The petitions of Mlle. Le Gras were changed into thanksgivings.

CHAPTER II

THE RULE OF THE SISTERS OF CHARITY

WE have seen the gradual degrees by which the Company of Sisters of Charity advanced to their position as a great institution. Collectively and individually they were to live in the spirit of humility and of obedience. M. Vincent himself is the best exponent of such a vocation; he knew its privilege and its difficulty, and when—in simple language—he summed it up for the benefit of one novice whose heart was failing her, he was expressing the lesson needed by all alike.

"I beseech you, Mademoiselle," he wrote, "reflect for a little on the Son of God, Who came down to earth not only to save us by His death, but that He might submit Himself to the Will of His Father, and draw us to Him by His example. If you will consider Our Blessed Saviour, Mademoiselle, you will see how ceaselessly He suffered, how He prayed, how He laboured, and how He obeyed. If you live after the flesh—S. Paul tells us—you die; and if you would live after the Spirit that gives life, you must live as Our Lord lived, and that is to say, deny yourself, do the will of another rather than your own, make good use of every difficulty, and prefer suffering to satisfaction. 'Is it not needful that the Christ should suffer these things?' He said to His disciples when they spoke of His Passion, and by that He shows us that as He came to His glory only by the way of affliction we may not hope to ascend without suffering."*

To pray, to labour, and to obey, was the whole duty of

* "Lettres," vol. ii., No. 431, June, 1658.

THE RULE OF THE SISTERS OF CHARITY

a Sister of Charity; and M. Vincent, while exhorting them never to aspire to equality with a Religious, reminded them constantly that their life was the closest imitation to that of Christ which was possible to a woman, for it was spent in travelling from place to place that they might heal the sick and comfort the despairing. Mlle. Le Gras, from her standpoint of close personal association, urged on them chiefly the necessity of charity among themselves. "You must love each other," she told them, "as Sisters whom Jesus Christ has united by His love, and you should try to understand that because God has chosen you and placed you together to do Him one special service, you must be as one body governed by a single will, and must regard each other only as different members of the same body."

The impression of the Company of Sisters of Charity left on us after study of the "Conferences" of the Founders is an inspiring one; we seem to be in sight of the fulfilment of a magnificent hope, but the reality was not as fine as the ideal. Great courage, sustained self-denial, pure and unquestioning faith—these qualities were to be found among the first Sisters of Charity, and not a few laid down their lives in the service of others. It would be easy, without departing from the truth, to draw a picture of them that would glitter with the glory of good works, and be free from any blots or shadows; but it would not be possible to see them in relation to M. Vincent and Louise Le Gras, and omit the deformities of their common life. For, indeed, M. Vincent never gives deeper proof of his knowledge of human nature than in his dealings with the Sisters of Charity. He might exhort them to the highest flights of aspiration, but he did not expect them to be perfect, and he was less disappointed than was Mlle. Le Gras when they gave proof of the weakness of human nature. There were so many possibilities of failure inseparable from their condition in that period of experiment. Organization and

Rule were not adjusted, and causes of disagreement might very easily arise; two or three women, drawn from different provinces and often from differing grades of society, and placed in close association in a country town to which all were strangers, were not likely to uphold the principle of brotherly love without a struggle. It is clear that frequently there were lamentable outbreaks of ill-temper; we find the proofs of it among M. Vincent's letters, for when a crisis was approaching appeal was always made to him. No instance of his intervention is more characteristic than a letter addressed to the Sisters at Nantes, a settlement where difficulties of many kinds were always present. Rumour, or perhaps clear testimony, seems to have accused the Sisters of conduct notably unworthy of their vocation, but the Superior-General does not approach them with any violence of reprimand.

"Continue to grow nearer to perfection, my dear Sisters," it is thus that he addresses them. "Consider the sanctity of your condition as truly the Daughters of God. It is so wonderful that human understanding can conceive nothing greater for a poor earthly creature.

"It seems to me, my dear Sisters, that here you reply that this is what you desire to do, but that you are disturbed by an infinity of temptations which overwhelm you. To which I answer that all these temptations are sent to you, or are permitted for you by God, for the same reason that they were sent or permitted to His Son —that He might have opportunity to give proof of His infinite love of His Father.

"'Yes,' you say, 'but it does not seem to me that all the other righteous souls in the world or in religion have the inward suffering that I have." Thereon I answer that there are no souls on earth who profess to have given themselves to God and to His creatures who do not bear trials outward and inward equal to yours, for it is God's

Will—not against, but in favour of righteous souls—that all whoever they be shall suffer temptations.

" And you answer, my dear Sisters: ' Bah! they may be tempted sometimes, but to be tempted always and everywhere, and by everyone with whom I am forced to live, this it is which is unbearable!' It is the good pleasure of God that the chosen souls who are so dear to Him should be tempted and afflicted daily. This is what He shows us when He says in the Gospel that those who would come after Him must deny themselves, and take up their cross —that is to say, must suffer—daily. Weigh that word *daily*, my dear Sisters.

" ' I will bear anything from outside persons willingly, Monsieur,' you say, ' but that it should be from my own Sisters, from those who should help me, but who are nothing but a care and a cross and a distress in all they do, and all they leave undone.' Alas! from whom should we suffer if not from those amongst whom we live? Did not Our Lord suffer from His Apostles, His disciples, and the people among whom He lived who were God's people?

" ' As to that,' you answer, ' I am better able to put up with the distress that is due to my Sisters than when it comes from the Sister in Charge. Her coldness, her harshness, her silence, the fact that she never says a gentle word to me, and if she does say anything it is only something severe or irritating—it is this which I find I cannot bear, and which drives me to seek consolation from those of my Sisters who suffer the same distress; it is this which causes me to talk as much as I can to my Confessor, and to tell my troubles to people outside.' To which I can only say, my dear Sisters, that we are poor weaklings if we must needs be flattered by our Superiors in all they say or order, and that instead of a Daughter of Charity seeking softness, she should feel that if the Sister in Charge humours her she is being treated as a child or an invalid. Our Lord led His own with severity, and sometimes even with hard words ... and He foretold for them nothing but the evils and trials that were to come. And yet—though that was so—we desire to be flattered by our Superiors, and we withdraw from them (as did the wretch who betrayed Our Lord) to make a party with other malcontents and with our Confessors! Oh, my very dear Sisters, may God preserve us from this!

"If you have not fallen into this miserable condition, I give thanks to God; but if you have so fallen, here are the means to rise out of it by the help of God:

"1. To devote your prayer three or four times to what I have said.

"2. Each of you shall confess to M. N. every fault in this connection of which you have been guilty, not only since your last confession, but also since your coming to Nantes, and shall resolve to accept the counsel he gives you and to follow it.

"3. After the Holy Communion you shall all kiss and ask pardon of each other.

"4. For a year your prayer shall once a month be devoted to this subject.

"5. You shall not follow inclination in choosing the Sisters with whom to hold intercourse, but those who attract you shall be avoided in favour of others.

"6. You shall not speak to your Confessor outside the Confessional unless it be one or two words for absolute necessity, following in this the rule of the other Sisters of our house in Paris with their Confessors at S. Lazare.

"7. You shall—each separately—write to me the thoughts Our Lord has given you.

"8. The Superior shall write to Mlle. Le Gras every month touching the progress of her family.

"Here, my dear Sisters, are my poor thoughts on your reason for praising God for your vocation, for persevering in it and perfecting it, and also a summary of those faults into which a Daughter of Charity might fall in a new settlement and the method for remedy.

THE RULE OF THE SISTERS OF CHARITY 235

" I ask you in all humility to accept what I have said to you for the love of Our Lord Jesus Christ."*

The Sisters at Nantes, however great the degree of their misdoing, were privileged; they were given direct touch with the mind of their Founder, and it becomes—by reason of his dealing with them—more possible to understand how he maintained the original spirit in his two great Companies in spite of their rapid growth. Probably there had been serious failure, and chattering tongues were busy with the proceedings of this new-fangled Order. There was opportunity for righteous wrath, for sharp severity. But instead there comes this letter from M. Vincent, with its suggestion of the true ideal, its graphic outline of the evil of short-coming, its homely recommendation for reform. It is a summary of his policy and of his spirit; sympathetic understanding and the most practical common sense are here, and withal that thirst for the imitation of Christ which was the secret of his energy of service.

Spiritually and practically it was a necessity that the charity of the Sisters should be an interior virtue; it was not sufficient that they should tend the sick and feed the hungry. It was magnificent that so many of them found the courage to brave peril and face death without flinching, but it was necessary that they all should also possess endurance of the weaknesses of others. Only a few were martyrs to their vocation, but all who accepted it were Sisters of Charity. One of the Articles of their Rule in its final form reminds them of the title (more familiar to their generation than to ours) of Daughters of Charity, and exhorts them to think often of it, and to be worthy of it. In one of his "Conferences"† on the Rule M. Vincent dwells especially on this with full comprehension of all that was involved:

" Is there, indeed, a title more honourable than that

* " Lettres," vol. i., No. 109, April, 1647.
† No. 86, March, 1658.

of a Daughter of Charity?" he asks. "Could any name be found approaching it in honour? No, my Daughters, and you never will hear of one more glorious. For, in fact, what do we mean by a Daughter of Charity? Nothing else than a Daughter of God. Oh, my Sisters, what a reason to yield yourself entirely to God, that you may be worthy of so noble a name!

"I do not know if you have ever fully considered the three things which are implied in this Rule. The first is love of God above all else, to be His altogether, to love nothing except Him, and if one does love anything else that it should be out of love of Him. If you love God thus it is the first mark of a true Daughter of Charity who really loves her Father. The second is love of our neighbours, to give real service to the poor; and when there is difficulty in so doing to force oneself to give it, that being the purpose for which one has given oneself to God. The poor must be regarded as lords and masters, and spoken of with deep respect; therein lies the second mark of a true Daughter of Charity. The third point is that you should never be at variance among yourselves to the degree of never allowing a single spiteful thought to rise up between you. Directly such thoughts rise up they must be stifled, my Daughters, and if, nevertheless, they still come back, you must be particular in disowning and rejecting them until such time as God shall give you grace to escape from your evil inclination. Be careful, also, to say nothing that can anger your Sister, nor hurt her, unless you do so officially, for officials not only may, but must, rebuke, even when they see they will rouse resentment. It would be a strange thing to see a surgeon not daring to use his lancet because a patient disliked the operation! And not less so if a Superior or an official dared not speak for fear a Sister should not take it in good part.

"And beware, my Daughters, for it will not do to listen to this which I am saying with indifference; it is a thing in which you have a special charge from God, and which you must force yourselves to practise. Otherwise, you will not be true Daughters of Charity; you will only be so in name and in dress. And as the saying goes, 'The cowl does not make the monk.'"

The lesson was extremely difficult to learn, and M. Vincent was obliged to elaborate and to insist, for he held that it was absolutely necessary for them to learn it. In another " Conference "* two months later he comes back to the same subject even more forcibly: " The very moment that you feel a little sense of antagonism, or that you see that one of your Sisters is slipping out of the friendliness that should prevail among you, let her know at once that it is so, and say to her with all the warmth that is in you: ' My Sister, if you only knew how I love you, and how greatly I desire to be friends with you! Oh, believe that it is with all my heart, and as God has required of me; love me as I love you, I beseech you.' If the Sister does not accept what you say the first time, tell her that you love her again, and God may grant that she will change. 'Ah, but, Monsieur,' say you, 'I do not feel like that in my heart, and it would be hard to tell her so.' Never mind, say it just the same, for it is the evil in your nature that makes it hard, and the Devil uses this evil to prevent you from loving each other.

" Be careful to be worthy of the name you bear, so that it shall not be said of you as to the man of the Apocalypse: 'Thou hast the name of living, and art dead.' You are Daughters of Charity; you bear this glorious name, and there is hate amongst you! You are false to it, then, for charity and hate cannot go together! Oh, my Daughters, offer yourself to God, that you may be made worthy of this name you bear. Say to yourself: ' It is true that my Sister annoys me, but I must put up with her because it is God Who bids me do so.' Say to yourself also: ' It is possible that I annoy her equally,

* No. 87, May 30, 1658.

and that it is more difficult for her to bear with me than for me to bear with her.' "

Let us picture the Sisters gathered together on a Sunday afternoon for the weekly " Conference," sitting with downcast eyes while M. Vincent, in this homely way of his, puts into words the half-formed remonstrance in their minds, or depicted in plain language the unacknowledged facts of their daily life. There was no escaping him; he assuredly was not of the race of surgeons who dare not use the lancet because the patient dreads the operation. Yet they could not have loved him more had he been less severe, and now and again, as he enlarged upon their Rule and illustrated special ways in which the breaking of it was to be apprehended, one of his hearers would humbly make acknowledgment that in just this way she had offended. In this there was an entire absence of sensationalism. Self-accusation of this kind was accepted calmly by M. Vincent, and by some mysterious method the fault immediately became his own. No details of the lives of these Daughters of his was too small to claim his attention. No one understood the difficulties so well as he did, nor the danger of that dread monotony which undermines and slays the enthusiasm of an impulsive nature; but we get glimpses of the individuality of his correspondents from his letters to them, and sometimes it is plain that they were very difficult people to deal with.

" You say that you have shed many tears, and made prayers, and kept novenas," he wrote to one of them; " all that is to the good. Our Lord said that the blessed are those who weep, and that those who ask receive. He did not say, however, that our prayers will be granted immediately, because He desires that we should go on praying. Therefore, my Sister, you must not allow yourself to say that the more you pray the less you get, for it betrays that you are not yet resigned to the Will of God, and do not confide yourself sufficiently to His promises. Often He is more gracious to us in His refusal of what we ask of Him than He would be in the granting of it, and we must be certain that what He sends us is the best, because He knows better than we do what is good for us, even though we dislike it, and all our hopes are disappointed.

" Ah, my Sister, how deeply I sympathize with you in your troubles, and how I pity our poor Sister Anne weighed down by discontent! But, surely, it is a trial which, as you say, God allows to test you! Accept it, therefore, as from the hand of your Father, and try to make good use of it. Help your Sister to carry her cross, as yours is a little lighter, reminding her that she is a Daughter of Charity, and that she should be ready to be crucified with Our Lord, and to submit to His pleasure, if she is not going to be utterly unworthy of Our Father.

" She should not—neither should you—be so much put about because the hospital is not well organized nor sufficiently provided for. You must do your best yourselves in the service of the poor, and leave the rest to the goodness of God.

" You are wrong in blaming Mademoiselle (Le Gras) for your troubles, and in resolving not to write to her again because you are not pleased with her letters, also in holding her responsible for the selection of you two instead of others, for it is solely due to the Providence of God that you are placed where you are. This you will realize when, for the love of God, you are obedient to your Superiors, and learn to think only of Him when you are given orders."*

As the sentences unfold themselves, the outlines of the mutinous Sister of Charity grows clearer—hating her work and the place where she is sent to do it, distrustful of her prayers because they bring no satisfaction to her rebellious wishes, bitterly angry with the Superior who had assigned her post to her. If the spirit of the Religious

* " Lettres," vol. ii., No. 441, August, 1658.

was in any way inculcated among the Sisters of Charity—and assuredly it was so—here was a case for uncompromising severity. Yet M. Vincent, though his gentleness hides here and there a little irony, could hardly be more gentle. No one, in truth, in all his immense and scattered family needs his compassion more than does this very discontented Sister—for had she not lost the joy of serving, which was the sole but satisfying treasure of all the Company of Mission Priests and all the Daughters of Charity?—and if by sympathy he might restore it to her it was not in him to withhold his sympathy, however serious her offence.

In circumstances such as these his tolerance and charity may have reconciled many a fretful soul to the lot that demanded sacrifice; but though in one direction he gives proof of his exceeding gentleness, in another we find him absolutely rigid in decision. It must always be remembered that the vow of the Sisters of Charity was taken annually, and did not involve the life-long dedication of the Religious. Each year on Lady Day they were renewed, and every Sister who renewed her vow did so by permission of the Superior. This regulation necessarily placed a Sister on an altogether different footing from that of a nun, but it is obvious that the Sisterhood must have declined rapidly if those that entered it had not regarded their renunciation of the world as being permanent. For five years they were tested before being recognized as fully trained and responsible Sisters; after that time their service was regarded as part of the established strength of the community. But it happened that some, even after long testing and association, did take advantage of the open door and return to the world. Mlle. Le Gras never got over the intense distress which these defections caused her. Sometimes there was an epidemic of desertion, and to her it may have seemed that if such a spirit could find acceptance by a few, there was no reason to hope for any limit on the spreading of it. But M. Vincent

THE RULE OF THE SISTERS OF CHARITY 241

did not share her apprehension. In his opinion all this wonderful growth of self-devotion which went on around him proceeded from the direct influence of Christ Himself on human souls, and any check therein was the concern of the invisible Head, and need not dismay his adjutants.

"You take the departure of your Daughters rather too much to heart," he wrote to her. "In the Name of God, Mademoiselle, try to acquire grace to accept these occurrences. Our Lord shows His mercy to the Company in purging it after this manner, and this will be one of the first things that He will reveal to you in Heaven. You must be quite certain that none of those whom Our Lord has really summoned into the Company will fail in her vocation. Why should you trouble about the others? Let them go; we shall not lack for Daughters."*

He was not, it must be owned, as tolerant of desertion among his Mission Priests, for the difference between the broken vow of the one class of defaulter and the broken purpose of the other seemed to him very material. And he had one rule to which he adhered unfalteringly. Neither Lazarist nor Sister of Charity who had once denied their vocation should ever be received again. He commiserated the despair which sometimes overwhelmed them when they discovered what they had done, but their repudiation once made was made for ever. There were many who, as he once told his listeners at a "Conference,"† "were incessant in their petitions through M. So-and-So and Mme. So-and-So to be received again." But in this matter he was relentless; the door that they closed behind them when they went forth could never again be opened.

It was necessary that the cloister, "built not of stone but of free will," should be thus defended; the escaped nun had no hope of support or protection from any but heretics, but no outward stigma rested on the renegade Sister of Charity: her penalty was the perpetuation of

* February, 1653.   † No. 42, July, 1652.

her self-chosen freedom. The only safeguard with which M. Vincent could provide the faithful Sisters was a reminder of their high vocation. " My Daughters, to my thinking you need greater perfection than a Religious," he said to them. " ' Eh, how can this be ?' you ask. ' How is it possible for us to need greater perfection than a Religious ?' For this reason: The aspirations of each one of us must be in proportion to the grace received from God. Now has any Religious ever received from God favours that equalled yours ? No; no one has been called to anything so great, and by such means as you have been called, and therefore God requires higher perfection from you than He does from them. You, my Sisters, serve those who are brought to you, and those whom you must seek. It can truly be said of you, as of the Apostles, that you go from one place to another, and that just as they were sent by Our Lord, so are you also in His Name by order of your Superiors, to the end that you should do what Our Lord Himself did upon earth. O my Daughters, if this is the call to you, realize how greatly you need to seek perfection."*

In the boldness of that recommendation we have a glimpse of the strength of M. Vincent. In those days the working nun was unheard of: " *Qui dit religieuse dit un cloître.*" It was tacitly admitted that the inhabitants of the innumerable monasteries were not so concentrated upon spiritual things as their profession and their garb implied, and the many splendid efforts at reform had been the means of directing public attention to the abuses that made such efforts necessary. Nevertheless the pious still cherished their ideal of the consecrated life, separated from contact with the world and devoted to prayer, and therefore M. Vincent's assertion that the Daughters of Charity were more highly favoured than the orthodox Religious was in defiance of public opinion; and many of them, in the performance of their daily

* "Conferences," No. 63, November, 1655.

THE RULE OF THE SISTERS OF CHARITY 243

duties, were by their own admission the prey of continual temptation. Their humble origin made the life of the streets attractive. Those who came from the country required superhuman self-control not to look about them as they hurried to and fro on their errands of mercy, but they were required to keep their eyes downcast, and to notice nothing. Vincent came to their "Conference" one day smiling and exultant. A gentleman had just left him, he told them, who had said: " Monsieur, I have seen two of your Daughters to-day; one of them carried a basket, and the other a bowl of soup for the sick. So great was the modesty of one of them that she never so much as lifted her eyes."

It would be very easy to prove the absurdity of such an exaggeration of self-repression, but undoubtedly for the accomplishment of M. Vincent's purpose it was the only way. Once permit the least distraction, and this dangerous experiment of his must have ended in utter failure, and the Sisters themselves were the first to admit that it was so. One of them, Sister Marguerite Laurence, acknowledged at one of their " Conferences "* that when she passed a troupe of mountebanks or a peep-show in the street, the desire to go and look was so strong that she had to press her crucifix against her heart, and repeat over and over again: " O Jesus, Thou art worth it all."

It was on the rock of simplicity such as this that the Company was founded, but even that virtue has its attendant failing, and it is easy to understand that the actions of Sister Marguerite Laurence and her compeers sometimes betokened undeveloped judgment. When the many demands for service necessitated that the Sisters should be scattered by twos and threes at great distances from each other, the task of directing them became a very anxious one. There is ample testimony to this fact in the letters of Mlle. le Gras and of M. Vincent. Small schemes were embarked upon without authority; accounts

* No. 5, August, 1640.

were confused because there was no method of keeping them; one Sister made an excursion to Orleans from Angers without leave; another journeyed to a place where a pious gentleman was dying, because she thought he might be induced to make a legacy to the poor. " The intention may have been praiseworthy," commented M. Vincent, " but the act was not permissible in one who has consecrated herself to God under a rule of obedience." Another Sister constantly makes little visits and little pilgrimages, and will not ask permission of her Superior. It was infinitely difficult to deal with such infractions of the Rule when distances were great, and means of communication very uncertain. The irregularity that the labours of the Sisters often necessitated increased the obstacles to direction, and Mlle. Le Gras was tortured by her misgivings as to the future conduct of her flock. It was fortunate for her that M. Vincent shared her burden, and reassured her by his cheerful acceptance of it. He did not lower his standard because his Daughters fell so far short of it : his " Conferences " at the Mother-House maintained their exalted level, but he knew the material out of which the Sisters of the Poor were being formed, and that the weaknesses inherent in their class did not vanish at the magic touch of their vocation. Moreover, though his faith in the Divine guidance of the new Company was absolute, he would have regarded its downfall as the Will of God no less than its success, and was convinced that human wisdom and experience could do very little to avert catastrophe.

The idea of separating the Sisters from the Mission Priests, and placing them under episcopal authority, was the outcome of M. Vincent's certainty that the Company was independent of his control; it was a species of independence to which he wished them to aspire both as individuals and as a Company; the human element which he thought had too great a place in their desire to be directed by the Lazarists was to be eliminated; they were

THE RULE OF THE SISTERS OF CHARITY

not to rely upon any particular Society, but completely upon God.

We have seen that the prayers and desires of Mlle. Le Gras overruled his intentions in this matter, but he never varied in requiring of the Sisters a conscious realization that the guidance of their lives must be Divine.

"Spiritual direction is of extreme value, it is true, my Sister," he wrote to one of them to whom it was denied; "it is an opportunity of receiving counsel in difficulty, and comfort when we are discouraged; it is a refuge from temptation, a support against despair—when the director is prudent and experienced it is, indeed, an infinite source of help and consolation. But do you realize that it is just where the help of man fails us that the help of God begins? It is He Who teaches us, Who strengthens us, Who is everything to us, and Who draws us to Himself. If He does not give you a spiritual father to whom you can turn in every difficulty, do you suppose He intends to deprive you of the benefit of such direction? By no means; it is Our Lord Himself who fills the vacant place, and of His infinite goodness directs you Himself."[*]

It was not easy for an isolated Sister of Charity at a difficult post to regard her deprivation as a benefit, but for all his gentleness M. Vincent had no wish to make life easy. Not only was he severe in his requirements, but his severity was of the most searching kind; he knew the intimate dangers of the life of piety, and had grasped some of the contradictions of a woman's character, therefore he intended to keep his Daughters out of reach of the snares that would surely be prepared for them.

"The Daughters of Charity must go wherever they are needed," he said in one of the "Conferences"[†] on their Rule, "but this obligation exposes them to many temptations, and therefore they have special need of strictness."

It was inevitable that they should be separated for long periods from the Mother-House, and they were scattered

[*] "Lettres," vol. i., No. 150.   [†] No. 75, October, 1659.

in such small detachments that it was hard to maintain the sense of Community life. Their possibility of loneliness had its own dangers, and with untiring insistence M. Vincent reiterates his warnings to them on the danger of any misuse of confession. The moment they found themselves seeking for sympathy, or tempted to pour out the distresses of their daily life, they must watch themselves carefully. Confession was a statement of sin, not of grievances. They went to the confessor appointed to them under obedience, and his individuality ought to be a matter of indifference.

"'But,' says someone, 'he is the kind of person who repels me!' But has his method done you harm, and has he not power to absolve you of your sins when you confess to him ? What more do you want ? Have you anything to do with him besides telling him your sins ? Do you expect him to relieve you of all your troubles ? Ah, my Sisters, you have no business to tell him about them; it is enough to confess your sins."*

If we go carefully through the series of "Conferences," the evidence of M. Vincent's astonishing knowledge accumulates. In these dialogues, which were often a part of his discourse, there is nothing mechanical; the phrase has the ring of individuality as if he had gleaned it from the lips of one or another of the Sisters. If any of them were ever tempted to resentment at his severity, they could not say that he was hard on them because he did not understand their difficulties; there can have been little in their lives that he did not understand, but he meant their sacrifice to have complete reality. Among their Rules was one that suggested they should deny themselves any satisfaction in the memory of enjoyment that had been theirs before they renounced the world, the pleasures of youth, the suggestions of marriage. Another required them to silence any expressions of gratitude from the sick whom they were tending, remem-

* "Conferences," No. 89, June, 1648.

THE RULE OF THE SISTERS OF CHARITY

bering that they were in very truth *servants* of the poor. (Mlle. Le Gras related with delight that one of the Sisters had been severely beaten by a patient, and had accepted this treatment uncomplainingly.) When they were ill themselves they were not to accept any luxuries that were not bestowed upon the poor even to gratify benevolent persons. They were never to receive reward for anything. They were never to pay a visit that was not part of their duty to the poor. They were never to receive a visit under any circumstances. Except under pressure of special necessity they were never to stand talking in the street, nor at the door of their own dwelling, nor in the houses of the poor, except in fulfilment of their duty. They must never go out without leave, and must report themselves to their Superior immediately on their return. They must not send or receive letters under seal except to their Superiors. And they must not ask to be permitted special indulgences of piety, to be admitted to Communion more frequently than others, to practise abstinence or some form of mortification that set them apart from their Sisters.

Surely there was clear evidence of that which is not human in the lives of these women. M. Vincent constantly averred it was so, but M. Vincent, with all his knowledge, was himself so far riveted on thoughts of Heaven, that he could not grasp the full difficulty of renouncing earth. The ladies of the Court tore themselves from folly and excitement, and gave themselves to God at Val de Grace or at Port Royal. Before them was the prospect of a life of devotion, sombre and austere enough, but surrounded with the dignity of great tradition, and inspired by the majestic ceremonial of the Church; and behind them was the torture and fever and passion of the years that had brought them to seek safety in the cloister. Their experience is indeed almost as old as Christianity itself. But the Daughters of the Poor came from a humble existence of ordinary labour and small, unexalted amusements to a service of unbroken hardship, and to them there was not permitted any form of sensuous gratification whatever, no sentimental rapture, no delight of the imagination.

" 'What, Monsieur?' cries someone—'what is this you tell me? Do you ask me to be my own enemy, to be for ever denying myself, to do everything I have no wish to do, to destroy self altogether?' Yes, my Sister, and unless you do so, you will be slipping back in the way of righteousness. 'Ah, but, Monsieur, it is so difficult to be always denying oneself.' Ah, yes, my Sister, but there is no avoiding it, for you must know that you have to make the choice either to live like an animal or to live like a reasoning being. To live like an animal you need only follow where passion and inclination lead, but if you are to live as a Christian, you must labour perpetually to deny yourself."*

So M. Vincent—simplest yet most austere of teachers—set forth the choice that must be made by all alike; and those who shrank before it might not aspire to be numbered among his children.

* "Conferences," vol. ii., No. 71, 1657.

CHAPTER III

M. VINCENT AND HIS DAUGHTERS

IT is only by following M. Vincent in his guidance of the Sisters of Charity that we can understand how they gained their position in France and in other countries with such rapidity. We are not regarding the development of a fine organization to meet an obvious need. The finest organization could not have found means to provide for some of the claims that were met by the Sisters. Dangerous and often revolting work was to be done, and, if the worker accomplished it without forfeit of life or health, there was no reward save that of appointment to some other task; even the barren satisfaction of personal credit was not to be allowed her.

"Observe, my Daughters," said M. Vincent, "that perfection does not depend on the multiplicity of one's work, but in doing it in the spirit that Our Lord did His. That is the root of true saintliness. Do everything you do well and in accordance with your vocation. The saintliness of a Daughter of Charity rests on faithful adherence to the Rule—I say *faithful* adherence—on faithful service to the nameless poor, in love and charity and pity, on faithful obedience to the doctor's orders; and on fulfilling all practices, both outward and spiritual, with the intention of acquiring those virtues which God has shown to be the spirit of the Company. It keeps us humble to be quite ordinary. It is right to desire to be better and more virtuous than anyone else, but to desire to appear so is vanity. Therefore I beseech you to be regular in virtue, but all the time regard yourself as worse than any of the others, believing that you do nothing of the slightest value."

The stirring of human pity, however sincere, the sense of duty, however deep, would not have been motives strong enough to keep a Sister of Charity at her task. Something that was not human was required, and it was the spark of the supernatural quiescent in these peasant women which M. Vincent was permitted to quicken and to sustain. It is awe-inspiring to consider how many heroic lives were spent—under that rigid Rule of his—in the daily drudgery of parish nursing, and in the struggle to maintain order in provincial hospitals. Such lives won little approbation, and seldom escaped criticism, and when their span was reached, they passed away unnoticed. The fact of them is among the strongest testimonies to the supernatural. "For the greater honour of Our Lord, their Master and Patron, the Sisters of Charity shall have in everything they do a definite intention to please Him, and shall try to conform their life to His, especially in His poverty, His humility, His gentleness, His simplicity and austerity." So runs a part of their Rule, and it suggests the key to the power that was in them, for if the Sister of Charity was seeking only the service of her neighbour, her resolution snapped beneath the strain; it was needful to hold before her that other deeply mysterious motive, "the honour of Our Lord, her Master and Patron."

In those early days of the Company, there were some special instances of devotion that stand out. For instance, after the siege of Arras in 1656, the inhabitants were left in so miserable a condition that some benevolent person implored Mlle. Le Gras to send help. Two only of the Sisters could be spared, and for them there was the utmost difficulty in obtaining shelter or daily bread. Disease and famine had done deadly work among the poorer folk, dirt and neglect of the most revolting kind prevailed. The work of eight parishes was on their hands, and at first they had to struggle with the overwhelming demands for their services without any assistance from the town authorities. Yet one of the two, having reported in a letter to Mlle. Le Gras how the other was sometimes obliged to cease working by reason of complete exhaustion, added: " I have never throughout heard a word of complaint fall from her lips or seen her face betray anything but the most serene content."

A little later, in 1658, after the French forces had encountered those of Spain in the battle *des Dunes*, there were 600 French soldiers, sick and wounded in the hospitals at Calais. Anne of Austria had accompanied the young King to the seat of war, and was so moved by the horrors of their condition that she sent to demand six of the Sisters from M. Vincent. Even to the Queen it was not possible to supply more than four, and considering the character and reputation of the soldiery in those days, there was opportunity for grave objection to sending any.

But the faith of M. Vincent soared above misgivings. " My Sisters, you are invited a hundred leagues away in one direction, forty leagues in another, sixty in another," he reminded them, ' and now the Queen has asked that you shall go to Calais to tend the wounded. How greatly is God blessing us ! Men take each other's lives and destroy each other's souls, and you are called to go and restore both. . . . I know that, by the grace of God, there are many among you who ask only to be told where they shall go. My dear Daughters, be sure that wherever you go God will take care of you. Even when you are in the midst of the army, have no fear that any harm will come to you."*

The Sisters obeyed the call readily, but the horrors that awaited them were indescribable, and—as was so constantly the case—their numbers were quite inadequate to the need. The conditions of the hospital at

* "Conferences," No. 49, June, 1658.

Calais had resulted in the outbreak of an infectious malady, of which the soldiers were dying by scores. Two of the Sisters caught it and died, and it was plain that no one could breathe the atmosphere of the wards without danger to life. M. Vincent read a report of the state of affairs to an assembly at the Mother-House. The result was a rush of volunteers. The worst horrors of an Army hospital awaited them, and they as nurses knew what such horrors were: there was the certainty of overwork and hardship, and the probability of death or of that permanent injury to health that makes life a burden; yet four more were sent, and all were eager to go. Sixteen years had passed since the first Sisters of Charity took their vows. The increase of their numbers had been very rapid, but the deepening of reality in them was even more remarkable. Not one of these volunteers would have been allowed to enjoy any token of admiration that might be offered to her if she survived her service to the soldiers. All that awaited her was return to the Mother-House, and reabsorption in the ranks of her fellow-workers. What she did she did without reward and without credit, " for the greater honour of Our Lord, her Master and Patron."

It is hard at the present day to understand all that was needed of them. It would not now be possible for suffering to continue unalleviated if money and good-will for its relief were forthcoming. But before the work of Mlle. Le Gras and of the Confraternities it was difficult for a rich lady—however benevolent—to make adequate provision for the sick on her estates. The small hospitals, that at an earlier period had been founded by pious persons in many of the smaller towns, had become useless from lack of supervision; in the homes of the people but little attention was paid to cleanliness; the most ordinary remedies were difficult to obtain, and there was small chance of recovery from serious illness. For maternity cases, it is true, a married woman was appointed for every parish; but the vacancy was made known from the pulpit, and the applicants were interviewed and the appointment made by the curé. The explanation of this system tells its own tale: so large a proportion of infants died a few hours after birth, that a chief qualification for a parish nurse was soundness in the faith, that their baptism might never be omitted.

It is easy to see that the great ladies of the period did well to remain in Paris or to be oblivious of their neighbours when they were in the country, unless they were proof against distress at the sufferings of others, for neglect and ignorance had gone too far to be combated in the intervals of a life of pleasure. The infection of benevolence spread rapidly, however, when the means of exerting it were discovered, and Mlle. Le Gras was overwhelmed by applications from the owners of great estates for Nursing Sisters to attend upon the poor. Only a proportion of such requests could be complied with, and many a small settlement begun in those early years of the Company, was sustained for a short time only; some because there was urgent need of Sisters at some other centre, and many more because the lady patronesses wearied of a novelty that was a drain upon their purses, and withdrew the modest sum required for maintenance. Here and there such work as this was of lasting benefit, but the great mission of the Sisters in the provinces was the reform of the hospitals. The work of the Confraternities was always closely connected with the hospitals; the tending of the sick in their own homes presented insurmountable difficulties when the very necessitous and degraded class was touched; but the hospitals in many places were so disorganized as to be useless, and had reached a stage when no amateur efforts could restore them to their original purpose. The remedy was an application to Mlle. Le Gras. Until her strength failed she went herself to readjust the methods that had prevailed and had been found wanting, and, when it was needed, to conciliate the authorities. She and her Sisters carried with them, in addition to their rules for the restoration of health, a new standard of personal life and of relation with the poor. The towns where need of hospital reform was recognized profited by their presence beyond the precincts of the hospital, and undoubtedly the Nursing Sisters did much to spread the spirit of M. Vincent's teaching in parts of the country where he was himself a stranger. The method pursued at Angers, the first of the hospitals placed in their charge, was typical of their work elsewhere, and though the form of abuse they discovered differed in different places, a fundamental readjustment was always a necessity. At Angers (a foundation due to the penitence of Henry II. at the murder of Thomas à Becket) the administration of the Augustinian monks had brought charity and religion into equal disrepute. At all periods pious Founders have recognized that sickness of body leads to a desire for spiritual health, and the priest was as closely connected with a hospital as the doctor. The Augustinians at Angers were, however, so unfit for their office, that the townspeople united in a petition, addressed to the King in Council, that they should be removed from it and replaced by secular priests to be chosen by the Bishop. Among those who were intimate with the affairs of the diocese were some who had made a Retreat at S. Lazare, who knew M. Vincent, and had heard of Mlle. Le Gras. The possibility of carrying out the practical and the spiritual reformation of the hospital simultaneously was suggested by remembrance of the new Company and its objects, and a petition for help was despatched to M. Vincent. This was in 1639, before any of the Sisters had taken vows, and the responsibility of a commission at such a distance was felt to be very great. Mlle. Le Gras left Paris with an advance-guard of two Sisters in November. The journey occupied fourteen days, and for some time after her arrival she was ill from fatigue. It was not until February that the reorganization was complete and the Sisters formally instated. Their Rule* (which is still in existence as drawn up by Mlle. Le Gras) declares " that they come to Angers for the honour of Our Lord, Father of the poor, and of His Holy Mother, and for the service, bodily and spiritual, of the sick at the Hôtel-Dieu." It requires that they shall live with the pure intention of pleasing God in all things, in absolute poverty, and in the most careful management of all that is provided for the poor as being the property of God; that they shall make their Communion each Sunday and hear Mass daily, reserve one half-hour for prayer in the morning and another in the evening. They were to rise at four every morning, be constant in care of their patients throughout the day, attempting whenever possible to teach them spiritually, as well as to tend them bodily. Those on night duty were to make their watching a time of prayer, but to remember that their duty to the sick came before anything else, and might be regarded as a part of their prayer.

This Rule was read every Friday, and it will be seen that adherence to it meant a claim on every hour of life. In framing it Mlle. Le Gras must have considered what complete renunciation it involved, and no doubt intended that the Sisters should understand from the beginning what lay before them. Nevertheless, when the time came for her return to Paris, she cannot have left them without misgiving as to their steadfastness. Much depended—at Angers and in all the other little colonies which year by year sprang up—on the capacity of the Superior. Mlle. Le Gras had a lively sense of the responsibility of those to whom authority was given. She bade them remember that the virtue of humility—so necessary to them all—must specially be studied by a Superior. She was to be known as the Serving Sister, and because

* "Lettres," vol. i., No. 42.

Providence had confided to her the guidance of others, she must show herself first in charity and always ready in their service. She should show herself gentle in intercourse with them, remembering that their delight in thinking of themselves as Servants of the Poor did not make it easy for them to take orders that were given sharply or unkindly. It should be the custom of the Serving Sister to ask rather than to command, to lead by example, to be ready with help and advice in small difficulties. Authority should be used in the spirit of charity, not in that of despotism. "And if we call ourselves Serving Sisters," she said, "it should mean that we bear the heaviest burdens in soul and body, and are to relieve our Sisters in any way we can, for they will always have a great deal to bear from us, whether by reason of our bad temper, or owing to a dislike of us with which Satan may tempt them. And if there be something that should need rebuke, we must give it in the spirit of charity at a convenient time, and not with any haste or possibility of prejudice."*

This was wise teaching, and the prosperity of the small companies of Sisters on their outpost duty depended on adherence to it. It was necessary that the Rule of obedience should be absolute, but the plight of a Sister of Charity serving at a long distance from the Mother-House under a Superior who was also an autocrat would have been most miserable. They were not women of refinement or with any tradition of good manners, the beauty of their lives, their gentleness to one another, was the gift of grace, and if the spirit of their vocation was lost or even overshadowed, they had no safeguards from misrule and mutiny. The amount of work that they accomplished—though their record is magnificent— is not so great a marvel as the fact of their continued growth, when all common likelihood suggests necessity of failure. In Paris every new scheme for the assistance

* See Gobillon, " Vie de Mlle. Le Gras."

M. VINCENT AND HIS DAUGHTERS 257

of the poor made a demand upon the Company—either for service or supervision. The Charity of the Hôtel-Dieu and of the Foundlings was entrusted to them. They were called upon to tend the miserable convicts waiting for deportation to Marseilles. When the Institution for the Aged (known as *Le Nom de Jesus*) came into being, they were responsible for maintaining its high standard of order and good government. But though these tasks were serious and responsible, they could all be performed by persons in close touch with the Mother-House and with S. Lazare. It was the work at a distance that laid on the Superior so heavy a burden of anxiety. Louise Le Gras was at all times afflicted by dark forebodings. M. Vincent's letters to her are full of suggestions of encouragement with regard to her personal affairs and the welfare of her son, as well as with reference to the Company; and without his support she could not have continued in her arduous office, for, to a woman of her temperament, the suffering involved by the continual sense of the possibilities of disaster was very severe. It was she who had the fullest knowledge of the material with which she had to deal, and of the circumstances involving danger, and it required lively faith to keep her mind at peace.

She is a pathetic figure despite—or perhaps because of —her great achievements, and in the later period of her life she is overshadowed, not only by M. Vincent, but by the array of Working Sisters, with their record of tasks fulfilled and dangers braved. Ill-health made life a burden, and the sense of demands that were quite beyond possibility of fulfilment robbed her of any satisfaction in her enterprise. There were no consciously fortunate years in her career. As a girl her great desire for the religious life had been thwarted; as a wife she was torn betwixt the sense of duty and regret for the conditions she had missed; and when at length God made His Will plain to her, obedience taxed her powers to their farthest limit. There does not seem to have been for her a moment when recognition from others or personal realization of success suggested self-importance. She was, indeed, less prominent after she had proved her powers than before. Perhaps the truest knowledge we can attain of the personality that was as the mainspring of that growing Company comes from the little collection of her Meditations in which she has set down her standard of conduct for herself, and for those who might truly be reckoned as her Sisters.

It is likely that after Mlle. Le Gras found herself the Superior of the Servants of the Poor, the point of view from which she had regarded life gradually altered. From the letters of her directors at an earlier period we grasp her as scrupulous and over-anxious, concentrated on the progress of her own soul and ingenious in self-torment. But she was brought into contact with the great world of human beings; she was forced to be a witness of their suffering and to have knowledge of their sin; she had constant intercourse with the rich as well as with the destitute, and became familiar with the differing temptations assailing each, and as a consequence her anxiety about herself fell into abeyance. The Servants of the Poor as they gathered round her became, indeed, her Daughters; she trembled for them in danger, suffered with them in hardship, and mourned—more deeply than they were able to mourn for themselves—over their failures and their sins. And thus she became—to a degree at least—merged in the being of the Company, and saturated with the spirit of humility which was its strength. The great desire and distress that, as we have seen, possessed her thoughts for years, concerned the Company, and when her prayers were answered, and she had secured for it the guidance she felt to be essential to its future welfare, she had no anxiety as to the methods of her own successor. At any moment she was ready to lay down authority, and there is no reason to doubt her sincerity when, time after time, she lays the blame of failure or desertion on her own maladministration. If we follow the record of the Company during her lifetime with any care, we must acknowledge not only that she used her power wisely, but that an immense amount of power lay in her hands and increased as the years passed. Among women-leaders in philanthropy there is not one to whom the world owes so much, but, because she was more than a philanthropist, she assumed less and less of personal prominence as her actual power grew. The real life of the Servant of the Poor must be a hidden one, she must have no self-assertion, above all she must never be self-confident. In the last passage of the Meditations, already referred to, we find her summing-up of the lesson of life :

"We have no knowledge of our way except we follow Jesus, always working and always suffering. And, again, He could never have led us unless His own resolve had taken Him as far as death on the Cross. Consider, then, whether we do well to spare ourselves, lest we lose whatever we have gained hitherto. When we have laboured forty-nine years, if we have relaxed in the fiftieth, and it is then that God calls us, the whole of life will have availed nothing."*

We meet here a sternness of regard that is suggestive of Port Royal rather than of that law of love which we connect with M. Vincent. But M. Vincent's softness was never towards himself, and Louise Le Gras owed her training to him; to some degree he had shared the fruit of his own experience with her. It is only those who have followed far along that difficult path where Christ is guide who reach the point where any relaxation of resolve implies denial of their Leader.

Mlle. Le Gras died in 1660, six months before M. Vincent, and therefore had the comfort of knowing that the affairs of the Company would be well ordered when her

* "Pensées," liv. v., chap. viii.

own guidance was removed; but the consolation of his presence as the last hour drew near was not allowed her. She endured a lingering illness without once seeing him, and it is said that the written word of encouragement which she implored that he should send her was denied. Towards weaklings he was all tenderness, but he knew that she was strong, and so left her in the Hands of the Master to Whose service she had given herself.

CHAPTER IV

THE LADIES OF CHARITY

THERE are many indications that—for actual work—whether as Nursing Sisters or as Mission Priests in country districts, M. Vincent considered the lower and middle class as the most useful. The Sister of Charity would be better able to whisper a word of advice or exhortation to those whom she attended if, by experience, she understood their point of view. The Mission Priest could stir the hearts of his hearers to more real purpose if he had actual knowledge of their trend of thought. " The best are those who really have the same nature as the villagers," said the Superior-General; " there are none more full of faith or who turn more readily to God in their time of need or hour of gratitude."

The Servants and Priests of the Poor were, therefore, according to the original desire of M. Vincent, to be, for the most part, humble persons not very widely separated by condition from those they served, but his intention of thus limiting them does not imply that he ignored the immense force that lay outside such limits; had he done so, his work would have been disastrously hampered. The period was one in which exaggerations of excitement and self-indulgence led directly to the extreme of reaction in practices of piety. The history of Port Royal furnishes many notable examples. The unflinching sincerity of the Port Royalists caught the imagination of an age when that virtue had fallen into disuse, and it was the reality of its asceticism that made its suspected doctrines so dangerous to orthodoxy. M. Vincent was vigorous in his condemnation of Port Royal, but he would not have denied that there was some element purer than mere excitement in the penitence of the heroines of the Fronde or in the renunciation of the lawyers and scholars who became the Hermits of Port Royal. In fact, the infection of spiritual aspiration that was responsible for the *Cabale des Dévots* was betraying its presence by many differing methods, and without its influence M. Vincent could not have maintained much of the work that was dearest to his heart. Money was an absolute necessity to him, and money cannot be obtained unless the springs of self-sacrifice are touched; but gifts of money are at best only the most elementary expression of spiritual awakening, and if M. Vincent's power with his high-placed contemporaries had been confined to the unloosing of their purse-strings, his connection with them would hardly merit record. In fact, the external generosity which he had the gift of inspiring was only a very small part of his effectiveness, although the traces of his dealings with individuals are not easy to disentangle.

Class distinctions at that time were very decided, and certain confusions did not lessen the division. The daughters of Colbert, in the later years of Louis XIV., married into the proudest houses in the realm; so—far less worthily—did the nephew and nieces of Cardinal Mazarin. At the Hôtel Rambouillet Princes and Dukes consorted with scribblers of humble origin, and considered that they were levelling society; but, in fact, the condescension which began in the Society of the Précieuses and continued amid the explosions of the Fronde had not the least effect in lessening the gulfs of division. The noble was only the more conscious of his nobility because he was magnanimous enough to recognize the existence of persons whom he had formerly ignored. The established customs of the time were all in favour of maintaining him on an exalted level. On his own estate he would have squires and pages, gentlemen-at-arms, a company

THE LADIES OF CHARITY

of guards, an endless retinue of servants. Among all these persons he was supreme, as the King was supreme in his Court. At table he and his lady would occupy armchairs, while his guests and relations sat on stools. If he went out, a bell was rung, and his suite lined the hall when he passed through, and followed at a respectful distance when he took exercise. As may be imagined, the whole welfare of the neighbourhood fluctuated with his coming and going. If he was cruel and a despot, his tenants trembled until the delights of the capital or the excitement of a war once more claimed him; if he was generous, they profited by his presence. The whole tendency was to teach him to look on himself as of different texture to ordinary human nature. Even in church he was privileged, for he took precedence in a religious procession, and could claim the first presentation of incense or of holy water.*

M. Vincent accepted the world as he found it. He had been a dependent in a great man's house, and was not less vigorous in his practice of the teaching of Christ because he breathed an atmosphere so antagonistic to its observance. And while he did homage, as was demanded of him, to the outward adornments of nobility, one may conjecture that he was all the time seeking for the real being behind the artificial trappings. It is significant that M. de Gondi—a representative type of the most superb of the courtiers of that day—spent his last years in complete retirement as an Oratorian. There are other instances of the same species of revulsion which may be linked with the personality of M. Vincent. As Mère Angélique, in her stern self-renunciation, seemed, from the shadowy cloisters of Port Royal, to arraign her contemporaries, so did M. Vincent, in his attempt to live the Christian life with direct simplicity, disturb the satisfied assurance of those with whom he came in con-

* Babeau, "Le Village sous l'Ancien Régime," and "Supplément aux Mémoires de Maximilien de Béthune, Duc de Sully."

tact. If, as a parish priest of humble origin, he had become engaged in large schemes of philanthropy, he would have been hampered by his ignorance of the real characteristics of the great folk with whom common interests brought him into contact; but his ten years with the de Gondi provided him with just that necessary external knowledge without which interior insight would have been impossible. A score of years lived within half a mile of the Luxembourg or the Marais Quarters might not have revealed even a faint reflection of what life meant to the high-born inhabitants of the great *hôtels;* they were of another race and of another world, and the Founder of the Company of Mission Priests and of the Sisters of the Poor had work enough to do for his generation without heeding them. But the mission of Vincent de Paul was not only to the poor; his own choice would have set that limit upon it, but he was not guided by his own choice. It is quite impossible to gauge the extent of his influence, but it is clear that for the thirty-five years during which he was a well-known figure in Paris he represented—all the more vigorously because there was about him no element of the picturesque—the power of religion on a human life. The demonstration that, simply and unconsciously, he was giving day by day drew men to him, not only the humble, but those whose traditions were completely different from his own, and the response of understanding was constantly required of him; and it was in the time of training, against which he had rebelled, that he had been taught to understand. He could be almost as severe with the wealthy women, whose work for others he had inspired, as with the Sisters of Charity, but it was his knowledge of their temptations and their inherent feebleness that made his severity so effective.

He did not mingle with the circle gathered round Mme. de Rambouillet, nor with the crowd that centred a little later on the rising sun of Royalty; but though his actual presence might be wanting, there was no condition of life and no grade of society at that time in Paris that was altogether untouched by the fact of his existence. One incident, lying entirely outside the orderly development of project and fulfilment, brings him into connection with the romance of those glowing days, and suggests how great a part he may have played in unrecorded drama. There was plenty of evidence to the strength of human passions; they swayed the fortunes of the State, and of necessity disturbed the peace of the most tranquil salon, but testimony to an opposing power was not so common. Vincent de Paul was a silent witness, but in the midst of clamour such silence appeals to the imagination more than eloquence. One instance of the power put into his hands must be recorded.

Among the brilliant group, of which Mme. de Longueville was the leader, there were numbered two sisters, daughters of M. de Vigean. The younger, Anne, contrived eventually to become Duchesse de Richelieu, and developed into an extremely clever woman of the world; but Marthe, her elder, eclipsed her in those early days, and was the most admired of all their circle. The young lady of quality at that period was trained for the winning of matrimonial prizes, and the esteem of her contemporaries depended on her success. Marthe de Vigean was pre-eminently fitted for a triumph of this kind, and her favours were the more coveted because she was known to have inspired Condé, the hero of the nation, with the great passion of his life. He was married, and she was both virtuous and prudent, therefore their connection cast a halo of romance about her career without disturbing it.* She was an acknowledged beauty, and it could

* *Cf.* lines by Voiture on Marthe de Vigean :

"Sans savoir ce que c'est qu'amour
Ses beaux yeux le mettent au jour
Et partout elle le fait naître
Sans le connaître."

truly be said of her that she had the world at her feet, and needed only to choose the form of glory that would please her most.

It chanced, however, that her mother, Mme. la Marquise, fell ill, and that M. Vincent came to visit her. At the end of his visit the eldest daughter of the house accompanied him to the door. It is not difficult to picture them descending the great staircase side by side, the girl radiant with youth and beauty, the natural possessor of the best of this world's gifts, and the priest in his shabby cassock, ugly and ungainly in his appearance, and with none of those graces of speech and manner that won popularity for the ecclesiastics of the salons. Probably there was no attempt at conversation between them; but before they parted M. Vincent had a message to deliver:

"Mademoiselle," he said, "you were not intended for the world."

Marthe de Vigean understood his meaning with a gasp of apprehension. She protested eagerly that she had not the faintest inclination for the religious life, and besought him not to pray that she should discover a vocation; but M. Vincent would give her no assurance, he went away in silence. For a time she continued to be a favourite in a society that had for her no taint of dulness. One very desirable marriage was suggested to her—other offers were certain. Two years passed before she gave her family any warning of what was in her mind, but before the end of the third year from M. Vincent's visit the doors of the Carmelite Convent in the Rue S. Jacques had closed upon her.*

M. Vincent's connection with her destiny can only have been known from the lips of Mlle. de Vigean herself, and we cannot trace the process by which that sudden warning of his ultimately bore fruit. It was not his

* For full details of this incident, see Victor Cousin's "Madame de Longueville," vol. i., note to chap. ii.

mission to go about the world gathering recruits for religious houses, and the detail of Mlle. de Vigean's experience was probably isolated; but, though it may have been to her only that he presented the supreme decision between the cloister and the world, the sight of him must have suggested to many a thoughtless pleasure-lover that a choice betwixt two masters must some day be made, and consideration of it might claim reflection.

The fate of Marthe de Vigean may inspire many minds with repugnance. That a young and charming woman should stamp out every natural desire and check the development of all the talents with which God endowed her may be regarded as a matter for infinite regret and a course which reason could not justify. There are innumerable arguments against such a choice as hers, there is only one in its favour; but M. Vincent, as he found his way back through the squalid streets that separate the Louvre from S. Lazare, would not have recognized that the fair young girl he had just left had any true possibility of choice as to the future. We must remember how closely and continuously he touched the problem of the world's miseries and inequalities, and that that problem cannot be met by those who adhere to accepted standards. A complete subversion of established ideas is necessary to the merciful man who sees life as it really is. M. Vincent believed that the one hope for the world was the realization of the Presence of Christ; his efforts for the temporal welfare of his fellows were all subordinate to his desire to give them understanding of the gift that only awaited their acceptance. It is easy to see, therefore, that the glittering prospects of a Court beauty would have no weight in the balance against the possibility that God was calling her to a life of painful fellowship with Him. In such a connection the language of mysticism was for M. Vincent the language of the plainest common sense; it was clear to him that he who would save his life must lose it, and therefore that the only prayer possible on behalf of Marthe de Vigean was that she might turn from the riches and pleasures of the world and obey God's summons without flinching.

The necessity of obedience to the claim for sacrifice has its most dramatic example in her story, but as a principle it rules all M. Vincent's dealing with himself and others. He was relentless in his searching demands on the members of the two Companies, believing that their only hope of peace lay in complete surrender, and we find that with such of the Ladies of Charity as showed themselves worthy of the name they had assumed he was hardly less insistent. It was not a small matter to be one of M. Vincent's Ladies of Charity. In early days it is likely that neither he nor they realized what an important step was taken by those who enlisted in that band. The field of philanthropy was unexplored, and the needs in all directions were so stupendous that the only course for a really prudent person was to ignore the thought of them entirely. But these Ladies were in their way as remarkable as the Servants of the Poor, and one great factor in their development was the enormous difficulty with which they had to contend. They had no tradition to help them, nor could they avail themselves of the experience of others, yet all the characteristics of the undeserving were present among many of those they desired to aid.

There had been a persistent endeavour on the part of State authority to cope with the evil of drunkenness. " What the men earn in the week they spend on Sundays in the tavern, while their wives and children are left to starve," so runs a village record in 1576;* and forty years before that date François I. issued an edict which condemned any man proved to be intoxicated to punishment of increasing severity until at the fourth offence he was deprived of his ears and banished. The measures prescribed were sufficiently drastic, but, as an old writer

* Quoted by Babeau, " Le Village sous l'Ancien Régime."

sapiently observes, " when a Sovereign makes a law of any kind it would be well that he should discover beforehand whether he has any chance of enforcing it," and the futility of the decree in question is proved by the prevalence a century later of the vice it strove to check. A very familiar difficulty was therefore presented constantly to the Ladies of Charity by the encouragement given to the drunkard by the assistance of the drunkard's family. The indiscriminate method by which former generations had administered charity had, moreover, encouraged the habit of idleness. The distribution of food from convent steps or at a rich man's gateway was the simple and obvious form of obedience to the teaching of the Gospels, and the founding and support of hospitals supplemented the provision for the active poor by affording to them a refuge in time of sickness. In theory the position was unassailable; but, as we have seen, the maladministration of the hospitals rendered them practically useless, and the daily doles of food supported sturdy beggars, who should have laboured for their bread, and did not reach the starving.

During the forty years which M. Vincent devoted to labour for the poor there were periods of abnormal distress which would have taxed the ingenuity of the most experienced of philanthropic leaders, but apart from these the difficulties that had to be met were very serious. The poor were there—in constant need of bodily and spiritual assistance—and all the old plans of providing for them seemed to have collapsed. The Ladies whom he had stirred to sympathy must have looked back with regret to days when it was possible to entrust alms-giving to the parish priest, knowing him to be the friend and leader of his flock. It will be seen that it was not only in spiritual matters that the degradation of the clergy affected the people. The astonishing system of bestowing the emoluments of a cure on a person who did not accept its responsibilities had destroyed the old relations of the curé and his flock. The ill-paid deputy, who owed his post to a condition of disorder, became himself disorderly. He was continually at strife on his own behalf, and was therefore no longer able to be arbitrator in the differences of others; he was often the slave of those sins against which it was his duty to warn his people, and was as eager a gambler as any of the tavern ne'er-do-wells. It was not to such as he that the bounty of the rich could be entrusted, if it was ever to be of service to the poor.

The Confraternities in the country and the Ladies of Charity in Paris had to create a system, and to work it out themselves; they had to face the fact that they were likely to make very serious mistakes, and that the onlookers who thought their attempts absurd would jeer at all their blunders, small and great. It was, moreover, extremely difficult for them to decide on a reasonable limit to their labours or to their gifts; more service and more money were needed than it was possible to give. With M. Vincent as their leader the drawing towards sacrifice might be gradual, but it was persistent. When once light had penetrated to a soul, he considered that response to it must never stop, and the obvious difficulties that hamper the advance of the wealthy were not, in his eyes, worthy of consideration.

"Nothing so alienates us from the Spirit of God as to live the life of the world," he said, in addressing an assembly at the house of Mme. d'Aiguillon. "The more one has of luxury, the less one is worthy of the indwelling of Christ. The Ladies of Charity must shun the atmosphere of the world as they would shun air that is tainted. They must show that they have chosen the side of God and of Charity; they must show definitely that they have done so, for those who are willing to remain ever so little on the other side are able to destroy everything. God will not accept a divided heart; He requires all—yes, He requires all."

We have seen that no allowance was made for the weaknesses of the *dévote*, and M. Vincent had as little tolerance for the harmless follies of the leisured class. A lady in whose company he chanced to find himself for a period of ten days showed so many symptoms of extreme melancholy that he was moved to ask her the reason of her grief. He found that it proceeded from the death of her dog, and in relating the experience* he inveighs against the vacancy of mind that could make such sorrow possible. It is quite plain that those who submitted to him at all were not allowed to reserve for themselves any sheltered territory of indulgence, that he was jealous of the completeness of an offering made to God; but the real dedication of a life lived in the world is so rare that the identity of some of those who achieved it is worth discovering. The Ladies of Charity were for the most part of the class that can command the indulgence of every whim; they lived in an age when women were attaining prominence in all directions, and excitement and variety were never lacking. Chief among them was Mme. la Duchesse d'Aiguillon, the niece of Richelieu.† After two years of wedded life she was widowed at eighteen. It was open to her to make a second marriage on a magnificent scale. She had great natural charm, great wealth, and, as the favourite of her uncle, was a desirable bride for an ambitious man; but she decided to remain single, and was immovable in her resolution. It is impossible to estimate the extent of the debt owed to her by the charitable organizations that were springing up in all directions. Not only did she display the greatest sagacity in the ordering of schemes of relief, but the magnificence of her generosity made it possible to put theories into practice. Her own personality, as well as the reflection of her uncle's glory, had made her a celebrated figure, and it is possible that at the outset the prestige of her presence among them won many recruits for the Ladies of Charity.

* Conferences," No. 64, June, 1656.
† She married Antoine de Combalet in 1622, and received her duchy in 1638.

Hardly less notable was Mme. de Miramion. The story of her abduction by Bussy de Rabutin, Grand Prior of France, had furnished most satisfying food for the chatterers, and that incident had a certain bearing on the work of M. Vincent. She also was a young widow, and she was strong enough to withstand and to defeat Bussy; but any charm the world had retained for her was dispelled by her violent contact with the manners of the period, and, like Louise Le Gras (to whose influence much of her development was due), she gave herself to a life of devotion and of good works. She was not as wealthy as Mme. d'Aiguillon, but she was not less generous, and she did not recognize the outward claims upon her time which the niece of Cardinal Richelieu could not escape. She might have proved the ideal of a Lady of Charity, and set a standard by which newcomers might form themselves. She missed this consummation, however, and the reason of her falling short is worthy of remark. It should always be remembered that those who were imbued with M. Vincent's spirit gave their service to the poor because they recognized a law of love, and were able to find Christ Himself in the degraded outcast whom they strove to succour; it was not in any way a means to an end. But Mme. de Miramion was a visionary, and at all times her own spiritual condition was a matter of more urgent anxiety to her than the amelioration of the miseries of the poor. She accomplished a vast amount of charitable work in the course of her long life, but its accomplishment was not the faithful fulfilment of tasks entrusted to her by the Council of Ladies. She was the inspired Foundress rather than the loyal follower; she left her mark on her generation, but she is an isolated being struggling after personal perfection rather than one of a company battling for others. The difference is of the same nature as that which divides the contemplative from the Sister of Charity, and the Church admittedly has need of each.

Madame de Miramion.

THE LADIES OF CHARITY

The strongest collective aid received by M. Vincent came from the legal and parliamentary class. The first President of the Ladies of Charity (and the foundress of those assemblies of deliberation which probably were the first ladies' committees that ever existed), was Mme. Goussaulte. Her husband had borne the office of President in the *Parlement*, and she and her most intimate colleague, Mme. de Herse, were associated with the busy practical side of city life. It was she who had compelled M. Vincent's interference in the affairs of the Hôtel-Dieu, and she was the confidential supporter of Mlle. Le Gras, who could turn to her and her circle of intimate friends in matters that were not sufficiently weighty to demand the attention of a great lady of the Court. It is unnecessary to attempt to apportion credit betwixt the nobility and the members of that great middle class whose force was then beginning to assert itself; the movement had need of both, but the Magistrates' Ladies were at least as ardent in their service as Mme. de Condé or Mme. de Liancourt. Undoubtedly they all looked to M. Vincent for their inspiration, but there was nothing enervating in his method of dealing with them. He desired their help and valued it, but he had no arts by which to draw them into the practice of self-sacrifice. It was his own uncompromising reality that stirred them, the honesty of purpose that takes for granted a corresponding honesty in others.

At first their Assemblies were held at S. Lazare, but it is likely that the crowd of waiting carriages and lackeys were an inconvenience at the headquarters of the Mission Priests, and the plan of meeting at the house of one or another of the group was adopted. One may imagine that the Citizen Ladies were touched to an excitement that was quite independent of their good work when they were summoned by Mme. d'Aiguillon to the Luxembourg Quarter and felt around them the aroma of the Court. In the Rue des Bernardins, where Mme. de Miramion was hostess, they would touch a note of exalted piety that echoed through the most practical detail of their undertakings; but possibly for real business they preferred the more familiar surroundings of the Rue Pavée, under the roof of Mme. la Présidente de Herse. M. Vincent was generally present at their conferences, but it was not his custom to pay any visits to individuals; he made this a rule, and only infringed it on some very urgent demand of illness. His strictness in such matters was exaggerated, and he never relaxed it even for Mlle. Le Gras, but the strength of his position towards his Ladies of Charity was undoubtedly increased by the fact of it. He regarded them as united for the service of God, and he guided them in their labours collectively. We have seen that they needed at times both restraint and exhortation. A new enterprise will sometimes appeal to the imagination when zeal for an old one is flagging, and these ladies were pioneers, and had not discovered their limitations. It was not easy to understand that every piece of successful work was a claim on their resources in the future, and an addition to their burden of responsibility; that, in fact, no one of their undertakings was possible to complete, but that each had a tendency to increase in its demand. Probably no other generation could provide an instance of sustained and united benevolence that could be compared to that of the Ladies of Charity; nevertheless, they could not completely be relied upon. It had needed a vigorous remonstrance from M. Vincent to prevent the abandonment of the Foundlings, and there were hours of stress when Louise Le Gras was in despair for lack of the funds which the Ladies had promised, but did not supply. There were periods when an infection of heedlessness spread among them. The Sisters of Charity had no alternative to the doing of duty. If they shirked it, they had no facilities for amusing themselves; but the Ladies were in reach of all the excitements of life, and occasionally there were signs of reaction which threatened to compromise all the labour of the dedicated workers. There were also

THE LADIES OF CHARITY 275

the times of national distress when money was very hard to find, and the majority had no thoughts to spare from personal anxieties. These were the crises when M. Vincent showed his real power. In 1649, when circumstances had combined to exile him from Paris, there seemed good reason to believe that all the organizations he had founded—for the love of God and in the service of the poor—would be abandoned. The pinch of poverty was touching the wealthy class, and the destitution among the ordinarily poor was appalling. The usual expedient of assembling all the Ladies could not be resorted to for fear that despair should spread among their ranks, and the situation teemed with difficulties. Under this pressure of anxiety M. Vincent wrote the following letter to a meeting that seems to have been a sub-committee of working members:

" LADIES,

" Being by God's good pleasure separated from you, I commend you and those dear to you to Our Lord at the altar, being assured that you of your charity pray for God's mercy upon me. Indeed, I ask you very humbly, Ladies, to do this for me, and I assure you that if it please God to hear my prayers for you, you will be specially protected in those afflictions with which He now visits us.

" You will have heard, Ladies, how God gave me opportunity to visit the houses of our little Company, and how I set forth with the intention of returning when the condition of affairs made it possible for me to do so. The question now arises: What are we to do with the work that God has put into your hands, especially the work of relief of the Hôtel-Dieu and of the poor Foundlings? Assuredly it looks as if individual distress dispensed you from any further care for that of others, and that we have a good excuse before the eyes of men for laying down this responsibility. But, Ladies, I do not know how the question will look before God, Who may surely ask of us, ' Have you yet resisted unto the shedding of blood ?' or as S. Paul asked of the Corinthians who found themselves in a similar difficulty, have you at least sold a portion of such treasures as you possess ? What am I saying to you ? I know well that there are some among you (and I can believe it of everyone) who have made offerings which would be considered immense, not only from persons of your own rank, but even from Queens; the very stones would proclaim it if I was silent, and it is by reason of the infinite charity that fills your hearts that I am able to speak to you like this. I should be very careful not to do so to persons who were less full of the Spirit of God.

" What, then, are we to do ? It seems as if it would be well to raise the question, Ladies, whether it is desirable that you should hold the great assembly that has been suggested ? Also when, and where, and how ? There are reasons for and against. It seems natural that it should be held, because it is our custom to have one about this time, and also because the need is abnormal we need some abnormal effort, like that of a General Meeting. On the other hand, this does not seem a good moment, because of the distress which is touching everybody, filling their minds with anxiety, and chilling their hearts. Possibly many Ladies would be afraid to come, and those who did so, unless they were filled with extraordinary charity, would only make each other more cautious. Moreover, Mme. la Princesse (de Condé) and Mesdames d'Aiguillon and de Brienne being absent is a serious drawback, especially if there is an idea of making any fundamental changes in your work. This, then, Ladies, is the for and against, as I see it. You will consider and decide it by vote."*

Contemporaries of M. Vincent claimed for him that he possessed an immense faculty of concentration; this letter

* " Lettres," vol. i., No. 135.

might be produced in support of such a contention. At the moment when it was written his own personal credit was threatened; he had defied Mazarin, and thereby forfeited the favour and protection of the Queen, and his rash attempt at arbitration had aroused the suspicions of the people, and destroyed the affection and confidence won by long years of labour. As a consequence S. Lazare had been pillaged, and the whole of his scattered Community ran risk of actual famine. In Paris and in every part of France the maintenance of order in the streets had become almost impossible, and the Sisters of Charity lived in constant peril. Responsibility for every disaster that might occur rested on the shoulders of the Superior and Founder of the two Companies, and at the same time his heart was wrung by the suffering that political troubles imposed upon the poor. If he had issued brief directions to the Ladies, or even been forgetful of the detail of their distresses, there was sufficient excuse. But it is plain that when he thought about them they were as vivid in his mind as if their concerns were the only care he had. He does not overstrain his right of interference or attempt definite prohibitions, though he foresaw that the terror of the times was likely so to affect the majority that, if they met together, the sparks of enthusiasm in a valiant few ran risk of being extinguished. He knew the need was desperate, and unless the Ladies made a superhuman effort all their past work would be rendered ineffective, and their failure would aim a blow at charitable enterprise which might check its development for generations; but there is no fretfulness in his petition, he dwells on what they have done in the past rather than on the overpowering demand of the present. And history testifies to his success. These Ladies performed prodigies of self-sacrifice, and thousands of persons would have died of starvation but for their assistance. We are less concerned with the statistics of result than with the springs of generosity to which the results bore witness. The fact that they had hesitated, and had had a moment of feeling that the demand made upon them as individuals was beyond reason, only deepens the reality of their offering. It is a well-known fact that a sudden awakening to the spiritual life, or the stabs of sincere repentance, have often induced an indifference to worldly possessions, which expresses itself in gifts to the Church; but the Ladies of Charity were not moved by such influences as these. There was nothing to disturb the tenor of their inner life; there was every inducement to more than ordinary prudence in outward affairs. Yet the cause of the starving poor prevailed, and the reserving of funds for the possible exigencies of an unsettled future was held to be unworthy caution.

It may be permitted to us to regard their action as directly due to M. Vincent. By her own choice each one had joined that courageous League of which he was the Leader, and already must have stood some testing by his uncompromising standards. Presumably, the faithfulness of each was due to her certainty that M. Vincent's life was animated by the Spirit of Christ to a degree unique in her experience. She saw in him the meaning of self-sacrifice, consistent and sustained, in human life, and when the hour of crisis came the thought of him broke down the barriers of calculation, and she also was possessed by the folly of the Cross.

There is far less material from which to gather knowledge of the Ladies of Charity than of the Servants of the Poor. Some of the former may have been under M. Vincent's spiritual direction, but he did not expend much time in writing letters to them, and therefore there is little record of any individual touch. The best idea of the conditions under which he required them to live may be gathered from his addresses to them. Almsgiving and good works by no means satisfied him. "Your first duty," he told them at the beginning, "is to labour for your own spiritual advance, to be always aiming at per-

THE LADIES OF CHARITY 279

fection, always to have the lamp kindled within you." He rejected those who cared greatly for frivolous amusements or were fond of gambling, and desired that each one should from time to time go into Retreat. In letters to Mlle. Le Gras one or another is commended to her by name, that they may be given the hospitality of the Mother-House, and assisted to escape from the clamour of the world; but there is no word that gives a glimpse of a personality. A few are historic figures. Mme. de Condé, mother of the great Condé and of Mme. de Longueville, was an active and loyal member of the Company, so was Mme. de Schomberg, wife of the Marshal. Mme. d'Aiguillon never slackened in her support. Mme. de Maignelay and Mme. de Miramion have both been the subject of separate biographies,* but these contain little reference to their connection with M. Vincent. Mme. Goussaulte and Mme. de Herse achieve a certain prominence in the record of work accomplished, but it is completely in relation to business. No one of them as an individual is shown in personal relation with M. Vincent. To a Sister of Charity he was a Father, grasping their troubles and temptations, and attempting to put himself in their place that he might help them; to the Ladies he is a Leader, and he claims allegiance from all equally.

The strength of the position he assumed towards them adds greatly to the dignity of their achievement. In their giving there was to be no commercial side; they had no reward of small adulation, nor were they allowed to use their outward liberality as a salve to their consciences—indeed, their personal life had to be purer because they aspired to make an offering of their possessions in the service of their neighbour. Previous generations provide examples of charity on the magnificent scale, and the

* "Vie de Charlotte Marguerite de Gondi, Marquise de Maignelais," by le Père "p.m.c." Paris, 1666. "Vie de Madame de Miramion," by François T. de Choisy. Paris, 1685.

devotion of self without any reservation, but the efforts of this Company of Ladies were on lines that were altogether new. They were hampered by the drawbacks of novelty, they were often fussy and imprudent, secure in their own opinion and restive under control; there were times when they must have tried M. Vincent's patience, and they added appreciably to the burden of his anxieties. But there is never an indication of contention or rivalry among themselves for authority or credit; the spirit that prevailed among them was strong enough to be their protection from the special temptations of the philanthropist.

It was a great need that summoned M. Vincent's Ladies of Charity, and not a desire in themselves that sought expression in outward service, and for this reason they cannot be regarded as the prototype of those who in later generations have laboured bravely and successfully in the same fields. The poor cried to them from the crowded wards of the Hôtel-Dieu, from the cribs of the Couche S. Landry, from the infected tenements in the byways of the city, and M. Vincent taught them that it was the voice of Christ Himself, and as Christians they must listen and respond, or be convicted of the most terrible of inconsistencies. Because their ears had been opened to this cry, he showed them that they might not share any longer in the indifference that was not a crime in others. That plea of his was extraordinarily potent. To those before whom he made it he was able to communicate his own complete sincerity. And as a result the charity that is pure from taint of self-consideration came into being.

CHAPTER V

THE COMPANY OF MISSION PRIESTS

IF M. Vincent had been forced to compare the importance and the value of those achievements which are connected with his name, it is quite certain that his view of them would not coincide with common opinion. In England the Sisters of Charity are assuredly the chief and probably the only recognized memorial of him, but while he lived it was the Company of the Mission Priests that was the foremost subject of his thoughts and prayers, and if he had desired remembrance at all, it is by their existence that he would have chosen to be commemorated. It is not in the least remarkable that they should have fallen into the background. Record can be kept of lives saved by opportune distribution of food in time of famine; the reconstitution of an hospital is so impressive a benefit that it needs no record; the rescue and tending of maltreated babies appeals too deeply to sentiment as well as to charitable instincts to be forgotten. But the Mission Priests were not responsible for any of these things; they had only two recognized objects—the training and reform of the clergy, and the preaching of Missions in country districts, and there was no possibility of scheduling the results of either endeavour. If we would understand M. Vincent's point of view towards them, we must again remind ourselves that he regarded spiritual starvation as far more terrible than lack of food or any bodily affliction, and his opinion was not shaken by the fact that the sufferers themselves did not share in it.

There is a well-known description by La Bruyère,* which

* " Les Caractères," chap. x.

brings before us the country folk of France as they were in the days of Vincent de Paul. " Here and there among the fields," says the satirist, " one may see certain wild beasts, male and female, black and parched and burnt by the sun, clinging to the ground which they poke and turn with unconquerable determination. They have the semblance of an articulate voice, and when they rise to their feet they display a human face, and they are actually human beings. At night they take refuge in hovels, where they live on black bread and water and roots; it is, indeed, thanks to them that other men are saved the toil of sowing and reaping that they may live, and therefore it is their due that they should not lack for the bread that they have grown." The living creatures so terribly depicted each represented to M. Vincent a soul which it was his duty to awaken. The discovery made at Montmirail, which resulted in his first experimental Mission, remained always vivid in his remembrance; he was haunted by the thought of the thousands who passed into eternity without opportunity of making their peace with God. To have any understanding of him it is necessary to grasp the complete simplicity of his view in matters such as these, and the extraordinary sincerity of effort that resulted. Innumerable souls in peril of being lost might be saved by his Mission Priests; their greatest danger was their ignorance of their own misery. There was no hope that they would recognize the Light until they understood they were in darkness; and the task that God required of the Sons of M. Vincent was to instil a knowledge of the need that the Church alone could satisfy.

Vincent de Paul, with his intimate knowledge of the wide realm of France and of human nature in many of its aspects, must have been fully alive to the stupendous difficulty of his enterprise. In the long years of his life at S. Lazare, when daily duties chained him to his post, his thoughts and hopes were following his emissaries as they

THE COMPANY OF MISSION PRIESTS 283

went out on their perilous journeys to carry the message of Christ to the poor. His letters to them will show us how close and individual was his consideration of their labours; each separate centre established in a provincial town, every Mission undertaken, however insignificant, was watched and realized as if there were no rival claims on his attention. The Company of Mission Priests, as we have seen, grew from indefinite beginnings into clear formation. Their final Rule was not given them until M. Vincent's life was near its close, and was the result of the deepest knowledge of their difficulties. In its opening we find this passage: " The Five Virtues necessary to the Congregation are Simplicity, Humility, Gentleness, Mortification, and a Zeal for Souls ";* and a little later: " The holding of Missions is our foremost and chief duty. The Congregation must never take up other good work as a pretext for evading this, no matter how useful the other may be; but each one must give himself whole-heartedly to it whenever obedience summons him."†

The Missions were to be preached in the villages and smaller towns; their object was not so much to encourage the religious-minded, as to pierce the indifference of those who did not appear to have any spiritual faculties at all. The peasantry were overworked and underfed, a constant struggle was demanded of them if they were to sustain their animal energies; from the cradle to the grave they fought for bare existence, and in a fight that brought them to the level of the brutes they ran the risk of losing their humanity. To the superficial observer they were little better than savages, dull of wit and gross of manner, with every characteristic, outward and inward, most calculated to repel a sensitive and high-strung temperament. Yet it was primarily for them that the Mission Priests existed. Assuredly each member of the Congre-

* " Règles Communes de la Congregation de la Mission," chap. i., art. 14. Paris, 1658.
† " Règles," chap. xi., art. 10.

gation needed the five virtues enumerated in their Rule, and most of all, perhaps, a Zeal for Souls, for if this last was to survive discouragement, it would only be by the ever-present remembrance that each of the unresponsive listeners who had been herded and driven into their parish church had special value before God, and possessed potential capacity of accepting his fellowship with Christ. No miracle of grace was too great to be claimed by M. Vincent's faith, and his confidence was imparted to his Sons.

From the very beginning, in days before the Company had recognized being, the first Missioners had realized the importance of discovering and fixing a method of preaching. The same method was always afterwards adhered to; the practice of it became a part of the Rule, and M. Vincent, in conference with his Sons the year before his death,* thought well to describe the circumstances of its origin.

"We assembled," he told them, "at the time of the birth of the Company, Monseigneur de Boulogne, Monseigneur d'Alet, and M. Olier being with us. The subject given was a particular virtue or vice. We each took pen and ink, and wrote down the *motive* and the reason there might be for avoiding the vice and embracing the virtue. Afterwards we sought the *definition* of them, and the *means* for evading or practising them. Finally, everything that had been written was gathered together, and we held a discussion. None of us made use of a book, but each worked out of his own head. M. Portail, having gathered up all that was said, then and in other conferences held by the Company, composed an easy method whereby sermons might achieve their purpose."

It was this method (which M. Vincent is so ready to attribute to M. Portail) which was the strength and the glory of the Company. Sermons had become an advertisement of the learning and wit of the preacher, and were sometimes incredibly elaborate. We have M. Vincent's

* In August, 1659.

theory of preaching in his own words as he imparted it to his Sons at S. Lazare :*

"How do we find that the Apostles preached? In friendly fashion, familiarly and simply. Now look at our manner of preaching: in homely language, naturally, in all simplicity. To preach as the Apostles did, Messieurs —that is to say, for any useful preaching—we must be simple and use ordinary words, so that everyone may be able to understand and profit. It was thus that the disciples and Apostles preached, it was thus also that Jesus Christ preached, and God has done great honour to this poor and paltry Company in allowing us to imitate Him in that.

"It is, then, on our little Company rather than on any other that God in His mercy has chosen to bestow His method. This method comes from God. Man can do nothing, and its results show us that it is God Who has given it to us. We must acknowledge, Messieurs, that this method is not in use elsewhere. The world's antagonism has forced the greatest preachers to resort to the use of fine phraseology and to subtleties of suggestion, that what is needful may seem attractive. They will employ every trick of oratory to catch and humour a wilful world. But of what good is a display of rhetoric? Is anyone the better for it? It serves no purpose except self-advertisement.

"And what does all this flourish consist of? Is someone anxious to show his power as an orator or as a theologian? If that is what he desires, he is choosing the wrong road; if he wants to win respect from the wise, and to have a reputation for eloquence, he must learn how to convince his hearers and to dissuade them from such things as they should avoid. Otherwise he is merely picking words, turning phrases, and rolling out periods in raised tones that are above everybody's head. Do these sort of sermons attain their end? Do they inspire

* August 20, 1655.

devotion? Are the people so moved by them that they are quickly drawn towards penitence? No, indeed! No, indeed!

"'But,' you say, 'this method is so insignificant! If I always preach like this what will be said of me? What will they take me for? In course of time everyone will despise me. I shall lose all dignity!'

"By so doing you will lose your dignity! In preaching as Jesus Christ preached you will lose dignity! It is to lose dignity to speak of God as the Son of God spoke of Him! What blasphemy is this!

"God is my witness that I have three times knelt at the feet of a Priest of the Company—who was of it then, but now is not—on three days following, to implore him to preach simply, but I was never able to persuade him. He was giving the addresses before ordination, so you can see how strongly this accursed inclination had hold of him. He forfeited the blessing of God, and his addresses and sermons were without any fruit—all this great hoard of words and phrases vanished in smoke."

M. Vincent's vehemence in repudiating everything that was elaborate, and in insisting on the Simple Method, reveals the immense importance he attached to this particular point. The original reason for the gathering of the Company had been the preaching of Missions, and the plan for the conduct of them was the result of his experience; but unless the actual preaching conformed to the spirit of the Company they were foredoomed to failure.

"Although we must practise simplicity at all times and in all places," says the Rule,* "we must be particularly observant of it in our Missions when we carry the Word of God to the poor folk in the country. We must be simple in the manner of our preaching and catechizing, suiting it to the people, and adhering to the Simple Method which the Company has used hitherto. There must be no affectations, no silkiness of speech, no

* "Règles," chap. xii., art. 5.

attempt must be made to take advantage of an opportunity given for preaching the truth to spread fantastic ideas, elaborate theories, and useless subtleties."

Copies of a pamphlet on the Simple Method of Preaching were distributed among the Priests of the Mission, and no true member of the Company could ever indulge himself in flights of rhetoric. The provisions of the Simple Method are in themselves elaborate, and its many warnings and suggestions bring before us the possible weaknesses of the first Sons of M. Vincent.* Much is to be treated briefly, " experience showing that the length of exhortations is not only useless, but even harmful, owing to the weariness it causes to the listeners." A story may advantageously be used for illustration, but care should be taken, firstly, that it has real relation to the subject treated; secondly, that it is absolutely edifying; thirdly, that it is authentic; fourthly, that it is not too long. The text also must be short and easy to understand, and the subject of the sermon should be connected with the text, and give occasion to repeat it several times.

The ingenuousness that is so characteristic of M. Vincent animates these directions of his; he realized the material from which his Mission preachers would be formed, and that he must take nothing for granted with them. But when he deals with the conclusion he strikes a higher note. Everything that has been said is then to be gathered up, so that the listeners may be left in the spirit of devotion. And for this it should be very short, and not like a fresh sermon; it should contain only a little reasoning, and it will be found well to end by addressing Our Lord Himself, asking for His grace and His help in the attainment of those things of which one has been speaking.

The idea of a Mission is as old as Christianity, but the form given to it by M. Vincent was new, and bears the impress of his personality. Close study of his method

* See "Sermons de S. Vincent de Paul," édité par l'Abbé Jeanmaire.

will reveal many points susceptible to criticism; it will be found very easy to inveigh against the tendency to sensationalism, and also to show that the result was likely to be evanescent. Probably the Missioners themselves would not have resented either suggestion. Possibly, however, the more experienced among them might have pointed out that the actuality and duration of spiritual results always remain outside the range of human knowledge, and with regard to the charge of sensationalism the best defence (if a defence be needed) lies in consideration of the type of mind to which the Missions were to make appeal. The message that was to be delivered was the most sensational that the imagination can conceive. If it was accepted, it would mean a complete reversal of habits and opinions; therefore to whisper it in a corner where there were none to listen, or to refer to it as if it was an ordinary and accepted topic, was to lose an opportunity of piercing the crust of custom that makes a peasant docile and inattentive, and with it the opportunity to save a soul.

The old method sanctioned by the Church of keeping the country folk in lively remembrance of their religion had been the celebration of the Mysteries.* From time to time the priest announced that the Mysteries were to be given, and from the moment of the announcement until the performance they were the chief subject of discussion. That intervening space corresponded crudely to the Preparation for a Mission. The theme of the Mysteries was Biblical; they consisted of tableaux representing scenes from the Garden of Eden onwards, the life of Christ and of the Blessed Virgin being treated with special care. Responsible persons went from place to place organizing the performances, but many of the inhabitants of the towns where they were held took part, and the priests were among the chief actors. They began by a procession through the streets and round the town;

* See Babeau, " La Ville sous l'Ancien Régime."

THE COMPANY OF MISSION PRIESTS 289

sightseers flocked in from all the neighbouring hamlets, and in some cases the celebration seems to have continued for several weeks on end, during which period ordinary labour was suspended.

The excellent idea on which this custom originated did not protect it from abuse. The suppression of the Mysteries is said to have been due to the criticisms of the Huguenots at the end of the sixteenth century, and it is likely that there was much ground for criticism, and that a solemn pageant had degenerated into a show which was grotesque and tawdry at its best, and not infrequently was blasphemous. Pious persons could not deplore their extinction, but the place they had occupied was left vacant, and for a generation no effort of any kind was made to awaken the labouring class to understanding of the faith that nominally was theirs. The Missions were preached to the grandchildren of men and women who had dressed up in strange attire that they might impersonate Scriptural characters, and take part in the masquerades that M. le Curé sanctioned. Public opinion had not been directed to anything higher in the interval, the popular imagination had been lying fallow, and the popular mind was without education either on religious or on any other subject.

It would be impossible to understand the scheme that was so important to M. Vincent if we ignore the condition of those for whom it was conceived. He had no ambition to set a model for all Missions to all sorts of people, but it was after concentrated study of the multitude (towards whom the clever and cultivated were utterly indifferent) that he made his rules for the guidance of the Priests of the Poor. Two Missioners, or three—according to the numbers awaiting them—were chosen from the Company at S. Lazare, and required to reach the scene of their labours by the cheapest possible method. They might not accept free quarters or gifts of any kind, but they were supplied during their stay with necessary furniture and cooking utensils, and their first duty on arrival was to instal themselves so that household care might not interrupt them when they had once entered on their labours. M. Vincent required that the practical things connected with spiritual work should be carefully ordered; he was solicitous also as to the authority which had demanded the Mission, and needed the consent of the curé of the parish and the approval of the Bishop of the diocese, believing that the lawlessness and indifference that prevailed only increased the necessity of strictness on such points. But whether the summons came from curé or from Bishop, the real commission was to be regarded as from God Himself. The Missioners were to concentrate all their thoughts and prayers and aspirations on the people who were given into their charge. It was inevitable that they should feel anxiety as to the number of their listeners at the outset, and that anxiety in various forms should remain with them till the days of opportunity were over.

M. Vincent's understanding of the possibilities of a Mission was unequalled. To him the call to this form of labour appeared as the highest call conceivable, and he considered that its acceptance involved a correspondence of personal sanctification. To preach a Mission was not an exercise or a part of the year's routine; it must be the expression of a personality. In his private intercourse with them we shall find M. Vincent exhorting his Sons to be on their guard against the self-love that brings in an element of private success and failure. Doubtless he had experience of the desire for conquest and sense of personal triumph in result, which is so easily confused with the true ardour of a zeal for souls, and so was constant in his warnings against this most insidious of temptations.

In all the details of these country Missions we are in touch with Vincent de Paul himself. One of his own preliminary sermons sketches for his hearers both his object and his method. The Missioners are come, he

THE COMPANY OF MISSION PRIESTS 291

tells them, for a short time, to preach, to catechize, to hear confessions, and to adjust quarrels. Two sermons were to be preached daily, one in the morning and one in the evening, at times suited to the convenience of the working people. The Catechism was always to be one hour after noon, and intended especially for those who had not made their first Communion. From the day of their arrival the Missioners invited confidence from any who might be at variance with each other, because no man may be at peace with God and continue to live at enmity with his neighbour.

After this most simple of warnings the Mission began; and again from a series of M. Vincent's own sermons, we can trace its progress. After a lapse of three centuries these sermons still produce an impression of extraordinary sincerity and force, and it is therefore possible to conjecture their effectiveness when delivered as a message from an unknown world to the country folk who never left their village. The first was on the general need of salvation, and the course goes on under the many heads that naturally suggest themselves. There is one on penitence, and more than one on self-examination; there is one—evidently intended to mark a definite stage in the listeners—on contrition, one on confession in its ordinary form, and one on general confession. In those times a sudden and violent end was the lot of a considerable proportion of the community, and therefore the theme of death and judgment could be given additional gravity by illustrations drawn from the recent annals of the district. It must always be remembered that the listeners were on the same intellectual level as the previous generations who had gaped at the Mysteries, and in this fact lies the explanation of the lurid studies of the Death of Sinners, of the Last Judgment, and of the Physical Pain of Hell. To the Rich Man of the parable the Almighty is represented as saying: " Remember that thou hast been a *gourmand* and a lover of luxuries, thou shalt therefore suffer specially by a hunger and thirst which shall cause thee to groan, to scream, and to cry in despair, and grinding of teeth, and God *shall never have pity upon thee.*"

The gift of imagination is latent in many uneducated persons, and it stirred in response to the description of the pains of hell. The Missioners set forth the fate of sinners as one of the great truths that composed their message with the most complete sincerity, but though it was not introduced for effect, it was extraordinarily effective. If the Mission had prospered, the preacher would be addressing a crowded church when he came to those topics of reward and punishment. For suffering human nature it has always been an easier task to depict punishment than reward; the heaven that would hold attraction for these half-awakened yokels was difficult to represent, and this may partially account for the disproportionate attention bestowed on hell. But the teaching, though it rings over-violently in modern ears, was both strong and simple.

" ' Tell us, you who are dead, where are you now ? ' we say. They answer: ' We are in the houses that during our life on earth we built for ourselves for all eternity.' "

This is the opening of a sermon on death, and it goes on with vigorous directness to point out to the living the possibility of founding their future house on present repentance. The object of the Lazarist Priest—whether accomplished by warning or persuasion—was one with that of S. John the Baptist: he came to call men to repentance that they might be prepared to receive their Lord. Everything else that might be accomplished by a Mission was secondary to this; a general awakening to the sense of sin was the supreme necessity if the Mission was to bear any real fruit at all. There was only a short period of time—ten or fourteen days—for the conquest of souls that appeared never to have been touched by any spiritual influence; but it must be remembered always that tradition or inheritance keeps alive in the children of the Church of Rome a certain subconscious knowledge, which may wait a lifetime for revival, but which is there waiting to be revived. It is easier to revive than to instil. The sermons of the Missioners of S. Lazare, although intended for the most ignorant of congregations, take a great deal for granted; they are reminders of what has been known and neglected rather than explanations of what is new. Also a good deal could be done outside the four walls of the church; the Missioners made it their aim to have as much personal contact with the people as possible. One of their Rules suggests that "one and all should desire ardently, and even, if necessary, make humble petition, to be allowed to visit the sick, as well as to endeavour to make peace wherever there have been quarrels."* M. Vincent urged upon them that all they did must be in the spirit of sympathy. "If God has given a blessing to our Missions," he said to one of the Company, "we must attribute it to the use of kindness and humility in dealing with all conditions of people. I implore you, Monsieur, to join me in giving thanks for this, and in asking His grace that every Missioner may always treat all with whom he comes in contact in public and in private with gentleness, humility, and charity, especially the sinners and those who show themselves hard of heart."

When the Mission was over, when, after a final procession, the last farewell, the last exhortation to perseverance, the last kindly word of encouragement had been spoken, the Missioners would return the household effects they had borrowed, pay the modest debts they had incurred, and go upon their way; and there, as a rule, their connection with the scene of their labours ended. When the Mission itself was over there came the time of test for the Missioner. Sometimes the concentration and excitement of the days of struggle were

* "Règles," chap. xi., art. 8.

succeeded by deep depression, but more often it is likely the thoughts that went back over the immediate past, noting the record of eventful hours, inevitably tended to elation. It had been impossible not to desire a success that meant the good of others, and when success had come it was impossible not to be uplifted by the thought of it; but the Father Superior had no tolerance for self-congratulation.* " This desire to be well thought of—what is it other than a desire for different treatment than was accorded to the Son of God ? It is an arrogance not to be permitted. When the Son of God was on earth what was said of Him ? How was He content to be regarded by the people ? As a madman, a rebel, a fool, a sinner. Keep that in mind, keep it before you, you who go to Missions, and you who speak in public. Sometimes, and often enough, one sees one's listeners so moved by what one has said that they are all in tears. . . . And at that it is one's instinct to be pleased, vanity shoots up and will grow strong if one does not crush these foolish satisfactions and look solely for the glory of God, for which only we must work—yes, *only* for the glory of God and the salvation of souls. For on any other terms you preach yourself and not Jesus Christ; and a person who preaches to be applauded and praised and flattered and talked about—what is this person doing ? This Preacher, what is he achieving ? A sacrilege and that only ! To make use of the Word of God and to speak of Divine things to win honour and reputation, I say that this is a sacrilege. O Father in Heaven, give such grace to this poor little Company that not one of its members shall fall into this misfortune ! Believe me, Messieurs, we shall never be fit to carry out the purposes of God without the most profound humility and complete distrust of ourselves. No, unless the Congregation of the Mission is humble and realizes that it can accomplish nothing of any value, that it is fit rather to mar than

* "Conferences," quoted by Abelli, vol. i., chap. xxi.

THE COMPANY OF MISSION PRIESTS 295

to make, it will never be of much effect; but when it has this spirit I have been describing, then, Messieurs, it will be fit for the purposes of God."

It was not easy to be a Mission Priest, it was no lip service which M. Vincent asked of his Sons. There are natures to whom the resignation of all that is soft and pleasant is repaid in full measure by the sense of great accomplishment, by the consciousness of supreme dominance over the thoughts and actions of others. The leader of a Mission had immense opportunity of such dominance, and he attained to it in the fulfilment of his vocation; it was the purpose for which he had renounced the world. It is worth while to realize this and thereby to see how searching was M. Vincent's demand. The Mission Priests renounced all choice in their career, all ordinary ambitions, every tie of blood; they were bound to a reality of poverty such as was rarely practised by professed Religious. But there remained to them one solace, one possible compensation: the joy in their own personal power for good. And this M. Vincent required that they should put away. "Otherwise," he said, "God will not use us for His purposes." It is impossible to know the depth of obedience that he won—he could not have known himself—but it seems certain that the Congregation was used for God's purpose in those difficult and troublous times, and therefore we may join M. Vincent in his simple faith, and believe that his Sons struggled for the hardest form of self-mastery, and that, in a measure at least, they did attain.

Year after year the number of the Lazarists steadily increased. That this should have been the case is a proof of the vigour of supernatural influence. There were far easier ways of engaging in Christ's service than the career of a Mission Priest; there were none that involved more complete renunciation. M. Vincent himself never attempted to discount a single detail of the severity of their vocation. "He who would live in the Company," he wrote, after many years' experience,* " must be prepared to dwell as a pilgrim upon earth, to sacrifice his reason for Christ's sake, to change all his habits, to mortify every passion, to seek God only, to be subject to anyone as being himself the least of all, to realize that he has come to serve and not to govern, to suffer and to labour, and not to live in comfort and idleness. He must understand that he will be put to the proof as gold is proved in the furnace, and that he cannot hope to persevere unless he desires to humble himself before God, knowing that by so doing he will attain to true happiness in this world and to life eternal in another." He was all tenderness and compassion toward the mass of his fellow-men, but he would tolerate no laxity in the conduct of the Company. In his eyes their call was absolutely sacred. The call to labour for others was null and void unless it was also a call to personal holiness.

"Consider the beauty of it," he exhorted them,† "that we should be striving first for the Reign of God for ourselves, and then that we should procure It for others. How great is the blessing on a Company which exists only that it may further the glory of God! But if, when we undertake a journey in the world, we are careful to choose the right road, how much more careful must we be in choosing if we aspire to follow Jesus Christ. All those who accept His maxims (especially that which bids them try all things whether they be of God) should consider what they are doing, and ask themselves: 'Why do you do this, or that? Is it to please yourself? Is it because you dislike something else? Is it to give satisfaction to some worthless being? Or is it rather to fulfil the Will of God and for His service?' What a life—what a life might be theirs! Would it be human? Nay, verily it would be that of the angels, for

---

* See " Abelli," vol. i., chap. xxxiv.
† "Conferences," quoted by Abelli, vol. i., chap. xix.

it would be all for the love of God that all things were done or left undone."

Truly, under such testing a faithful Son of M. Vincent might hope to go far on the road to perfection; but not all had capacity for complete faithfulness. At first he accepted almost all who came to him expressing a desire to join the Company, but—as he was always ready to acknowledge in later years—he had not at the beginning formed any idea of the future that lay before them or of the need for the self-consecration of all who bore their part in it. It was, indeed, only with the deepening of his experience as a Superior that he acquired knowledge of those weaknesses that are masked by outward piety. Among his letters we may find proof of all that he had to bear from the unfaithful, and a suggestion of the pain that desertion caused him.

With that question of desertion we touch a point of special importance in the history and progress of the Company. We must remember the simple manner in which it had originated. Three or four priests, who had united to live a life of poverty and preach the Gospel to the poor, made their headquarters at a house in a small street in Paris. This house and a certain sum of money was given them by a pious lady, who greatly desired the spiritual welfare of the poor. Their main object was clearly defined, but every other detail connected with them was left absolutely indefinite. Their numbers grew; the place of their headquarters altered; as the career of their Superior developed, the scope of their labours widened; but it was all gradual, there was no special moment at which they claimed special recognition. And thus it came about that to all intents and purposes they formed a powerful Community under a Superior when, in fact, they had no definite Rule and were not bound by any recognized vow. That their existence was of benefit to the nation is above doubt. The work they did for the poorest of the people had hitherto been left undone, and, armed with the experience of their country Missions, they formed a sort of reserve force that could be called upon in such disasters as the civil war or the outbreaks of pestilence for special service towards the sufferers. But if they were to preserve their collective force as a Company, it became obvious that a vow was necessary. How otherwise was it possible for a number of persons scattered in little groups of twos and threes all over Europe to maintain a common standard of poverty and simplicity? The more we consider the conditions of their lives the more we shall see the difficulty of faithfulness. M. Vincent's insistence on the necessity of vows has sufficient explanation in mere common sense.

It was, nevertheless, extremely difficult to obtain the Papal sanction for the vow, or the formal recognition of the Company of Priests of the Mission. It was considered that there were already too many religious orders in France; for the most part they were decadent and tended to lower the standards of discipline and morals—already low enough. M. Vincent was aware of this fact, and had not originally intended to require any vow from those who joined him; it was the experience of the years as they passed that convinced him of its necessity.

"Lately I have been talking to a man of great wisdom, intelligence, and knowledge," he wrote, in 1651, to M. Almeras,* one of his earliest companions, who was then in charge of the Mission at Rome. "He thinks that we require some sort of chain that unites us each to the other and collectively to God as a defence against the natural inconstancy of mankind, and to prevent the destruction of the Company. Unless we have this many will join us merely to gain experience and to fit themselves for public work, and will then be off; and others who were strong in purpose at the beginning will none the less give up at the first drawback or at the chance

* "Lettres," vol. i., No. 182.

THE COMPANY OF MISSION PRIESTS

of a good opening in the world, there being nothing to hold them. We have only too much experience of such failures, and even now as I write we have one who, having been trained and schooled for thirteen or fourteen years, now asks for funds to help him to start, and only waits till he has them to leave us. What remedy is there for this evil? How shall we avoid wasting the funds, that are given us to strive for the salvation of the poor, on people of this sort who have their own objects in view, if we have no means of holding them by some strong bond of conscience, such as a vow of perseverance."

It is seldom that M. Vincent permits himself to express such deep discouragement. It should be remembered that in 1651 the heroism of some of the Mission Priests on the battlefields had won honour for the Company, but that, simultaneously, the insidious poison he describes threatened to destroy their power for good. Two years later he was still petitioning for the Papal sanction. M. Berthe had replaced M. Almeras at Rome, and the petition had become more definite, but His Holiness remained unmoved. Even at this distance of time M. Vincent's arguments in favour of his cause carry conviction. "There is such great variety in our undertakings, they are so trying and so prolonged, those employed in them are so rebuffed and confronted with so much opposition, that it is hard for them to be steadfast if they are not bound to the Company. And it will happen with us as it has happened with some other Congregations where individuals had no obligation to obey: the members will go as they like, and when the Superior intends to send some of them—be it far or near—for the glory of God, he finds he had no hold, having no claim on their obedience. Therefore, as the case stands now, the Missioners being free to do or to leave undone the good work offered to them, to go or to remain as they may feel inclined, and to go off altogether when the fancy takes them, it becomes impossible to maintain the work begun (much less undertake anything new), for many are so light-minded that what they choose to-day they will weary of to-morrow.... This is why we are imploring the Holy Father very humbly to make our vows impossible of dispensation save by His Holiness himself or by the Superior of the Congregation."*

The picture suggested by this letter is in sharp contrast to M. Vincent's ideal for the Priests of the Mission. To him their vocation was so clearly a privilege that each instance of unfaithfulness caused him poignant suffering. It was in bitterness of spirit that he wrote to M. Berthe to plead for that support which the Vatican authorities were so slow in giving. Yet in his plaint he reveals unwittingly the marvel that he himself had wrought in gathering and controlling his great Company by the sole force of his own influence. When (in 1658) his hopes were at last fulfilled, and His Holiness made the vow of the Mission Priest both obligatory and binding, the Company was already strongly and firmly established, and, in spite of his moments of dejection, M. Vincent knew that it was so. The retrospect of the thirty-three years that preceded the formal recognition of their existence will be found in his own address to the Assembly at S. Lazare when he gave them their Rule and their Constitution:

"Our Rule,"† he told them, "seems at first sight to bind us only to an ordinary life, nevertheless, it contains enough to lead those who practise it to the highest perfection.... Our Rule is almost all—as anyone can see for himself—taken from the Gospel, and its object is to make your life an imitation of that which our Lord led on earth, for it is written that our Saviour came, and was sent by His Father to preach to the poor. It is this that our little Company is endeavouring to do, and herein

---

* "Lettres," vol. i., No. 245.
† See "Abelli," vol. i., chap. xlvii.

THE COMPANY OF MISSION PRIESTS 301

is great reason for humiliation and self-abasement, for, so far as I know, there is no other that has chosen for its object to take the message of the Gospel to the very poorest. This is the call to us. . . .

"It is full thirty-three years since God gave us our beginning, and all that time we have, by His grace, been practising the Rule which we are now going to give; indeed, there is nothing in it that is new, nothing that you have not practised for many years with great edification. If we had given this Rule at the beginning and before the Company had tested it, it might have been thought that there was something human rather than Divine about it, and that here was a plan of human origin, and not the work of Divine Providence; but, my Brothers, this Rule and everything else that is part of the Congregation has come to pass I know not how, for I have originated nothing, and it has all developed little by little in a way that one cannot explain. Now, S. Augustine says that when one cannot trace the origin of a good thing we must attribute it to God Himself. According to that, is not God the Author of our Rule, which has come in suchwise that we cannot tell how or why ? Indeed, I can assure you, my Brothers, that the thought of this Rule, or of the Company, or even of the very name of Mission, never came to me; this is the work of God, man had no part in it. For myself, when I contemplate the means by which it has pleased God to found the Congregation in His Church, I confess that I know not where I am, and all that I see seems like a dream. Ah no ! this thing is not ours, it is not human, it is from God ! That which does not come from man's understanding is not human. Our first Missioner had no more thought of it than I; it has grown, apart from all our plans and hopes. If you were to ask me how all the Practices of the Company were introduced, how the thought of all these exercises and undertakings came to us, I should say to you that I do not know, and that I cannot understand. Here is M. Portail, who has seen as much as I have of the beginnings of the little Company, who will tell you that nothing was farther from our thoughts than that which has come to pass. It has all happened as if of itself, little by little, one thing after another. The number of those that joined us increased, and each was striving after virtue, and as our numbers grew we learned the regulations needful for our common life and for order in our employments. These regulations, by the grace of God, we are still using. Oh my Brothers, I am so overwhelmed by the thought that it is I who give this Rule that I cannot imagine how it has come about that I stand where I am; it seems to me that I am once more at the very beginning, and the more I think, the farther it is all withdrawn from human origin, and the more clearly I see that it is God alone Who has given this Rule to the Company. If it be so that I have added to it anything, I tremble lest it be that which shall hinder its perfect observance in the future."

It was Friday evening, May 17, 1658. M. Vincent's life was near its close, and these are the words of an old man, possessed by one thought, repeating it again and again in his homely language. " This thing is not human, it is from God." That is the burden of it, and that, indeed, was the thought he desired so earnestly to instil into his Sons with regard to their vocation, and all that concerned it. Their Rule seems to leave no circumstance of their life untouched, and there could be no better guide to understanding of the sacrifice entailed by their vocation. By it they were bound to accept no benefice; they were not to write books or to seek distinction in theological controversy; their preaching was to be always for the poor and the ignorant; they were not to talk of public affairs either among themselves or with any whom they might meet; they were to give prompt obedience in all things, not only in the letter but in the spirit, and they were to eschew all social diversions

THE COMPANY OF MISSION PRIESTS 303

absolutely. This is the rough outline of their renunciation, " and "—so runs the Rule itself—" in the end it is needful we should realize clearly that, in the words of Jesus Christ, when we have accomplished all these things that are commanded us we are but unprofitable servants, and also that but for Him we could accomplish nothing at all."*

It is hard to be in the world and not be of it. In those days of feverish political excitement it was not a small test of resolution to abstain from asking or repeating news of the *Parlement*, of the Court, and of the war; nor was it a small deprivation for a Frenchman, possessed of wit and of eloquence, to relinquish all hope of the response of the cultivated mind, and devote himself to awaking the dulled faculties of " the poor and simple."

Some of the Priests of the Mission were men of intellect and learning; some had social gifts, and loved intercourse with their fellows; some were of independent spirit, and found the chain of implicit obedience infinitely galling. There was great diversity among them in spiritual development as much as in brains or in rank, and if we would realize them as individuals we must turn once more to M. Vincent's letters. We shall find these letters charged with remonstrance, with pleading, and with rebuke, but so clear in insight and true in sympathy that very often it is the personality of the recipient rather than of the writer that they unveil.

* "Règles," chap. xii., art. 14.

CHAPTER VI

M. VINCENT AND HIS SONS

"THERE are certain souls which are most difficult to guide, and there are natures of different types which tend to things that are unusual and often undesirable. You must bear with these, and endeavour by gentleness and patience and skill to teach them love of the Rule and of obedience. And in doing so humble yourself before God, recognizing that you are nothing save a useless tool who may spoil everything. But such as you are, yield yourself to His Divine guidance, being confident that it will be your guide in guiding others, your strength both of soul and body, and the spirit of all your Company."*

Such was M. Vincent's teaching to the Superior of the Mission Priests at Genoa, a year before his death, and the letter reads like a summary of his own position towards the task of ruling. We must remember that very many of those he ruled had in their turn to rule others. As soon as the real usefulness of a Mission had declared itself, and also the capacity of the Mission Priests in the control of Seminaries, demands for help came to S. Lazare from every part of France, and also from Italy, from Poland, and from the British Isles. The difficulty of travelling was great, and it was not possible to send to and fro from the headquarters in Paris;† Branch-Houses were of necessity established, both within the kingdom and outside it, and for each a Superior was necessary. The Rule required implicit obedience to the Superior, but the Branch-Houses became so numerous that not infrequently

---

* "Lettres," vol. ii., No. 477.   † See Appendix, note iv.

M. VINCENT AND HIS SONS

authority was wielded by those who were not fit for their responsibility. M. Vincent was aware of the difficulty. We find him writing, in 1647, to one of the senior members of the Company a sort of defence of the state of things that prevailed. " I acknowledge," he says,* " that the offices of Superior in our houses are not well filled, but remember that in newborn Communities this always happens. Grace follows Nature in many things, and much that Nature allows to be rough and unpleasant at birth is perfected by time."

In fact, very many of his letters are full of remonstrance or advice to these Superiors, and, possibly because the more mature needed less guidance, and therefore were favoured with fewer letters, the impression produced is that the recipients were unduly young for their position, their age (quoted in footnotes to the volumes of correspondence) being usually under twenty-eight. After 1640 M. Vincent very rarely left S. Lazare—though he had originally intended to conduct much of the Mission work himself—and the threads of all the multifarious labours he had inaugurated were held by him. It is obvious how much must have depended on the wisdom and tact of his representatives, and it becomes evident as we read the Letters how constantly wisdom and tact were lacking. It was a rule of the Company that letters might always be sent by any individual in a Branch-House to the Superior-General in Paris without inspection before their despatch. M. Vincent was specially insistent on this point, and his own comments on it show its importance; but it is easy to understand that the Superiors did not share his eagerness for its observance. To one of them who may perhaps have interposed some obstacle he wrote:† "*Au nom de Dieu*, do not check the most complete freedom in writing to the Superior-General; it is a custom for which there are very good reasons, and entire liberty in this respect is one of the chief consolations of those

* " Lettres," vol. i., No. 111. † *Ibid.*, vol. i., No. 70.

under authority, and one to which they have undoubted right. Do not imagine, Monsieur, that anything is believed against a Superior without giving him a hearing, or that any action is taken on guess-work. No, by no means! I can assure you that I give no rebuke save on the testimony of the individual Superior himself. It is greatly to be desired, Monsieur, that all Superiors in the Company should copy the practice of one among you, who from time to time desires those under him to inform the General of whatsoever displeases them in his private conduct or method of governing, that with the help of God he may correct it."

M. Vincent had been through many years of the discipline of life before he attempted to rule others, and it seems certain that he did not covet authority. His ambition was to inspire and control rather than to command, but it was very difficult to instil the same spirit into his representatives.

"Be on such simple and cordial terms with the others," he wrote to M. Durand,* "that when you are all together it would be impossible to say which is the Superior. Do not decide business of any importance without asking their advice, and particularly that of your Assistant. For my own part I always summon my colleagues when there is any difficulty to be decided, whether it be in spiritual and ecclesiastical matters, or in things temporal. When these last are concerned I take counsel with those who have them in charge. I take the advice of the lay-brothers on the housekeeping because of their experience in it. Thus the decisions, which are reached by mutual agreement, receive God's blessing."†

And, again, to the Superior at Sedan: "Those who are at the head of the Houses of the Company should not look at the others as below themselves, but on each as a brother. Our Lord said to His disciples: 'I call you no longer servants, but I have called you friends.' Your

---

* Superior at Agde. † "Lettres," vol. ii., No. 419.

conduct towards them should always be humble, gentle, and kindly. I do not mean to say, Monsieur, that I always keep to this rule, but when I break it I know that I am failing."*

It is evident that the Priests of the Mission (like the Sisters of the Poor) found the preservation of mutual charity extremely difficult. If they allowed themselves to descend from the supernatural level, the monotonous routine of some of the Branch-Houses, the hard fare and lack of bodily ease that prevailed in all, induced an irritability which was destructive to social peace. M. Vincent knew the danger, but he knew also that the most incompatible temperaments can maintain good terms if self-love is not allowed to triumph, and therefore he has no sympathy for those who cannot be friendly. As he wrote on one occasion: "It is well to take as an unassailable maxim that our difficulties with our neighbour arise rather from our own ill-controlled tempers than from anything else."†

In fact, the Mission Priests who squabbled among themselves were falling short of their vocation, and no possible excuse would justify them in the eyes of M. Vincent.

But the difficulties arising between Superior and subject could not be disposed of by the application of any maxim. Sometimes there were real grievances, sometimes the complainant was moved by discontent, and the Superior was the injured party. But while M. Vincent ruled at S. Lazare there was no real fear of injustice if a question was brought to his notice. Every one of the scattered groups of his children was clear in his mind, and, though he acknowledged the incompetency of many of his representatives, it is evident that he had tested the character of each before giving him office, and could judge what likelihood there might be of accusations against him being just. In all cases his advice to a Superior is to take a

* "Lettres," vol. i., No. 164. † *Ibid.*, vol. i., No. 40.

humble attitude, to ask malcontents to warn him of his failures, " not only as a Superior, but also as a Mission Priest and as a Christian," and he does this, not from the elevation won by his own long experience and tried capacity, but as being the equal of those who make the worst mistakes. " Ah, Monsieur, how deep is human weakness, and what patience is needed by a Superior!" so ends a letter to one of them. " I conclude by asking for your prayers that God may forgive the innumerable faults that I myself commit in that office every day."*

Among the many figures gradually revealed by M. Vincent's correspondence there is not one more interesting than M. Codoing, who was chosen at a very early period to hold responsibility, but who seems at all times to deserve a place in the category of "souls which are most difficult to guide." He was born at Agen in 1610 of the *bourgeois* class, and joined the Congregation when he was twenty-five. His deep attachment to his own family is one strongly human point about him, and this M. Vincent attacked at the very beginning of their connection, for he would not permit family affection to dominate the heart of the true Mission Priest. In 1639 we find M. Codoing in charge of a new centre of the Company at Annecy, and by the letters directed thither we are initiated into one of those curious little dramas of development of which M. Vincent must have had such constant experience. M. Codoing had only been four years in the Company in 1639, and can have held no other post as Superior before going to Annecy. His after-career makes it plain that he was hot-headed and impulsive, devoted to the Company, but more faithful to the spirit than to the letter of its Rule, and disposed to make his own interpretations of its spirit.

There was sent to him at Annecy a certain M. Escart, a little younger than himself, but with equal experience of the Company. Before M. Escart had been in residence

* " Lettres," vol. ii., No. 461.

very long he seems to have become possessed with the idea that it was his mission to oppose and counteract the misdoings of M. Codoing. He approached the task with enthusiasm. He wrote to the Superior-General that all the minor rules were being broken, that laziness and sensuality prevailed, that two of the Company had been given permission to make a journey when such permission ought to have been denied. It is likely that M. Vincent—having studied the character of M. Codoing—had doubts as to his fitness for authority, but at Annecy he had special advantages for obtaining real knowledge of the position of affairs, because Mme. de Chantal, then very near the end of her life, was living there, and was in close touch with the Priests of the Mission. The responses to M. Escart's first letter of accusation temporizes, because M. Vincent was applying to Mme. de Chantal for advice. In due course he received from her the fullest reassurance as to the wisdom of his choice of M. Codoing; but meanwhile the self-appointed reformer had discharged another catalogue of charges against his Superior, and in reply to this M. Vincent expresses himself with invigorating clearness: "I give thanks to God, Monsieur, for your eagerness in the observance of the little rules, and your zeal for the advance in virtue of him of whom you write. But because zeal, like some other virtues, becomes a vice when carried to excess, it is well to be on one's guard against that possibility, and the zeal that passes the bounds set by the claim of charity to our neighbour is no longer zeal, but rather a fervour of dislike. I will allow that it may have been zeal to begin with, but its exaggeration has degraded it into this."*

The Mission Priests were bidden, in their relations with each other, to consider those of Christ and His disciples, and M. Vincent draws attention to the later development that began with constant criticism of Our Lord's teaching. "Why was it," he asks, "that those

* "Lettres," vol. i., No. 44.

who should have followed Christ persistently misunderstood Him? Was it not that they would not try to grasp the spirit in which He worked? Because they had allowed themselves to be out of sympathy with Him, they allowed criticism to go unchecked, until their minds were so filled with it that they could no longer distinguish between false and true. Whatever was in agreement with their twisted judgment they accepted gladly, and so there gathered the suspicion and hatred which had such terrible results."

M. Vincent must have been very clear in his conviction that M. Escart had taken up a thoroughly false position, or he would not resort to such severity of condemnation. To one who had constituted himself the defender of Christian conduct, the form of this rebuke must have been difficult to swallow, and it speaks well for the character of M. Escart that the Superior-General congratulates him—in a letter dated a few weeks later—on his complete submission and conquest of himself. It is, of course, quite impossible to form any judgment as to the justification for the charge that the minor rules were neglected and there was too much laxity; from further knowledge of M. Codoing we may conjecture that there were irregularities wherever he held authority, but a humorous light falls on the incident with another appearance of M. Escart among M. Vincent's correspondents.

One of the primary points of the Rule was the complete withdrawal of members of the Company from family life; they were never to visit their homes by their own desire. Yet M. Escart, that champion of strict conformity, becomes insistent that he should return to his native place. He was informed that one of his sisters was threatened with loss of faith, and it became imperative that he should reason with her. As a type M. Escart is wonderfully consistent. His self-assurance had induced him to make a formal complaint against his companions for deviation from the Rule; the same quality gives him

M. VINCENT AND HIS SONS

so high an estimate of his own powers of persuasion that the Rule itself must not be allowed to check their exercise. He was so decided in his intention of defiance that the Superior-General was forced to intervene. A firm reminder that members of the Company must adhere to its Rule would probably have been effectual, but M. Vincent preferred that his Sons should understand as well as obey. " Mme. de Chantal tells me you have heard of the apostasy of one of your sisters," he writes.* " I have been very much distressed, but—though I know not why it is—I find it rather hard to believe that this is the case. I fear the Enemy has suggested this means of attracting you home to those who would like to have you there." And thereupon the Superior proceeds to make it plain that M. Escart, who professes to renounce all things for his vocation, must remain quietly at Annecy. " You say," he adds, " that ' perhaps you may be able to draw this dear sister of yours back within the pale of the Church.' Indeed, you do well to say ' perhaps,' for you have reason to be very doubtful of it, and if you imagine you can of yourself do her any good, the only result will be your own injury. You may do this, however : it would be an excellent thing that you should write and ask the Capuchin Fathers at Lyons to see your sister and your relations and to do their best to win your sister back."

We can see, without aid of deep knowledge or experience, that the schooling of a Mission Priest was—to M. Escart and to natures such as his—the greatest opportunity conceivable. If within them there was enough true metal to stand the test, they might emerge from the fire of discipline with a real knowledge of themselves and with a grasp of the meaning of renunciation; and the debt that some of its members owed to the Company was greater than any advantage they could bring to it. The obvious and rather ludicrous faults of the less promis-

* " Lettres," vol. i., No. 46.

ing recruits were not, however, nearly so difficult to deal with as the brilliant qualities of the few who, like M. Codoing, had capacity for ruling. M. Escart might be malicious, pompous, inordinately vain, but his self-righteousness melts beneath a touch from M. Vincent; and, where he was concerned, there were no uncertain issues and very little reason for anxiety.

M. Codoing was a valuable acquisition to the Company, but there were times when he seems to have strained the powers of guidance, and even the patience of the Superior-General. The greatest cause of danger with M. Codoing was his high estimate of his own business capacity; this would appear to be the most innocent form of vanity, but in the life of a Mission Priest there was no room for vanity of any kind. As M. Vincent's representative and in control of a Branch-House, considerable powers were in his hands, but such powers were meant to be used after consultation; M. Codoing used them on his own initiative. It is very likely that his deep veneration for the Superior-General as a spiritual leader betrayed him into an under-estimate of the practical value of advice from headquarters. When he was rebuked for his independence, he replied that an answer which might have reached him in a month had not arrived after six months' delay, and that valuable opportunities had been missed in consequence. He may have gone from S. Lazare to take up his first charge at Annecy full of confidence that his abilities would secure temporal advantage for the Company, and the indifference with which his suggestions were received became intolerable. As the Superior-General was so slow in giving support to the interests of the Company, M. Codoing decided that it was his part to supply the deficiency, and he embarked on a promising financial scheme, unauthorized save by his own judgment.

M. Vincent was taken by surprise—he never expresses any confidence in M. Codoing's wisdom—and he regarded the undertaking in question (it was concerned with a species of mortgage in the town of Annecy) as altogether outside the province of a Mission Priest. " It may be true," he wrote,* " that I am too long in answering and over other matters, but even so I have never yet seen any undertaking damaged by my delay; I see rather that everything gets done in its own time and with the care it needs. I mean, however, in future to send an answer as soon as may be after I have received your letters, and have considered what they contain in the Presence of God. It is due to Him that we should take time to weigh those things that concern His service—that is to say, everything with which we have to do. You will therefore, if you please, correct your impatience in decision and action, and I will try to reform my slackness. And, above all, I implore you, in the Name of God, to give me news of all that happens, with the for and against of anything that is matter for question. Be very careful not to add to or take away from or in any way to change the system of our common life without having written to me and received my answer."

M. Vincent's knowledge of M. Codoing may have led him to direct greater severity towards him than towards others; yet, though the letters to him are concerned chiefly with rebuke, he is still selected for difficult posts. There was business at Rome, and he was sent thither in haste (though he seems in this instance to have desired delay).† On his journey we find he contravened his orders and borrowed money at Lyons,‡ and when he reached his destination it is quite evident that the Superior-General was extremely uneasy as to the result. There was good cause for uneasiness. M. Codoing may have made real surrender of personal ambition, but his enthusiasm for the Company betrayed him into a desire for its success; and even while he had every intention of

---

* " Lettres," vol. i., No. 57.   † *Ibid.*, vol. i., No. 59.
‡ *Ibid.*, vol. i., No. 62.

being loyal to its Founder, he failed to identify himself with the spirit that was its real foundation. In Rome especially there were many opportunities for dangerous errors, even in a humble Mission Priest not closely connected with the hot-bed of intrigue. The House of the Company there was an experiment. Missions had been held in Italy, and a centre for the Missioners was needed; but M. Vincent shrank from extending the scope of their labours or allowing them any prominence. M. Codoing, on the other hand, desires that they should claim importance, and have Seminaries that would compete with the Jesuits. He had the fullest belief that the methods of the Company were the best methods possible, and drew from this the conclusion that the more they could undertake the better. It must be acknowledged that M. Vincent needed all his faith in the Divine ordering of the affairs of the Company to keep his mind at peace while M. Codoing represented him at Rome.

"I beseech you to submit to the decisions we arrive at here," he wrote.* "I do not mean with regard to one special point, but in everything; and not to do anything of importance without writing to me and until you have received my answer."

It was a difficult command indeed for young impatience. So many opportunities had time to slip while the question went from Rome and the answer came back from Paris, and it seemed so unlikely that the decisions reached in Paris, with only partial knowledge of the circumstances, could be so good as those arrived at on the spot. M. Codoing was severely tested, and a firm belief in his real sincerity of purpose is the only explanation of his selection for his great responsibility.

"We let ourselves be too much carried away by our opinions, you and I," wrote M. Vincent, somewhat mendaciously; but it was his custom to associate himself with the misdeeds of those whom he reproved. "You

* "Lettres," vol. i., No. 63.

are, however, at a post where you need immense reserve and circumspection. I have always heard it said that the Italians are the most cautious people in the world, and the most distrustful of the hasty. Reserve, patience, and gentleness win in the end with them, and because they know that we French folk are too hasty they stand aside a long time before they will deal with us. In the Name of God, Monsieur, take heed of this, and also of the orders that we send you."

It seems that money had been sent for a certain M. Thevenin, also a member of the Company, and M. Codoing, deciding that a purpose for which he required it was more important, had appropriated it. M. Vincent indicated, with some vehemence, that this form of insubordination could not be permitted. "A thousand inconveniences and disorders must result when the will of the Superior is not obeyed," is the conclusion of his reprimand, and then, with one of the sudden outbursts that we may believe to have strengthened his hold immeasurably over his wayward Sons, he adds: "I seem to have said a great deal, Monsieur, but to whom could I speak simply and with complete openness if not to another self who is dearer to me than myself; indeed, I shall always show you my heart and keep nothing back, because I know the depths of yours and the charity towards me that Our Lord has given you."

Again and again M. Codoing makes complete surrender, and letters of warm gratitude and approval are despatched from Paris to Rome; but his desire for the recognized success of the Company is not easy to uproot, and again and again he unfolds fresh projects that present themselves to his imagination. He plans a Seminary, a House of Retreat like the one in Paris, a different method in the holding of Missions; finally, that the Mother-House should be transferred to Rome! The motive for some of his suggestions is avowedly the acquisition of favour among powerful people who may be useful; for some it is the most transient expediency; and no principle of the Company, however fundamental, is safe from his enthusiasm for novelty. We have no recorded instance of the Superior-General giving consideration to any one of his ideas, but he gives reasons for refusal, and these contain the fruit of deep experience of life. One private letter of rebuke has special significance.

M. Codoing had gone out of his way to obtain the notice of Cardinal Lanti, and to this end had disobeyed instructions. M. Vincent disapproved. " It seems to me," he says,* " to be a contradiction of Christian simplicity. I have always avoided works of piety in one direction that are to win credit in another, except in one instance, when we held a Mission in a particular place to gain the interest of the late M. le Président de Paris, which we believed ourselves to need. It was the Will of God that the effect should be contrary, for some of the Company gave such proof of our weakness that it was necessary for me to go to the place after the Mission, and, on my knees, ask pardon of a priest for an affront he had received from one of the Company. Thus did Our Lord show me by experience that which I had realized in theory, that we must look straight ahead without calculations in what we do and let His Hand guide us. . . ." The young Superior at Rome, reading those words amid so many very different influences, had opportunity to learn the real secret of the writer's power; but his fund of original ideas was so inexhaustible that no rebuff and no reasoning could convince him that they were wasted; the failure of one only seems to have encouraged him to produce another. M. Vincent was always ready for him, however:

" You may have plenty of arguments to bring against me," he told him; " but, believe me, Monsieur, I can supply an answer to every one, and therewith the experience which my sixty-six years and my own sins have

* " Lettres," vol. i., No. 67.

brought me, which may not be without its uses for you."

We may be sure that among the fruits of M. Vincent's experience was his understanding of an ardent nature and the difficulty with which it learns reliance on the Will of God. He had, indeed, much clearer knowledge of the full meaning of such reliance than have most human beings, and, because he had gone so far towards its attainment, he knew it to be unattainable in its completeness; but he insisted on it as the goal of aspiration, and he believed that for the hot impulsiveness of M. Codoing the constant remembrance of such a goal was specially necessary. For a Mission Priest to have his head full of schemes and to occupy his time in bringing them to a successful issue meant the destruction of the spirit of the Company. In a letter of remonstrance to M. Codoing we find one of his rare lapses into self-revelation and reminiscence. He goes back to the period after his return from Châtillon, when the plan for the first establishment at the Collège des Bons Enfants was under discussion, and, all his suggestions for a first Superior having been rejected, it had become clear that he himself was to be the Founder.

"The idea of the Mission was so perpetually in my mind," he says,* " that I began to fear it was proceeding from self-will, or even from the Devil. Full of this apprehension, I went into Retreat at Soissons, desiring that it might please God to take away the excitement and delight the enterprise was giving me. It did please God to grant my prayer, and by His Mercy my feelings were altered entirely; and if God gives any blessing to the Mission and I am no injury to it, I believe this to be the reason, and desire to make it my practice to undertake nothing and to decide nothing while I am full of enthusiasm and hopes about it. . . . . Our Lord casts down to raise up, and gives every kind of suffering to purify

* "Lettres," vol. i., No. 64.

us. He may often desire an object more than we do, but we must win grace to accomplish it by the practice of virtue and by many prayers. Will you let me say to you, Monsieur, that I have often detected the same fault in us both—that of following a new idea too easily and clinging to it too ardently. It is this which has caused me to pledge myself to do nothing of any importance without taking counsel, and God shows me every day the necessity of so doing, and deepens my resolve to adhere to it."

That Retreat at Soissons had taken place twenty years earlier—in 1622, when M. Vincent was forty-six; his reference to it gives us a glimpse of the interior contest which the restraint and discipline of his daily life hid so efficiently. He also, it would seem, knew what it was to be eager, to desire immediate action, to picture a completed building of his own devising before the foundation stone was laid; and on his knees he had implored for strength—not to attain, but to yield; to give up the plan with all the golden opportunities for good it was to offer; to stamp out the glory of the projected service; to desire nothing but that which the voice of God from day to day should claim of him. Looking back over that intervening score of years he may have seen the perils of shipwreck from which his prayer had saved him, and therefore have desired to detect in others and to repress with unflagging energy the instincts he knew so well by personal experience.

It would appear that M. Codoing was too strongly imbued with a real love of his vocation to fall intentionally into the sin of disobedience, and it was deliberate defiance of authority for which M. Vincent has no mercy. Some of the instances of this offence in the early years of the Company were certainly peculiarly flagrant. The vagueness of their vows, the novelty of their vocation, and the fact that their Rule had no tradition of observance to strengthen it, combined to provide Superiors with a certain number of open questions, and to give them some excuse for misapprehension as to the degree of their authority. Nothing could justify the licence that was taken, however. At Sedan, for instance, where the townsfolk were hospitable and the routine of the Mission-House became monotonous, the Superior moved a Resolution that invitations to dinner should in future be accepted, and put it to the vote among his brethren, despite the categorical provision of the Rule in this matter. The little detachment of the Company at Sedan being sociably disposed, the Resolution was carried, but one of the minority lost no time in reporting to headquarters.

It was at moments when his trust was betrayed to such a degree as this that the difficulty of M. Vincent's position must have seemed overwhelming. His letter to the Superior at Sedan is full of indignation: " I have been exceedingly astonished, and distressed beyond power of expression. You must allow me to tell you, Monsieur, that you have done wrong."* Adequate words to condemn wrong-doing of this type were indeed hard to find, for its results might well have dishonoured the whole Company; but it served to deepen M. Vincent's sense of the absolute necessity of obedience.

It must not be imagined that it was personal obedience to himself on which he was insistent; it is a remarkable characteristic of his method that his own judgment is only prominent when there is a question of advocating delay. Although he was the Founder and inspirer of such vast undertakings, and his reputation was so firmly established that his decisions would never have been questioned, it is evident that he was honest in consulting others and deferred to the opinion of his appointed advisers. Once a decision was reached, however, he exacted obedience to it from all the Company, and his gentleness, of which we have so many proofs, assumes

* " Lettres," vol. ii., No. 330.

a different aspect when we understand the capacity for resistance that went with it.

With reference to the position of the Superior-General he expressed himself once very clearly in a private letter* as follows: " There is this difference between the opinion of an individual and that of the General, that the first only sees and feels the things entrusted to him and is given grace only for that, while the goodness of God must give grace to the General for the whole of the Company. The individual may see all that the General sees—it is possible he may see more—but humility should make him distrustful of himself; while the General must have confidence that, as God proportions grace according to vocation, he will be given sufficient to choose what is best for the Company, especially in matters of great consequence to which he has devoted long reflection and much prayer."

It was by virtue of his office that M. Vincent asserted authority, and the submission that he required was to be made before God; it was not the yielding of one human will to another. With M. d'Horgny (who succeeded M. Codoing at Rome, and proved even more difficult to manage) it was necessary to be explicit on this subject. He had been guilty of setting aside instructions sent to him from headquarters, and M. Vincent explains the gravity of the offence:† " May I venture to say to you, Monsieur, that it is more important than I can describe that you should offer yourself to God to be made exact in following all the orders of the General, whatever they are, however much they go against your judgment, and whatever excellent reasons you may have for differing, or whatever may be the consequences; for no consequences can be so serious as is disobedience itself. The other day a Captain told me that if he saw that his General was giving mistaken commands, and knew that obedience to them would be likely to cost him his life, he would not say

---

* " Lettres," vol. i., No. 73.   † *Ibid.*, vol. i., No. 86.

a word, even if speech would alter his General's decision, because he would say it only at the price of his honour, and so ought rather to die than speak. You will realize, Monsieur, what a disgrace it will be to us in Heaven that military obedience should be so perfect and ours such a failure. I assure you that if two or three Superiors acted as you have done, it would be enough to wreck the Company altogether."

Rebukes of this nature are not given twice. M. d'Horgny had his choice between complete submission and the repudiation of his vows, and he was evidently strong enough to bear severity, for in later years there are many confidential letters to him from the Superior-General, and he continued to hold positions of trust. It was defiance such as his, however, that showed the necessity of a sanctioned Rule, and a vow that was absolutely binding.

It should be remembered that when the first Mission Priests gathered at the Collège des Bons Enfants they were animated by the deepest spirit of self-dedication, no other reason could have brought them there, and each one remained steadfast; then, when the numbers increased and the Company had become well known, the idea of it made appeal to the imagination, and there were some who obtained admission without having counted the cost. Months of monotony and uncongenial labour convinced them that they had made a mistake, and they applied to the Superior for release. M. Vincent was unmoved by any loss that the Company might sustain by such disaffection; it was the loss to the individuals of which he took a serious view. Discontent rather than open rebellion was the common prelude to desertion, for the culprit was always able to offer full justification for his own action. One phase of this temptation was the idea that the capacities which God had given were being wasted, and that retirement into another condition of life was a command of conscience. There was a certain priest, who must be referred to as M. X., who complained to the Superior-General that he had not sufficient opportunity for study. M. Vincent never desired to develop a love of learning among his Sons, and in this case he replied that the call to their vocation was an infinitely higher one than that of the student. " If you make progress in the school of our Lord, He will give you higher knowledge than you can get from books."* A year later, however (in 1652), the Bishop of Treguier was anxious to institute a Seminary in his diocese, and M. X. was selected as an assistant. We have no knowledge of his previous history, or under what circumstances the call to join the Priests of the Mission had come to him. He may have been carried away by one of those waves of aspiration that will disturb the balance of the sanest mind, and because his regard for his vocation was mental, and based on a reasoned conclusion that he was choosing the best manner to use his gifts for the service of God, it failed to give him the courage and endurance that were needed in the passing of the years. Interest and variety were essential to him, and probably he insisted to himself that his powers would be crippled by deprivation. On his appointment to the new Seminary, M. Vincent found it necessary to write plainly to him:†

" I beseech you, Monsieur, to make surrender of yourself to Our Lord in good earnest, that you may bear some fruit that is worthy of your vocation. Is it worth while for the vain satisfaction of coming and going, of paying and receiving visits, to fail in your duty towards God? Is it worth while, for the sake of your body (to which, perhaps, you give in too much) that your soul should cease to strive for the salvation of an infinity of others? If I had ever seen anyone the better for continuing in self-indulgence I would say to you: ' Do the same, by all means.' But, on the contrary, everyone is ruined who chooses that path; it is a wide one, and often leads to

---

* " Lettres," vol. i., No. 180.   † *Ibid.*, vol. i., No. 214.

perdition. The time has come, Monsieur, for you to follow Our Lord in the narrow path of a life that corresponds to your profession. It is nine months now since you began to show signs of slackness, in spite of the fact that you are under special obligation to make an effort after perfection. Firstly, because God calls you; secondly, because He has given you a very good disposition; thirdly, He has bestowed on you special inward grace and outward gifts; fourthly, there has been particular blessing on your past undertakings, and so great was His goodness towards you that He gave you strength to consecrate yourself to His service and that of His Church in a special manner.

"Remember, if you please, that you began well, and went on even better; and that, to let self get the upper hand now, would be lack of loyalty to God. It would be abuse of His grace, and would be at the risk of His indignation; and you would repent of it while your life lasts and afterwards. I imagine, Monsieur, that you will be greatly disturbed by what I say to you, and that the Evil One will do his best to break your courage and to overthrow you; but I hope that you will resolve at once to respond to God's purpose for you, and to bring it to effect everywhere and always. If you do this, Monsieur, be certain that He will give you grace beyond your need. I make this appeal in the name of His love for you, of the rewards He promises you, of the grace He has already given you, of the good work you have already done among priests and ordinary people. You delay too much; lost time never returns. Death comes; the harvest is plenteous, the labourers are few, and Our Lord depends on you. Remember, also, that Our Blessed Saviour said that He sanctified Himself that His own might also be sanctified. From this we learn that to work fruitfully for others we must needs practise good living ourselves. You have the chance of doing this without any hindrance. If you will let me suggest it, you should begin by making a good Retreat, and continue in serious endeavour to reawaken your own zeal and fervour."

The Mission Priest whose zeal and fervour could not be reawakened was worthy of all pity. To M. Vincent it may have seemed that he grew lax by his own consent, and was making choice between the two masters deliberately and fatally. But M. Vincent's vocation to the service of God and of his kind was so strong that the sense of reaction never affected him. The only remedy he could suggest for restlessness was immediate repentance and renewed self-dedication. There are further letters to this unsatisfactory Son of his, and about two years later there is one* that is partly congratulation on a resolve to remain loyal, and partly warning against an opposite choice :

"I give thanks to God for the grace He has bestowed on you, and to you for resisting the temptation that threatened to drag you from your vocation, and cast you back in the world; and I pray that you will be ever more and more confirmed in your promise to Our Lord to live and die in your vocation. One may not play at making promises to God, and then break one's word; and therefore I beseech you, Monsieur, to be steadfast in the vocation to which you are called. Remember all the high desires Our Lord has given you. Life is not long, the end comes quickly, and the judgment of God is heavy on those whose life here is over, and of whom He says: 'They have not fulfilled My commands.'"

The note of uncertainty is plain. This was not a faithful member of the beloved Company. He had been weighing and considering too long, and to hesitate at all in such a choice was fatal. That letter, with its covert warning, failed in its mission or came too late. Its recipient broke his vows. Probably he was allowed to go in silence, and justified his conduct to himself as he went. But M. Vincent could not condone this offence.

* "Lettres," vol. ii., No. 281.

The renegade Mission Priest remained a priest, and the capacity that had made him useful in the Company would, humanly, continue to be his when he had renounced a vow which at that period was only voluntary. His real fruitfulness for good was, nevertheless, destroyed by his refusal to bear the burden of self-sacrifice which he accepted with his vocation. Vincent de Paul shared with the Port Royalists the belief that suffering was an honour, the special mark of the design of God upon the individual. This doctrine, admirable as the theme of a religious exhortation, presents difficulties in application to daily experience. A man of sensitive nature, who also possessed high intellectual ability, may have found the Rule of the Mission Priest intolerable the moment that the glamour of the consciousness of sacrifice had faded. It was a Rule designed expressly to stamp out every tendency towards self-love and make half-measures impossible, but it would press far more heavily on a high-strung temperament than on the phlegmatic. According to M. Vincent, the finer nature had the more reason to glory in his vocation; but, as we have noticed already, M. Vincent's capacity for sympathetic comprehension of others failed him when the temptation to seek escape from the Company was in question. If they yielded, they had deserted from the service of Our Lord. In the case which we are regarding the culprit seems, after his desertion, to have applied to M. Vincent for help to get a particular cure. Possibly he found that, without M. Vincent's interest, he was debarred from any preferment, and if that were the case, his condition was melancholy. The following is the reply to his application:*

"I have given the cure for which you ask to a good priest, who is determined to live there and to do well. I should have been very glad to serve you, after having seen you offer yourself and your possessions to God for

* "Lettres," vol. ii., No. 294.

the salvation of the poor, if you had not, by withdrawing your offering, given me reason to fear that you were not more likely to be faithful in a new pledge to God than you were in the old. When you say that you left us with the desire of doing greater service to souls, who do you think will believe you, seeing that you could find in the Company opportunity to help both in the training of priests and in the work of the Missions that benefit the poor folk in the country?"

The verdict may seem pitiless, but the issues involved were too serious for leniency. The value of the Company lay not only in work accomplished, but in its meaning for its members. Experience had taught the Founder the degree to which their Rule was a protection from temptation, and if he appeared merciless to a deserter, he was so that he might deter others from choosing destruction under the guise of liberty.

"The priests who live in the world," he said,* "love their ease too much. They shirk work, and are always trying to collect benefices, their chief object being the satisfactions of this present life." It was a somewhat sweeping indictment, and not intended, probably, for literal acceptance, but it was founded on very intimate knowledge, and sufficiently explains his severity with those who had chosen a higher way and then rejected it. And underlying all M. Vincent's judgments in these matters is the sense of vocation, which in a nature such as his is an incalculable force. It was his sense of the priests' vocation which inspired him in his leading of the Ordination Retreats at S. Lazare, and in his control of the celebrated Tuesday Conferences. It was his sense of his own individual vocation that supported him through the intricacies and disappointments of his dealings with the Queen and Mazarin. Above all, it was his intimate and overwhelming realization of the true

* "Lettres," vol. i., No. 268.

vocation of a Priest of the Mission that taught him (unhindered by the number of its fools and waverers) to guide the Company towards fulfilment of its great purpose of saving souls, but which would not let him seek excuse for the weaklings who found the path too steep and had turned back.

CHAPTER VII

THE VOCATION OF A MISSION PRIEST

THE letters of M. Vincent to the Priests of the Mission declare to us his mind on the subject of vocation. One meaning of vocation to him was a love of Christ so burning that it consumed all desire other than His Will. Close examination of his recorded words suggests that in his view there were no degrees of vocation, because nothing could be more perfect than the perfect following of the Will of Christ. His desire not to exalt the Companies of which he was the human Founder led him into the use of expressions indicating the superiority of other Orders, but in fact no classification was consistent with his actual point of view. It is worth while to follow him into the detail of his direction of his Mission Priests that we may understand how searching and intimate was his representation of this claim of Christ upon them. If they neglected details, it was a sign that their vocation was not being faithfully followed. Unless the fire of the love of Christ was near extinction, there could be no desire to snatch the sweetness of small indulgences; and by the lowering of purpose in one member the whole Company suffered, for they were knit together by the acknowledgment of a claim that touched them all equally. As the first fervour that delights in exaggerated self-immolation died away, there appeared in many of these souls a tendency to rely on their vocation in its spiritual aspect, and neglect its external demands. In 1650 there is a letter from M. Vincent* (it is addressed to the Superior

---

* "Lettres," vol. i., No. 145.

THE VOCATION OF A MISSION PRIEST

at Richelieu, but it was sent to all the Branch-Houses of the Company) on the question of the rigorous observance of the Rule and the reason for such observance. This letter touches a principle which was a matter of difficulty to many, and though much of it is concerned with the minutiæ of the semi-monastic life of a Mission Priest, it would lose weight if given merely in extract.

"MONSIEUR,

"You know that everything is constantly undergoing change, that even men are never in exactly the same state, and that God often allows the most sanctified of societies to suffer loss. There have been examples of this in some of our houses, and it has come to our knowledge from visits made to them, although at first we did not discover the reason of it. It has taken some study and attention to find it out, but at last God has made it clear that a bad result has proceeded from the freedom with which some of you have indulged in more rest than the Rule allows. All the more because, in consequence of not joining the others in prayer, they forfeit the advantage of prayer in common, and very often pray very little or not at all by themselves. It follows that, as these persons are less watchful of themselves, they grow slack in conduct, and the Community no longer holds its life in common. To check such disorder, the root must be removed, and to that end you must require punctuality in rising, and insist on its observance, so that, little by little, each house will change its character, growing more attached to the Rule, and every individual will learn to prize his own spiritual privilege.

"All this caused us to make this opening act of the day the subject of our first 'Conference' in this new year, that we might become more resolute in all making four o'clock the invariable hour of rising, and so attain the sooner to the good effects of such faithfulness. This having been the subject of our discussion, I thought it well, Monsieur, to inform you of it, and to take counsel with you on the possibilities of objections to it, and the best means of impressing it on your family, so that they may maintain the same practice (or adopt it, if they are not doing so at present), and have their share in the blessing on it.

" The first advantage in rising at the moment of call is that it is fulfilment of the Rule, and consequently of the Will of God.

" The second, that the more prompt the obedience at that hour, the more acceptable is it to God, and it will bring a blessing on all the other doings of the day, as we see in the promptitude of Samuel, who, having risen three times in one night, won the praise of Heaven and earth, and special favour from God.

" The third, that one gives first place to that which is most worthy of honour, and as all honour belongs to God, we should give to Him this first act of the day, otherwise we shall be handing it to the Devil, allowing him to come before God. This is why he prowls around our bed when the day begins, that even if he have no more of us later, he may be assured of our first act.

" The fourth advantage is that, once one is accustomed to a time, there is no difficulty in waking or in getting up, habit taking the place of a clock, if none is to be had. While, on the other hand, Nature presumes on all we yield to her. If we rest one day, the next she will ask for the same indulgence, and continue the demand so long as we give her opportunity.

" The fifth is that mind and body are the better for the regulating of sleep. Those who allow themselves much become effeminate, and open the door to temptation.

" If the life of man is too short to serve God worthily and to atone for the waste of the night, it is melancholy that we should desire to curtail even such time as we have. A merchant will get up early to attain to riches; every moment is precious to him. A robber will do the same, and will be up all night that he may waylay travellers. Is it well that we should have less industry for good than they for evil? In the world there is much eagerness to be up to attend a great man's levée. *Mon Dieu!* how can we face the shame of losing the appointed hour for intercourse with the Lord of Lords, our patron and our all, because of our laziness?

"When we take part in prayer and office we share in Our Saviour's blessing, Who gives Himself freely, being present, as He Himself has said, among those who assemble in His Name. The morning is the fittest time for this employment, as being the quietest in the day. The hermits of old and the Saints, following in the steps of David, used it for prayer and meditation. The Israelites had to rise early to gather manna, and we, being without grace or virtue, why should we not do the same to attain to these things? God does not bestow His favours equally at all times.

"It is unquestionable that since He has given us grace to rise all at the same moment, we are all more punctual, more recollected, more humble, and in this there is reason to hope that so long as we are agreed on this matter there will be continuous growth in grace, and each one of us will find his vocation deepening. There are several who have left because, as they could not get enough ease, they could not content themselves with their condition. How can there be any eagerness for prayer in those who are only half-awake, and only get up under protest? On the other hand, those who rise promptly are those generally who persevere, who never grow slack, and make good progress. The reality of vocation depends on prayer, and the reality of prayer depends on getting up. If we are faithful in this first act, if we come before Him all together as the first Christians did, He will give Himself to us, He will give us of His light, and will Himself bring to pass in us and by us the good which we are bound to do in His Church. And He will give us grace to attain that degree of perfection which He requires of us, that we may be one with Him in eternity.

"You will see, Monsieur, how important it is that all the Company should rise at four exactly, because the worth of our prayer depends upon this opening action, and the worth of everything else we do rests on what our prayer has made it. He who said that he could tell what all his day would be from the prayer that began it, spoke with knowledge.

"In some, however, the love of soft living will not surrender without remonstrance, and because there is some excuse for saying that the rule of rising should not be equally binding on strong and weak, I foresee that it will be urged that the weak need longer rest than others. To that the best answer is the opinion of doctors, who all agree that seven hours' sleep is enough for all sorts of people, and also the example of all religious Orders, who limit sleep to seven hours.* There are none who take more, there are some who do not have so much, and with most it is interrupted, as they rise two or three times in the night to go to chapel. That which most of all reflects upon our weakness is that nuns do not have any more indulgence, although they have less strength and have been brought up more luxuriously.

"'But, surely, they sometimes take an extra allowance of sleep?' No, I have never heard that they do so, and I can assert that the nuns of S. Mary do not, except in the case of those who are ill and in the infirmary. 'What, Monsieur!' cries someone else, 'must one get up when one is ill? I have a terrible headache, a toothache, an attack of fever that has kept me awake all night!' Yes, my brother, my friend, you must get up if you are not in hospital, or have not received a special order to remain in bed; for if you have got no relief from seven hours' sleep, one or two hours more prescribed by yourself will not cure you. But if, in fact, you do require relief, it is needful that you should praise God with the others in

THE VOCATION OF A MISSION PRIEST

the appointed place of prayer, and that you there make your need known to the Superior. Unless this is the rule, we shall be perpetually forced to begin all over again, because so many will very often feel some illness, and others will pretend that they do, that they may pamper themselves, and so there will be endless opportunities for irregularity. And if one does not sleep soundly one night, Nature is very well able to make up for it the next.

"'Do you mean also, Monsieur,' I hear someone asking, 'to forbid any extra rest to those who have come off a journey or have just completed some arduous task?' I answer, Yes, where the early morning is in question; but when the Superior thinks there is weariness that demands more than seven hours' rest, he can give leave to retire earlier than the others. 'But when they come in very late and very tired?' In that case there would be no harm in allowing longer rest in the morning, because necessity is its own rule. 'What! must we always get up at four o'clock, in spite of the custom of resting till six once a week, or at least once a fortnight, to get a little refreshed? This is not only very annoying, but it is enough to make us all ill!' There sounds the tongue of self-love, and here is the answer: Our Rule and custom requires that we all have the same hour of rising. If there has been any laxity, it has only been so of late, and only in some houses, by the fault of individuals and the indulgence of Superiors, for in others the rule for rising has always been adhered to faithfully, and these are the prosperous ones. To think that illness will result from there being no intermission in observance is merely a fancy; experience has proved the contrary. Since the Rule was enforced there has been no illness here or elsewhere that there was not before, and, moreover, we know, and the doctors repeat, that oversleep is bad both for the dull and the high strung. Finally, if it be urged against me that there may be some reason which prevents someone from going to rest at nine or ten o'clock, I answer that such reasons must, if possible, be avoided; and if there be impossibility, it will be so rare that the loss of an hour or two of sleep is insignificant compared to the harm done by one remaining in bed while the others are praying.

" Have I not made a great mistake, Monsieur, to have expressed myself at such length with regard to the importance and usefulness of early rising, when your family is perhaps the most regular and the most fervent in all the Company? If that be so, I have no other object than to urge on them a humble thankfulness towards God for the faithfulness that He has given them; but if they have fallen into the fault against which we are fighting, I have good reason, I think, to require them to raise themselves from it and to ask you, as I am doing, to uphold them.

" May it please God, Monsieur, to pardon our past failures, and to give us grace to amend, that we may be like those fortunate servants whom the Master shall find watching when He cometh.

" Here, indeed, is sufficient for one letter; I ask the prayers of you and of your little Company."

Two points are here made clear to us: First, that the Mission Priests—though many of them were marvels of courage and self-devotion—were, in ordinary life, very human in inclination and in weakness. In consequence of this we see in truer proportions the miracle of guidance performed by M. Vincent. We may be tempted to think of him as controlling a huge machine which, from distant and scattered quarters, was connected with S. Lazare. Instead, we must recognize that his control was over a company of human beings, each with a very definite individuality, and each with his special struggle to maintain against familiar and ordinary temptation.

And then, by his insistence on a detail, we see how M. Vincent required the testimony of vocation to shine

THE VOCATION OF A MISSION PRIEST

in every thread of the fabric of a life. The truly dedicated life, under whatever conditions, is offered whole. There can be no treasured indulgence, however small, kept in reserve; even the wish to save out of the sacrifice is enough to spoil its value. A lengthy dissertation on the advantages of early rising is not, perhaps, a valuable contribution to spiritual literature, yet M. Vincent's exhortation to his Sons on the necessity of exact obedience to the Rule that a Mission Priest got up at four is one of the most characteristic expressions of himself that has been preserved to us. It is an exhortation to obedience, but it is much more than that. In the headquarters at S. Lazare the Superior-General, in spite of the innumerable claims upon his time, was living a life of prayer. In so far as the strength of the Company emanated from him, it was not on his experience and administrative capacity that it depended, but on his faithfulness in prayer. The evidence of his letters, as well as the witness of those who knew him, leaves no uncertainty on this point. Every distress and every difficulty was with the most complete simplicity laid before God, and he had discovered that there was no other method of guarding a vocation from the perils of distraction, of ennui, and of self-indulgence; his sense of peril was his motive for summoning his Sons to prayer. At the same moment every one of that great troop of combatants must be united (despite all division of distance) in asking for the aid they would all need before the day ended; if indifference crept in here the Company was doomed. It was, therefore, not only the enforcing of an order, but the comprehension of its spirit and the real desire to fulfil it which M. Vincent considered necessary, and this was by no means a small demand.

That obedience as obedience was required of a Mission Priest no less than of a Religious has been demonstrated in many of the letters already quoted. In its aspect as an exercise in humility it was specially cherished by

M. Vincent; he himself relates* that one of the seminary students was so full of zeal for his own spiritual advance that he desired to attend the lectures to ordination candidates. He asked leave to do so from the Director, but it was not immediately accorded to him, and he ventured to gratify his desire without leave. He was at the end of his last year, but for this misdemeanour he was required to remain an additional six months, " not having had strength to subdue himself in this matter."

The unnamed culprit seems to have been an ardent youth athirst to realize the spirit of the vocation which he hoped might be his own, snatching at every chance of external assistance and eager in every devotional exercise. Probably he would have been foremost in upholding M. Vincent's theory that the Mission Priest must be a man of prayer, and would have given intellectual assent to the assurance that humility is the necessary concomitant of the true spirit of prayer; but, when it was a question of deferring to the judgment of another where his own spiritual needs were concerned, his intellectual apprehension proved insufficient, and his professions of humility showed themselves to be unreal. By this one instance, insignificant enough in itself, we can judge of the innumerable questions that must have come before M. Vincent, in which his decision had lifelong effect on the spiritual life of those concerned; and of the impossibility of bearing such a burden solely by the aid of reason and experience. Rebuke was so very often necessary, and among the many responsibilities of authority there is none in which the grace of God is more essential than in the giving of rebuke. The vagaries of error were endless. Besides the heresy, the disloyalty, the disobedience, which were self-evident temptations to those who made profession of self-surrender, there were unexpected outbreaks originating in failings that were inconsistent with the most elementary understanding of

* " Lettres," vol. ii., No. 347.

THE VOCATION OF A MISSION PRIEST

the vocation of a Mission Priest. It was hard always for M. Vincent to believe that a real understanding, however faint, of what it meant to be a Mission Priest, could ever be clouded by any other consideration. As he expressed it to one of them who was tempted by the ambition of a scholar :*

"You must make yourself realize that there are thousands of souls who are stretching out their hands to you, who are saying, ' Alas, Monsieur ! God has chosen you to help to save us; have pity on us and give us your hand to draw us out of our present misery. We are left to rot in ignorance of our chance of salvation, and in sins which we have been ashamed to confess. If we lack your help we are in peril of damnation !' "

This is a very simple presentment of the position as M. Vincent understood it. The horrors of ignorance and vice were very vivid in his own mind, and it was the part of the priest to remedy them. It was the duty of his Company not only to be physicians themselves, but to train others to the same office, and both labours were equally important. We have an instance of the varied difficulties of the Superior-General in connection with this work of training. One of his priests employed therein was dominated by a violent temper, which expressed itself in abusive language and in blows. The need of plain rebuke was clear, the whole Company was likely to suffer by the scandal; but the sinner was the more difficult to deal with because he was not convinced that he was wrong, and M. Vincent became more forcible than was his habit in consequence :†

" If you say that you have not observed these faults in yourself, Monsieur, that is only a sign that you have very little humility; if you had as much as our Lord requires of a Priest of the Mission you would regard yourself as the faultiest of all, you would know yourself capable of these things, and would assume that the reason you do

* "Lettres," vol. i., No. 21 (1634).   † *Ibid.*, vol. ii., No. 393.

not see what is seen by others, especially since you have
been criticized, is some secret blindness in yourself. And
with regard to criticism : I am informed also that you
will not tolerate any from your Superior and still less
from others. If this be so, Monsieur, your condition is
indeed serious, and very far removed from that of the
Saints who humbled themselves before the world and were
glad to be shown any defects."

In truth, the condition of very many of them was very
far removed from that of the Saints, and yet the Call of
God upon them was one that demanded saintliness. The
work of village Missions alone required a specially consecrated body; and this need of sanctification becomes, if
possible, even more evident if we turn to that other
missionary enterprise that had its centre at Marseilles.

With the possible exception of the Foundling Hospital
in Paris, the most celebrated labour undertaken by
M. Vincent was that connected with the convicts at
Marseilles. It is in a measure detached from the accepted
tasks of the Company, but by its difficulty, and by the
conquest of inclination that it demanded, employment in
it was the most real test of spirituality. The idea that
M. Vincent's sympathy was first drawn towards the
captives in the Hulks by the recollection of his own years
of slavery is not a straining of probability; there is a
story that his pity once moved him to change places
with one of these wretched beings. We do not have it
on his own authority, and the question of belief in it
may be left to the discretion of the individual; his real
claim on the gratitude of the convicts had a far deeper
basis than a passing act of quixotism.

That which is humanly described as chance gave Vincent de Paul his original link to the Hulks at Marseilles.
M. de Gondi was General of the Galleys, and as a member
of his household, access to them, which otherwise might
have been denied, was accorded to him. Whether his
first visit was by the desire of M. de Gondi or at his own

THE VOCATION OF A MISSION PRIEST

request we have no means of knowing, nor does it signify; the work was waiting for him, and somehow he was brought to it. It would be an offence to transcribe the record of conditions prevailing in those days at Marseilles and at Toulon. The King's ships were rowed by malefactors; it was necessary that they should be rowed, and volunteers for the office were not forthcoming, therefore the stock of malefactors could never be permitted to run low, and the list of crimes which were visited by condemnation to the galleys became a formidable one.* When the term of the sentence was reached, there was no guarantee of release for those whose services were still required. An edict of Louis XIII.† ordains that the first two years of a convict's labour should not count as part of his sentence, because it took that period to train him as a seasoned and accomplished oarsman, and there seems to have been no protest against this singular inversion of the principle of punishment. When we add that the training, and the subsequent labour of those who were trained, was under the lash, that the rowers were chained to their oars, and that no change of climate altered in the slightest the conditions imposed upon them, we can form some idea of the despair which descended on the prisoner who heard this doom pronounced upon him.

As far as the process of the law was concerned, Vincent de Paul did not effect any improvement in the position of a convict. It is well to admit this fact at the outset; but it is difficult to decide whether any interference was within his power. We know that at the very beginning of his intercourse with them‡ he received a special ap-

* For example: An innkeeper lodging a stranger for more than one night without informing authorities; an able-bodied beggar giving a false name or simulating disease; anyone who could be proved to have caused a woodland fire, even accidentally (Simard, "Vincent de Paul à Marseilles").

† Clement, " La Police sous Louis XIII., Les Galères."

‡ 1619.

pointment from Louis XIII. as Royal Almoner to the Galleys, and also that M. de Gondi was extremely influential, and he stood high in favour with M. de Gondi. Even in those days, moreover, it was possible to appeal to popular sentiment to check a monstrous abuse, and a priest with the reputation that M. Vincent already possessed had the best opportunity for circulating such an appeal; his observations would be listened to and repeated until his cause became a public one. On the other hand, he was a member of the household of M. de Gondi, and an outcry raised against the conditions of the convicts was of necessity an attack on the General of the Galleys. At the time of his first connection with them he had made his attempt to retire into obscurity, and had just accepted the decision that the place he held was assigned to him by God. Moreover, at all times he was influenced by the instinct of deference from the peasant to the noble, and he would not have assumed the position of mentor towards M. de Gondi without the actual compulsion of his conscience. It is clear that he felt no such compulsion, nor, when M. de Gondi himself was no longer concerned, did M. Vincent attempt to move the authorities; and thirteen years after his death we find a Bishop of Marseilles presenting a humble petition in favour of certain prisoners whose term of servitude had expired ten years earlier, but who were still chained to their oars, which suggests that the barbarities practised in 1622 had not lessened half a century later.

The explanation of M. Vincent's quiescence is not to be found in a failure of compassion. He realized what sentence meant to the future galley slave, he knew that many died by their own hand rather than face the penalty, and that the lives of many more were wasted from lack of the bare necessities of existence, while all were brutalized by the cruelties to which they were subjected. He suffered in the thought of their sufferings, but there seems to have been in him a touch of something akin to fatalism; we find evidence of it in his unwillingness to interfere with the administration of the Hôtel-Dieu at the call of Mme. Goussaulte, and again in his abstinence from protest when Jean François de Gondi became a candidate for priesthood. To the onlooker in these very differing cases his duty appears obvious, but in the first he only took action under obedience, and in the second he never attempted any action at all. In fact, we must believe that he waited always for the call of God, and that complete reliance (which we have seen sustaining him under responsibilities that were too great for human strength) withheld him from interference in disorder, unless he was assured that interference was required of him by God. This position of absolute quiescence is, of course, difficult to reconcile with the theory of the pure philanthropist; it is not one that can be adopted lightly, for it assumes the long and diligent practice of prayer which safeguards the soul from self-deception. If M. Vincent's life was in any degree consistent, we must recognize that that which he left undone was so left as the result of prayer.

The fact being admitted, then, that the cruelty meted to the convicts was not lessened by M. Vincent, it is desirable to ascertain the actual value of his sympathetic intentions towards them. It was the custom to assemble the prisoners destined for the Hulks in Paris until there were a sufficient number to be worth escorting southward; then *la chaine* started on its miserable pilgrimage. But great as were the horrors of the road, they were not greater than those which were endured in the time of waiting in the dungeons of the capital; and here M. Vincent was able to interfere to some purpose. For the good of the State it was desirable to preserve these future oarsmen from disease, and the conditions to which they were abandoned made disease inevitable. Contemporary writers revel in revolting details, but it is sufficient to note that in this intermediate stage between condemnation and the fulfilment of their sentence, the culprits were kept chained to a wall in prisons that in some cases were underground. M. Vincent collected money, and a building in the Rue S. Honoré, near the church of S. Roch, was dedicated to the purpose he desired. Thenceforward a galley-slave obtained his first knowledge of the charity of the Mission Priests before he reached Marseilles; moreover, when the Confraternities had developed, benevolence to the convict was one of the duties of a Lady of Charity; and if they fell ill while still in Paris, they were tended by Sisters of the Poor. By this means the way was opened for nearer approach when they were established at Marseilles.

The earliest scenes in the history of the Mission to the Convicts are personal to M. Vincent. He could use the memory of his own imprisonment to give him a footing of equality, and even at that period he had so far attained humility that the most resentful of tempers could not detect in him any tokens of condescension. He desired to approach them as comrades who had fallen on evil days, and by that method opened a door to their hearts that might have appeared to be hermetically sealed. It is impossible to imagine a less promising scene for spiritual awakening than the Hulks at Marseilles and Toulon, but the surprise that proceeds from violence of contrast has a peculiar power. Men who were habitually treated as brutes were astonished at the approach of a stranger—even though he was only a priest in a shabby cassock—who spoke to them as if there was some favour they might confer upon him, and appeared oblivious of the horrors that made them loathsome to themselves and to each other. In Paris one of them threw a dish at one of the Sisters of Charity, and in return she besought the guards not to punish him.* This was the method which M. Vincent desired in dealing with them. He knew that even the most righteous severity would be misplaced.

* "Conferences," No. 102.

THE VOCATION OF A MISSION PRIEST

" It is when I have kissed their chains, sympathized in their sufferings, and showed them my sorrow for their misfortunes, it is then that they have listened to me, that they have given glory to God, that they have sought salvation." So he wrote in after-years to the priest* who was carrying on his labours at Marseilles, and the description probably is almost literal. He was doing that which was folly in the eyes of the world, and he could only do it by such an effort of the spirit as should show him Christ in the most miserable and the most guilty of the unfortunates to whom he ministered.

His scheme for the holding of Missions was new in his mind at the time of his first knowledge of the convicts, and in 1622 he applied it for their benefit. He had the fullest support from de Gondi, and from Cardinal de Sourdis, Archbishop of Bordeaux. He was allowed to choose twenty Religious to help him, and had free entrance to the galleys for himself and them. He appointed two to each vessel, and himself passed from one to another, working continually. His Mission lasted a month, and whatever may have been its permanent effect on the prisoners themselves, the effect upon M. Vincent was to imbue him with a strong desire to resume the attempt that he had made, and to provide some permanent aid and means of consolation for these the most wretched of his fellow-countrymen. No claim, in fact, could make sharper appeal to the instinct of pity, but M. Vincent did not rule the order of his undertakings by any obvious human instinct. It may be that the work at Marseilles was crowded out by the rapid march of events, and by his own separation from the General of the Galleys, but it is quite equally likely that, having brought his own great inclination for this enterprise before God, he was not convinced that he was called to embark on it; and, in fact, it was left in abeyance for ten years. The position of M. Vincent between 1620 and

* M. du Coudray.

1630 was a strange one. He was awaking, first, to a sense of the miseries, physical and spiritual, endured by the majority of his fellow-countrymen; and, second, to the comprehension of his own mission as God's agent for their assistance. The effect of the double revelation upon him resembles the consternation expressed by Isaiah, rather than the ardour of the successful leader of reform. He was always afraid to assume that, because he saw the existence of an evil, it was necessarily his part to interfere with it. Later on, when he held in his hands the threads that could guide great forces of benevolence, the response to cries for help was accorded with less misgiving; but in that earlier time he was, in his own phrase, "afraid to encroach upon the purposes of God." His vocation was only gradually accepted. It came to him with an understanding of its difficulty that was as a fire for the burning of his self-esteem. In the time of transition, although there were many possibilities of service within his reach and within his capacity, he chose to set them aside deliberately.

When he resumed his work for the convicts, there is evidence that M. Vincent was no longer single-handed. As far as it is possible to disentangle the confusion of record, it would appear that the *Cabale des Dévots* had been in advance of him in practical effort for lessening the horrors of the galleys, and that it was chiefly their efforts which achieved the building of a hospital for the tending of the convicts in sickness. As Abelli never makes any reference to that strange secret society, and he is responsible for the contemporary record of M. Vincent, it is quite possible that credit has been unfairly apportioned in this as in other matters; but there is no doubt that, when public attention had once been directed to this particular abuse, all responsibility for spiritual ministration to the prisoners was assigned as a matter of course to the Priests of the Mission. It was in 1643 that the hospital was actually opened, and at the same

Marie de Vigneron.
(Duchesse d'Aiguillon)

THE VOCATION OF A MISSION PRIEST 345

time, by the generosity of Mme. d'Aiguillon, a permanent house in connection with it was established for the use of the Lazarists, four of whom were to be always in residence. Then at length M. Vincent was able to send labourers to the field on which he himself had entered twenty years earlier with such energy and enthusiasm.

By general consent it was decided that the new conditions should be inaugurated by the holding of a Mission. One of the Oratorians — Jean Baptiste Gault — had recently been made Bishop of Marseilles, and his extreme enthusiasm for the work resulted in his death from exhaustion and overstrain.

The Mission lasted twenty days, the first eight being given to instructing the prisoners collectively; afterwards opportunity of individual intercourse was allowed by the authorities. Even with every facility for investigation a spiritual balance-sheet is of questionable value, and it is not at this distance of time possible to form any estimate of the result. The Director was M. du Coudray, one of the first companions of M. Vincent, and pre-eminently fitted for his task, and we are told that scarcely a soul upon the Hulks remained unaffected. It is evident that a wave of emotionalism passed over them, and there are picturesque accounts of the prayer meetings held among themselves by the convicts, and the intervals of leisure devoted to the singing of hymns and to spiritual reading. Only a little knowledge of the criminal class is sufficient, however, to discount a reckoning of wholesale conversion.

All that we can know is that the twenty days' Mission made a great impression, and that the work that followed it was worthy of the highest tradition of the Mission Priests. The fact that the hospital was under their supervision was an immense assistance to them. The galley-slave who escaped thither from the horror of illness on the Hulks found himself under merciful conditions of which he had had no experience. It was the most opportune moment conceivable for delivering to him that message of interior peace with which the Lazarist was commissioned. But the deceptive faculty draws its most luxuriant growth from the soil that nourishes the criminal instincts, and spurious penitence no doubt was common in the convict hospital, and disappointment the most ordinary experience of the Mission Priest. It was, indeed, admitted that the most arduous post for a member of the Company was that of Superior to the Mission at Marseilles, and that the labour that set the severest tax on spiritual vitality concerned the prisoners in the galleys. But it might be admitted with equal justice that there was none more suited to a true Son of M. Vincent, for it forced him into a supreme reality of aspiration. Constant failure might be relied upon to weaken his self-love, and the ugliness of the life he was forced to look at schooled him in detachment. So trained, he had the fullest opportunity of living up to his vocation.

There were difficulties besides the difficulty of their spiritual labour. Certain townsfolk of Marseilles were associated with them in the government of the hospital, and local jealousies and disagreements disturbed its peaceful ordering. Graver questions were involved by their connection with the Hulks. Here the appointment of the Almoner (necessarily a priest) was in their hands, but the Captain of a galley was supreme with a kind of supremacy that has no parallel in civilian life; and the office of Almoner, though it had long had nominal existence on every galley, was not recognized with any respect. The Almoner had a place at the Captain's table, and, despite his priesthood, was under the Captain's orders. He was sometimes required to take his turn of watch, and it was extremely hard for him to assert the real immunity from any service of the ship which was his right. It was, in fact, such an anomalous position that vacancies, when they occurred, were very difficult to fill,

THE VOCATION OF A MISSION PRIEST 347

and the candidates were not of a type that could be imbued with the missionary spirit. Yet, when the galleys put out from port, the rowers had no spiritual assistance except from the Almoner, and the whole object of the Mission Priests on shore was so to stir them from their apathy that they would need spiritual assistance. When Colbert was Chief Minister there were forty galleys in the harbour, and more than 8,000 prisoners manning them. The responsibility resting on the little Company of Lazarists established at Marseilles was, therefore, very heavy, and it is evident that the naval authorities resented any interference from them, and interposed every hindrance to the fulfilment of their charge.

There was another consideration for those posted at Marseilles besides the constant test of tolerance and temper. The danger to health was abnormal. Bishop Gault may have fallen a victim to overwork, but many of the deaths there were clearly due to infection. One of the Company—M. Robiche—a man of thirty-five, and in vigorous health when he arrived, forfeited his life after a few months of service. He was noted for his devotion to the prisoners in the hospital, and from them he caught what is termed a " purple fever," and died of it. Of necessity his companions and his successor must have realized that his fate was always hovering very near themselves. Marseilles was, indeed, no place for waverers, and even the most faithful may have flinched sometimes at the sharpness of the demand life made on them.

In 1649 there was so terrible an outbreak of the plague as to cause a sort of stampede among the inhabitants. The condition of the Hulks reached a point of horror from which the imagination recoils. There was no one to perform the most ordinary offices for the dying or the dead, but the prisoners remained prisoners still without opportunity to snatch a chance of life. A few words record the fact that the Sons of M. Vincent stuck to their post, but it is a fact that implies much. In those days terror of the plague amounted to a passion, and their numbers—there were but four of them—were utterly inadequate. If they had retired on the plea that the situation was beyond their power to remedy, the excuse could hardly have been challenged; instead, they did their part to establish the standard of the Company. Aided by Simiane de la Coste, a Provençal gentleman who was a prominent member of the *Cabale des Dévots*, they laboured incessantly, endeavouring specially to preserve the living by burying the dead. It is remarkable that only two—M. de la Coste and one of the Lazarists—died, for the mortality was abnormal, and the peculiar horrors of this particular outbreak of the pestilence is still one of the traditions of Marseilles.

M. Vincent loved his Sons individually, and waited day by day in eager expectation of news from the South; but he was at peace concerning them, whether he ever saw them in the flesh again or not, for they were showing that spirit of entire self-offering which should be inherent in the priest, and justifying for all time the vocation of his " paltry Company."

CHAPTER VIII

THE FOREIGN MISSIONS

A CERTAIN infection lies in the display of courage. The Lazarists at Marseilles, who held their lives so lightly, were partly responsible for the fine indifference to danger which came to be recognized as characteristic of the Company. It is probable that M. Vincent was affected by this development among his Sons, and that their readiness to sacrifice themselves suggested those perilous enterprises on which he embarked in the last fifteen years of his life. It was also a natural sequence of idea which drew him from the criminal captives on the galleys to their innocent companions in adversity, the Christian slaves in Tunis and Algiers. In those days the Mediterranean was infested by Turkish pirates, who made as much profit out of the crew and passengers on board their prizes as out of the merchandise. Their prisoners were sold in the market at Algiers as cattle are sold, and were treated afterwards as having less value than cattle. No difference of degree was recognized between the gently born and the roughest seaman, and no pity was shown to women. Only the width of the Mediterranean separated French subjects from their native land, but no effort was made to deliver them from a bondage that was daily torture. At Algiers there are said to have been about 20,000 slaves, and the majority of them were French; yet France was nominally on peaceful terms with the Sultan, and had her Consuls to represent her in his dominions. The position was singular, and it would require intimate knowledge of the practices of diplomacy at that period to understand it.

M. Vincent cannot have had much experience of the administration of foreign affairs, but his connection with Marseilles brought the plight of the Christian slaves in Africa before his attention, and the memory of his own youth sharpened his perception of this horror. It was not only compassion for their pain that moved him. He thought of them as Catholics in the hands of infidels, and he determined to put within their reach the only consolation that could be of real value in the midst of such suffering as theirs. This enterprise was the most risky of all that he undertook. The actual loss of life involved was less than in the missionary expedition to Madagascar, but in it he touched issues which were outside the office of a priest, and the Company at times ran serious risk of discredit. It is easy to understand the motive of his action—he was venturing where others dared not venture, because unhappy souls pleaded to him for succour—but it was utterly at variance with his habitual prudence. His first measure was not so reckless as that which followed. It was by the terms of a treaty with the Sultan that France was represented by Consuls both at Algiers and Tunis, and the Consul had permission to bring with him a priest of his own faith. The Consuls had shown no eagerness to avail themselves of this privilege, but it gave opportunity to M. Vincent, who obtained the appointments for Priests of the Mission. No plan could have been more wise and reasonable. A Mission Priest sent by the French Government, and officially attached to the French Consul, should have had every opportunity of ministering to French subjects unmolested. But, although something was achieved, the obstacles thrown in the way of the Lazarists almost nullified their efforts, and M. Vincent, in far-away Paris, came to the conclusion that it was mainly due to the Consuls that no progress was being made. It is possible that this decision was a just one. The position of a Consul was exceedingly precarious. Either Sultan or Dey would break faith if the inducement

THE FOREIGN MISSIONS 351

were sufficient, and any infringement of the treaty with France would inevitably mean death to the French Consul. The successive holders of the office were mainly occupied in endeavours to escape from it without damage to their future career, and incidentally they were sometimes able to acquire fortune by a trading venture. It was not to be expected that they would welcome the advent of the priests from France, nor that they would do anything to facilitate any plans that concerned the spiritual consolation of the Christian slave. The Queen Regent might be reputed to have pious proclivities, but it was a far cry from Algiers to the Palais Royal. The reward accruing to those who aided the Lazarists was problematical, while the risk of so doing was obvious and immediate. As a result, the reports of the Lazarists, while they deepened M. Vincent's conviction of the need of missionary labour in Algiers, did not satisfy him that their actual presence there was being of much benefit to the Christian captives.

It would appear that the Turks were anxious to win converts for Mohammedanism, and that the plight of the slaves was aggravated by intermittent religious persecution. We find M. Vincent embarking on action which appears ill-judged and hasty, and it is interesting to see that he did not do so to prevent bodily suffering. It is plain that he was haunted by the thought of the constant danger of apostasy that shadowed these unhappy captives. He knew the isolation and the hopelessness of their lot, and could realize that the great amelioration that would reward them for denial of their religion was a temptation not easily withstood. He was not able to deliver them from their distress, but he believed himself to be under a sacred obligation to provide them with the consolations of their faith. Without the Sacraments it was hard for them to continue steadfast, yet, if they yielded to their tempters, they condemned themselves to punishment for all eternity. His point towards their dilemma was absolutely consistent with the principles by which his life was ruled, and it was the zeal of a faithful priest that prompted him to his great adventure; nevertheless, it is with something of a shock that we find him buying, on behalf of the Congregation of the Mission, the office of Consul at Tunis and at Algiers, and appointing to each a member of the Company that was pledged to hold aloof from politics. " It was a mistake of his piety to imagine that the qualities essential to a Consul could co-exist with those essential to his monks," says M. Eugene Plantol in his chronicle of the relations between Algiers and France.* " Christian humility and the thirst for martyrdom are not the best qualifications for a Consul," is the suggestive phrase of another of his critics.† Possibly the mistake is explained by the difference between M. Vincent's estimate of " the qualities essential to a Consul," and that of the normal observer, and no word of his ever suggests that he regarded his experiment as a failure.

" If it is worth risking a life for the salvation of one soul," he wrote,‡ after nine years' experience of the difficulty of the enterprise, " how can we give up so vast a number because we count the cost ? And even if the only result of our attempt was to show the glory of our faith to that accursed land by the testimony of men who cross the sea and leave their home and brave a thousand dangers to comfort their unhappy brethren—even so I should hold the money and the men were well employed."

From the outset he needed all his courage. There were remonstrances from Propaganda at Rome on the plea that the Church forbade a priest to hold secular office in a heathen country. The fact that the Mission Priests

* " Correspondance des Deys d'Alger avec la Cour de France, 1579-1833," Introduction.
† H. de Grammont, " Relations entre la France et la Regence d'Alger au 17me Siècle," part iv.
‡ " Lettres," vol. ii., No. 423.

THE FOREIGN MISSIONS 353

were Consuls proves that their Superior was able to overcome these objections, but one may imagine that he did so by the weight of his character rather than his arguments, for reason was against him, and the Lazarist Consuls were not successful as officials.

The history of this Mission, as it was under M. Vincent's control, is a very curious one. His successor realized that there were business faculties required, even from the point of view of the captives, which members of the Company did not possess, and the right of appointment was sold to Colbert in 1669; therefore the real experience of the experiment was gained in M. Vincent's lifetime. The clearest example of its drawbacks may be found in the history of M. Barreau, who was appointed to Algiers in 1651, and appeared to be a promising pioneer for the new scheme. M. Barreau was a native of Paris, belonging to a family of wealth and established respectability; he had no vocation for the priesthood, but a strong instinct of self-sacrifice urged him into becoming a Brother at S. Lazare. He seemed to have every qualification that M. Vincent most desired for the post. He was sure to give loyal support to the priests of the Company, and to be zealous in softening the lot of the Christian slaves in any way that might be possible. But, unfortunately for Frère Barreau, it was part of his duty to buy the release of those captives for whom money could be collected. Mme. d'Aiguillon (to whose generosity the purchase of the Consular appointments was due) was specially ardent in this matter, and vast sums were given, in the name of religion and of charity, to save the Christian captives from the risk of martyrdom or of apostasy. S. Lazare became a sort of agency for the transport of ransoms, and in many cases the relatives of a slave contributed all the money they could raise to secure his liberation. It will be seen that the business side of M. Barreau's commission required very careful handling; but his personal touch with individuals moved him to the most astonishing negligence of the ordinary principles of justice. He deduced, from the fact that all men are equal in the sight of God, the theory that all had equal rights, and that therefore he might apply for the liberation of one slave (whose plight was specially dangerous or deplorable) the money that had been contributed for the benefit of another.

The distance from S. Lazare to Algiers, and the length of time required for communication, increased the difficulty in which M. Barreau involved his Superior. In vain M. Vincent reminded him that a year had elapsed since the sums necessary for the release of such and such persons had been acknowledged, and still nothing was heard of their return, and "their relatives, who are justified in requiring news of them, are giving trouble, and we know not what to say."*

M. Barreau may not have intended to appropriate what did not belong to him, but in actual fact he did make use of the ransom intended for one unfortunate that he might have the happiness of delivering another, and the explanation that he regarded his action as consonant with the strictest principles of Christian charity did not pacify the father who had sold his goods for his son's release, or the wife whose support depended on the speedy deliverance of her husband. Living as he did in daily association with the prisoners in Algiers, M. Barreau might congratulate himself that the money entrusted to him was applied to the most urgent and deserving cases; but M. Vincent, in Paris, had to deal with the disappointed kinsfolk of those whose captivity had not aroused M. Barreau's pity, and a note of indignation is apparent in the letters despatched from headquarters. The Lazarists were unfortunate in their choice of a representative; the reaction from constant obedience seems to have combined with inherent unworldliness to destroy any common sense that he may ever have possessed. Not only did his compassion move him to borrow largely to liberate the slaves, but he

* "Lettres," vol. i., No. 243.

THE FOREIGN MISSIONS 355

was weak enough to go surety for a merchant from Marseilles. The merchant went bankrupt and prudently decamped, leaving liabilities to the extent of 12,000 crowns, for which the Consul was imprisoned by the Turks.*

"Never before," wrote M. Vincent to the Superior at Marseilles,† "have I had so fine a lesson in the evils of disobedience as has been given me in these matters. They have involved and discredited the Company to a degree beyond possibility of telling."

The Company was not really implicated in the matter of the Marseilles merchant, but the arrested debtor was their representative, and it was impossible to leave him to bear the penalty of his own folly. Money, that was so sorely needed in other directions, had to be collected to set M. Barreau free, and, when his release had been effected, he received a vigorous letter of advice from his Superior. "I give thanks to Divine goodness," wrote M. Vincent,‡ "that you have preserved your reputation and can still protect the slaves for whom you have so much feeling. You must be very careful not to divert sums of money to other purposes than those for which they are sent to you (for instance, not to take from one to give to another), but you must keep for each that which belongs to him, and be ready to give it up when he claims it. And with regard to what you say of slaves released by the merchants to whom you cannot refuse the thirty piastres they need for their return, I must tell you that you can only advance it if you have the money of your own; you may neither borrow it nor take it from what is intended for others, nor must you go surety for others. If you do so, we shall be just where we were before, with the drawback that it would not be possible for us to deliver you again. There must never be another suggestion of raising money in Paris on your behalf. Whether you

* "Lettres," vol. ii., No. 384. † *Ibid.*, vol. ii., No. 420.
‡ *Ibid.*, vol. ii., No. 488.

can continue or whether you should give up depends upon yourself. It will be easy for you to continue if you will listen to what is said to you. Have no dealings that are outside your office; do no business, nor make any arrangements with people in the world, except when your office requires it of you; and do not involve yourself in what is beyond your powers. It is with good reason that I give you this special charge not to go outside your Consular business, for, besides the trade for diamonds and other things that you entered upon, I find that you have quite recently written to your brother about undertaking to send pearls to France. This, my dear brother, is out of place, and against the Will of God. He called you to fulfil your duties—not for bargaining."

This letter, gentle though it is, shows us to what extreme of folly M. Barreau had been tempted. Money meant liberty to the captives, and the harassing thought of their captivity destroyed in him all scruple as to the means of obtaining money. It was a malignant fate that caused the credit of S. Lazare to fall into the hands of one in whom the honest spirit of devotion could be so distorted; yet M. Barreau's errors were not the only ones that checked the success of M. Vincent's enterprise. The impression produced by a first association with the Christian slaves in Africa was overwhelming, but its effects on different temperaments were curiously varied. While M. Barreau was moved to compassion of the most unbalanced kind for their sufferings, a fellow-labourer, Philippe Le Vacher, Priest of the Mission, was so appalled by their depravity that pity seems to have sunk into abeyance. Pain may have power to bring men down to the level of the brutes, and some of these slaves had sunk to the same condition of despair as the convicts at Marseilles. Among them were priests and Religious who failed entirely to profit by the opportunity afforded them of sanctifying suffering. Le Vacher was young, and his training had imbued him with a vigorous view of the obligation of a priest; much that he saw roused him to righteous indignation, and he seems to have gone among the broken wretches he was intended to encourage, with the flail of ecclesiastical discipline.

Again it was necessary for M. Vincent to despatch a letter of remonstrance. " Draw what good you can from priests and Religious by gentle means," he wrote.* " Use no severity except in extreme cases, lest the discipline which your position gives you the power to exercise, joined to the misery of bondage which they have to endure already, drives them to despair. You are not responsible for their salvation, as you seem to think; you have been sent to Algiers to comfort unhappy souls, to help them in their suffering, and to give them courage to be steadfast in our holy religion. . . . It is impossible to enforce rule without adding to the wretchedness of these poor fellows; it would hardly be possible to do it without putting them out of patience with you altogether. Above all, you must not be in such a hurry to interfere with their habits, even though their habits may be bad. Someone repeated to me the other day a passage of S. Augustine, which says one should be very careful not to begin by an attack on the vice that is prevalent in a place, because one will not only achieve nothing, but will repel all those to whom vice is habitual, and thereby become incapable of effecting any good at all. Whereas, by a different method of approach, much might have been accomplished. I implore you, then, to be as considerate as you can to human weakness. You will be far more likely to win these captive priests by showing compassion than by reproach and rebuke. It is not understanding that they lack, it is strength; and that is best conveyed to them by good example and friendly intercourse. I do not say that you should sanction what is evil, but I say that the cure should be a gentle and a kindly one because of their circumstances, and should be applied with infinite precaution. . . . Good work is so

* " Lettres," vol. i.. No. 179.

often spoilt by too much haste; impulse runs away with wisdom and makes us think that because a good thing needs doing, it is therefore practicable immediately. It is not so, and one finds it out by the failure of result. . . . Ah, Monsieur, how deeply I desire that you should restrain your eagerness and weigh each enterprise carefully in the scales of the sanctuary before you begin it. Be patient rather than ardent; thus will God achieve by you alone that which all mankind could not accomplish without Him."

It is when M. Vincent is required to demonstrate the obvious that we see the sort of material from which those workers of his were moulded. We find that one can break faith and disobey in affairs of infinite importance, while another can associate with men who live in torture of mind and body and desire to sit in judgment on their moral failure rather than console them in their miseries. Probably M. Vincent had more sympathy with Jean Barreau in his recklessness than with Philippe Le Vacher in his self-righteousness, but to feel that the work, for which —beyond all the rest—his own heart yearned, lay in such hands as these must have made his burden of anxiety almost too great for bearing.

Fortunately, there is another side to the picture. The Company of the Mission, whether at home or abroad, might furnish abundant evidence of the weakness of human nature, but it could also show the heights of achievement to which the Christian soul can rise, and in the African Mission the quality of the workers was drawn out to a peculiar degree. Philippe Le Vacher himself learnt charity from his Superior, and became valuable; but in his brother Jean Le Vacher we find the purest strain of the missionary spirit. Of him it is related that when, in deep despondency over a broken love affair, he went to S. Lazare to ask counsel, he was pressed by M. Vincent to enter the Company—the only instance of such an occurrence that was known. He was only twenty-eight when he was sent to Tunis. He held the office of Consul from time to time, but his spiritual capacity was too great for purely secular labour to be his vocation. He may be said to have given his life to the slaves. Thirty-seven years of it were passed among them, and he finally suffered martyrdom by being blown from the cannon's mouth at Algiers in 1683. The danger of martyrdom was close at hand for every Mission Priest in Africa, for all the force was held by the Turks; and if a wave of fanaticism swept over them—as happened periodically—the Christians were completely at their mercy. " They can harm you," M. Vincent wrote to one of them,* " but I beseech you to have no fear. For they will do you no harm save that which Our Lord wills that you should suffer, and that which comes to you from Him is only to prepare you for some special favour which He designs to bestow upon you. It is rare for anything good to be accomplished without loss; the Devil is too clever and the World too corrupt not to be determined to smother such good work as this in its cradle. But take courage, Monsieur, it is God Himself who has set you where you are; if your purpose is for His glory, what have you to fear ? Still more, what may you not hope for ?"

This is, in truth, the simplest of messages, and as old as Christianity itself. Yet one may picture with what new force it came from M. Vincent to those Sons of his in their perilous exile. They knew his heart was with them, and that he would willingly have made their lot his own. In his extreme old age his sense of the sufferings of the Christians in Africa was so acute that he attempted to start an expedition against the Turks, and had obtained some sort of promise of support from the King and Mazarin, but he died without having transmitted his own fervour of courage to any individual among his survivors, and the expedition never took place.†

* " Lettres," vol. ii., No. 278.
† For full detail of this abortive scheme, see Bougaud, " Vie de S. Vincent de Paul," vol. ii., liv. 5, chap. i.

There is much that is astonishing in the long career of Vincent de Paul, but the vigour and enterprise of his last years is perhaps the greatest of these marvels. The shadow of failure was over him, but it cannot be attributed to the dwindling of his powers, but rather to the supreme development of his conception of the duty of a priest. The vast sums of money spent in the African Mission, and the corresponding sacrifice of life, had for their object the saving of souls in imminent danger; the idea of bodily relief was altogether subservient. In the Mission to Madagascar there was no philanthropy at all, it was the most desperate of ventures; and yet M. Vincent dedicated to it the picked men of his Company, and judged that he was according to them a special honour.

The reality of missionary ardour is, like the religious vocation, beyond the understanding of those to whom it has never been a matter of experience, but in his later years M. Vincent was possessed by it. It was, indeed, the natural growth from the deep love of souls at home of which his life-work was the evidence. He had ministered to the most crying needs of those who were at hand. It had always been his principle so to adjust the machinery of every new foundation that it depended on the joint efforts of persons he had chosen; and as it was his firm belief that each one was directed by the Hand of God, he could feel that its success no longer rested on the guidance of its nominal Founder. He was, therefore, not moved by any idea that the claim of a distant country was inferior to that of his native land. The fulfilment of the one obligation only made the other more evident.

The claim on the Lazarists to go as Missionaries to Madagascar came in this manner. The Eastern Trading Company obtained the concession of the island, with exclusive commercial rights, shortly before the death of Richelieu. There had been no settled rule over the natives since its discovery two centuries earlier by the Portuguese, but in 1646 Comte de Flacourt was appointed as Governor,

THE FOREIGN MISSIONS

and at his suggestion Cardinal Bagin, the Papal Nuncio, invited M. Vincent to attempt to carry the Christian faith to the inhabitants. The failure of former attempts at government was due primarily to the climate, which proved fatal to the majority of Europeans, but the determined hostility of the natives was partly responsible. The population numbered about 400,000—Kaffir, negro, and Arab. They were idolaters, and in the extreme of moral degradation. A hundred priests would have seemed insufficient for such a work, yet only two were sent to open it.

From that inadequate beginning there was no intermission in the misfortunes of the Madagascar Mission. It cost the Company twenty-seven valuable lives, and the continual deaths by disease or violence left the people for long intervals without a priest, so that any foundations of conversion laid by one had ceased to be distinguishable before the arrival of another. The records are so confused that it is impossible to explain the apparent folly of sending men in pairs. It may have been that no facilities were given for transporting larger numbers, and M. Vincent, even when he realized the forlornness of the hope, would still, for this purpose, have sent his Sons across the seas to certain death. The first to be chosen for Madagascar was M. Nacquart, and in the letter he received announcing his appointment we are allowed a share of M. Vincent's thoughts on this particular subject. M. Nacquart was thirty-one, and had been eight years in the Company. M. Vincent was then seventy-two. He writes from Paris on March 22, 1648:*

"MONSIEUR,

"Long ago Our Lord put into your heart the desire to serve Him in some special way. And when the suggestion was made at Richelieu of opening Missions among the Jews and idolaters, it seemed to me that you

* "Lettres," vol. i., No. 121.

felt you had a call. The time has come for the sowing of this heavenly vocation to bear fruit. Monseigneur the Nuncio has, with the authority of the Congregation for the Propagation of the Faith, of which His Holiness the Pope is chief, chosen the Company to go and serve God in the Isle of St. Lawrence, otherwise called Madagascar, and the Company has regarded you, and another priest as your companion, as the best sacrifice it can make for the glory of the Creator and for His service. Ah! my very dear sir, what does your heart say to this news! Is it fitly overwhelmed and humbled by so great a favour from Heaven? This is a vocation as high and as great as that of the chief Apostles and Saints of the Church of God—a design from eternity fixing itself in time on you. Such a favour can be met only by humility and the complete abandonment of all that you are or may be in absolute confidence in our Creator.

"You will need the strongest courage; you will need faith as great as that of Abraham. The charity of S. Paul will be necessary. Zeal, patience, diffidence, compassion, austerity, discretion, moral discipline, and an immense desire to be completely sacrificed to God—these are as essential to you as to S. François Xavier.

"This island is nearly 400 leagues long and 160 wide. The people have not heard of God, but they are intelligent and open-minded. To get there you must cross the Equator. Authority over the island is in the hands of Parisian merchants, who are like kings there.

"The first point for your attention is to mould yourself by the journey of that great Saint, François Xavier; to help and to serve those who are on board with you; to establish public prayer, if it be possible; to pay great attention to the distresses of others, and always sacrifice your own comfort to theirs; to bring as great a blessing on the voyage (which lasts four or five months) by your prayers as do the sailors by their labour. As regards the Directors, always pay them the greatest respect. Be faithful to God, and never go against your conscience for any consideration; but take special care not to injure your work for God by being too impulsive in it. Take plenty of time and learn to wait.

"When you have lived and worked with those around you, so as to set a good example, your great aim must be to teach these poor people, who are born in all the gloom of ignorance, the truths of the Faith, not by the subtleties of theology, but by reasoning drawn from nature; for one must begin there, trying to make them understand that you seek only to develop the traces of God in them which have become hidden by long yielding to the corruption of nature. And to do this, Monsieur, you will need to turn continually to the Father of Light, and say to Him that which you say to Him daily—*Da mihi intellectum ut sciam testimonia tua*. By meditation you will be able to arrange the light revealed to you, that you may be able to declare the truth of the Supreme Being. . . .

"And with this I give myself to you, if not to follow you in the flesh, of which I am unworthy, at least to pray God daily that He will leave me on earth to aid you, and (if it please Him to have mercy on me) that I may meet you in Heaven and do you honour, as one whose high vocation has raised him to the level of the Apostles. There is nothing on earth that I desire so much as to go as your companion in the place of M. Gondrée."

The enthusiasm and the soaring hopes of the writer are evident in every sentence. It is not for the honour of the Company, but for the glory of God, that he sends his much-cherished Son to the other end of the world; but it is clear that he sends him with exuberant confidence in the result. The natives—intelligent and openminded—will assuredly flock to hear the message that brings light to their darkness.

It is evident also that M. Vincent did not at that time realize the mortal danger that lay before the Missionaries. He plans the report that they shall send, and the news from home they shall receive annually; but M. Gondrée died in a year, and M. Nacquart did not survive him very long. It is impossible altogether to explain the divergence between the hopes aroused by the prospect of this Mission and the actual conditions under which it was carried out. There must have been some intermediary, whose identity is now impossible to trace, who was too sanguine; for the actual authorities in the island (at whose supposed invitation the Missionaries went out) made no preparation for their arrival, and gave them very little support. Moreover, small rivalries between the Eastern Company and the Marshal de la Meilleraye, who had interest in the island, led to threats of rejecting the Mission Priests, in spite of the sacrifices they had already made, and sending members of a religious Order.

M. Vincent, having spurred his Sons towards this supreme offering of themselves, saw it undervalued and rejected. It would be hard to imagine a sharper form of humiliation, and it came to him when he had already been through eight years of disappointment. "I do not know what God will make of our Madagascar Mission," he wrote in 1657 to M. Jolly at Rome.* "I have been told that M. de la Meilleraye has asked for twelve of the Capuchin Fathers, and they have been promised him. There may be some truth in this, because I have ventured to write to remind him that our Missionaries were holding themselves in readiness, awaiting his summons to proceed to Nantes, and he has not made any reply. Whatever comes to pass will be according to the Will of God."

All that had come to pass was heartrending. The letters from the Missionaries to their Superior are extraordinarily graphic. Each one is hopeful. The people seem to have been sufficiently responsive, and they were

* "Lettres," vol. ii., No. 413.

THE FOREIGN MISSIONS

in such an extreme of ignorance that the opportunity given him had its own delight for the writer. But the courage of these champions, fighting, as some of them did, single-handed against overwhelming odds, only adds to the tragedy of their inevitable failure. The fate of those who, like M. Nacquart and M. Bourdaise, were able for a time to sustain life in that poisonous climate, was the hardest, for they saw their companions perish, and were left to the desolate realization of a task too great for a hundred men, and dependent upon one.

"Oh my dear Father," wrote M. Bourdaise, "how often I long that all the able priests who remain in idleness in France, and who know of this great need for labourers, would realize that Our Lord Himself has this reproach for each of them: 'Oh priest, if you had been in this island, many of my brothers bought by My Blood would have been saved from everlasting death.' No doubt the thought of it would rouse their pity, and perhaps their fear."

Such appeals as these fell on deaf ears. M. Bourdaise, in his desperate fight against idolatry, pictured the Guardian Angels of the natives who died unbaptized reproaching him for negligence; but on the other side of the world the responsibility did not bear the same aspect, and year by year he waited for aid that did not come, and at last, when relief was on its way, he also died.

M. Vincent had not been heedless, but a force stronger than any human agency was against him. One after another the chosen companions who started for Madagascar were driven back, shipwreck or capture having deprived them of their means of transport. At best the journey occupied six months, and involved enormous peril. But again and again a fresh party volunteered, for the missionary spirit had seized upon the Company, and their Superior would not hear of discouragement.

"It is a strange sort of army that turns back," he

told them, "because it has lost two, three, or four thousand men. Such an army would be a pretty sight—a gathering of cowards and runaways! And so also with the Mission—it would be a pretty sort of Company that gave up the work of God for five or six deaths! A worthless Company, heeding nothing but the things of flesh and blood!"

There are times, nevertheless, when even a gallant army must turn back, and, despite his resolute words, it is likely that M. Vincent realized before his death what must be the end of the Madagascar Mission. In fact, the conditions became worse as the years passed. The feeling of the natives towards the French colony lost its friendliness, and the Mission Priests, though they had no part in the causes of the change, were included in its effects. Constant danger of murder was added to the other perils to existence, and their converts returned to the practice of idolatry. There was one moment when, as we are told by a contemporary chronicler,* of all the hundreds of natives baptized into the Church there remained only three who were not renegade. The French occupation of Madagascar had proved a failure, and the colony was preparing to withdraw. It became necessary for the Missionaries to abandon their position, and in 1676 the remnant of them reached France—there were two only out of the twenty-nine who had in twenty-five years offered themselves for the service of the heathen; for the others their offering had been a literal offering of life.

The story of that last enterprise of M. Vincent's is not a subject for easy criticism. It is well to set it down—and indeed, the record of his life is incomplete without it—but not to apply the ordinary tests of expenditure and profit. It was the greatest venture of faith he ever made, and its outward failure should not be confused with the idea of loss either to him or to the Company.

* J. Grandet. See "Les Saints Prêtres Français du 17me Siècle."

CHAPTER IX

S. LAZARE AND PORT ROYAL

THE history of the foreign Missions undertaken and directed by M. Vincent brings home to us with new vividness the extraordinary quality of his capacity for detachment. His manner of dealing with each separate enterprise suggests that he was concentrating interest on it. His letters in many instances betray the unmistakable ardour of the enthusiast; his whole heart is intent on a ten days' Mission on the Hulks at Marseilles, on a project for softening the lot of the captives at Algiers, or on choosing from among the numbers of the Lazarists the priest most fitted for service in Madagascar. And then there were Branch-Houses established in Poland, and there were expeditions, even more definitely missionary, sent to Ireland, to the Hebrides, and to Scotland. M. Vincent followed each with close attention. The account of labour and hardship in the Hebrides is written by M. Duguin, Priest of the Mission, to his Superior at S. Lazare, with just the same confident claim on sympathy and comprehension as if he were writing of familiar things from Agen, from Annecy, or from Rome. M. Le Blanc, the Missionary to the Highlands, nearly lost his life at the hands of the Puritans in Scotland; and M. Vincent is torn with grief and anxiety even while he glories in the possibility of martyrdom. Events that moved him deeply in differing ways happened simultaneously. The year when the Mission to Madagascar was taking form was the year of the beginning of the Fronde; and afterwards, while he was struggling with his immense organizations for relief in Paris and the provinces, and making his valiant efforts to obtain peace for the suffering people, he was also forced to keep watch over his representatives in Tunis and Algiers, and was striving to readjust the maladministration of Consular affairs. It is as if we were dealing with separate and differing lives—and all the time it may be true to say that the real life of M. Vincent continues unrecorded.

It is not a new discovery that that which is deepest in the life of man is likely to remain hidden—spiritual revolution may take place within him, and those of his own household will not know it—but it is not this admitted duality, mysterious as it is, which is evident in the case of M. Vincent. He was, openly and under every condition, the Servant of God. He did not, as so many sincere Christians are forced to do, spend a large proportion of his time among persons to whom the spiritual life is as a closed book. All his employments and all his intercourse with others were linked with his religion; it was not necessary for him to pretend to a respect for material things which he did not feel. But in spite of this declared and recognized position, it remains true that his ministry, as we find it recorded by his own letters and by the testimony of his contemporaries, does not represent him. True, he was wise and sympathetic as a Superior; he had genius for organization; he could arouse and sustain the dormant spirit of charity in others—in short, he did not fail in showing the sincerity of his faith by the outward testimony of good works. Yet, when all that is admitted, he might remain only a fine example of a type familiar in every generation, and his exceptional celebrity might be explained by the unusual opportunities which came within his reach.

It is not easy to summarize the points of difference between Vincent de Paul and the rest of the great army of those who spend themselves in the service of their neighbour, but the fact that he always regarded such service as subordinate to a higher claim removes him from the rank and file. He proved sufficiently that he desired to labour for the well-being of others, but he only desired their well-being if he was convinced it was the Will of God; therefore the practical point of view seemed to him to consist in the attainment of knowledge of the Will of God—the formation of a plan of action was a secondary consideration. He could not have lived through his many years of wide experience without formulating some social theory, and dreaming of a future when the injustice and inequalities that were hourly before his eyes should be done away. But his theory was a very simple one; he dreamed of a time when all men should be seeking to understand and to fulfil the Will of God. By such means the great revolution that he desired would take place without the strife that he abhorred; and in the darker period where his own lot had fallen he did what he could to prepare for the halcyon age he pictured. In fact, he did that which no other man living could have done, and he was able to do it because he demanded of himself far more than he did of others. We shall see him in his closing years refusing to accept the legitimate satisfaction that, humanly, his well-spent life had earned for him, increasing rather in the deep sense of his own unworthiness—" Si je n'étais pas prêtre je ne le serais jamais." That point of view in one possessing so clear a record could proceed only from the constant contemplation of the Ideal of Christian life.

Here, then, is the clue to the mystery of his strength. The man who can with real desire centre his thoughts on Christ will of necessity forget himself, and so he will be spared the wear and tear of personal considerations and fears as to success or failure; for if he is assured that he is working as His Master wills, he cannot consistently be anxious as to results. In practice it is hard to achieve to this position, although the verbal statement is extremely simple, and M. Vincent did not maintain his foothold unfalteringly. There were times when he was troubled, when his heart failed him, and his burden seemed too heavy to be borne. If it had been otherwise, perhaps he would not have understood the struggles and downfalls of his followers so well; but a favourite and oft-repeated phrase of his suggests his remedy for faint-heartedness, as well as many other ills: " My Son, weigh it in the Scales of the Sanctuary." Before the Altar the vexed question was to be reconsidered, the overwhelming task offered up and then quietly resumed. For every Catholic, whether priest or layman, there was this unfailing source of consolation, and the sorrow or the difficulty which could not thus be brought before his Lord ought not to continue to disturb his life. The Scales of the Sanctuary was the surest of all tests.

If we turn from the thought of M. Vincent in the church of Lazare, claiming the Divine support his life-work needed, to those who dwelt outside among the excitements and temptations of the city, the difficulty of applying his remedy to their ills becomes apparent. They might plead with reason that both constitution and disease were different, and must demand a different cure. But M. Vincent was able to look beyond his own experience, and he thought otherwise. In his simple view the only real disease was sin, and for that there was only one Physician. If the sufferer came with an honest desire to be healed, he might be confident of cure, whatever the stage of the disease that he had reached. It was not his custom to place himself on a different plane from those with whom he came in contact, and therefore it was his method to apply the principle of that which was of assistance to himself as a means of assisting others. In the early days of his tutorship he had made silence and retirement his safeguard against the distractions of the world that then came so near to him; when he was offered the buildings of S. Lazare he was ready to renounce them rather than allow his Mission Priests to relinquish their habit of silence. His great remedy for the laxity of the secular priests was, as we know, the provision of an annual time of silence in which they might consider their vocation and their own failures in its fulfilment; and as his two great Companies grew under his direction, he never wavered in his insistence that they needed periods of silence to recruit their spiritual forces. "Oh my Daughters, there is no practice to be compared to that of silence," he said to the Sisters of Charity; "it is through it that you may hear God speaking in your hearts." He had much opportunity of discovering the degree to which the ears of men were deafened to the Voice of God by the clamour of their fellows, and his letters give many instances of the effect on himself and on others of days of silence spent in an endeavour to learn the Will of God. It is evident that he regarded a Retreat as a great opportunity of advance, and therefore, when his mind was occupied with the question of awakening the sleeping souls of average mankind, it was natural that the idea should occur to him of offering to them the privilege hitherto reserved for priests and Religious.

Let us consider the aspect in which the hurrying life of the Paris streets presented itself to Vincent de Paul. In every face he read the tragedy—realized or unrealized—of the vagrant soul; to him the objects that filled men's hearts and minds were void, and the disorder of which all, in differing degrees, were conscious proceeded from their indifference to the object designed for them by God. And this was not merely a theory for sermons and meditations, it was the basis of active enterprise. He believed that his own deep content had come to him as the fruit of his opportunities, and that opportunity was all that others would need to attain to their share in it. Being imbued with this belief, he would not have been true to his deepest instinct of charity if he had failed to make provision for a great spiritual need. Thus it came about that Retreats for laymen were instituted at S. Lazare, and, between 1635 and the date of M. Vincent's death, it was computed that 20,000 retreatants had been received. It may be imagined that this was a labour very dear to M. Vincent's heart, for in this he believed he touched the form of service to his neighbour which had reality of value. The definition of the meaning of Retreat, which he left in writing for the enlightenment of the Company, explains his sense of its importance :

"This term Retreat, or Spiritual Exercise, should imply entire detachment from all worldly matters and occupations. The object is that a man may gain real knowledge of his inward state, and be able to examine his conscience, to pray and to meditate, and so to prepare his soul for purification from all sin and from all evil desires and habits, that it may be filled with a longing for goodness. Then he may seek to know the Will of God, and when he knows it he will submit and unite himself to it, and so will advance and eventually attain to the State of Perfection."*

Here M. Vincent gave words to the picture that was cherished in his own mind. If they would resign themselves to outward silence, the souls of men would hear the Voice of God; and if that grace was once accorded to them, the old life of sin must of necessity be left behind. It was to be his privilege to make a period of outward silence possible to all who might desire it, and to set the visible gates of S. Lazare as widely open to all comers as was the entrance to his own heart. This particular expression of his charity produced a curious position. He would have no payment asked for the cost of maintenance during a Retreat, for he held that the question of expense might turn the scale in the case of a waverer, and a soul might thus be lost. But the great establishment at S. Lazare was often in sore straits from lack of funds, and the more practical among the Company resented the additional burden, and sometimes remonstrated with their Superior. If they urged that at such a rate of expenditure there was

* Abelli, part ii., chap. iv.

S. LAZARE AND PORT ROYAL 373

no escape from actual ruin, M. Vincent replied that, if it was necessary, they must all depart, " and put the key under the door." If they represented that many of those who came on the plea of spiritual need were merely seeking board and lodging, M. Vincent answered that, if only a few of those who came were faithful, the enterprise was worth all it could cost. Probably it was more difficult to form an estimate of the real result in this work than it was even in that of the Missions; but each individual in the constant stream of men of all conditions which passed through S. Lazare must have received some impression from the atmosphere of pure religion that prevailed in the home of Vincent de Paul; and—though even his unfailing panegyrist Abelli considers M. Vincent's hospitality to have been " somewhat excessive "— the real generosity of the welcome to all comers was probably not without its usefulness even to those who were least worthy of the trust their host reposed in them.

Not only did M. Vincent maintain his enthusiasm for his undertaking until his death, but also he exhorted his Sons not to let it fail when he was gone, but to regard this opportunity of winning souls as one of the greatest favours that God had bestowed upon the Company. Probably he knew that the office of directing others in the most important hours of their life could not fail to have its effect upon the directors; a high standard was a necessity for each one on whom that responsibility was laid. He would need to learn—as the Superior pointed out— complete distrust of his own personal capacity, and therefore the Company would gain in proportion as it gave. Collective Retreats that corresponded to those given to Ordination Candidates were arranged for laymen, but it seems as if the more ordinary method was to give each retreatant into the hands of a Mission Priest, who was to be at once his director and his servant during his stay. In no case was future direction to be promised, nor was any guest to be invited to return. At S. Lazare each one had

had his opportunity of reviewing the past and learning all that the future, by the Grace of God, contained for him; it rested with himself to make those days of strange experience the starting-point of a life completely different from all that had gone before. A few, no doubt, went away with dispositions that differed very little from those with which they came; a few fulfilled M. Vincent's high conception of the possibility of a Retreat, and, passing through the stages of self-knowledge and purification that he indicated, set forth on the steep path that leads towards perfection; but the greater number gained the knowledge of what might be within their reach, and real reformation remained in abeyance. It depended on individual character whether it was achieved eventually; for S. Lazare was no place of miracles, and M. Vincent was prepared to have his message to his fellow-wayfarers rejected. It was only here and there that Christ had found the listeners who would respond to Him, and the Mission Priests did not aspire to be greater than their Master. But the place of S. Lazare, as a centre of spiritual life for all who sought it, was assured by the system of Retreats. There were many havens for the priest or the Religious overtaken by spiritual storm, but for one of the people, without respect of condition or profession, if the Call of God had come to him, and he desired to pause and consider what It meant—there was no refuge except S. Lazare, no other certain friend but its Superior.

It is, perhaps, this close and peculiar touch which M. Vincent gained with the laity as well as the clergy, by means of his Retreats, which explains the violence of his action in a question of very deep importance and of infinite difficulty. The Jansenist controversy had a prominent place as a subject for thought during the last thirty years of his life, and the cause of the Jansenist made appeal to the same minds as were stirred by his message; it was therefore impossible that he should ignore it.

The facts of this celebrated dispute have now become

extremely difficult to disentangle. To the contemporaries of S. Cyran* there were clear issues involved, and those who sided with him were sufficiently convinced of the goodness of their cause to suffer persecution for it; but their violence and that of their opponents has obscured the evidence for both sides, and there is a tendency at the present day to attribute to " the poison of Jansenism " many heretical opinions that would have found no favour with the original Port Royalists.

It should always be remembered that the Convent of Port Royal had won celebrity before it had any connection with Jansenius.† Angélique Arnauld transformed the Benedictine Community assembled there from laxity to the extreme of adherence to the Rule. The austerity of Port Royal stirred the imagination of innumerable persons who had no desire to share in it, and created a unique position for Mère Angélique and the Sisters; and when it became known that the Perpetual Adoration of the Blessed Sacrament was maintained in one of the Houses of the Community, the respect which these mysterious nuns excited was mingled with awe. In 1636 S. Cyran became Director to the Community. He had been the friend and companion of Jansenius at the College of Louvain, and afterwards in Paris, and was the exponent of his book on S. Augustine. His whole mind centred on his realization of the dishonour brought upon the Church by the unworthiness of the priests and the false administration of the Sacraments, and his knowledge of the first centuries of Christianity intensified his horror of the conditions that he saw around him. So violent was he in denunciation that it was easy to represent him as making an attack upon the Church. Port Royal had attracted a great concourse of well-known persons, some of them the highest intellects and the finest characters that society could produce, and through these his theories spread with

* Duvergier de Hauranne, Abbé de S. Cyran.
† Jansenius was Bishop of Ypres, and died in 1638.

dangerous rapidity. Richelieu was intolerant of those who aspired to any kind of leadership, and some of the accusations against S. Cyran were well founded; therefore he gave an order for his arrest and imprisonment at Vincennes.* Probably his action was a wise one, but he failed to weaken the influence of the offending priest; it was the essence of the spirit of Port Royal " to covet suffering," and S. Cyran was regarded as a martyr in the cause of truth. His imprisonment lasted five years,† and he died almost immediately after his release.

Even at this early stage of the Jansenist difficulty Vincent de Paul was implicated. He was on terms of friendship with S. Cyran, they were natives of the same province, and they were both moved by the same desire for the purifying of the Church. The enemies of Jansenism suggest that S. Cyran had a definite intention of using the Mission Priests to spread his theories, and there is some evidence that he did make an attempt to alter M. Vincent's aim for the Company. But, in fact, the two natures were unsympathetic, and the regrets and desires that they held in common acted upon them in wholly different ways. S. Cyran was strangely ignorant of the character of Vincent de Paul if he imagined that his fidelity to the Church was easily shaken; their friendship was, in fact, destroyed by certain reckless words of his, recorded years after in a letter from the Superior of S. Lazare to a Mission Priest in Rome :‡ " He said to me one day that it was God's intention to destroy the Church as it is now, and that all those who labour to uphold it are working against His intention; and when I told him that these were the statements made by heretics such as Calvin, he replied that Calvin had not been altogether in error, but that he had not known how to make a good defence."

It is quite plain that after a lapse of twelve years M. Vincent's horror was still burning, for no member of the

* May, 1638. † Till February, 1643.
‡ " Lettres," vol. i., No. 124.

S. LAZARE AND PORT ROYAL

Society of Jesus upheld the authority of the Church in its entirety more vigorously than he did. But even this attitude towards S. Cyran has been made a matter of animated controversy, and probably the exact truth of their relations has never been stated. It seems certain that when the animosity of Richelieu was beginning to declare itself, M. Vincent visited S. Cyran and attempted to reason with him on his opinions; possibly a generous intention betrayed him into excessive zeal, for a subsequent letter shows that the object of his solicitude had not received his visit in good part.

"The one thing that impressed me," wrote S. Cyran afterwards,* "was the fact that you, who profess to be so gentle and considerate to all, that you should have seized the moment when the storm has burst over me to join yourself to my assailants, and should even exceed them in their outrages by intruding upon me under my own roof, which no one else has dared to do."

Later, there is a question whether Vincent de Paul was a witness at the trial of S. Cyran, and the testimonies on this point are contradictory; it is clear, however, that after the prisoner was released, M. Vincent hastened to visit him, and remained on friendly terms with him until his death. Even when the facts are authentic, it is difficult to form from them any clear idea of M. Vincent's position at that period, and this may be accounted for by our knowledge of his character. He did not foresee the troubles that were coming; he believed his old friend to be in error; but he had suffered disgrace and captivity, and it was a natural instinct to give him every possible proof of affection. Moreover, S. Cyran had been the friend of François de Sales, of de Bérulle, and of Mme. de Chantal, and his strict and regulated life accorded well with the Lazarist standard for the priesthood; therefore it is likely that if, after his death, there had been no fruits of his influence, the existence of real friendship between

* Quoted by Abelli, vol. ii., chap. ii., sect. 12.

himself and M. Vincent would never have been contested. The fact that that most ardent of Port Royalists, Claude Lancelot, was at pains to prove the reality of the alliance between his Leader and the Superior of S. Lazare is a tribute to the reputation of the latter;* but the opponents of Jansenism, among whom may be numbered all the biographers of Vincent de Paul, are not inclined to give prominence to the evidence of his tenderness towards S. Cyran.

The real truth seems to be that M. Vincent did not declare himself in the matter till it had reached a later stage, and his reasons for doing so are in close connection with the whole intention of his life. The history of events may be given briefly. Shortly after the death of S. Cyran, Antoine Arnauld, the youngest of that celebrated family, himself a priest and Doctor of the Sorbonne, wrote his "Livre de la Fréquente Communion." The Jansenist controversy, which had not attained to its full celebrity, centred until then on the "Augustinus" of Jansenius, which was read only by a few scholars; but when Arnauld's book appeared, it was received with enthusiasm and devoured eagerly. It was against this book that M. Vincent directed his attack, and it is noteworthy that Pascal—to whose genius the real importance of the Jansenist struggle is due—has claimed no notice at all from one who is described as "the most dangerous enemy of the disciples of S. Augustine."†

His opinion on the subject of the book by Antoine Arnauld can be given in his own words, for it chanced that a valued member of the Company, M. d'Horgny, of the Mission at Rome, was infected by the new heresy, and his Superior wrote to him on the subject at length and with great distinctness:‡

" Your last letter says we have done wrong to go against general opinion. You say that this concerns the book ' De

* "Mémoires," par M. Lancelot, part iii., chapters xxxiii., xxxiv.
† Gerberon, " Hist. de Jansenisme," vol. i., p. 422.
‡ " Lettres," vol. i., No. 124. June, 1648.

la Fréquente Communion' and Jansenius; that as regards the first you have read it twice, and that the common abuse of this Most Holy Sacrament has given occasion for it.

"It is true, Monsieur, that there are only too many who misuse this Divine Sacrament. I am myself guilty beyond any man alive, and I beseech you to join in my prayers for God's pardon. But the reading of this book, instead of drawing men towards frequent Communion, is calculated to alienate them. People do not frequent the Sacraments as they used to do—not only at Easter, but at other seasons. Many curés in Paris are saying that they have many fewer communicants than in former years. There are 3,000 less at S. Sulpice. M. le Curé of S. Nicolas du Chardonnet has told me recently that, when visits were paid after Easter in his parish by himself and others, he found 1,500 of his parishioners had not made their Communion; and it is the same elsewhere. Also, there are none now who approach the first Sunday of the month or on festivals, or very few, even at the religious houses, except a few with the Jesuits. This is what the late M. de S. Cyran was aiming at to bring the Jesuits into discredit. The other day M. de Chavigny said to an intimate friend that this gentleman had told him there was an agreement between himself and Jansenius to discredit the Order on all points concerning the administration of the Sacraments. I have myself heard him say things to this effect constantly. . . .

"You say also that, as Jansenius read all the works of S. Augustine ten times, and his treatises concerning Grace thirty times, the Mission Priests are not fit to question his opinions.

"To which I reply, Monsieur, that those who desire to establish new doctrines always are learned, and give deep study to the authors of whom they are making use; that this Bishop should be acknowledged to be very learned, and that he may have read S. Augustine as many times as you say, with the intention of discrediting the Jesuits. But that does not prevent him from having fallen into error, and we shall have no excuse for sharing in his opinions in defiance of the censure of his doctrine. All priests are bound to repudiate and contradict the doctrine of Calvin and other heretics, although they have never read either their books or the authors from which their doctrines are drawn.

" And when you say, Monsieur, that we do not need to know whether there be Grace Sufficient, I beg leave to answer that it seems to me of great importance that all Christians should know and believe that God is so good, that by the Grace of Jesus Christ all may obtain salvation; that by Jesus Christ He has given them the means, and that this is a great manifestation of the goodness of God."

Arnauld's book had power to grip the minds of its readers, however, and M. d'Horgny ventured to write another letter to S. Lazare in its defence. The second reply was as vigorous as the first:*

" It may be (as you say) that certain persons in France and Italy have drawn benefit from this book; but for a hundred in Paris to whom it has been useful in teaching more reverence in approaching the Sacrament, there have been ten thousand, at the least, whom it has injured by driving them away. . . . It is absolutely certain that if anyone holds his maxims to be true, he must of necessity be hindered in frequenting the Sacraments. For my own part, I tell you frankly that, if I paid the same respect to M. Arnauld's book that you do, I should give up both Mass and Communion from a sense of humility, and I should also be in terror of the Sacrament, regarding It, according to the book, as a snare of Satan, and as poison to the souls of those who receive It under the usual conditions that the Church approves. And if we discard all other considerations and confine ourselves solely to what he says of the perfect disposition, without which one

* " Lettres," vol. i., No. 128. September, 1648.

should not make Communion, is there anyone on earth with such a high opinion of his own virtue that he would think himself worthy ? Such a position is held by M. Arnauld alone, who, having made the necessary conditions so difficult that S. Paul might have feared to approach, does not hesitate to tell us repeatedly that he says Mass daily. In this his humility is only equalled by the charity that he displays towards so many wise directors, secular as well as religious, and towards their penitents."

It is very rarely that we discover M. Vincent moved to real indignation, but we shall see that the attack of the Jansenists threatened the deepest injury to the work of the Mission Priests, and he could see in it nothing but evil. It was a great source of danger that the Jansenist assault was levelled at abuses recognized by the Lazarists, which it was part of their mission to correct. M. Vincent's distress at the light-mindedness of many of those who administered and of those who received the Sacraments was as deep as that of S. Cyran or of Antoine Arnauld; but he believed that spiritual advance and ultimate salvation depended on the grace imparted in the Sacrament of the Altar, and, further, that that Sacred Mystery was to be approached only by those who, having in penitence confessed their sins, had been cleansed by Absolution. His touch with the dying sinner at Folleville had been a turning-point in his own life, and it was inevitable that questions concerning the use and abuse of the confessional should have occupied him continually. His charges to the Mission Priests, and his warnings to the Sisters of Charity, show us how fully he saw the power for evil which lay in the hands of an unworthy priest; but the chief aim of the Lazarist was, nevertheless, to direct the people towards the sacramental life. A Retreat was, as we have seen, primarily a summons to repentance; and a series of Mission sermons, however much instruction they had conveyed to the ignorant, had failed of their purpose if they did not awake the slumbering consciences of the listeners. It is experience such as had fallen to the lot of M. Vincent that teaches the value of the Sacrament of Penance. Sorrow for sin is possible to all men, but only the Catholic is taught to bring his burden, at whatever cost of shame, to the feet of the Saviour Who has bought redemption for him. The sinner had no assurance of forgiveness until he had bent his will to the avowal of guilt, and again and again M. Vincent had seen the alteration of a life as the result of a reconciliation won at the cost of long and bitter struggle.

To him it seemed that the Jansenists, in the ferocity of their attack, were destroying the treasures of the Church, and that none of the evils that cried for remedy were to be compared for danger to the means employed to extirpate them. It should be remembered that modern opinions regarding the standards and teaching of the Jesuits of that period have frequently been based on Pascal's "Provincial Letters"; but every student of devotional life will acknowledge that the Jesuit of that inimitable work is an extreme type, and may not be regarded as representative. The secret power of the Society of Jesus was being used to silence the Jansenist writers, and Pascal, spurred by a sense of justice as well as by an intense conviction of the righteousness of his cause, used his weapon of ridicule relentlessly, and involved the innocent in the ignominy he desired to heap upon the guilty. Probably the particular forms of abuse against which the attacks both of Arnauld and Pascal were levelled did not come under M. Vincent's notice. His dealings were with the ignorant, with the *dévote*, or with the sinner at the crisis of conversion; the subtleties of casuistry did not concern him deeply. What did concern him was the spread of any opinion which could alienate the souls of men from the means of grace, and he believed there was proof that the advance of spiritual life was being arrested by the doctrines promulgated from Port Royal. He had seen with delight his ideal of the vocation of the parish priest fulfilled by M. Olier at S. Sulpice, and the religious revival that had resulted; and there was no denying that S. Sulpice suffered by the spread of the new opinions. It might be true that the free dispensation of the Sacraments in that period of scandalous living had given fair excuse for protest, and that even the most devoted priests were too anxious for numerical result; but M. Vincent preferred that the way should continue to be made too easy, if the alternative was that closed door of the Jansenist penitence through which a sinner might hardly gain entrance.

"For three months I have made the doctrine of Grace the subject of my prayer," he told his Company at one of their Conferences, "and each day God has strengthened me in my faith that Our Lord died for us all, and that He desires to save the whole world."*

And yet it should be remembered that the Mission Priests did not depict the way of salvation as an easy path. If we follow the process they adopted in their Missions we find that if they are less sensational than the Port Royalists, they are hardly less forcible. They did not begin with description of the pains of hell, and denunciation of the sinners for whom these were reserved; but the course of the Mission was not complete if such description and such denunciation were omitted. Sin in its various forms was their most frequent theme, and when they dwelt on sin and its terrors, it was to lead their hearers to the reality of penitence, which was the way of escape. Those to whom M. Vincent entrusted the conduct of a Mission were experienced in the guidance of human souls; the deepest part of their personal work was done in the confessional, and the virtues of patience and of charity were essential to its accomplishment. But they were not taught to be tolerant of sin. They reiterate the necessity of the offering of shame and

* See "Process of Canonization," evidence of Antoine Durand.

sacrifice; they were not satisfied with a mere outward semblance of contrition, with a superficial survey of past errors and their causes. "Everywhere nowadays Christians throw the burden of their faults on each other. The husband on the wife's fancies and caprices; while to hear the wife you would believe her to be a saint, if the ill-temper and irregularity of her husband had not spoilt her temper. The father throws blame on his children, and they on him and on their mother. Those who live in continual enmity allege the incompatibility of their neighbours. One excuse for oaths is the stupidity of servants, the other the violence of masters. Force of habit, youth, bad companionship, poverty—all serve as excuses. There are some who lay the blame on their destiny and the course of the stars, others who will confess the sins of others to shield their own. Such as these come as counsel for the defence, not as a prisoner pleading guilty, and they are reversing the order of penitence ordained by God Himself." So runs one of the Mission sermons of M. Vincent's earlier time,* and it holds more than a suggestion that the way would not be made too easy. In fact, the Lazarists themselves and the new order of parish priests whom they had trained were severe in their dealing with their penitents; but the excesses of some of the prominent Jansenists produced a panic, and brought those who practised the most ordinary strictness under suspicion of belonging to the new sect.

It may be seen, then, that from M. Vincent's point of view the doctrine of Port Royal did and could do nothing but harm, and was directly subversive of all his hopes for the future. In the Rule of his Company we find† that "one of the principal points of our Missions is to inspire others to receive the Sacraments of Penance and of the Eucharist frequently and worthily. It is fitting, therefore, that we go beyond others and give the

* "Sermons de S. Vincent de Paul," No. 10.
† "Règles," chap. x., art. 6.

example in this matter. We will endeavour to attain to greater perfection in each; and that order may be maintained in all things, every priest shall confess twice (or once at the very least) every week, and shall celebrate Holy Mass every day." But avowedly one of the principal points of Jansenist teaching was to inspire such awe of the Sacraments that they could only be approached very rarely by the pastor as well as by his flock. In short, the religion of Port Royal—full as it was of pure aspiration—was the religion only of the few, and it was calculated to alienate those for whom it was not suited from the practice of any religion. It was not the erudite few, but the great mass of the people, for whom M. Vincent spent himself; it was their immense need for which he prayed continually; and it was against them that he believed the Port Royalists were closing the door of salvation.

If it were possible for us to realize this fully, we should cease to wonder that this apostle of charity took the side of persecution. No other threat of danger ever moved him as did this one. The horrors of civil strife, the cruelty of unjust laws, aroused his pity and sometimes his indignation; but through every bodily suffering he could see the possibility that God might work upon a human soul. It was the thought that the means of grace would be made more difficult of access that kindled his wrath into active violence. The Jansenists recognized him as their most dangerous opponent, and in this they are the more likely to have been accurate because he was not a controversialist, but entered the lists at the prompting of intense conviction. It is a manifest absurdity to suggest that he chose his part on a motive of worldly wisdom, that he might stand well with the Jesuits at a moment when their fortunes were on the ascendant. M. Vincent at all times was a faulty diplomatist, and we cannot find one instance when he conciliated the possessors of power to serve the interests of the Company. His faithful support of Cardinal de Retz and its penalty is sufficient proof to the contrary. It is not necessary to follow his course of action in detail; from the day when he first grasped the meaning of the doctrine of Jansenius until his death he was unchanging in his opposition.* It was said by a French Bishop that, "just as S. Ignatius and his Society were raised up by God to combat Luther and Calvin, so were Vincent de Paul and his Company for the battle against Jansenism."†

His position on the Council of Conscience gave him peculiar power. When the Sorbonne had condemned the Five Propositions drawn from the "Augustinus," a petition signed by eighty-five French Bishops was forwarded to Rome. It was to ask for the Papal confirmation of the sentence on the Jansenists, and if the plea was granted (as eventually it was), it meant the ruin of Port Royal. This petition was the work of M. Vincent, and was forwarded by him for signature. The labour and correspondence in which it involved him must have been immense, but his zeal and determination were unflagging. At all costs, also, he purified his Company from the insidious poison of the new opinions. Lancelot, the disciple and biographer of S. Cyran, had been trained by M. Bourdoise in his Seminary at S. Nicolas du Chardonnet; M. Bourdoise himself—impressed by the austere practices of the Jansenist priests—had wavered in his disapproval of their doctrines; the Oratorians were so deeply infected as to be past hope of recovery; while Antoine Singlin passed from intimate relations with Vincent de Paul himself to be Confessor and Director at Port Royal. There were gaps in the ranks of the Ladies

* "Qui ne se jettera sur ce petit monstre qui commence à ravager l'Église et qui enfin la désolera, si on ne l'étouffe à sa naissance?" À l'Évêque de Luçon: "Lettres," vol. i., No. 193.

† See "Process of Canonization," quoted by Maynard. "Vie de S. Vincent de Paul," vol. ii., liv. v.

of Charity also, and laymen who were regarded as staunch supporters of the Church were discovered to be eager partisans of the rebels. The danger was too great for temporizing, and M. Vincent gave no quarter where he held authority.

" As to your idea that each one of the Company should be left free to form his own conclusions on this subject," he wrote to M. d'Horgny,* " I reply, Monsieur, that it is not submission to your Superior that is required of you, but to God, to the Pope, and to the Saints; and if there be any who refuse to yield, it will be well for him to withdraw from the Company, or else for the Company to require him to do so."

In fact, a Lazarist must oppose Port Royal, or he must cease to be a Lazarist. M. d'Horgny capitulated, but the Company became the poorer by fourteen of its members who were not equally submissive.

The triumph of the Jesuits is a matter of history. All the force of Papal condemnation was levelled against Jansenism, and Port Royal was ruined. This is not the place to enlarge on the struggle and suffering by which the nuns and hermits of Port Royal bought their influence upon their age. Whether the opinion of the individual upholds or condemns them, it is impossible to study their lives and to deny that they were seekers after truth in belief, and holiness in practice, for themselves and others; and it is no small addition to the irony and the tragedy of their fate that Vincent de Paul should have been numbered among the most implacable of their enemies. Perhaps in this he failed in insight, or blinded himself on principle. To him faith came simply, and obedience was inevitable. If he had had to contend with doubts and questions in himself, he could not have served others in the manner that God required of him. He saw the few bringing injury to the many, the gifted minority threatening the ignorant masses; and because he was the

* " Lettres," vol. i., No. 124.

friend and defender of the ignorant, it was not his part to dwell on the motives of those who harmed them. He had accepted it as his vocation to help the poor to save their souls, and therefore against any who might hinder them in such endeavour he was pitiless.

CHAPTER X

THE LAST DAYS

WE have seen that the closing years did not bring outward peace into M. Vincent's life; the tragedy of the Madagascar Mission overshadowed him, and he was never free from anxiety regarding the Jansenist peril. But in many directions the seeds that he had sown sprung up, and there were signs of steady growth. In their differing tasks and widely separated dwelling-places the Mission Priests and the Sisters of Charity were testifying that it was by God's prompting that their Founder had drawn them from the ways of ordinary life into the path of consecrated service. In Paris many dreams for the linking of rich and poor had been fulfilled, and S. Lazare itself had become a centre for work of a kind not attempted anywhere else. It is hard to summarize all the varied endeavour that the mere name of S. Lazare suggests. M. Vincent, referring to the gathering of retreatants, observed that the house resembled Noah's Ark, because it sheltered specimens of every kind; yet it was not among the retreatants that its strangest inmates were to be found, nor was their claim the most searching that their hosts were required to meet.

M. Le Bon had accepted the care of a few insane persons who were lodged within the precincts of S. Lazare, and it was part of his contract with Vincent de Paul that this responsibility should be continued. It had, in fact, a special attraction for the new Superior. As he told the Company, the service of the insane had this peculiar merit: that, besides being repugnant to natural inclination, it excited no admiration from onlookers nor gratitude from its recipients, and that therefore it was specially acceptable to God. At a moment when their right to the great Augustinian Monastery was contested by another Order, he had tried to discover in the recesses of his own mind the chief reason for regret if their adversaries were successful, and he had found that there was nothing of all that they would lose so precious to them as this task of caring for those whom no one else would care for.* In addition, by the choice of the Superior the Company undertook the charge of those whose moral capacity was lacking. Although it might be less hopeless, this was a more difficult enterprise than the tending of the insane. The black sheep of a respected family is not a welcome guest either in a private house or a public institution, and may be an endless source of misery so long as he is left at large. The idea of assuming a responsibility that was repudiated by everyone else appealed to M. Vincent. Mental deficiency was not more pitiable in his eyes than its moral counterpart, and he was indifferent to the damage that might result to S. Lazare if it was regarded as a place of detention for bad characters.

We have no statistics relating to this experiment of M. Vincent's, and a good deal of mystery necessarily attached to it. Young men were confided to his care by their relations on an order from a magistrate, and he was authorized to detain them so long as he thought well. They were not sent to him unless they were thoroughly depraved, and it was his intention not to let them return to the world until they were really reformed. In the interval there was time for the patience of the Mission Priests to be tested on lines that differed from their ordinary experience. But there seems to be evidence that the culprits did really profit by the influence of S. Lazare, and though this imprisonment there lasted for long periods, they looked back on the scene of it with affection, and not with resentment. This labour ap-

* Abelli, vol. ii., chap. vi.

peared to the contemporaries of Vincent de Paul as another work of charity undertaken to relieve despairing parents of a difficulty with which they could not cope; but this was not the only aspect in which he himself regarded it. He desired that the Home of the Mission Priests should be a House of Prayer, that prayer as much as any of their special activities should be characteristic of them, and he argued that, if this desire was realized, the atmosphere of S. Lazare must have power to cure moral disease and restore the sufferer to his normal place among his fellows. In this, as in his generous welcome to retreatants, he did not always secure the agreement of the Company. Sometimes it was represented to him that one of these inmates was a hopeless case, and that it was both dangerous and a waste of labour to allow him to remain; and sometimes there would be remonstrance against the arduous burden as a whole, on the plea that there was nothing in the Rule that claimed the charge of lunatics and malefactors. On the one point M. Vincent replied that the culprit would be the cause of greater danger and distress outside S. Lazare than he was within, and that the difficulty of control proved how essential it was that he should be retained in safe keeping. The other point touched a principle, and for it he had a deeper answer.

"As to our Rule," he said, "in regard to this our rule is Our Lord Himself. He chose to be surrounded by madmen and idiots, by the tempted, and by the possessed. They were brought to Him from all parts that they might be healed, and in His loving-kindness He healed them all. How is it that we are criticized and blamed for trying to imitate Him in a thing that was His chosen work? If He received the lunatic and the possessed, shall we not receive them also? We do not go out to look for them, they are brought to us; and how can we be sure that God, Who has so ordered it, does not intend to use us for the healing of these poor souls for whom Our Saviour had such great compassion that He seems to have desired to have part with them ? Ah ! my Saviour and my God, grant us grace that we may see in these things even as Thou Thyself didst see !"*

There is an indication here of the strength that lay beneath all M. Vincent's gentleness—the strength that made him able to rule others even when he was most distrustful of himself. A little world of differing characters and interests was contained within the walls of S. Lazare, and M. Vincent, who had been the visible agent for its formation, presided over it, and guarded it from evil up to the hour of his death. He had tried once to lay down his charge,† and at an Assembly of the Company had resigned his office of Superior; but by a unanimous vote he was re-elected, and it was plain that any further effort at retirement would have been meaningless. Therefore he ruled, and while he held the responsibility he required compliance with his directions from the Company. We have seen that he could be severe when the occasion demanded severity, and that he was able to disregard the opinion of others. He had shown this in his dealings with the Court and with the people, and had in the process of time earned the highest possible tribute of respect from every class. In long-ago days he had been independent of the opinion of M. de Gondi; he had dared to interfere with the prejudices of class on the question of duelling; he had ignored the possibility of his patron's wrath when a spiritual prompting called him to Châtillon. There is little doubt that it was because he had touched the real strength of Vincent de Paul that M. de Gondi himself in due course renounced his rank and riches, and accepted a life of hardship and humility. The same capacity that gave M. Vincent power in the world served for the moulding of the Company; it was his aim to offer himself hourly to God, and to spread out every action and every decision when he knelt in those

* Abelli, vol. ii., chap. vi. † In 1642.

THE LAST DAYS

long hours of prayer that began the day, and afterwards to act on that which he had learnt with courage. This system involves the danger that ensnared the followers of Mme. Guyon, but M. Vincent guarded himself against it.

"Among the crowd of thoughts and ideas that come," he said, "some appear to be good which in fact do not come from God and are not according to His Will. By what means can these be recognized? Our only chance is to reflect very carefully, to refer everything to God in prayer, asking Him to give us light, and then to consider the motive, the end, and the means of that which we intend to do, to see if it is in conformity with His good pleasure. We should also ask advice of those who are wise and possess the knowledge of God. If we do this, we may be sure we are following His Will."* "If you ever want to know why you have failed in any undertaking, you will find it is because you relied upon yourself. If a preacher or a Superior or a confessor trusts to his own wisdom and learning and capacity, you will see how God deals with him. He will leave him to himself, and, however much he works, there will be no real result until he sees his own uselessness and understands that all his experience and all his cleverness are nothing unless God is working with him."†

It was this particular species of humility which made M. Vincent confident in enforcing the decisions that nominally were his. In his old age he attained to a position of self-distrust that seems to have required neither consideration nor effort, and he insists on the immolation of conceit in his Sons as the essential preparation for faithful living. "I give thanks to God," he wrote to one of them,‡ "because He has shown you how to tear yourself to pieces—that is to say, the means of becoming really humble by realizing and acknowledging your faults. You are right to regard yourself as you do,

---

* Abelli, vol. iii., chap. v.   † *Ibid.*, chap. iii.
‡ "Lettres," vol. i., No. 272.

and to consider yourself quite unfit for any sort of office. That is the foundation on which Jesus Christ can build up His purpose for you. At the same time, while you consider your own inward state, you should lift up your soul towards realization of His supreme goodness. There is great reason that you should distrust yourself, but there is much greater reason that you should have entire trust in Him. It is well that you should devote more thought to His love than to your own unworthiness, to His strength than to your weakness."

As a basis of prayer the direction had its value, and, indeed, M. Vincent would have desired all his spiritual direction to his Sons to rank merely as suggestion for their prayer. As we have seen in his exhortation on the subject of early rising, he regarded this as the chief duty of their day. He knew very well, however, that time nominally given to prayer may be time wasted, and that the fact of routine and obligation would tend to check the possibilities of fervour in some natures. For this reason, and also because he desired to increase his own intimacy with the members of the Company, he instituted certain meetings—two in every week—where the subjects and the fruits of prayer might be discussed; and it was his custom to question three or four of those present on their own recent experiences during their time of meditation. In hands less dexterous than his these meetings might have been productive of harm—the devout would have been tempted to pose and the wilful to invent; but M. Vincent had deep knowledge of human frailty, and he watched over the conference with the utmost care.

In any detailed biography of a pious individual of that period (and of these many have been written) there will be found some reference to a nun or a recluse with the reputation of being specially illuminated in the ways of prayer. These were the product of an epoch of extremes, and were probably genuine in their profession of sanctity.

But M. Vincent did not encourage a tendency to eccentricity in this direction; he acknowledged that special gifts were bestowed upon a few, but he thought that they were claimed by many who had not received them. It was better, he once observed,* to be incapable of anything but the simplest form of prayer and to be diligent in the correction of one's faults, than to go into spiritual ecstasies and to speak evil of one's neighbour. His system of discussion, while it served to awake the stagnant soul to effort, was also a defence against spiritual vagaries. Simplicity was as needful in prayer as it was in action, and on this subject he opened his mind to his Sons of S. Lazare when the period of his visible presence with them was drawing near its end.

"If you are seeking fine ideas in your prayer," he said, "and amusing yourself with complicated thoughts—particularly when you do this with the intention of advertising yourself when you are giving an account of your prayer—you are guilty of a sort of blasphemy. In fact, you are making an idol of yourself, for in your intercourse with God your object is to foster self-complacency; you are using time that should be sacred for your own satisfaction. In flattering yourself that you have beautiful sentiments you are offering a sacrifice to the idol of your own vanity.

"Ah! my Brothers, let us be clear of such follies as these. Let us realize that we are full of all that is evil, and let us seek only that which may teach us to be more humble, and to do the thing that is right. In prayer let self become nothing, and when we speak of our prayer let us relate our thoughts humbly; and if there are any that seem to us to be fine, let us be distrustful of them and afraid, lest they were suggested by vainglory or by the Devil himself. And because there is always this possibility, directly we think we have a fine inspiration, we must humble ourselves utterly, whether it comes to us in

* Abelli, vol. iii., chap. iii.

prayer, or when we are preaching, or when we are talking to others.

"And then, when our prayer has brought us to the making of resolutions, we must implore the Grace of God, and be free of the least suggestion of trust in ourselves. And when in spite of this we fail, not once or twice only, but repeatedly during long spaces of time, and even when we have never brought one to any real fulfilment, we must none the less renew them, and throw ourselves on God's mercy, that we may have His Grace to help us. It is well that past sins should humble us, but they must not rob us of our courage; and however deep the sin into which we fall, it is not a reason for abating the confidence that God requires we should place in Him. We must always resolve afresh, and trust to His Grace to save us from another fall. We do not find that doctors cease to treat the ills of the body because at first their remedies appear to do no good; and if they persevere with physical maladies, although there are no signs of improvement, how much more must be we patient with our spiritual diseases, for which the Grace of God can work wonders of healing?"*

There was, indeed, only one remedy, only one source of strength and of wisdom. The Superior of S. Lazare had undertaken far too much for human capacity—a brief review of all that was in his hands will prove that it was so—but it was not on human capacity that he depended. The direction of a single soul would have seemed too high a task for his unaided powers, and he feared always lest the success of a system should tempt his Sons to forget that they needed constant renewal of inspiration. If the spirit of dependence became clouded, the service of the Mission Priests to God or to their fellows would have no further value.

"How may we hope to do our work?" he said. "How can we lead souls to God? How can we stem the tide of

* Abelli, vol. iii., chap. vii.

wickedness among the people? How can we instil the idea of virtue and discipline in those who are entrusted to our care? Let us realize that this is not man's work at all—it is the work of God. It is the same work as Christ came to do, and human energy will only hinder it unless God directs.

"The most important point of all is that we should have real touch with Our Lord in prayer. When we are in any doubt turn instantly to God and say: ' Lord, Who art the Source of knowledge, teach me what I ought to do in this matter.' And this not only in moments of difficulty, but also that we may know directly from God what we ought to teach. And, further, we must turn to God in prayer to preserve in our own souls the love and the fear of Him, for, alas! it is necessary that we should know that many who intend to bring others to salvation come to destruction themselves. To avoid this we must be so closely united to Our Lord that we cannot lose Him, lifting up heart and soul towards Him constantly, and saying: ' Lord, do not suffer that I myself should fall in trying to save others. Lead me Thyself, and do not withhold from me the grace that by means of me Thou hast given to others.' We must resort to prayer also that we may place the needs of those whom we direct before Our Lord. It is quite clear that we shall gain more result by this means than by any other. Jesus Christ—Who should be our guide in all things—did not think it sufficient to preach, to labour, to fast, and to die for us, He prayed also. For Himself He did not need it; it was for us that He prayed so continually, and to teach us to do the same on our own behalf, and also for those whom He is helping us to save."*

This is simple teaching; but M. Vincent's life, in so far as it has been possible to gather knowledge of it, appears to have been formed on the lines that are here laid down. He never suggests that he had spiritual experiences that

* Abelli, vol. iii., chap. xxiv.

were denied to others; his teaching on prayer is insistent, but it is given in terms of his own knowledge, and his hearers may always infer that his knowledge is easily within their reach if only they will seek for it. Yet perhaps there were some who, if they tried to follow in his footsteps, discovered that the way on which he led them was not an easy one. " To be so closely united with Our Lord that we cannot lose Him, lifting up heart and soul to Him continually," is a condition that demands more capacity for detachment than the majority of mankind possess. M. Vincent was never sensational in his method of instilling the principles of the spiritual life. His listeners were not always aware of the full import of his maxims, but when he was dealing with those who aspired to the vocation of the Mission Priest his intention was to draw them onwards to the heights of real self-surrender.

" Indifference," he said, " is a state wherein we are almost free of desire for one thing rather than another. As a virtue, it is not only very valuable, but also of infinite assistance for advance in the spiritual life. It may be said, indeed, that for those who would give perfect service to God it is indispensable, for how may we seek the Kingdom of God and devote ourselves to converting sinners if we ourselves are clinging to the comforts of this present life ? How shall we accomplish the Will of God so long as we cling to our own ? How can we deny ourselves as Our Lord has bidden us if we are always looking about for praise and recognition."*

We have seen that the sacrifice of life itself was required not infrequently of a Mission Priest, and such sacrifice was to be made as part of the vocation he had accepted. " If there be one of us," cried the Superior, " who fears to lose his comforts, who is so dainty that he grumbles at anything that may be lacking, and desires to change his post because the air is unhealthy or the food is bad, or because he is not sufficiently free to come and

* Abelli, vol. iii., chap. v., sect. 2.

go—if, in short, there is anyone who is still the slave of his own desires, let him realize that he is unfit to hold the office to which God called him. We see others risking their lives for the service of God, and we remain as fluttered and as timid as so many damp hens."*

This was the vigorous spirit of renunciation which supported M. Vincent's prayer, and if we are able to form an idea of its reality, we shall understand the motives that prompted François de Sales to choose the peasant priest before all the learned ecclesiastics then in Paris as Director of his Order of the Visitation. It was a deep testimony to his position as a man of prayer and of that wisdom which real prayer engenders. The honour was one which M. Vincent would gladly have escaped, and it was only his reverence and affection for the Founder and for Mme. de Chantal, the first Superior, that induced him to accept and to retain the charge, for he looked on the guidance of Religious as an office outside the sphere of the Mission Priests, and the members of the Company were forbidden to undertake it.

The nuns of the Visitation had dedicated their lives to prayer, and therefore their conditions differed entirely from those of the Sisters of Charity; also, their Community was intended for women of gentle birth, and this intensified the contrast to the homely order of Servants of the Poor. It is plain that it was not among these well-born ladies within their convent walls that M. Vincent felt himself at home. In their reminiscences of him,† which cover a period of thirty-eight years, we hear much of his wisdom, his intuition, his careful maintenance of discipline; but the record might apply as well to M. Olier or M. Bourdoise, or even to François de Sales himself. There is no touch of description distinctive of that singular personality, so uncouth of aspect, yet possessed of such infinite attraction, which was known to the world of Paris as Vincent de Paul. With his Sisters of Charity M. Vincent spoke what was in

* Abelli, vol. ii., chap. i. † *Ibid.*, vol. ii., chap. vii.

his mind without reserve, and it is to them—though they were devoid of culture or literary attainment—that we owe the most living portrayal of him. He has no place among the writers of Spiritual Letters, and among his contemporaries he was never known as a confessor and director of the devout. Many of the avenues to intimate knowledge which are open in the case of François de Sales, of Bossuet, of Fénelon, or of many other saintly natures, are closed when we consider Vincent de Paul. The brilliant women of the world whose difficulties and honest aspirations called forth words of wisdom from those whom they consulted were not part of the charge of the Superior of S. Lazare. His letters to the great ladies of the period are letters of business. As a rule he did not undertake the spiritual direction of private individuals, and all his intercourse with women was limited with extraordinary strictness. Nevertheless, there was in his own nature both the tenderness and the intuition that are characteristic of the woman rather than the man. Throughout his life as a priest—from the moment that he said his first Mass in the lonely chapel of Our Lady at Buzet—he had had a special devotion to the Mother of Our Lord; and there was reason that in his active life he should place deep confidence in the courage and self-devotion of women. No one, perhaps, has ever had more real understanding of a woman's character.

The absolute command which M. Vincent exercised over the wayward and undisciplined natures that were to be found among the Sisters of Charity was not due to his eloquence or to his reputation so much as to his habit of taking them into his confidence and of making them feel that they really had part with him in the " Conferences " where he met them face to face. With his Mission Priests he sets a standard, but with his Sisters of Charity he seems to unveil himself with the desire to make the way easier for them by the knowledge of his difficulties. It is no wonder that his confidence in them pro-

THE LAST DAYS

voked response, and that the sealed and hidden chambers of their hearts were thrown open at his summons. A veteran Sister at the close of one of their assemblies knelt down before him and confessed, so that all might hear, that in long past times she had taken a book from one of her companions, and then denied possession of it, because she desired to keep it. The original owner being dead, she there and then restored it publicly to M. Vincent.* This avowal entailed a complete sacrifice of reputation, and is hard for us to estimate the cost. It would have been very easy for the offender to acknowledge her fault in secret on the plea that a younger generation might be harmed, but she had touched reality as she sat listening to M. Vincent, and she could not rest till she had made the fullest reparation that was possible. It was not his method to calculate the possible ill-effects of honesty. " It is well to have the habit of stating things as they actually took place," he said. " For my own part God has given me so strong a conviction of this that I call it my Gospel, and I am specially helped in telling the exact truth because to do so is in conformity with the Spirit of God." † Accordingly he does not hesitate to tell his hearers of his repeated loss of temper with the Brothers or Priests of S. Lazare, of his sense that he must try the patience of many of his Company, of the forgetfulness that has brought him unprepared to a " Conference," or the mismanagement of time that has caused him to neglect them for so long.‡ The note of unworthiness is present as much in rebuke as in exhortation; his own weakness is a hindrance to them and to his own Company: " *Tout le mal qui se fait à la Mission, dites que c'est Vincent qui le fait.*"§

It is the consequence of his own strong sense of sin that he is so infinitely compassionate towards sinners. In many varying directions all through his ministry we have proof of it; it was a foundation of his power with the

* "Conferences," vol. i., 45. February 24, 1653. † *Ibid.*, vol. ii., 53.
‡ *Ibid.*, vol. i., 26, 41, 86, 87.   § *Ibid.*, vol. i., 72. May, 1657.

ignorant. He might preach the fear of God and uphold the necessity of penitence, but it was by love and patience, not by the threat of penalty, that he drew offenders to him; and it is by the understanding of their weaknesses that he made the Sisters of Charity so inseparably his own. We have a special instance at the time when some of them had failed notably in the house at Nantes; the violence of their quarrels had become a scandal in the town, and warnings and reprimands from headquarters produced no effect. It became necessary to send a chosen few from Paris to reform the existing condition and bring the rebels to a better mind; but in doing so M. Vincent's sympathies went out to those under rebuke; he was fearful that the representatives of order might fail in tact, and his charge to them as they set forth is characteristic of his tender heart:

"Because you are Sisters of Charity you are bound to aim at perfection," he told them;* "that is expected of you. And, because you are so, you have been chosen to go to the help of the wounded. You know that in war we take up arms, we fight; and some are killed, some wounded; some conquer, and others are conquered. In this way our Sisters have been wounded in the battle, our Enemy has declared against them. They are not to be despised for that, they are still worthy of admiration; but the demon of contention made a cruel attack upon them."

It is a heavy blow for those who hold office to be superseded because of failure, but under M. Vincent's authority the penalty lost some of its harshness, and the law of love had opportunity to gather force. We have, of course, only a little knowledge of his dealing with his children during the last seven years of his life, but it is enough to show us that his hold upon their hearts must have grown closer with every month that passed. In those

* "Conferences," vol. i., 49. November, 1653.

THE LAST DAYS

years he was no longer distracted by claims to attend the Queen's Council; Mazarin had triumphed, and Vincent de Paul had lost the influence at Court that he had once possessed. Moreover, the Regency had ended, and with it the time of transition wherein enthusiasts had hoped to lay the foundation of a glorious future. The enthusiasm of Vincent de Paul never waned; his faith in the power of righteousness could not be disturbed by any passing events; but he had to learn that the new order of which he dreamed was not to come while his earthly eyes might look on it, nor was he to have any part in bringing it about. After the Fronde was ended he withdrew more and more into seclusion at S. Lazare. He had never been courted for his brilliant parts, he was not eloquent nor very learned, and death had thinned the ranks of those who were ready to support a scheme of his at any sacrifice. It was inevitable that in his extreme old age his hold on the great world should loosen, and he was the more ready to accept retirement because of the ecclesiastical dislocation which had set the authority of the Church and the Crown at variance. Vincent de Paul had preached loyalty unswervingly all his life, but Mazarin and de Retz had brought about a situation which forced him to keep silence; and if he, who had been labouring for reform for thirty years, must hold his peace in sight of terrible abuses, it was better that he should also hide his eyes.

A cloud of sadness and of disappointment hangs over him in his relations with the world in those final years, though there is no failure of hope. "The spirit of charity is lessening in Paris," he wrote in 1657, "and where we used to gather 16,000 livres we now get no more than 1,000."* Possibly the shrinking of generosity was due chiefly to his absence from the assemblies where charitable undertakings were discussed, and such absence was inevitable, for in 1657 he was eighty-one and in a state of

* "Lettres," vol. ii., No. 409.

extreme bodily infirmity. But if his outward work had not fulfilled its promise, the close of his life was cheered by the final touches to the foundation of his Company. It was in September, 1655, that the Pope sanctioned the Constitution of the Mission Priests, and in May, 1658, M. Vincent gave the Rule to his sons. It was the last great event of his career. In the year that followed he lost M. Portail, his closest friend and companion, and in the spring of 1660 Mlle. Le Gras, and he knew the hour of his own departure must be near. His position forced a certain loneliness upon him. He was Founder and Superior, and it was for him to give encouragement and inspiration; there was no one from whom he might receive it. But his faculties were not enfeebled to the very last. Two months before his death he held a " Conference "* for the Sisters of Charity, in which his capacity for eliciting their real opinions is still apparent, and in the spring of that year he had guided them through the time of uncertainty and consternation consequent on the loss of Mlle. Le Gras. He had thought to spare, also, for the distresses of private individuals. There are letters of his at this period that go into the detail of difficult family affairs as if these were his sole concern. His bodily condition does not occupy his thoughts any more than it had done in the prime of life. His only complaint is at the luxuries that are forced upon him. Of his own free will he would never have relaxed the extreme austerity of his habitual practice, but superior authority compelled him, when he had reached the age of eighty-two, to accept a fire in his room and a coverlet in the cold weather.

He had been afflicted for years with a malady of the feet and legs which made walking a matter of infinite difficulty, and he never recovered from the hardships of his perilous wanderings in 1649 (he is said to have increased them voluntarily that he might make an offering of his bodily suffering in the hour of national disaster). In his

* " Conferences," vol. ii., 108. July, 1660.

THE LAST DAYS

last weeks many ills took possession of him, and he spent long periods in torture. He was of very strong constitution, and lingered on for days after those about him had believed that death was imminent. On Monday, September 27, 1660, he died.

The manner of his end was in keeping with his life. There was nothing that was dramatic or could appeal to the imagination. He took his share in the dire experience of suffering which comes sooner or later to the ordinary human being; he had to bear the long strain on faith and fortitude, the humiliation of protracted helplessness; and he was patient under it. It is worthy of remembrance that his followers were so imbued with his spirit that they give us the simple history of an old man's last days without elaborate eulogy of the courage and self-restraint that was a part of his being.

When his body lay in state in the church of S. Lazare, rich and poor flocked thither in such numbers to look for the last time on the familiar face, that the six Mission Priests who watched over him had hard work to defend the coffin from the pressure of the crowd; and not only the poor whom he had loved, but Princes of the blood and civic dignitaries, were at his funeral. All Paris mourned for him.

But though the manifestation of national regret was due to him, he had never cared for public honours. The tributes of sorrow he would have valued were paid, one may believe, when the news spread to distant country places; when Mission Priests, stirred to new effort by their sense of loss, faced once again the searching claim of their vocation; and Sisters of Charity, those homely, nameless Servants of the Poor, knelt down, at the first impulse of their love and grief, to pray for the departed soul of him who had taught them to renounce the pleasant things of life and choose the way of unremitting labour—for the soul of their friend and leader, Vincent de Paul.

APPENDICES

NOTES—LIST OF AUTHORITIES—
CHRONOLOGICAL TABLE—INDEX

NOTES

NOTE I. TO PART I., CHAPTER III., P. 46

Acte d'Association passé éntre S. Vincent de Paul et ses Trois Premiers Compagnons

Nous Vincent de Paul p'bre et principal du Collège des Bons Enfans fondé à Paris, joignant la Porte St. Victor, faisons foy à tous qu'il appartiendra: que selon la fondation faicte par Mgr. Philippe-Emmanuel de Gondy, Conte de Toigny, Général des Galères de France, et de feue Dame Françoise-Marguerite de Silly, Baronne de Montmirail et d'autres lieux, son espouse; pour l'entretien de quelques ecclésiastiques quy se tient et unissent ensembles pour s'employer en manière de mission, à catéchiser, prescher, et faire faire confession genérale au pauvre peuple des champs, selon qu'il est porté par le contract de fondation, passe pardevant Jean du Puis et Nicolas le Boucher, notaires et gardenottes du Roi au Chastelet de Paris le dixseptiesme avril mil six (cent) vingt cincq. La dicte fondation approuvée et autorisée par Mgr. l'illustrissime et révérendissime Jean François de Gondy, Archevesque de Paris, du vingt quatriesme du dit mois mil six cent vingt six; par lequel contract il nous est donné pouvoir de faire choix de tels ecclésiastiques que nous trouverrons propres à l'employ de ce bon œuvre. Nous, en vertu de ce que dessus après avoir fait preuve, un temps assez notable, de la vertu et suffisance de François du Coudray, p'bre du diocèse d'Amyens, de M. Antoine Portail, prestre du diocèse d'Arles, et de M. Jean de la Salle, aussy p'bre dudit diocèse d'Amyens; avons iceux choisy, éleu, aggregé et associé, choisissons, élisons, aggregeons et associons à nous et au dit œuvre, pour ensemblement vivre en manière de congrégation, compagnie ou confrairie; et nous employer au salut du dit pauvre peuple des champs, conformément à ladite fondation, le tout selon la prière que les dits du Coudray, Portail et la Salle nous en ont faict, avec promesse d'observer la dite fondation et le règlement particulier quy selon iceluy sera dressé; et d'obéir taut à nous qu'à nos successeurs Supérieurs comme estant sous nostre direction, conduite et jurisdiction. Ce que nous susnommez, du Coudray, Portail, et de la Salle aggreons, promettons et nous soumettons garder inviolablement. En foy de quoy nous avons réciproquement signé la présente de nostre propre main; et faict mettre le certificat des notaires.

Faict à Paris, au Collège des Bons Enfans ce quatriésme jour de septembre mil six cent vingt six.

Signé. Vincent de Paul, Du Coudray, Portail, de la Salle.

(The original document is preserved in the Archives of the Mission, Rue du Seine.)

NOTE II. TO PART I., CHAPTER III., P. 54

Avis pour les Ordinand—1628.

I. Avant les Orders.

1. Reconnaitre si l'on a vocation à l'état ecclésiastique.
2. Prier Dieu et le faire prier pour connoître cette vocation.
3. Consulter son confesseur ou quelque notable personnage pour cela.
4. La vocation reconnue, l'embrasser avec pureté d'intention de la gloire de Dieu et de son salut.
5. Avoir un titre qui ne soit ri feint ni faux.
6. Faire publier les bans un mois avant l'ordination, porter le certificat de la publication, et de ses vie et mœurs.
7. Se présenter à l'examen, avec l'esprit d'indifférence soit à l'admission ou à l'exclusion.
8. Approchant le temps des exercises, produire quantités d'actes de renoncement au monde et de désir de se donner à Dieu.

II. Durant les Exercices.

1. Entrer aux exercices avec grand désir d'apprendre les fonctions et les vertus propres de chaque Ordre, et celles qui sont convenables et communes à tout l'état ecclésiastique.
2. Les Ordinands prieront Dieu chaque jour qu'il leur donne un cœur docile pour bien apprendre ce qui sera enseigné.
3. Feront chaque jour des notes de ce qu'ils auront appris de plus remarquable.
4. Emploieront fidèlement tout le temps pour faire tous les exercices.
5. Demanderont quelque temps opportun à celui qui dirige les exercices pour penser et écrire leur confession générale.
6. Demanderont au même permission de faire quelques humiliations, comme de servir à table ou balayer.
7. Pendant qu'ils recevront les Saints Ordres, ils s'offrirent et consacreront à Dieu, sans réserve ni exception aucune en la manière qui leur sera enseignée.

APPENDICES

III. Après le Exercices.

1. Rendre actions de grâces de l'Ordre qu'ils ont reçu et des instructions qu'ils ont eues pour cela, à l'exclusion d'un millier d'ecclésiastiques qui ont reçus les Ordres en divers quartiers du monde sans cette préparation.

2. Se proposer de bien pratiquer les dites instructions qu'ils ont reçues.

3. De dire ou d'ouïr tous les jours la sainte messe.

4. Se confesser deux fois tous les huit jours à un même confesseur.

5. Avoir un emploi de la journée et l'observer.

6. Étudier de sorte qu'on puisse faire tous les dimanches une prédication ou un catéchisme.

7. Avoir un directeur auquel l'on communique les difficultés de son intérieur.

8. Accepter les charges et conditions auxquelles le prélat emploiera, et y demeurer en attendant un autre emploi, tel que le prélat le voudra donner.

9. Faire son possible pour entrer dans les Conferences qui se feront, pour conserver la dévotion qu'on a reçue de Dieu pendant les exercices.

NOTE III. TO PART I., CHAPTER IX., P. 173

ORDONNANCE DU ROI (FAIT À PARIS, 14 FÉVRIER, 1651).

De par le roi :

Sa Majesté étant bien informée que les habitants de la plupart des villages de ses frontières de Picardie et de Champagne sont réduits à la mendicité et à une entière misère, pour avoir été exposés aux pillages et hostilités des ennemis et aux passages et logements de toutes les armées; que plusieurs églises ont été pillées et dépouillées de leurs ornements, et que pour sustenter et nourrir les pauvres et réparer les églises, plusieurs personnes de sa bonne ville de Paris font de grandes et abondantes aumônes qui sont fort utilement employées par les prêtres de la Mission de M. Vincent et autres personnes charitables envoyées sur les lieux où il y a eu le plus de ruines et le plus de mal, en sorte qu'un grand nombre de ces pauvres gens a été soulagé dans la nécessité et maladie. Mais qu'en ce faisant, les gens de guerre passant ou sejournant dans les lieux où lesolits missionnaires se sont trouvés, ont pris et détroussé les ornements d'église et les provisions de vivres, d'habits et d'autres choses qui étaient destinés pour les pauvres, en sorte que s'ils n'ont sûreté de la part de Sa Majesté, il leur serait impossible de continuer une œuvre si charitable et si importante à la gloire de Dieu et au soulagement des sujets de Sa Majesté. Désirant y contribuer de tout ce qui peut être en son pouvoir, Sa Majesté de l'avis de la reine régente, défend très-expressément aux gouverneurs et ses lieutenants-généraux en ses provinces et armées, maréchaux et maîtres de camp, colonels, capitaines et autres chefs et officiers commandant ses troupes, tant de cheval que de pied, Français, et étrangers, de quelque nation qu'elles soient, de loger ni souffrir qu'il soit logé aucuns gens de guerre dans les villages desdites frontières de Picardie et de Champagne, pour lesquels lesdits prêtres de la Mission leur demanderont sauvegarde pour assister les pauvres et les malades, et y faire la distribution des provisions qu'ils y porteront, en sorte qu'ils soient en pleine et entière liberté d'y exercer leur charité en la manière et à ceux que bon leur semblera. Defend en outre Sa Majesté à tous gens de guerre de prendre aucune chose aux prêtres de la Mission et aux personnes employées avec eux ou par eux, à peine de la vie, les prenant en sa protection et sauvegarde spéciale, en enjoignant très expressément à tous les baillifs, séné chaux, juges, prévôts des maréchaux et autres officiers qu'il appartiendra, de tenir la main à l'exécution et publication de la présente, et de poursuivre les contrevenants, en sorte que la punition en serve d'exemple. Veux Sa Majesté qu'aux copies de la présente duement collationnées foi soit ajoutée comme à l'original.

("Récueil cangé, Ordonnances Militaires," vol. xxviii.)

NOTE IV. TO PART II., CHAPTER VI., P. 304

Establishments of the Company of Mission Priests during the Life of Vincent de Paul

1625. Paris: College des Bons Enfants.
1632. Paris: S. Lazare.
1635. Toul.
1637. Notre Dame de la Rose.
1638. { Richelieu. / Luçon. / Troyes.
1639. Annecy.
1641. Crécy.
1642. Rome: Monte Citorio.
1643. { Marseilles. / Cahors. / Sedan. / Montmirail.
1644. Saintes.
1645. { Le Mans. / Saint Méen. / Paris: S. Charles. / Genoa. / Algiers. / Tunis.
1648. Tréguier.
1649. Madagascar.
1650. Agen.
1651. Warsaw.
1652. { Montauban. / Turin.

CHIEF AUTHORITIES FOR LIFE OF VINCENT DE PAUL

ORIGINAL SOURCES

Vie du Vénérable Serviteur de Dieu, Vincent de Paul, par Abelli, Évêque de Rodès. Paris, 1664.*
Vie de Saint Vincent de Paul, par Collet, Prêtre de la Mission. Nancy, 1748.
Conférences de Saint Vincent de Paul. Paris, 1882.
Les Lettres de Saint Vincent de Paul. Paris, 1882.
Règles Communes de la Congregation de la Mission. Paris, 1658.
La Vie de Mademoiselle Le Gras, par M. Gobillon, Curé de Saint-Laurent suivie des Pensées de Mademoiselle. Paris, 1676.
S. Vincent de Paul : Sermons.
La Vie de Madame de Miramion, par François T. de Choisy.
Mémoire touchant la Vie de M. de S. Cyran. Claude Lancelot. 1788.
Mémoires de la Régence. Gui Joly. Amsterdam, 1718.
Mémoires de Madame de Motteville.
Mémoires de Jean François de Gondi, Cardinal de Retz.

RECENT AUTHORITIES

Saint Vincent de Paul : sa Vie, son Temps, ses Œuvres, son Influence. L'Abbé Maynard.
Histoire de Saint Vincent de Paul. Mgr. Bougard, Évêque de Laval.
Saint Vincent de Paul et sa Mission Sociale. Arthur Loth.
Saint Vincent de Paul et ses Œuvres à Marseille. H. Simard.
Saint Vincent de Paul. Emmanuel de Broglie.
Saint Vincent de Paul et le Sacerdoce (un Prêtre de la Mission).
Saint Vincent de Paul et les Gondi. R. de Chantelauze.
La Vénérable Louise de Marillac, Mademoiselle Le Gras. Mgr. Baunard.
La Sœur de Charité. A. de Pistoye.
Le Cardinal de Retz et son Temps. Leonce Curnier.

---

* The basis of the present volume.

Histoire Généalogique de la Maison de Gondi. J. de Corbinelli.
Théophraste Renaudot. Eugène Hatin.
T. Renaudot d'Après des Documents Inédits. Gilles de la Tourette.
Un Oublié : T. Renaudot. Gaston Bonnefont.
Jean Jacques Olier. G. M. de Fruges.
Vie de M. Olier. Faillon.
M. Olier de la Congrégation de S. Sulpice.
La Cabale des Dévots. Raoul Allier.
La Misère au Temps de la Fronde. Alphonse Feillet.
Histoire de la Fronde. L. C. de Beaupoilde Saint-Aulaire.
L'Esprit de la Fronde. J. B. Mailly.
Histoire de la Ville de Paris, vols. i. and ii. Michel Félibien.
Histoire des Antiquités de la Ville de Paris, vol. ii. Henri Sauval.
La Police sous Louis XIV. Pierre Clement.
Correspondance Administrative Louis XIV., vol. iii. G. B. Depping.
Histoire de la Vie Privée des François. Le Grand d'Aussy.
Le Village sous l'Ancien Régime. Albert Babeau.
La Ville sous l'Ancien Régime. Albert Babeau.

CHRONOLOGICAL TABLE

PERSONAL LIFE.	CONTEMPORARY EVENTS.
1576. Birth of Vincent de Paul.	1574. Accession of Henri III.
1588. Begins Education at Dax.	1589. Death of Henri III.
1596. Receives the Tonsure.	Death of Catherine de Médicis.
1600. Ordained Priest.	
1605. Captured by Turkish Pirates.	1590. Battle of Ivry.
	1593. Henri IV. abjures Protestantism.
1607. Liberated, and goes to Rome.	
1609. Returns to France.	1600. Marriage of Henri IV. and Marie de Médicis.
1610. Appointed Almoner to Marguerite de Valois.	1610. Assassination of Henri IV.
1612. Curé of Clichy.	1611. De Bérulle founds Congregation of the Oratory in Paris.
1613. Tutor to Sons of M. de Gondi.	
1617. First Mission Sermon. Becomes Curé at Châtillon les Dombes. Returns to M. de Gondi.	1622. Death of S. François de Sales.
	1624. Richelieu becomes First Minister.
1625. Foundation of Congregation of Mission Priests. Death of Mme. de Gondi.	1638. Birth of Louis XIV.
	1639. Death of Marie de Médicis.
1632. Mission Priests established at S. Lazare.	1641. Death of Sainte Chantal.
	1642. Death of Richelieu.
1640. Foundlings adopted by Ladies of Charity.	1643. Death of Louis XIII. Publication of Arnauld's "Frequent Communion."
1642. First Vows of the Sisters of Charity.	
1643. M. Vincent appointed to Council of Conscience.	1648. Beginning of Fronde Rebellion.
	1653. Imprisonment of De Retz. Mazarin returns to Paris.
1649. First Mission to Madagascar.	1656. Publication of Provincial Letters.
1660. Death of Mlle. Le Gras. Death of M. Vincent.	1661. Death of Mazarin.

INDEX

ABELLI, LOUIS, first biographer of Vincent de Paul, 22, 29, 32, 344, 373
Aiguillon, Marie de Vigneron, Duchesse d', niece of Cardinal Richelieu, 111, 158, 270, 273, 276, 279, 345, 353
Albret, Jeanne d', Queen of Navarre, mother of Henri IV., 13
Almeras, René, Mission Priest, 298, 299
Angoumois, Philippe d', 105
Anne of Austria, Consort of Louis XIII. and Queen Regent, 14, 18, 82, 108, 114, 118, 120-134, 138-155, 158, 160-162, 164-168, 176, 183, 188, 197-201, 251, 277, 326, 351
Arnauld, Angélique, Abbess of Port Royal, 135, 138, 263, 375
Arnauld, Antoine, Doctor of the Sorbonne, 378, 380-382
Arnaulds, the, 171
Augustine, St., 30, 375, 379
Augustinian Monks, the, 47-49, 390

Bagin, Cardinal, 361
Barreau, Jean, 353-358
Bassancourt, M. de, 113
Beaufort, Duc de, 140, 182
Berthe, Thomas, Mission Priest, 299, 300
Bérulle, Cardinal de, 18, 20, 22, 27, 28, 33, 35, 38-40, 47, 135, 377
Berzian, Seigneur de, 114
Beyrier, M., 36
Boileau-Despreaux, Nicolas, 79, 171
Bon, M. le, Superior of Augustinian Monks, 47-49, 65, 389
Bossuet, Jacques Benigne, Bishop of Meaux, 28, 59, 61, 400
Bourbon, Henri de, 50

Bourdaise, Toussaint, Mission Priest, 365
Bourdaloue, Père, 61
Bourdeille, François de, Bishop of Périgueux, 5
Bourdoise, M., Curé of S. Nicolas Chardonnet, 113, 386, 399
Bourgoing, Père, 18
Breton, M. le, Mission Priest, 149
Bretonvilliers, Mme. de, 177
Brienne, Mme. de, 276
Broussel, M., Magistrate, 149, 150
Buckingham, George Villiers, Duke of, 128
Bussy de Rabutin, 272

Calvin, 376, 380
Capuchins, the, 105, 364
Carmelites, the, 44, 144, 247, 266
Chantal, S. Jeanne de, 309, 311, 377, 399
Charlet, Père, 42
Chevreuse, Mme. de, 127, 128, 178, 182
Codoing, Bernard, Mission Priest, 308-310, 312-318, 320
Colbert, Jean-Baptiste, Minister to Louis XIV., 79, 171, 262, 347, 353
Commet, M. de, 46
Company of the Blessed Sacrament, the, 104-111, 138, 169, 262, 344, 348
Concini, favourite of Marie de Medici, 209
Condé, La Princesse de, 273, 276, 279
Condé, Prince de, 139, 140, 145, 150, 158, 160, 161, 182, 183, 201, 265, 279
Condren, Père de, Superior of the Oratorians, 107
Conti, Armand de Bourbon, Prince de, 160
Corneille, Pierre, 171
Coste, Simiane de la, 348

Coudray, François du, Mission Priest, 46, 53, 74, 343, 345

Descartes, 171
Desmoulins, Père, 70, 71
Dominicans, the, 12
Ducourneau, Frère Bertrand, Secretary to M. Vincent, 152, 153, 155
Duguin, M., Mission Priest, 367
Dumas, Alexandre, 128
Durand, M., Mission Priest, 306

Epernon, Duc d', 6
Escart, Pierre, Mission Priest, 308-311

Fénelon, François de, 28, 400
Ferrier, M. du, 113
Fiesco, Gian Luigi, 187, 198, 199
Fiesque, M. de, Curé of S. Sulpice, 112
Flacourt, Comte de, 360
Francis of Assisi, S., 179
Franciscans, the, 4
François de Sales, S., 22, 60, 117, 135, 216, 377, 399, 400
François Xavier, S., 362
Fresne, M. de, 40

Gaston d'Orleans, brother to Louis XIII., known as "Monsieur," 111, 182, 201
Gault, Jean Baptiste, Bishop of Marseilles, 345
Godefroy, M. Charles, 59, 60
Gondi, Jean François de, Archbishop of Paris, 42, 43, 56, 73, 187-190, 202, 228
Gondi, Jean François Paul de. See Retz, Cardinal de
Gondi, Mme. de, 27, 28, 30-35, 38-44, 51, 73
Gondi, Philippe de, General of the Galleys, 20, 22, 27, 29, 32-35, 39-44, 263, 338, 340, 343, 392
Gondi, Pierre de, 185
Gondrée, Nicolas, Mission Priest, 363, 364
Goussaulte, Mme., 73, 74, 76, 77, 273, 279, 341
Guéménée, Mme. de, 182
Guyon, Mme., 393

Henri IV., 11, 13, 15, 25, 61, 78, 82, 108, 113, 120, 178
Herse, Mme. de, 273, 274, 279

Horgny, Jean d', Mission Priest, 321, 378-380, 387
Hospital of Charity, 12, 15, 16
Hospital, Convict, 110, 344-347
Hospital " du Nom de Jésus," 85, 257
Hospital, Foundling, 89, 90, 257, 274, 275, 288
Hospital of "La Salpêtrière," 82-86
Hospital of the Trinity, 86, 90
Hôtel Dieu, 72-75, 99, 218, 257, 273, 275, 280

Ignatius Loyola, S., 386
Innocent X., Pope, 162-164, 166, 197, 198, 202

Jansenius, Cornelius, Bishop of Ypres, 375, 378, 379, 386
Jesuits, the, 42, 314, 377, 379, 382, 385-387
Jolly, Edmé, Mission Priest, 364
Joseph, Père, Counsellor of Cardinal Richelieu, 94, 97

La Bruyère, 281
Lancelot, Claude, 378, 386
Lanti, Cardinal, 316
Laurence, Marguerite, Sister of Charity, 243
Le Blanc, M., Mission Priest, 367
Le Camus, Bishop of Bellay, 210
Le Gras, Antoine, secretary to Marie de Medici, 209, 212
Le Gras, Mlle., 76-78, 157, 207-229, 231, 239-241, 243-245, 247, 250-260, 272-274, 404
Lestocq, M. de, 48
Le Vacher, Jean, Mission Priest, 358, 359
Le Vacher, Philippe, Mission Priest, 356-358
Liancourt, Duc de, 111
Liancourt, Duchesse de, 273
Longueville, Anne Geneviève de Bourbon, Duchesse de, 145, 182, 191, 279
Longueville, Duc de, 145, 160
Louis XIII., 61, 78, 94, 96-98, 121-123, 125, 127, 128, 139-141, 183, 339, 340
Louis XIV., 115, 128, 140, 150, 156, 162, 164-168, 182, 200, 201, 203, 251, 262, 359
Luther, Martin, 386
Luynes, Constable de, 127
Luynes, Mme. de. See Chevreuse, Mme. de

INDEX 419

Maintenon, Mme. de, 28, 61, 209
Marillac, Louise de. See Le Gras, Mlle.
Mazarin, Cardinal, 109, 110, 118, 124-130, 132, 140-155, 158, 160-162, 164-168, 181, 182, 184-186, 190-194, 197-203, 229, 262, 277, 326, 359, 402
Medici, Catherine de, Queen of France, 13, 185
Medici, Marie de, Queen of France, 28, 76, 92, 97, 120, 121, 209
Meilleraye, M. de la, 364
Meilleraye, Mme. de la, 23, 279
Miramion, Mme. de, 89, 272, 273, 279
Molé, Mathieu, Magistrate, 147, 148, 154
Montbazon, Mme. de, 182
Montorio, Pierre, Papal Legate, 9, 11, 22
Moras, Bertrande de, mother of Vincent de Paul, 3, 16
Motteville, Mme. de, 141-144

Nacquart, Charles, Mission Priest, 361-365
Naseau, Marguerite, Sister of Charity, 224

Olier de Verneuil, 113
Olier, Jean Jacques, Curé of S. Sulpice, 36, 59, 61, 75, 107, 111-120, 149, 167, 181, 284, 383, 399
Oratory, Congregation of the, 18, 40, 42, 44, 70, 71, 118, 263, 345, 386

Palatine, Anne de Gonzague, Princess, 182
Pascal, Blaise, 171, 382
Patin, Gui, 25, 79
Paul IV., Pope, 11, 18
Paul, Jean de, father of Vincent de Paul, 3, 5
Pichery, Henri de, 105
Plantol, M. Eugene, 352
Portail, Antoine, Mission Priest, 45, 150, 284, 404
Port Royal, 28, 35, 37, 108, 118, 138, 169, 247, 259, 261-263, 325, 375-387

Potier, Augustin, Bishop of Beauvais, 53, 54

Racine, Jean, 171
Rambouillet, Hôtel, 182, 183, 262
Rambouillet, Mme. de, 183, 264
Renard, Frère Mathieu, 176
Renaudot, Théophraste, 91-103, 121, 141, 148
Retz, Jean François de Gondi, Cardinal de, 24, 27, 140, 148, 181-203, 229, 386, 403
Reynie, Nicolas de la, 79
Richelieu, Armand Jean du Plessis, Cardinal, 29, 59, 62, 94, 97, 98, 101, 102, 107, 121, 122, 128, 139, 141, 271, 272, 341, 360, 376, 377
Robiche, Louis, Mission Priest, 347
Rougemont, Comte de, 36-38
Rousseau, Marie, 114, 117

St. Cyran, Jean Duvergier de Hauranne, Abbé de, 138, 375-379, 386
Saint-Martin, M. de, 6, 16
Saint-Simon, Duc de, 122, 124
Salle, M. de la, Mission Priest, 46
Schomberg, Mme. de, 279
Singlin, Antoine, Director of Port Royal, 386
Sourdis, Cardinal de, 343

Talon, Omer, Magistrate, 147
Tallemant des Réaux, 25
Thevenin, M., Mission Priest, 315
Tronson, M., 59

Urban VIII., Pope, 46

Val, M. André du, 48, 49
Valois Kings, the, 13, 28, 195
Valois, Marguerite de, first wife of Henri IV., 12-15, 20-22
Ventadour, M. de, 105
Vigean, Anne de, 265
Vigean, Mme. la Marquise de, 266
Vigean, Marthe de, 265-268
Visitation, the Order of the, 135, 332, 399

www.ingramcontent.com/pod-product-compliance
Lightning Source LLC
Chambersburg PA
CBHW031323230426
43670CB00006B/223